THE INVENTION OF
THE FAVELA

A book in the series

LATIN AMERICA IN TRANSLATION /
EN TRADUCCIÓN / EM TRADUÇÃO

This book was sponsored by the Consortium in
Latin American and Caribbean Studies at the University
of North Carolina at Chapel Hill and Duke University.

THE
INVENTION
OF THE
FAVELA

Licia do Prado Valladares

Translated by Robert N. Anderson

THE UNIVERSITY OF NORTH CAROLINA PRESS

Chapel Hill

Translation of the books in the series Latin America in Translation / en Traducción / em Tradução, a collaboration between the Consortium in Latin American and Caribbean Studies at the University of North Carolina at Chapel Hill and Duke University and the university presses of the University of North Carolina and Duke, is supported by a grant from the Andrew W. Mellon Foundation.

Designed by Jamison Cockerham
Set in Arno, Scala Sans, and Museo
by Tseng Information Systems, Inc.

Manufactured in the United States of America

The University of North Carolina Press has been a member of the Green Press Initiative since 2003.

Cover illustrations: concrete wall © iStockphoto.com/Andrei Berezovskii; brick wall © iStockphoto.com/Dmitrich; buildings © iStockphoto.com/Lindrik

Originally published in Portuguese by Editora FGV, Rio de Janeiro, Brazil, with the title *A invenção da favela: Do mito de origem a favela.com*, © 2005 Licia do Prado Valladares.

LIBRARY OF CONGRESS CATALOGING-IN-PUBLICATION DATA
Names: Valladares, Licia do Prado, author. | Anderson, Robert Nelson, translator.
Title: The invention of the favela / Licia do Prado Valladares ; translated by
    Robert N. Anderson.
Other titles: Invenção da favela. English | Latin America in translation/en traducción/
    em tradução.
Description: Chapel Hill : The University of North Carolina Press, [2019] | Series: Latin
    America in translation/en traducción/em tradução | Translation of: A invenção da
    favela : do mito de origem a favela.com. Rio de Janeiro : Editora FGV, 2005.
Identifiers: LCCN 2018052926 | ISBN 9781469649979 (cloth: alk. paper) |
    ISBN 9781469649986 (pbk.: alk. paper) | ISBN 9781469649993 (ebook)
Subjects: LCSH: Slums—Brazil—Rio de Janeiro—History. | Rio de Janeiro (Brazil)—
    Social conditions. | Poor—Brazil—Rio de Janeiro.
Classification: LCC HV4075.R53 V3513 2019 | DDC 305.5/69098153—dc23
    LC record available at https://lccn.loc.gov/2018052926

To

GIZELLA DO PRADO VALLADARES,

a great woman!

(IN MEMORIAM)

Contents

Figures, Graphs, and Map

GRAPHS

MAP

Foreword: Deciphering the Favela

This book by Licia Valladares is probably the broadest and most systematic study yet published on the phenomenon of the favela. Since she was a young university student, Valladares has investigated the issue of housing among the popular social classes in Brazil. From there, she has undertaken a series of studies, and many of her works have become basic references for all fields of the social sciences. Sociologists, anthropologists, political scientists, economists, urban planners, architects, social workers, journalists, and others have benefited from and dialogued with this body of work of international resonance.

The Invention of the Favela observes and analyzes the evolution of the "favela" as a category of social problem and as a problem for her field of study. The result is a work that is truly historical and archeological in its review of images, stereotypes, prejudices, and common places as well as a review of various actors' attempts to overcome these. This book provides an exhaustive and stimulating survey of more than a century of denunciations, critiques, polemics, and efforts to find solutions for this dramatic dimension of Brazilian society's process of urbanization. Although Rio de Janeiro is the main focus of the work, Valladares also seeks to understand aspects — particularly striking ones — of Brazilian society as a whole.

It is worth highlighting her Herculean effort to include most everything relevant that has been written about the topic of the favela, both by academics and by writers of public policy. It therefore constitutes an invaluable exercise in the sociology of sociology and in the history of ideas and social policy. It is also worth pointing out the breadth of her academic references, both in theoretical terms and in terms of the research itself. This book not only treats these issues generally but also presents vividly the activity of institutions and the trajectory of individuals who had significant roles in this complex process of identification, construction, and analysis of a tense, conflictual area of study and political debate.

This book is already a landmark in the history of social sciences in Brazil. Its importance pushes our boundaries, to the extent that it raises questions of great importance for the analysis of urban life and its dilemmas in the contemporary world. It is a valuable contribution to the study of the living conditions of the poorer social classes and their relationships with other classes and with public and private institutions. Its critical dimension stands out in the face of the ongoing social crisis that we in Brazil have been living through for decades. All of this is presented in a clear, objective style accessible to diverse segments of the reading public.

Gilberto Velho (1945–2012)

Most everybody has an idea of a favela nowadays. Successful movies, from *Black Orpheus* to *City of God*, have shown them to international audiences. Newspapers like the *New York Times, Le Monde,* and *El País* regularly publish articles about them. There are Favela Chic restaurants and nightclubs in London, Paris, and Tokyo. The favelas of Rio are announced in international tourist guides, from *Lonely Planet* to its French equivalent, the *Guide du routard*. In Rio, favela tours pick up visitors in all major hotels. Several favelas with a nice view have hostels, many have restaurants, and there is even a gastronomic guide to the favelas. One can even take a virtual tour of major favelas on the Internet, using Google Maps and Google Street View. Many websites and blogs offer images and information about them.

The favela has become an internationally established, attractive representation of poverty. It exposes otherness (poverty, Brazil) in a pleasant and exotic setting (weather, landscape), with a tinge of danger and adventure (violence, drug traffic prowling around), but with positivity and creativity (music, community, warm social relations, collective mobilizations).

The purpose of this book is to show that this image of the favela is not the simple straightforward reflection of a social reality but the outcome of a long process of production and diffusion of representations of the favelas by the media, policy makers, experts, social scientists, and community and nongovernmental organization (NGO) activists. Students from around the world rush to the favela dreaming they will find some form of social innocence within the city, like the anthropologist discovering a forgotten tribe deep in the Amazon forest. They should be aware that thousands of students, researchers, NGO activists, and journalists have been there before; that hundreds of books, PhD dissertations, and academic articles have been written and published; that all these writings, and media headlines and articles, and politicians' discourses, and public policy statements, and programs have contributed to shape the "favela as a problem" and the everyday representations they will be collecting.

As important as deconstructing the stereotype is to understand how the stereotype has been constructed. This book claims that historical depth is essential to understand the present state of favelas, today's representations of favelas and their inhabitants (the *favelados*), as well as prejudices and discrimination against them. Favelas began more than a century ago and with them came public discourses and public policies, mostly against them. Debate after debate, conflict after conflict, policy after policy, ideas, images, and projects have accumulated. They have also changed, but always carrying with them the weight and tensions of previous debates. The book is a historical inquiry into this process, identifying the actors in each phase and analyzing their discourses. It shows how the scene changes, from the initial stages involving journalists, politicians, architects, and medical doctors, to the present-day complex interaction of planning agencies, academic researchers, police organizations, NGOs, media, churches . . .

One striking result of this inquiry is how much has been written on favelas. Based on quasi-exhaustive bibliographical research covering the twentieth century, the book discusses this vast literature over three periods: the genesis of the favela and of the favela as a problem, and the first public policies, mainly during the first half of the twentieth century; the first surveys of favelas when fieldwork was experimented with, in parallel with political mobilizations valorizing the social qualities of favelas, during the 1960s and 1970s; and the favelas of the social sciences, when favelas became a key object of academic research stimulated by public policy programs and NGO activism, over the last two decades of the twentieth century and the beginning of the twenty-first. The epilogue presents the most recent changes that took place after the original publication of this book in Brazil and sketch out the major contributions in the ever-expanding social science literature.

Another result of the inquiry is that much of this literature is redundant. This is largely due to the widespread underestimation or sheer ignorance of research already published, which produces a constant (re)discovery of things already studied and discussed. This is true of many foreign scholars who come to the favela as if it were a new and undiscovered land and are only aware of the limited literature in their native language. But this is true also of Brazilian researchers, as the produced work in the social sciences is somewhat undervalued in Brazilian academia. The book is intended to convince the reader of the importance and interest of this accumulated literature and its ability to help us understand the present situation and representations of favelas. It can be used as an introduction enabling the reader to find his or her way into it, identifying the sources most useful for one's project.

The book is also a critical analysis of the literature. It shows that, over the years, most publications have tended to establish and reinforce three dogmas that define the academic stereotype of the favela. They are dogmas in the sense that they are structuring representations that are taken for granted, hardly ever discussed, with major consequences for research design and generalization of results. The first is that of specificity: the favela is a different place from the rest of the city. The second is that the favela is the urban locus of poverty. The third dogma is that of unity: unity between favelas, unity within the favela.

The conjunction of the first and third dogmas has produced a remarkable outcome regarding the vocabulary used in Brazil over the last decade to discuss favelas. The word *favela* has been largely replaced by the word *comunidade* (community). This is all the more remarkable since, unlike for U.S. cities, the word *community* is very seldom used in the urban context. Evidently there is much political correctness in this avoidance of the words *favela* or *favelado*, which carry the stigma of poverty, illegality, marginality, or violence. On the contrary, *community* has the positive connotation of moral values of unity and solidarity. The word *community* expresses an identity that goes against the stigmatizing word *favela* (Gondim 1982). It attaches value to the favela and its inhabitants, who are neither "barbarians" nor "marginals." This positive denomination, originally used by the Catholic Church during the Vargas period, has been put forward in recent decades by NGOs and militants, by residents' associations, by international agencies that value residents' participation, and by many scholars who tend to mix a militant ethos with the scientific one. Social scientists have a strong responsibility in the reinforcement of this dogma, despite being the first ones who should question it and evaluate empirically the validity of such a representation.

There are cases where the residents themselves use the stereotypes in order to attract the attention of public agencies and claim their rights (Goldstein 2003). Fernanda Delvalhas Piccolo (2006) calls attention to this and shows that only as a "community" can the favela compete politically (for social projects), economically (through finance), and socially (through prestige). The media now use *community* much more than *favela*—during one month in early 2016, the newspaper *O Globo*, for example, used the former term 213 times and the latter only 63 times. *Favela* is more often used in association with negative events, such as confrontations between the police and drug traffickers. As a resident of Santa Marta put it, "The word *community* was invented by the government and by institutions [NGOs]. The idea is that the residents should be included in the society, they should be more accepted" (quoted in Fiell 2001, 24). Patricia Birman (2008), however, stresses that the notion is polysemic, that it can be used both favorably and unfavorably in reference to the favela inhabitants. *Community* both upholds the good moral qualities of the residents, of their way of life and their "culture," and stresses that they live in a territory different from the rest of the city, that *favelados* have a different social profile and their own cultural values. The difference between "we, of the community," and "you, of the city," then reinforces the dualism in the common perception.

The book goes beyond the discussion of the ambivalence of the political correctness of naming favelas "communities" and presents arguments from the (minority) portion of the literature that has focused on inequalities within and between favelas. There is increasing social stratification inside the larger favelas, whose population is comprised not only of a diverse working-class majority, many of whom work in commerce and services, including many domestic and food service employees, but also, increasingly, of more skilled workers, shopkeepers, business owners, and landlords. There are also strong internal inequalities, with some areas being now well equipped with the proper urban infrastructure, buildings with several floors made of good material, and other areas less so, there being sites in each favela where there are no paved alleys, where garbage accumulates around wooden shacks and the population is very poor indeed.

The differences among favelas are also quite noticeable, particularly between the oldest ones close to the center of Rio or the upper-class areas of the Zona Sul (South Zone) along the beaches, and the more recent ones north or west of the city and its suburbs. The former, the most noticeable and disturbing for the powerful elite living nearby, have over the last three decades received a lot of public attention and investment; they are close to employment areas, public transport, and many public services. The latter are more recent, have a weaker infrastructure, are farther from transport and services, and are much farther from employment areas; they are often in very polluted areas; and they do not have a postcard view.

Favelas are also areas with diverse social groups, sometimes in competition or even conflict, far from the dreamed-of solidarity of the "community." Voluntary associations compete for followers and sometimes fight each other. Evangelical churches verbally and sometimes physically attack Afro-Brazilian religious sites. Some favelas have two or three competing residents' associations, and many residents do not take part in any of them. The violence of drug dealers, militias, corrupt and violent police, young people attacking people in the streets of the city center or along the beaches is not an external violence imposed on a peaceful, united, and solidary population; it is part of the social experience of the favela, of its mode of violent socialization (Machado da Silva 2012). This violence has attracted much attention in the last fifteen years and will be discussed more thoroughly in the epilogue, since it has generated a large amount of new scholarship, particularly related to the recent public policy of placing Unidade de Polícia Pacificadora (UPP) stations in favelas to "pacify" them.

Licia do Prado Valladares

Acknowledgments

This book represents many years of research and reflection, begun with my Habilitation à Diriger des Recherches thesis, defended in France in 2001. Throughout the years, the collaboration of friends, colleagues, assistants, student workers, and librarians has been enormous and fundamental. The list is long both from Brazil and France. The participants mobilized for this journey are so numerous that some surely will be absent here.

I begin with the long-standing friends who watched me grow up with them during all those years in Rocinha: Ariete, Sandra and Igor, Grilo, Cristina, Leandro, Anderson and William, Dona Geni and Eraldo, Auri, Dona Miquelina and Dona Maria Aparecida, Maria Helena and Luiz Kleber, with whom I share a great interest in the favelas.

Adriane Macedo, Alberto Passos Guimarães Filho, Araci Moema Seljan, Carlos Alberto de Medina, Catherine Bruant, Celso Lamparelli, Diana Brown, Elisabeth Leeds, Gilberto Velho, Gizella do Prado Valladares, Henrique Miranda, Jane Souto de Oliveira, José Arthur Rios, Luiz Antonio Machado da Silva, Luiz Werneck Vianna, Margareth da Silva Pereira, Maria Coeli Tavares de Moura, Maria Hortência do Nascimento e Silva, Maria Lais Pereira da Silva, Maurício Abreu, Michel Marié, Nadia Peralva Abreu Teixeira, Renato Boschi, Rogério Aroeira Neves, Suzana Pasternak Taschner, and Wanda de Mattos Pimenta Pompéia granted me long hours of interviews and testimony as well as informal conversations that helped me clarify doubts.

I am grateful to Alzira Abreu, Angelina Peralva, Bianca Freire-Medeiros, Denise Stuckenbruck, Dominique Vidal, Elina Pessanha, Estella Abreu, Filippina Chinelli, Gilberto Hochman, Jean-Pierre Gaudin, Luis Senna, Lucio Kowarick, Luiz Nogueira Barros, Magda Prates Coelho, Martha Aimée Rangel Batista, Marco Antonio da Silva Mello, Nair Telles, and Nísia Trindade Lima for their suggestions and clarifications.

Thanks to Altidório Silva — "Silvinho" — and the staff at the Instituto Universitário de Pesquisas do Rio de Janeiro (IUPERJ), which has become the Instituto de Estudos Sociais e Políticos (IESP), joining the Universidade do Estado do Rio de Janeiro (UERJ), for the operational support and the goodwill with which they always honored my requests. Beatriz Garrido Guimarães and Simone de Oliveira Sampaio of the IUPERJ library, Lia Riedel of the Dominican Convent Library in Rio de Janeiro, and Maria Aparecida Rosário de O. Ferreira of the Center for Documentation at the Fundação Escola de Sociologia e Política de São Paulo (FESPSP) always answered my bibliographic queries and promptly met my requests for materials.

Paulo Fernando Cavallieri, Gustavo Perez, and Adriana Vial of the Sistema de Assentamentos de Baixa Renda (SABREN) at the Instituto Municipal de Urbanismo Pereira Passos (IPP) also kindly helped me with all of my requests for recent data on the favelas of Rio de Janeiro.

The team at URBANDATA-Brasil collected the bibliographic data that served as the basis of chapter 3. The Conselho Nacional de Desenvolvimento Científico e Tecnológico (CNPq) and the Fundação de Amparo à Pesquisa do Estado do Rio de Janeiro (FAPERJ) fellows Ana Lúcia Saraiva Ribeiro, Claudia Cruz, Luiz Kleber Farias, Márcia Farias, Mario Danner, Monique Batista Carvalho, Natalia Gaspar, and Raíza Siqueira proved ever-enthusiastic collectors of information.

Suelyemma Franco, research assistant at URBANDATA-Brasil, efficiently organized the bibliography and list of acronyms for this book. Rodrigo Farias de Sousa provided all necessary support in information technology and Internet research.

The images reproduced here come from several sources: Eduardo Augusto de Brito Cunha kindly provided the caricatures by J. Carlos. The National Library Foundation Archive gave permission to reproduce the three images from the book *Habitações populares* (Popular dwellings) by Everardo Backheuser. I thank the Historical Archive of the Museum of the Republic and the Center for the Conservation and Preservation of Photography at the Fundação Nacional de Artes for access to the Flávio de Barros Archive. To the Museum of Image and Sound and the Department of Cultural Heritage of Rio de Janeiro's Mayor's Office I owe the picture of the Morro da Providência from the Augusto Malta collection. The Department of Documentation at the Casa Oswaldo Cruz Victor Tavares de Moura Fund granted me permission to use photos of theirs, and TV-ROC allowed the reproduction of an earlier homepage, now offline.

In France, I relied on the participation of Anita Joussemet, Isa Aldeghi, Françoise Imbert, Suzanna Magri, colleagues at the Cultures et Sociétés Urbaines program of the Centre National de la Recherche Scientifique (CSU-CNRS), where I was a research associate for many years. I was a professor from 1998 to 2001 at the Institut d'Urbanisme de Paris (IUP), Université de Paris XII, where I benefited from the support of colleagues, including Jean-Pierre Frey, Michèle Jolé, and Anne Fournié, as well as the secretary of the Laboratoire Vie Urbaine, Anita Becquerel. The late Isaac Joseph, of the Université Paris X Nanterre, was a friend with whom I discussed many of the ideas presented here. In the École des Hautes Études en Sciences Sociales, Christian Topalov and Afrânio Garcia invited me to present some of the chapters of my research to their students during their seminars. More recently, the Sérgio Buarque de Holanda Chair at the Maison des Sciences de l'Homme made it possible for me to continue my academic activities in France, where I became professor of sociology at the Université de Lille 1 in 2003.

I cannot neglect to mention the institutions in Brazil that have always supported my work: IUPERJ, where I taught for twenty years and could count on intellectual stimulation from my colleagues and students; the Universidade Candido Mendes (UCAM), which maintained URBANDATA-Brasil and was understanding of my coming and going between Brazil and France; and the Coordenação de Aperfeiçoamento de Pessoal de Nivel Superior (CAPES), which gave me a postdoctoral fellowship in 1997–98. As a visiting professor in the Graduate Program in Anthropology and Political Science at the Universidade Federal Fluminense (UFF), I had the opportunity to give a course, Cem anos pensando a favela (A Hundred Years of Thinking about the Favela), while I was preparing part of this book.

Finally, I want to express my thanks to Lidia Medeiros, a researcher at URBANDATA-Brasil, whose efficiency and faithfulness have been proved over the years. Maria de Lourdes Menezes served not only as translator but also worked with me on the updating and adaptation of this work from the French-to the Portuguese-language edition. Margareth da Silva Pereira has acted as a true collaborator, discussing the various chapters of the text and taking care of access to almost all of the images reproduced here. Lena Lavinas, Anete Leal Ivo, and Claudia Menezes contributed so much with friendship and intellectual support.

Diana do Prado Valladares, of the Municipal Secretariat of Health, of Rio de Janeiro's Mayor's Office, introduced me to another Rocinha. My sons Leonardo and Paulo Valladares Pacheco de Oliveira have put up with my absences and have accompanied my work as a researcher. Gizella do Prado Valladares gave me unconditional support at every moment.

Edmond Préteceille, my partner, and Michèle Ferrand, my French sister, have been a continual source of intellectual stimulation, in Brazil and in France. Indeed, they are my partners in this (ad)venture.

For the English edition of this book, I would like to thank institutions and professionals: the Programa de Pós-graduação em Ciências Sociais at UERJ, which gave me support as visiting researcher for two years; my editor, Elaine Maisner, for her patience and assistance; Robert Anderson, my translator, who did a great job; Raíza Siqueira, for her friendship and continuous help; Nathalia Curvelo who did the research on the UERJ database; and, again, Edmond Préteceille, who did everything possible to encourage me — I owe the energy to complete the English edition of this book to him.

Note from the Translator

Installment 15 of the *Guardian*'s series "The Story of Cities" showcased not just Rio de Janeiro but specifically Morro da Providência, formerly Morro da Favella (5 April 2016). The story's title, "The Rise and Ruin of Rio de Janeiro's First Favela," is somewhat misleading because, as the article reveals, and the present book traces in detail, the history of this favela and others in the Marvelous City is more complex than a simple trajectory of growth and decline. Bruce Douglas's brief but interesting portrait in words of images has many points of intersection with Licia Valladares's *The Invention of the Favela*. Both remind us not only that the favela (generically speaking) has had a particular history in the long twentieth century but also that the history of thought and study about the favela has had its own particularities of the same period. In fact, like the mysterious vanished film *Favela dos meus amores* (Favela of my loves), awareness and understanding of this latter history has faded in and out of view. At the same time, this intellectual, political, and scholarly history has determined the representations of the favela that both professionals and lay people have been heir to. Thus we use *favela* in the present translation because of its particular history and its trajectory in the popular imagination, scholarly inquiry, and public policy.

Valladares's task was to write a history of the "favela" of public policies and the social sciences. As such, she had recourse to both a long professional and personal engagement with this object of study and also more than a hundred years of primary documentation and published secondary sources in Portuguese, French, and English. The author's exposition is rooted disciplinarily in sociology, public policy, and the social sciences. Though a sociologist by training and practice, she succeeded in weaving a historical narrative that brought together vast evidence from a range of discourses that included testimonial, journalism, government and law, medicine, literature, religion, urbanism, and so forth, through several distinct periods spanning about 125 years. Such discursive variety might have posed special challenges for a translator.

The translator's task was to work from the Portuguese translation of the original French publication. This publication history provided several benefits. First, the original work targeted a French-reading audience not necessarily familiar with Brazil that might include both social scientists and nonspecialists. The audience of the Portuguese translation would include more readers familiar with Brazil, with Rio, and possibly with the favelas, but these would not necessarily know the North American or French intellectual background to much of the present story. The exposition of the original was straightforward and not unnecessarily technical, and yet it does not eschew substance or insult the reader's intelligence. The citations and reproduced images were not arcane, and they are explained in the text. As such, my task was easier than it might have been, and I hope that readers of the English translation will find it accessible yet informative.

First, some observations about word choice. As noted above, this book is about a category, a construct, a concept—one that manifests in a range of representations and is subject to a dynamic of reification and change. "Favela" in the singular can thus be this category or a specific such residential cluster. I have used the English neologism *favelization*—the process of a settlement becoming a favela—for the Portuguese *favelização*. Similarly, readers will see *favelado(s)* alternate with "favela resident(s)."

I have also alternated *cortiço* and "tenement" and "Carioca" with "Rio" (used adjectivally as a more obvious equivalent). Although *cortiço* and "tenement" denote similar phenomena in Brazil and the United States, respectively, and they have similar connotations as a "locus of the poor," they have different "flavors" in the two countries; *cortiço* is defined legally in the present work, and the *cortiços* in Rio's city center were precursors to the favelas. I have alternated *morro* and "hill," the former exclusively in proper names and in its metaphoric sense and association with the favela; the latter is used more topographically. A few other words that are used occasionally seemed better to use in Portuguese with a gloss or explanation in the text or a note.

Some recurring terms demand explanation here at the outset. Specialists understand that, despite many similarities on our histories, race, ethnicity, and color are constructed and negotiated differently in Brazil and the United States. The present book and many works in the field of Brazilian studies address this complex matter. These differences in how the people of the United States and Brazil think about race, ethnicity, and color are inscribed, therefore, in words that superficially resemble each other across languages. In most recent decades, the Brazilian census has used the following "color or race" categories: *branca* (white), *parda* (brown), *preta* (black), *amarela* (yellow [*sic*], referring to persons mostly of Japanese, Chinese, and Korean descent), and *indígena* (indigenous, Indian). In popular usage, *pardo* is usually substituted by *mulato* (mulatto) if the descent is mixed Euro- and Afro-Brazilian, *caboclo* if the indigenous presence is noticeable, or *moreno* (more generically — and euphemistically — brown). Intellectuals will often substitute mestizo or mixed (*mestiço*) for *pardo, mulato, caboclo,* and *moreno*. In this translation, I use the Portuguese terms that Valladares uses, trusting that the reader will refer to this note. I have used *moreno* and "mulatto" only in quotations from primary sources as the former is vague and the latter is frequently pejorative and misused. Both historically and in recent designations of an African-descended group and political identity, *negro* (Black) is used, though often ambiguously. *Negro* thus basically subsumes *preto* and *pardo* as shorthand for "African-descended." Historically, though, *negro* and *preto* were used synonymously and interchangeably. In the translation, if the English terms are used above, I use "Black" for this ethnopolitical identity term *negro* and "black" for the skin color or census term *preto*. One should be aware, regardless, not to conflate U.S. and Brazilian color or race constructs. The readers should know, for example, that in Brazil "white" and "brown" cover a wide range of descent configurations, phenotypes, and identifications; whereas "black" (*preto*) is a color category that presupposes predominant African ancestry. What lies behind this is a tripartite color distinction that underlies and even competes with biracial, "color blind," or multicolor formations in Brazil. The terms *indígena* and *índio* appear as "Indian," following common current usage in the United States. These, like *negro* and *amarelo* are panethnic and even political constructions, with implications of descent as well. They refer to those who have chosen to identify primarily with indigenous Brazilian descent, and who might credibly convince others to identify them as such as well based on cultural, linguistic, and residential criteria. Finally, one can assume that mention of *pardos* or *mestiços* in the present work could include *caboclos* or persons of indigenous descent.

I have rendered *município* as "municipality," the basic unit of local government in the Brazil's "trinitary" federation. The reader should understand, though, that this is essentially a city or town and the suburban and rural areas under its control. This might be understood as a "township" in the U.S. context, but such a translation would obscure its fundamental importance in the structure of government. To render *município* as "city" or "county" would be technically inaccurate. Similarly, "municipal" will have the same jurisdictional scope as a municipality. Confusingly, the republic's Federal District was coterminous with Rio de Janeiro, which had a municipal government. When the federal capital was moved to Brasília and a new Federal District was established in 1960, the old Federal District became the state of Guanabara, which had unitary state government and no municipalities. The state of Guanabara merged with the state of Rio de Janeiro in 1975, and the state of Guanabara became the municipality of Rio de Janeiro.

The second sort of intervention is to elucidate details of the Brazilian context that the original work may have taken as general knowledge. Thus, I have frequently made interpolations in the original texts—rearrangements and substitutions for the sake of the readership. I have added contextual information either in the running text or in notes for the sake of the English-language public. Such additions are meant to illuminate, not change, the original essay, and, of course, any errors in these are mine and not the editors' or author's.

Finally, a note about orthography: Portuguese has undergone a number of orthographic reforms in the chronological scope of this book. When using Portuguese words in the running text and notes, including proper names for which an alternate preference is not indicated, I have used the post-2009 orthography. In publication titles, I have used original title as cited in the bibliography. Some proper names use the preferred spelling if an alternative to the standard is known or indicated. One special case is Morro da Favella, which retains the double 'l' because of its status in the myth of origin and to set it off from the generic favela.

In closing, I want to acknowledge my late father, Robert N. Anderson Jr., a city and regional planner, whose career included regional land-use plans, public housing, and urban renewal. Through him I came to this translation task well acquainted with the world of urban planning, including both the idealism and the challenges when projects meet the real world. I also acknowledge the late Tim Lopes, my friend, who introduced me to the real Rio de Janeiro and later lost his life reporting on the drug trade and prostitution recruitment in Complexo do Alemão.

Robert N. Anderson III

Abbreviations

AI-5	Ato Institucional n° 5 (Institutional Act no. 5)
ANPOCS	Associação Nacional de Pós-graduação e Pesquisa em Ciências Sociais (National Association of Graduate Study and Research in Social Sciences)
ANPUR	Associação Nacional de Pós-graduação e Pesquisa em Planejamento Urbano e Regional (National Association of Graduate Study and Research in Urban and Regional Planning)
BEMDOC	Brasil–Estados Unidos Movimento para o Desenvolvimento e Organização da Comunidade (Brazil-U.S. Movement for Development and Community Organization)
BNDES	Banco Nacional de Desenvolvimento Econômico e Social (National Bank for Social and Economic Development)
BNH	Banco Nacional da Habitação (National Housing Bank)
CAPES	Coordenação de Aperfeiçoamento de Pessoal de Ensino Superior (Coordination for the Improvement of Higher Education Personnel)
CARE	Cooperative for Assistance and Relief Everywhere
CDI	Center for Digital Inclusion (known in Brazil as the Comitê para a Democratização da Informática)
CEASM	Centro de Estudos e Ações Solidárias da Maré (Maré Center for Study and Action in Solidarity)
CEBRAP	Centro Brasileiro de Análise e Planejamento (Brazilian Center for Analysis and Planning)
CEDAE	Companhia Estadual de Águas e Esgotos (State Water and Sewer Company)

CEDEC	Centro de Estudos de Cultura Contemporânea (Center for Contemporary Culture Studies)
CEE	Comissão Estadual de Energia (State Energy Commission)
CEF	Caixa Econômica Federal (Federal Savings Bank)
CENPHA	Centro Nacional de Pesquisas Habitacionais (National Center for Housing Research)
CEPAL	Comisión Económica para América Latina y el Caribe / Comissão Econômica para a América Latina e o Caribe (Economic Commission for Latin America and the Caribbean)
CERIS	Centro de Estatística Religiosa e Investigações Sociais (Center for Religious Statistics and Social Research)
CHISAM	Coordenação de Habitação de Interesse Social da Área Metropolitana do Grande Rio (Office of Social Interest Housing of the Greater Rio Metropolitan Area)
CINAM	Compagnie d'Études Industrielles et d'Aménagement du Territoire (Company for Industrial Studies and Land-Use Planning)
CLAPCS	Centro Latino-Americano de Pesquisas em Ciências Sociais (Latin American Center for Research in Social Sciences)
CNBB	Conferência Nacional dos Bispos do Brasil (National Conference of Brazilian Bishops)
CNDU	Conselho Nacional de Desenvolvimento Urbano (National Council for Urban Development)
CNPq	Conselho Nacional de Desenvolvimento Científico e Tecnológico (National Council for Scientific and Technological Development) (until 1974 Conselho Nacional da Pesquisa [National Council for Research])
CNRS	Centre National de la Recherche Scientifique (National Center for Scientific Research)
CODESCO	Companhia de Desenvolvimento de Comunidades (Community Development Company)
COHAB-GB	Companhia de Habitação Popular do Estado da Guanabara (State of Guanabara Affordable Housing Authority)

CPDOC	Centro de Pesquisa e Documentação de História Contemporânea do Brasil (Center for Research and Documentation of Brazilian Contemporary History)
CREDAL	Centre de Recherche et de Documentation sur l'Amérique Latine (Center for Research and Documentation on Latin America)
CSU	Cultures et Sociétés Urbaines (Urban Cultures and Societies)
CUFA	Central Única de Favelas (Central Favela Confederation)
DESAL	Centro para el Desarrollo Económico y Social de América Latina (Center for Latin American Economic and Social Development)
DESCO	Centro de Estudios y Promoción del Desarrollo (Center for the Study and Promotion of Development)
ECLAC	Economic Commission for Latin America and the Caribbean
ELSP	Escola Livre de Sociologia e Política (Free School of Sociology and Politics)
FAFEG	Federação das Associações de Favelas do Estado da Guanabara (Federation of Favela Associations of the State of Guanabara)
FAFERJ	Federação das Associações de Favelas do Rio de Janeiro (Federation of Favela Associations of the State of Rio de Janeiro)
FAO	Food and Agriculture Organization of the United Nations
FAPERJ	Fundação de Amparo à Pesquisa do Estado do Rio de Janeiro (Rio de Janeiro Research Foundation)
FASE	Federação dos Órgãos para Assistência Social e Educacional (Federation of Organs for Social and Educational Assistance)
FAU	Faculdade de Arquitetura e Urbanismo (College of Architecture and Urbanism)
FFCL	Faculdade de Filosofia, Ciências e Letras (College of Philosophy, Science, and Letters)
FGV	Fundação Getúlio Vargas (Getúlio Vargas Foundation)
FIESP	Federação das Indústrias do Estado de São Paulo (Federation of Industries of the State of São Paulo)

FINEP	Financiadora de Estudos e Projetos (Financing Agency for Studies and Projects)
HSFR	Swedish Council for Research in the Humanities and Social Sciences
IAB	Instituto de Arquitetos do Brasil (Institute of Brazilian Architects)
IBASE	Instituto Brasileiro de Análises Sociais e Econômicas (Brazilian Institute for Social and Economic Analyses)
IBGE	Instituto Brasileiro de Geografia e Estatística (Brazilian Institute of Geography and Statistics)
IBOPE	Instituto Brasileiro de Opinião Pública e Estatística (Brazilian Institute of Public Opinion and Statistics)
IBRD	International Bank for Reconstruction and Development
IDESP	Instituto de Estudos Econômicos, Sociais e Políticos de São Paulo (Institute of Economic, Social, and Political Studies of São Paulo)
IHEAL	Institut des Hautes Études de l'Amérique Latine (Institute of Advanced Studies of Latin America)
INSEE	Institut National de la Statistique et des Études Économiques (National Institute of Statistics and Economic Studies)
IPEA	Instituto de Pesquisa Econômica Aplicada (Institute for Applied Economic Research)
IPLAN-RIO	Instituto de Planejamento Municipal da Prefeitura da Cidade do Rio de Janeiro (Institute for Municipal Planning of the Office of the Mayor of Rio de Janeiro)
IPPUR	Instituto de Pesquisa em Planejamento Urbano e Regional (Institute for Research in Urban and Regional Planning)
IRFED	Institut International de Recherche et de Formation en vue du Développement Harmonisé (International Institute for Research and Training for Harmonized Development)
ISER	Instituto de Estudos da Religião (Institute of Religious Studies)
IUP	Institut d'Urbanisme de Paris (Paris Institute for Urban Planning)
IUPERJ	Instituto Universitário de Pesquisas do Rio de Janeiro (University Research Institute of Rio de Janeiro)

JUC   Juventude Universitária Católica
      (Catholic University Youth)
LAP   Laboratório de Estudos sobre Urbanização,
      Arquitetura e Preservação (Laboratory of Studies
      on Urbanization, Architecture, and Preservation)
NGO   nongovernmental organization
PAC   Programa de Aceleração do Crescimento
      (Growth Acceleration Program)
PADF Partido Autonomista do Distrito Federal
      (Autonomist Party of the Federal District)
PCB   Partido Comunista Brasileiro
      (Brazilian Communist Party)
PIR Villes Programme Interdisciplinaire de Recherche sur la
      Ville (Interdisciplinary Research Program on Cities)
PT   Partido dos Trabalhadores (Workers Party)
PTB   Partido Trabalhista Brasileiro (Brazilian Labor Party)
PUC   Pontifícia Universidade Católica do Rio de Janeiro
      (Pontifical Catholic University of Rio de Janeiro)
RA   região administrativa (administrative region)
SABREN Sistema de Assentamentos de Baixa Renda
      (System on Low-Income Settlements)
SAGMA Société pour l'Application du Graphisme et de la
      Mécanographie à l'Analyse (Society for the Application
      of Graphics and Information Technology in Analysis)
SAGMACS Sociedade de Análises Gráficas e Mecanográficas
      Aplicadas aos Complexos Sociais (Society for Graphic
      and Machine Analysis Applied to Social Complexes)
SEBRAE Serviço Brasileiro de Apoio às Micro e
      Pequenas Empresas (Brazilian Micro- and
      Small Business Support Service)
SERFHA Serviço Especial de Reabilitação das Favelas e
      Habitações Anti-higiênicas (Special Service for
      Recovery of Favelas and Antihygienic Housing)
SERFHAU Serviço Federal de Habitação e Urbanismo
      (Federal Housing and Urban Planning Service)
SESI Serviço Social da Indústria (Social Service for Industry)
SMDS Secretaria Municipal de Desenvolvimento Social
      (Municipal Secretariat of Social Development)

TV-ROC	Televisão Rocinha
UCAM	Universidade Candido Mendes (Candido Mendes University)
UDN	União Democrática Nacional (National Democratic Union)
UERJ	Universidade do Estado do Rio de Janeiro (Rio de Janeiro State University)
UFBA	Universidade Federal da Bahia (Federal University of Bahia)
UFF	Universidade Federal Fluminense (Federal University of the State of Rio de Janeiro)
UFMG	Universidade Federal de Minas Gerais (Federal University of Minas Gerais)
UFPE	Universidade Federal de Pernambuco (Federal University of Pernambuco)
UFRGS	Universidade Federal do Rio Grande do Sul (Federal University of Rio Grande do Sul)
UFRJ	Universidade Federal do Rio de Janeiro (Federal University of Rio de Janeiro)
UNB	Universidade de Brasília (University of Brasília)
UNESCO	United Nations Educational, Scientific, and Cultural Organization
UNICAMP	Universidade de Campinas (University of Campinas)
UNICEF	United Nations Children's Fund
UPA	unidade de pronto atendimento (urgent care center)
UPP	Unidade de Polícia Pacificadora (Pacifying Police Unit)
USAID	United States Agency for International Development
USP	Universidade de São Paulo (University of São Paulo)

THE INVENTION OF
THE FAVELA

INTRODUCTION

The title of this book will almost certainly surprise the reader: The favela was *invented*? How could this be if today favelas are quite obviously present? The municipality of Rio de Janeiro has 752 such clusters, and 18.7 percent of its population lives in these areas, which are growing faster than the city as a whole.[1] How is it possible to speak of the *Invention of the Favela* in the face of the daily news transmitted by print and electronic media about the violence associated with *favelados* (favela residents), about the drug trade, and about conflicts with the police? How is it possible to deny the sociospatial segregation in the Rio metropolitan area of which the favela is the prime symbol? How is it possible to ignore the concreteness of favelas if, within the scope of urban policies, they receive special attention from government administrations and public agencies? How then can we speak of the favela as *invented*?

Doubtless, I owe the reader an explanation. My intention is not to analyze the evolution of the phenomenon of urban spaces becoming favelas (or "favelization"), its causes and consequences, the proliferation of data and the comparison of indicators, or even the supposed threat that such areas represent to the city. What I intend to introduce and discuss in this book are the social representations that the Rio favela has stirred up during the last hundred years. My objective is to show how the construction of these social representations occurred historically and to treat the "discoveries" of the favela by diverse social actors. I also will analyze the change witnessed in the evolution of the categories "favela" and *favelado* and of the notions they express beyond their synonyms, associations, and oppositions. I intend to give special attention to the favela of the social sciences and to the agenda of the academy, keeping in mind their weight in the whole of scholarly production and in the dissemination of paradigms of poverty in urban Brazil.

In the construction of social representations, the author's biography has its place, as do the implicit and explicit ideas and discourses of her time. One can only understand the thought of a given author when one takes into account her time period, class origins, social, political, and religious characteristics, and the intellectual context in which she circulated. Thus my own trajectory has a relationship to my "invention" of the favela. For this reason, I offer, as an aperitif, the history of a journey in search of my own construction.

In 1966 I first set foot in a favela in Rio de Janeiro. I was twenty years old and was studying sociology and political science at the Pontifícia Universidade Católica of Rio de Janeiro (PUC). I was born in Salvador and lived in Bahia until I finished high school. I then moved to Rio de Janeiro to attend university. As a middle-class Bahian girl, according to the criteria of the Instituto Brasileiro de Geografia e Estatística (IBGE), I was a migrant.

I arrived in Rio in 1964, the year of the military coup. With the move of the capital of Brazil from Rio to Brasília in 1960, the erstwhile Federal District became the state of Guanabara. Governor Carlos Lacerda turned Rio upside down, hoping to show that even though it had lost the status of federal capital, the Marvelous City should nevertheless modernize and take on the air of a great metropolis.[2] The earthworks of the Aterro do Flamengo caused terrible traffic jams, and in my first months at PUC, during the daily commute from the district of Fátima to Gávea, the district where PUC is located, I watched Pasmado Favela being removed. Tractors moved in and destroyed the shacks while families were hurriedly put on trucks as they tried to gather their few possessions. These images have stuck with me forever. The newspapers of the time announced the events in headlines. Questioning the governor's decisions, the Federação das Associações de Favelas do Estado da Guanabara (FAFEG) tried unsuccessfully to counter the removal of residents to distant Vila Kennedy and Vila Aliança. These names were not chosen by chance: since he had gotten resources to carry out his long-planned favela removal from the Alliance for Progress, funded by the U.S. Agency for International Development (USAID), Lacerda decided to pay homage to the U.S. president and the international funding program.[3]

The military regime and dictatorship years of 1964–78 were times of much debate but also considerable fear. As a private institution, PUC somehow managed to preserve itself during this period, maintaining a certain degree of autonomy in how it trained its students. I thus got a classic sociology education that included not only Émile Durkheim and Max Weber but also Karl Marx. At the same time, U.S. sociology made inroads through the work of Talcott Parsons and Robert Merton.

I have always been attracted to fieldwork, and it was because I thought of becoming a researcher that I chose to study sociology. However, this was not the emphasis of the training in the sociology and political science program at PUC. The course in research methods and techniques taught how to carry out a good survey, and the statistics courses that were part of our curriculum reinforced quantitative methods requiring data set calculations. At this time in Rio, the classic texts of the first Chicago School—now widely taught in master's and doctoral programs—were not known.[4] Only Donald Pierson's textbook *Teoria e pesquisa em sociologia* (Theory and research in sociology), revised after 1945, was recommended for classes.

At the same time, right beside the building where I studied, there was a veritable social science laboratory. From the third floor, I could watch the comings and goings of the residents of the Parque Proletário da Gávea (Gávea Proletarian Park), built in the 1940s during the Getúlio Vargas era. It was supposed to have been a temporary housing upgrade for the dwellers of several favelas. However, an enormous contrast separated what we saw from what we were taught and were interested in. The most engaging debates for us had to do with the historical moment of the nation and the sociopolitical tendencies of Latin America. What was most important was to discuss and understand Brazil, the so-called Brazilian reality. In fact, in the midst of the military dictatorship, PUC was a place where students could breathe easily and escape the repression bearing down so heavily on the public federal universities.

In 1966, a research center that operated at PUC announced it was recruiting interns to conduct a survey at three favelas—Brás de Pina, Mata Machado, and Morro União.[5] I did not think twice; I applied. It was thus, with a questionnaire in my hands, that I stepped into a favela for the first time. The instructions were to knock on the door of every tenth shack and give the questionnaire to the head of the household. We were carrying out the socioeconomic survey delegated to PUC by the Secretariat of the Economy of the Guanabara state government.

I have few memories of this first experience aside from the inhabitants' reticence to receive young university students seeking information about numbers of household residents, family composition, income, occupation, and education level. By its very nature, the survey did not allow a more intimate connection with the families selected for the sample, and quite rightly there was mistrust of our intentions in collecting this information.

For me this first experience was frustrating. I wanted to carry out another sort of work in the favela, one that could to help me understand that intriguing reality, which remained unknown to me even after that initial contact. Indeed, at that time, many myths populated my thoughts. In short, these were that the favela represented the world of the "people," the authentic locus of Rio life, of the samba schools, of popular religiosity, of the *jogo do bicho* ("animal game," popular but illegal, analogous to "numbers" in U.S. cities), and of *malandragem* in the best sense of the term.[6] A different world concentrated on Rio's hillsides, the favela seemed strange to me, quite distinct from the middle-class reality that was my way of life.

The following year, fieldwork led to me to a series of hits and misses that culminated in participant observation conducted in Rocinha favela.[7] Carlos Alberto de Medina offered me this opportunity in 1967 and served as a true adviser.[8] I had met Medina at the Centro Latino Americano de Pesquisas em Ciências Sociais (CLAPCS), an organ of the United Nations Educational, Scientific, and Cultural Organization (UNESCO) based in Rio, where I was a scholarship intern at its Center for Documentation.

At that time, there were few extant, accessible studies of Rio favelas. Of these rare available texts I had already read the diary of Carolina Maria de Jesus's *Quarto de despejo*, first published in 1960 and released in English translation as *Child of the Dark: The Diary of Carolina Maria de Jesus* in 1962. This national and international bestseller recounted the life of a favela dweller in the city of São Paulo. I had also read the work of the Sociedade de Análises Gráficas e Mecanográficas Aplicadas aos Complexos Sociais (SAGMACS), *Aspectos humanos da favela carioca* (Human aspects of the Carioca favela), published by the newspaper *O Estado de São Paulo*, whose authors include Father Louis-Joseph Lebret and José Arthur Rios; Carlos Alberto de Medina's *A favela e o demagogo* (The favela and the demagogue; 1964); and the essay by Andrew Pearse, "Some Characteristics of Urbanization in the City of Rio de Janeiro" (1961).

In contrast, I had read very little about fieldwork in urban areas, although there were texts in English dealing with the subject, notably the methodological appendix to *Street Corner Society*, published in the second U.S. edition in 1955. It was thus that I began to practice my "anthropology at home," without yet knowing the rules of how to turn the exotic into the familiar and the familiar into the exotic, and not having studied otherness or the challenges of fieldwork in the city. At that time, in 1967, several articles that every student of methodology should read had not yet been published: "O ofício de etnólogo; ou como ter *anthropological blues*" (The ethnologist's trade, or how to have the anthropological blues) by Roberto da Matta and "Observando o familiar" (Observing the familiar) by Gilberto Velho, both published in 1978. I had not yet been introduced to "On Intellectual Craftsmanship," the appendix to *The*

Sociological Imagination by C. Wright Mills (1959; first edition in Portuguese, *A imaginação sociológica*, 1965), to the classic texts of the first Chicago School, or to *The Craft of Sociology* by Pierre Bourdieu, Jean-Claude Chamboredon, and Jean-Claude Passeron, to which I only had access many years later (in the 1980 French edition).

Although I was supported by my adviser, I now see that, in fact, I was unprepared to face the complexity of this experience of participant observation. Naive at first, I believed everything I was told. I felt like an adventurer taming a new land. I also recall the envy of most of my university classmates, who only knew the middle-class neighborhoods—except for those who had worked in grassroots education in some Rio favelas. It took several months for me to find my place as a researcher and observer and several more to resolve the question of my indebtedness to the residents and intermediaries who were my informants, who helped me in my research into daily life, without receiving anything in return unless it was—as I came to learn later—the friendship of a Bahian university student who had moved to Rocinha and the status that this friendship brought in the eyes of the other residents.

The Centro de Estatística Religiosa e Investigações Sociais (CERIS) was doing this study for the Conferência Nacional dos Bispos do Brasil (CNBB). The Vatican was worried about losing ground among the faithful in Brazil, and the CNBB had this research program in its five-year plan.[9] I soon learned that I needed to make it clear to the residents what had brought me there, bearing in mind that in those years it was important not to raise any sort of suspicion. Mistrust was natural due to the military regime and the antifavela policy Governor Lacerda had begun with the removal to Vila Kennedy and Vila Aliança, but it was also unsurprising when faced with people of another class who viewed one's neighborhood as an object of study.

Having worked on religion in the favela (Medina and Valladares 1968), I became interested in the favela itself. After a long phase of immersion, I was accepted in my role as observer and outsider. Here is not the place to tell all of my adventures and misadventures in Rocinha. However, it is worth mentioning that it was in conversations with my adviser, far from the field, and in the company of other researchers, many of whom were young like me, especially anthropologists and architects, that I could share my discoveries and distress, broaden my knowledge of Rio's favelas, and discuss theories and interpretations about poverty and squatter settlements in Latin America, notably through the recently published texts by the architect John Turner (1969) and the anthropologist William Mangin (1967), which we all were reading at the time.

There were at least three meeting places: (1) the CLAPCS, thanks to its excellent library and the recently created master's program in social anthropology at the National Museum of the Universidade Federal do Rio de Janeiro (UFRJ), a program initially headquartered at the CLAPCS; (2) the apartment of anthropologist Anthony Leeds, where he held informal seminars that brought together people working with and in favelas; and (3) the office of the Quadra architectural group, which carried out the pilot experiment in urban planning in the favela of Brás de Pina. Everyone, I included, published our research: Lucien Parisse, a French Dominican doing his doctoral thesis for the University of Strasbourg; Jean-Pierre Bombart, who was in Brazil for the Coopération Technique Française (French Technical Cooperation); Anthony Leeds and the group of Peace Corps volunteers, including Elizabeth Leeds, Paul Silberstein, Lawrence Salmen, Diana Brown, and Janice Perlman, who were writing their dissertations for various U.S. universities; and a group of Brazilians, including Luiz Antonio Machado da Silva, who was engaged in various surveys in the favelas, and the architects Carlos Nelson Ferreira dos Santos and Rogério Aroeira Neves.

At that time, we all knew each other and broadly shared the same ideas: (1) that characterizing favelas as marginal did not make sense since, in addition to emerging alongside the city, they exhibited great economic dynamism and gathered a population that was integrated into the dominant political, economic, and social system, even if this participation was partial and had its own characteristics; (2) that the favelas represented a very important segment of the working-class housing market, a market that had its own rules, different from those of the regular housing market and constituted in the absence of the public sector; (3) that the favela residents were against removal and in favor of urban improvements and the extension of public services to their homes, with their collective labor proof of the residents' collaboration with efforts already carried out by some institutions; (4) that only by anthropological fieldwork or work with the assistance of the residents was it possible to come to know the favelas, their residents, and the functioning of their organizations and networks.

Having already moved away somewhat from religious topics, I was increasingly interested in the phenomenon of the favelas themselves, their internal organization, both spatial and social, their different social and political actors, be they local or not. In the favela where I was doing research, I turned my gaze and interest toward the structuring elements of this social space and toward institutions other than the Catholic Church, with the intention of understanding better the structure of the place. In an article "Associações voluntárias na favela" (Voluntary associations in the favela; Valladares 1977), I analyzed the many associations existent in Rocinha in 1969 and the competition for clientele in a divided and heterogeneous locale. This essay questioned the idea of the favela as a community, a notion that Medina (1969) and the Leedses (1978) also opposed.

The period during which I lived in Rocinha coincided with the favela removal policy of Governor Francisco Negrão de Lima (1966–71). What had been at first a local government initiative (that of Lacerda) with U.S. aid became a federal policy led by the Coordenação de Habitação de Interesse Social da Área Metropolitana do Grande Rio (CHISAM) financed by the recently established Banco Nacional da Habitação (BNH), a creation of the military government. A cleansing operation was prepared for the South Zone of Rio de Janeiro, with a view to eliminating its favelas. Notwithstanding its distance from Lagoa Rodrigo de Freitas, the focus of the intervention, Rocinha ended up being partially affected by the construction of the Dois Irmãos Tunnel (now Zuzu Angel Tunnel), now linking two sides of the hill on which Rocinha is located and guaranteeing the expansion of the South Zone in the direction of Barra da Tijuca.

For an observer interested in understanding the mechanisms of urban and housing policy and at the same time involved with the daily life of the favela, the partial removal of Rocinha was impossible to ignore. I began to register in my field diary everything I saw, heard, and felt, noting the mobilization of social workers and the government technicians in preparation for what would be happening. I specifically noted all of the informal relations developed after the announcement of the intervention in the area, including residents' associations, important local groups, and the "last-minute *favelados*" — those who moved into the favela for the sole purpose of being included in the relocation program. The stir caused by the external intervention caught my attention, as did the informal relations and different interests that directly affected the local housing market.

In *Passa-se uma casa* (Passing by a house; Valladares 1978a), I described and analyzed in detail the removal of a favela, the residents' settlement in a public housing block, their integration into the housing financing system, and their return to the favela. The book, which grew out of my doctoral thesis defended in France, led me to broaden my horizons and enabled me to experience the feeling of distancing. The long stay in Europe was, for me, an introduction to a new group of authors as well as to these authors' critical reflection on the city, to the issue of housing, and to the role of the United States in urban policies. These authors were Raymond Ledrut, Henri Lefebvre, Manuel Castells, Jean Lojkine, Christian Topalov, Francis Godard, and Edmond Préteceille. With Ruth Glass, I entered the world of poverty and philanthropy in Victorian England, discovering the importance of this philanthropy to understanding social welfare for the poor.

These experiences altered my course and changed my way of working on my object of study. From an interest initially molded on a case study and on the understanding of what a favela is (the conceptual aspects linked to the nature of this reality, the structure, and relations with the outside world), there followed a concern with the favela as an object of urban policies. These policies, throughout a range of circumstances, changed both in their instruments and purposes and in their social actors (Valladares 1976, 1977, 1978b, 1981). In fact, understanding such policies, which at first glance appeared to be local, required a comparative and international point of view (Valladares 1985).

During the 1980s, with Rocinha as a point of reflection, I turned to studying a phenomenon considered relevant to Brazilian sociology: urban social movements (Boschi and Valladares 1982, 1983), which in the last phase of the military dictatorship were understood as a struggle for full citizenship. So I returned to Rocinha in 1988 to study the socialization of children in the face of violence (Valladares 1990a), a topic that had an important place in the literature on poverty in Brazil. In addition to this, and in opposition to a dominant view that poverty necessarily brings with it delinquency—that poor people in Rio de Janeiro must choose between the world of work and a career as a gangster—I posited the hypothesis of another possible route by way of a work ethic transmitted and inculcated mainly by mothers.

From there, it became increasingly clear to me that the urban question should not and could not be separated from the international social question. Analyses done in several countries on "spontaneous" housing, popular mobilization in its various forms, and the impact of neighborhood associations demonstrated that a broader analysis would necessarily take into account the effects of poverty, social inequalities, and public policies.

The importance of social representations, of the history of ideas and their circulation, and the formation of a scholarly understanding also came to influence my reflection. Frequent contact with European colleagues opened up new perspectives that underscored the need to understand the genesis and history of thought about social phenomena as well as the constitution of thematic areas and the circulation of ideas (Depaule and Topalov 1996; Topalov 1999). In this way, after having analyzed the matrices (discourses and interpretations) of reflection on urban poverty in Brazil, their relation to the several stages of the urbanization process, and their corresponding spatial forms (Valladares 1991), I was led to rethink the favela—more precisely, its field of study, the reasons for constituting this field, the actors who have contributed to this reflection process — that is, the favela before and after the advent of the social sciences. And so I decided to work on a sociology of the sociology of the favela.

At the Instituto Universitário de Pesquisas do Rio de Janeiro (IUPERJ), where I was teaching, I was able to carry out a study of trends in urban research in Brazil, thanks to URBANDATA, the bibliographic database on urban Brazil. By critically reading intellectual production in texts in the fields of sociology, anthropology, geography, history, and urban planning, I was able to delimit the field of urban studies and grasp its origins and constitutive paradigms based on a large number of studies and analyses. I also could show how a field of urban studies in Brazil was institutionalized by public and private organs. Finally, I studied the role assumed by Brazilian universities in the development of the field and the imposition of certain topics to the detriment of others (Valladares and Coelho 1995).

During the 1990s, the subject of the favela came into fashion, with more and more graduate students becoming interested in the topic. The number of new academic research projects about the favela caught my attention. A large portion of these projects were funded by governmental agencies. The Programa Favela-Bairro (Favela to Neighborhood Program), launched by the Rio Mayor's Office in 1993, stimulated the production of these studies, with funding from the Financiadora de Estudos e Projetos (FINEP) to evaluate the program to be implemented by the Municipal Secretariat for Housing.

But could this sudden interest in favelas, on the part of graduate students and researchers and of governmental and nongovernmental institutions, be explained by the rise of Programa Favela-Bairro? Or was this interest "independent," a reflection of the intense favelization occurring in Rio not only in the multiplication of the number of favelas but especially in the increasing density of these clusters? Indeed, the proportion of Rio's population that lived in favelas was increasing: from 16 percent in 1991 to 18.7 percent in 2000.

In the face of this renewed interest, most surprising was the lack of awareness or forgetting of the previous work on this topic, especially among the younger generations who sought me out as an adviser. Over and over again, I encountered students and researchers who gave priority to "objective" indicators, as if these were not, in and of themselves, historically dated social productions, always developed in specific contexts. What is more, they appeared to be the very "discoverers" of the favelas in the midst of the city, as if nothing had been published in the decades before.

All of the contributions of the authors who, in the past, had broadly dissected the topic, questioning the very definition of what was called "favela," comparing this space with other forms of working-class housing, describing its housing market, analyzing previous experiments in urban planning and relations among residents, representatives of associations and the public sector — all this production had been forgotten. With some exceptions, the new authors treated the history of research on the favela as a tabula rasa, remembering only the history of the favela, according to the political circumstances and within the restrictive perspective of resituating current policies in relation to the policies of the past.

In parallel, since the 1980s, accounts and news stories depicting violence, the drug trade, and criminality in and around the favelas came to dominate front pages in Brazilian newspapers to the point that they became a Rio specificity — a fact that no doubt contributed to researchers' renewed interest. The almost systematic association between poverty and violent criminality made the favela a synonym for outlaw territory, where gangsters and police are in constant struggle. But could the development of this new interest in the favela be explained by the escalation in violence alone? Or could it be that violence and the favela had not already been systematically associated for a long time?

It seems that the subject of the favela may have been reactivated by the importance of issues related to sociospatial segregation. In a metropolis in which geographic space is so particular — the sea and the hills — the presence of favelas in the midst of middle- and upper-class districts provides a violent contrast between the way of life of the poor and that of the wealthy. The increase in violence reinforces the fear that inhabitants of the formal urban area feel with respect to the population of the hills, accentuating a dualistic view quickly reduced to concise formulations like the "divided city" (*Cidade partida*; Ventura 1994). The favelas thus come to be perceived as "the other half of the city," appearing to be, first and foremost, spaces of violence and poverty, of illegality as opposed to the "legal" city.

This representation of the favela as a space of violence, of all sorts of illegality, as a pocket of poverty and social exclusion, seems to me a premature generalization, contrary to my observations over a long time and to certain data from the 1991 census. Not that the favelas do not have poor residents and crime, but a large part of the poor population of Rio de Janeiro is concentrated in the suburbs and in peripheral, irregular parcels of land, not to mention those who are homeless. Moreover, violence occurs in many other neighborhoods: the drug trade also exists outside the favelas.

During my thirty years regularly spent in Rocinha, I witnessed, overall, the development of great diversity, visible in spatial as well as social differences. Within Rocinha itself, there were various "Rocinhas." The expansion of built space, the increase in masonry, and the verticalization of construction—reaching as high as six stories—are testimony to an intense dynamism in the housing market. This process is accompanied by development of commerce and specialized services by professionals from within and without, and by the numerous domestic and foreign nongovernmental organizations (NGOs) that, side by side with the residents' association, try to mobilize the local population. This is not to mention the up-to-date technology, widely disseminated, such as cable television and the internet.

This contrast between representations and my perceptions led me to resume my fieldwork in a more systematic way, in order to deepen my observations that had led me to doubt the dominant representations. In July 1997, I spent ten days without leaving Rocinha, staying in the home of a former neighbor who over time had become a friend. This experience confirmed for me not only changes that I had already observed but also many others that I had not noticed until then, revealing to me positive and surprising ties with globalization (Valladares 2002a).

I considered then that the modes of production and persistence of the stereotypes linked to the images of the favela should constitute a motive for reflection. To understand better how scholarly production was able to maintain these conceptions, with the help of the URBANDATA-Brasil team, a colleague and I edited an analytical bibliography showing what was already known about the Rio favela (Valladares and Medeiros 2003). This precious material revealed a voluminous and quite heterogeneous production, suggesting historical consistency in the different representations of favelas.

Immersion in this production led me to shift my questions from the favela to the way the favela had been perceived and imagined in various historical and political contexts; that is, from sociology of the favela to the social history of thought about the favela. This procedure begins with the idea that the category of favela used today, in both scholarly production and the media, is the more or less cumulative and more or less contradictory result of successive social representations, originating from the constructions of social actors who have mobilized around this urban social object. In appearance, that so-evident favela is, in a certain way, an "invented" favela. It is this process of invention that I intend to elucidate, tracing, throughout the twentieth century, speeches, images, representations, and analyses that have accompanied the hundred years of the favelas' concrete existence in Rio de Janeiro.

CHAPTER ONE

GENESIS OF THE RIO FAVELA

From Country to City, from Rejection to Control[1]

Favelas, now seen as a typically urban phenomenon, were viewed during the first half of the twentieth century as a veritable "rural world in the city." This chapter analyzes the early representations of these spaces in Rio de Janeiro, where they have existed now for over a hundred years.[2] I argue that the dominant representations of the favela in the second half of the twentieth century broadly depended on those of the first decades of the century and that these representations organized a founding myth of the favela's social representation.

By reviewing nonspecific literature on the topic, I will stitch together notes and information that confirm the favela's growing importance in the social imaginary and show how this social construction of representations of the favela occurred. This happened at a time when knowledge and action were inseparable, and the concerns of the intelligentsia, both local and national, were centered on the future of the young republic — on the health of society, on the hygiene of the country, and on the beautification of the city of Rio de Janeiro.

This multiplicity of views and interpretations — a legacy of journalists, medical doctors, engineers, and urban planners who wrote even before the social sciences came on the scene — attests to the representations, associations, images, and vocabulary used at various times by diverse social actors.

Taken as a whole, the bibliography of writings about the Rio favela suggests a periodization, widely disseminated, of relations between the state and the favela, and between the latter and the various political regimes peculiar to each period. This evolution may vary according to the authors,[3] but it is generally broken into the following stages: (1) the 1930s — the beginning of the process of favelization of Rio de Janeiro and the recognition of the favela by the 1937 Código de Obras (Building Code); (2) the 1940s — the first proposal of public intervention, leading to the creation of the Proletarian Parks during the Vargas era; (3) the 1950s and the early 1960s—uncontrolled expansion of favelas under the populist aegis; (4) from the mid-1960s to the end of the 1970s—the elimination of the favelas and removal of their residents during the authoritarian regime; (5) the 1980s—urbanization of the favelas by the BNH and by the social service agencies after the return to democracy; (6) the 1990s—urbanization of the favelas by means of Rio de Janeiro's policies and the Programa Favela-Bairro (Favela to Neighborhood Program).

My intent is to reconstruct the evolution of the representations of this social space based on landmarks and monuments that are exceptions to the generally used periodization. In other words, the history of reflection on the favela should not be confused with the history of the favela properly speaking, based on dates, events, and sociohistorical conditions, characterized moreover by various actions or interventions implemented by governments in distinct political and administrative moments.

Based on a reading that does not follow established historiography, I propose a break with the traditional periodization without wholly discarding it. To this end, I propose a sociology of the sociology of the favela that examines the origins and constitution of learned thought about this social phenomenon, privileging its actors, connections, interests, representations, and actions.

The history of reflection on the favela here follows another logic, and its periodization is constituted on the basis of a myth of origin: the image of the settlement of Canudos described by Euclides da Cunha in *Os Sertões* (1902; published in English as *Backlands: The Canudos Campaign*, 2010). This is an image that corresponds to those glimpsed by the first visitors to the favela in Rio, when they transposed their descriptions of the duality coast-versus-backlands to the duality city-versus-favela.

Following this period of discovery comes a second moment of transformation of the favela into a social and urban planning problem, followed by a third period, in which an administrative approach to the problem takes the shape of concrete measures and policies. A fourth period relates to the production of official data by way of the 1948 census of the favelas of the Federal District and the General Census of 1950, which generalized the definition of this sort of urban residential cluster.

When the social sciences came on the scene, other periods followed. In this chapter, however, I intend to consider only the first four periods, with the goal of pointing out the representations that inspired the social sciences or that, not always consciously, they inherited.

Neither in Europe nor in Brazil were the social sciences at the roots of the "discovery" of poverty (Leclerc 1979; Himmelfarb 1984; Bresciani 1984; Barret-Ducrocq 1991; Valladares 1991). In the nineteenth century, when urban poverty became a concern of European elites, it was professionals in the press, literature, medicine, law, and philanthropy who came to describe poverty and propose measures to fight economic misery. This knowledge was used to a practical end: to understand, to indict, and to act; that is, knowledge was for proposing solutions, for ministering to and managing poverty and those affected by it. And so science placed itself at the service of reason, of urban order, and of the health of urban populations.

In Rio de Janeiro, as in Europe, those first interested in portraying the urban scene and its characters in detail turned their gaze to the *cortiço*, or tenement.[4] As the locus of poverty par excellence in the nineteenth century, these were residences inhabited both by workers and by *vagabundos* (bums) and *malandros* (hustlers) — members of the so-called dangerous class. Defined as a "social hell," the tenement was seen as the gateway to idleness and crime, as well as an environment that favored epidemics. It was thus cast as a threat to social and moral order. As a space believed to propagate disease and vice, it was denounced and condemned through medical and hygienist discourse, which led city governments to adopt administrative measures.[5] Figure 1, a caricature by J. Carlos, confirms this negative image of the world of the poor, present in Rio de Janeiro since the turn of the nineteenth to twentieth century.

In Rio de Janeiro, laws were passed to block the construction of new tenements.[6] At the end of the nineteenth century, a veritable war was unleashed, leading to the demolition of the most important *cortiço*, Cabeça de Porco (Pig's Head). Later, Francisco Pereira Passos, mayor of Rio from 1902 to 1906 and known as the "Tropical Haussmann,"[7] became the great agent of urban social reform. One of his principal goals was to sanitize and civilize his city by eradicating countless dwellings of the poor.

Studies of the Rio de Janeiro tenements show that this type of residence could be considered the "seed" of the favela. According to a study by Lillian Fessler Vaz (1994, 591), the Cabeça de Porco tenement, destroyed by Mayor Cândido Barata Ribeiro in 1893, had shacks and precarious dwellings of the sort identified in Morro da Providência (later Morro da Favela). Other authors also established a direct connection between the demolition of tene-

Figure 1. "Typical Personages of the Idle Poor" (from *Revista para Todos*, no. 630, January 1931, Archive of Eduardo Augusto de Brito e Cunha).

ments in the city center and the illegal settlements in the hills in the early twentieth century (O. Rocha 1986; L. Carvalho 1986; Benchimol 1990).

It was only after this iron-fisted campaign against the tenement that interest was awakened in the favela as a new geographic and social space and the most recent territory of poverty. From the beginning, such interest was directed toward a certain favela that catalyzed everyone's attention. This was Morro da Favella, which had already existed under the name Morro da Providência, and which earned its place in history through its connection with the Canudos Campaign. Former campaign combatants took up residence there, with the goal of pressuring the Ministry of War to pay their back salaries. Gradually, the name of Morro da Favella was extended to any group of shacks clustered without a street plan or access to public services, on invaded public or private land. These clusters began to multiply in the center and the North and South Zones of the city of Rio de Janeiro.

According to Maurício de Almeida Abreu, who researched the newspaper *Correio da Manhã* between 1901 and 1930, it was only in the second decade of the twentieth century that the word "favela" became a generic noun no longer referring just to Morro da Favella.[8] A new category thus arose to designate a poor urban habitat of illegal, irregular settlement, without regard to norms, and generally on hillsides.

It is important to note that the phenomenon of the favela existed before it appeared as a category. The occupation of Morro da Providência dates from 1897. In 1898, Morro de Santo Antônio showed signs of a similar favelization process. According to Abreu and Lillian Vaz (1991), soldiers from another battalion returning from the same Canudos Campaign built shacks—with authorization from military chiefs—on Santo Antônio Hill, between Evaristo da Veiga and Lavradio Streets in central Rio. In 1898, a member of a hygiene commission pointed out the disturbing development of shacks in an already occupied area, while in 1901 the press denounced "the development of a completely new neighborhood, built without permission from municipal authorities and on property belonging to the state. . . . It contains a total of 150 shacks . . . and about 623 inhabitants" (*Jornal do Commercio*, 14 October 1901, qtd. in M. Abreu 1994b, 37).

The favelas of Quinta do Caju, Mangueira,[9] and Serra Morena also date from the nineteenth century, all before Morro da Favella. Occupation of these areas began in 1881, and nothing proves that they were the result of illegal settlement. In the cases of both Quinta do Caju and Mangueira, the first inhabitants do not appear to have been from the Brazilian countryside. They were Portuguese, Spanish, and Italian immigrants, leading one to suppose

Genesis of the Rio Favela

Figure 2. Oswaldo Cruz sanitizing Morro da Favella
(*Oswaldo Cruz Monumenta Histórica*, vol. 1, no. 188).

that their settlement in these areas was authorized.[10] Notwithstanding, it was Morro da Favella that went down in history. Already by 1900, the *Jornal do Brasil* proclaimed it to be "infested with vagrants and criminals that are shocking to families." According to Marcos Luiz Bretas (1997, 75), a police officer pointed out in his report that "even though there are no families in the designated locale, it is impossible to do policing there because in this locale, which is a focal point of deserters, thieves, and common soldiers, there are no streets, the hovels are built of wood and covered with zinc roofs, and there is not a single gas outlet on the entire hill."

Morro da Favella, which was photographed as early as the first decade of the twentieth century, not only drew considerable attention but also gave rise to initiatives by authorities, such as the sanitation campaign of 1907, under the direction of Oswaldo Cruz,[11] illustrated in important caricatures published in the press.[12]

A caricature in the magazine *O Malho* (fig. 2) shows Oswaldo Cruz well-dressed, wearing shoes, with hair combed, bearing a Red Cross armband on his left arm, while, with his right hand, he sweeps the population out of Morro da Favella, with a comb that reads "Hygiene Police." Morro da Favella is rep-

Genesis of the Rio Favela

resented by the head of man with a surly expression, perhaps even with the look of an evildoer. The image suggests that the inhabitants are as lice to be removed. A short text accompanies the caricature: "An indispensable cleaning: Hygiene will clean Morro da Favella, next to the Central Railway. For this reason, the residents were told to move within ten days."

In the early decades of the twentieth century, journalists, engineers, medical doctors, and public figures connected with management of the capital, including chiefs of police, gradually lost interest in the tenements, which became "a thing of the past," of less importance for hygienism. The tenements survived only residually.

The favela then came to occupy first place in the debates about the future of the capital and of Brazil itself. It became the object of discourse of hygienist doctors who condemned the unhealthy dwellings. The ecological premise that the environment conditions human behavior was applied to the favela, and the perception persisted that the poorer classes were responsible both for their own ills and those of the city.[13] This leads one to see that the debate about poverty and the environment of the poor, which had stirred up the local and national elites since the nineteenth century, would give rise to specific thinking about the Rio favela.

THE DISCOVERY OF THE MYTH OF ORIGIN: EUCLIDES DA CUNHA, CANUDOS, AND THE RIO FAVELAS

The process of constructing social representations of the favela began with descriptions and images that were left to us by writers, journalists, and social reformers at the beginning of the twentieth century. Their writings, widely distributed at the time, caused a collective imaginary to develop about the microcosm of the favela and its residents, at the same time that they set up the opposition between favela and city.

Although they belonged to differing ideological and political schools of thought and pursued distinct objectives in their visits to the hillsides, these writers shared a view of what these areas and their residents represented in the context of the federal capital and the young republic. Their points of view referred to a group of conceptions to the same world of values and ideas. Their representations converged to establish an archetype of the favela, a different world that emerged on the Rio landscape, against the current of the established urban social order.

To better understand this process, we must attend to a series of questions: What was the common origin of this understanding? Why did a certain view

Genesis of the Rio Favela

become consensual? And why did such a social construction attach itself to a myth, referred to by practically all of the authors who spoke of the favela at the beginning of the twentieth century—the myth of Canudos?[14]

Reading the texts from beginning of the century leads one to associate Morro da Providência, in Rio de Janeiro, with the town of Canudos, in the backlands of the state of Bahia. In fact, the two histories overlap, since it was the former federal combatants in the Canudos Campaign who settled in Morro da Providência, thereafter called Morro da Favella. Most of the commentators present two reasons for this change of name: (1) the favela plant, which had given its name to Morro da Favella in Canudos, was also found in the vegetation that covered Morro da Providência,[15] and (2) the fierce resistance during the Canudos war of the entrenched fighters on the Bahian Morro da Favella, which had slowed the final victory of the Army of the Republic (the army's taking of this position was decisive in the battle).

If the first explanation speaks to a physical similarity, the second has a powerful symbolic connotation that suggests resistance, the struggle of the oppressed against a powerful and dominating adversary. In Rio de Janeiro, the demobilized soldiers of the Canudos Campaign settled Morro da Providência, a strategic position in relation to the War Ministry, in hopes of receiving their overdue payment.

The mark of Canudos on this founding moment is quite evident. What I intend to demonstrate, however, is that Canudos's mark on the Rio favelas' myth of origin was more than a simple allusion to the Bahian town and the final battle. It also incorporated additional elements from the account of the campaign by Euclides da Cunha in *Os Sertões* (see note 14).

Considered Brazil's "number one book" (R. Abreu 1998), with more than thirty editions in Portuguese—the first in 1902, the second in 1903, and the third in 1905 published by Edições Laemmert—*Os Sertões* was read by virtually every intellectual of the time, putting the Canudos Campaign very much in the collective memory. Berthold Zilly (1998, 14) observes that Cunha and his seminal epic of the Bahia backlands, whose events occurred in the closing years of the nineteenth century, would not have had the importance today that it was accorded in the First Republic. The impact at the time was considerable and can be measured by the number of texts *Os Sertões* inspired, as surveyed in bibliographies by Irene Monteiro Reis (1971) and by Maria Japor de Oliveira Garcia and Vera Maria Fürtenau (1995), to which we can add recent publications on the role of Euclides da Cunha in Brazilian social thought and on his influence past and present (N. Lima 1999; R. Abreu 1998; Fundação Oswaldo Cruz 1998).

Cunha's book was published after Morro da Providência was rebaptized Morro da Favella (1897), but this event would have passed unnoticed and word "favela" would not have had the legacy it has had without the forceful, striking images that *Os Sertões* transmitted, images that could allow Brazilian intellectuals to understand and interpret the emerging favela. By way of example, let us consider the article "Os livres acampamentos da miséria" (The open camps of misery) by João do Rio, man-about-town and columnist, published in the *Gazeta de Notícias* in 1908, reprinted in the book *Vida vertiginosa* (Dizzying life) in 1911, and collected in *João do Rio: Uma antologia* (Martins 1971). The article tells of the author's visit, on the occasion of a music festival, to Morro de Santo Antônio, which had become a favela, like Morro da Providência, during the last years of the nineteenth century.

> I had the idea that Morro de Santo Antônio was a place where poor workers gathered while awaiting housing, and the temptation arose to attend the serenade. . . . The hill was like any other hill. A wide, poorly maintained path, on one side revealing, in layers that spread out ever, the lights of the city. . . . I followed [the people] and came upon another world. The lights had disappeared. *We were in the country, in the backlands, far from the city.* The path that snaked down was sometimes narrow, sometimes wide, full of troughs and holes. On either side, narrow houses, made of planks from wooden crates, with fences indicating yards. The descent became difficult. (Martins 1971, 51, 52, 53; emphasis added)

Our man-about-town continued:

> How did that curious village of indolent misery grow up there? It is certain that today it shelters perhaps more than 1,500 people. The houses are not rented, they are sold. . . . The price of a normal house is 40–70 *mil réis*. All are built on the ground, without regard to depressions on the lot, with wood from crates, sheet metal, and bamboo. . . . *One had, in the luminous shadows of the starry night, the studied impression of the entrance to the village of Canudos* or the acrobatic idea of a vast, multiform chicken coop. (Martins 1971, 54–55; emphasis added)

What would become the model of the favela was already, therefore, quite present in the spirit of these Rio intellectuals, who discovered new spaces in the city through Euclides da Cunha's gaze on Canudos. The source of inspira-

Figure 3. A *sertanejo*'s house in Canudos. Photo by Flávio de Barros,
army photographer (Historical Archive of the Museum of the Republic,
Photographic Conservation and Preservation Center—FUNARTE).

tion is quite evident in the way of representing not only the geography but also
its population.

In the reports of visits by journalists, the hills are described as spaces endowed with a particular geography. In the 1924 *crônica* (a piece for a column)
"A favela que eu vi" (The Favela I Saw), Benjamin Costallat (1995, 34) described the difficulties he had in getting to the top of Morro da Favella because
of its irregular topography: "It's a goat trail. One doesn't walk, one gravitates.
The feet lose their normal function of walking, they become claws. . . . I was
always told of the danger in going up Favella. . . . The greatest risk that I found
on Favella was the risk, at every step, of plunging from up there into the quarry
or down the hill."

In Rio, as in Canudos, the hill offers a strategic position. It looks out over
the city and, isolated, hides from those below who watch what takes place up
there. All who arrive at the most elevated part, as around Canudos, experience
a sensation of fear mixed with a sort of fascination. For Euclides da Cunha
(2010),

> There is an unexpected vista awaiting the traveler crossing this
> region. One will get the feeling that one is treading the ruins from an

Figure 4. One of the first photographs of Morro da Favella
(Departamento Geral de Polícia da Capital / Morro da Providência,
Memória da Favela, Museum of Image and Sound, Augusto Malta Collection).

earthquake as one climbs now up the hills closest to Canudos [34]. . . .
[Seeing Canudos,] at first glance, before the eye could accustom itself
to the maze of huts and labyrinth of alleys leading to the big square
where the churches were located, the visitor would have the impression
of coming upon a large city [258]. . . . General Arthur Oscar de Andrade
Guimarães, mounted on horseback next to the cannons, gazed for the
first time through the dazzling moonlight, at the mysterious backland
city [306]. . . . They counted: one, two, three, four, five thousand huts!
Five thousand or more! It might be six thousand. There were about
fifteen thousand to twenty thousand people dug into that Babylonian
weed patch. They were all invisible [342].

Journalists were likewise awed by the mazes of shacks, with the impoverished citadels in Rio. Luiz Edmundo, the author of several books on political
and cultural life during Rio's Belle Époque, was no less explicit in his perception of the favela as a reminder of Canudos in the city. As João do Rio had done,
he visited Morro de Santo Antônio. Afterward he wrote in his book *O Rio de
Janeiro do meu tempo* (The Rio de Janeiro of my time, 1938) that *"a large majority of the dwellings are improvised, made of scraps and rags, tattered and sad, like*

       Genesis of the Rio Favela

their dwellers. Among them live beggars—true ones—when they are not stationed in the lodgings on Misericórdia, capoeira fighters, rogues, vagrants of all sorts, women without the support of relatives, the elderly who can no longer work, abandoned children, and among them sound people who, almost worse, however, are without the aid of work, truly despised by fortune and forgotten by God" (Edmundo 1938, 246–47; emphasis added). This journalist continued the story of his visit:

> Finally we reached a more or less flat part of the settlement *where the wretched citadel spreads.* The ground is rutted and harsh, the grove of trees lacking in foliage, carpets of sedge or grass growing around the twisted and poorly traced paths. Mediocre sights. All a grim and tumbled-down group of dwellings without design or value.... Buildings generally of used lumber, unusable boards torn from crates that had been used to transport lard or codfish, poorly attached, patched up, of different colors and qualities, some popping up here, others leaning over there, rotten, splintered, or blackened. Coverings of old zinc, rarely corrugated, scrap sheet metal taken from used vessels. Everything coarsely woven together, without form or fancy. (Edmundo 1938, 2:251–52; emphasis added)

Once again it is possible to see an analogy: in Rio as in Canudos, one arrives at the top of the favela after a long march during which one must survive the *tiriricas*—sedges that produce rashes just as the leaves of the favela bush do, cross arid spaces, finally to reach a remote, unknown location. The favela described by Luiz Edmundo draws together the two "citadels of misery"—the redoubt of "fanatics" in the *sertão* and the enclave of poor people in the great coastal city. These chroniclers, when they described the new, impoverished neighborhoods of the capital of the republic, sought to show that the backlands were present in them. Indeed, the medical doctor Afrânio Peixoto affirmed in 1918, "we should not fool ourselves—our backlands begin at the edge of the Avenue."[16]

Such examples, which are countless, show the deep influence of Euclides da Cunha's book on the earliest observers of the favela. To understand better the elements of the founding myth of the Rio favela, constituted through this transposition, consider the main characteristics of Canudos as seen by the author:

1. The specificity of a process of urban growth, even though it was a settlement in a rural area, that was rapid, disorganized, and precarious: "The settlement grew at a dizzying pace, spreading over the hills. The improvised dwell-

ings were so crude that the homeless crowd was able to put up as many as a dozen a day" (Cunha 2010, 151).

2. The topography of a hilly region that makes it a veritable bastion, very difficult to access:

> The wild city was surrounded from the beginning by a formidable circle of trenches carved into all the slopes, offering a line of fire level with the ground and a commanding view of approaches from all directions. Hidden by a growth of thorny macambira trees or by stone mounds, these were not visible from a distance. Anyone approaching from the east would think that the tiny huts scattered like sentry boxes were the approach to a ranch house and its outbuildings, the home of peaceful cowboys. He would be taken aback when he suddenly came on the compactly built village, as if walking into an ambush. (Cunha 2010, 154)

In Rio, there had been an association between the terms "favela" and *morro* since the beginning of the twentieth century, from the time of the appearance of the first favelas. This happened almost automatically since the two words were long used as synonyms. In the journalistic writing of authors such as Lima Barreto and Olavo Bilac (Zaluar and Alvito 1998, 11–12), and in samba lyrics from 1928 to 1994,[17] the favela *is* the *morro*, in the geographic sense. So, in the metaphorical sense, the favela appears as a bastion, like Canudos. Costallat stated, "I was always told of the danger in going up Favella. . . . Of its terrible ruffians. Of its rogues who would rob you as easily as they might say, 'Good day'" (Costallat 1995, 34).

3. The absence of private ownership of land, replaced by collective ownership: "They wanted nothing from this life, which is why private property was a type of exaggerated tribal collectivism common to Bedouins. Personal property was limited to moveable property and their individual dwellings. There was absolute common ownership of land, pastures, and herds" (Cunha 2010, 256). "The land belongs to no one, it belongs to everyone," Costallat (1995, 35) similarly observed of a favela he visited in Rio.

4. The absence of dominion of the state and of public institutions (law, police, municipalities, and so forth) in this territory in rebellion against the republic (Cunha 2010, 185–87). As for Antônio Conselheiro himself, the author is emphatic: "He preached against the republic, that much is certain" (Cunha 2010, 167).

5. A specific political order characterized by the dominion of a chief, Antônio Conselheiro, a charismatic leader who steered his people away from

their obligations (Cunha 2010, 134–49), openly preaching insurrection against the law.

As in Canudos, the favela had a chief who controlled a citadel where public institutions were not respected. As the journalist Costallat (1995, 37) reported, "One day, a man arrived at the favela—Zé da Barra. He had come from Barra do Piraí [a municipality in the state of Rio de Janeiro]. He had already garnered great fame. His feats were well known. He was a ruffian, but with a great heart. And so Zé da Barra came and dominated the favela.... And so the favela, which had not known police, or taxes, or authorities, came to know Zé da Barra, and he was to be obeyed. And Zé da Barra became the undisputed chief of Favella."

Respective proportions aside, it is the same story of the outsider who arrives, imposes order, directs and administers a space in which recognition of constituted authorities and obedience to national laws are excluded, and comes to dominate the local population. Note that Antônio Conselheiro began his struggle against the local authorities in the state of Bahia, questioning the recently decreed autonomy of the municipalities, and he later struck out into the *sertão*, where he could have his own laws and rules prevail.

6. A space that can condition the behavior of individuals, integrating the recent arrivals into the collective, homogeneous, uniform group identity:

> The simple *sertanejo* (backlander), when he set foot in the place, was transformed.... He was taken over by the collective psychosis. ... The population was made up of the most diverse elements, from the fundamentalist believer who abdicated all the comforts of life elsewhere to the loose bandit who arrived with his rifle on his shoulder, looking for a new field of action. The place became a homogeneous community, an unconscious, brute mass growing without evolving, without organs and specialized functions, a mechanical conjunction of successive layers, like a human polyp. (Cunha 2010, 155–56)

The idea of community, so present in the field analyzed by Euclides da Cunha, wound up likewise being associated with the Rio favela, and it served as a model for the first observers who tried to characterize the social organization of the new territories of urban poverty. As we see in his description, Cunha viewed the settlement of Canudos as a community of the abject poor marked by a common identity. Luiz Edmundo (1938, 255–59), "in a pilgrimage through the distressing favela," narrated his impressions and conversations with washerwomen and illiterate single mothers, living in conditions of extreme precariousness but fatalistically accepting their lot: "Have you ever seen a poor person happy, sir? We go on carrying on our lives by the grace of God."

7. Moral behavior that the observer finds revolting, characterized by debauchery, promiscuity, lack of work, and an economy based on theft and pillaging:

> It is no surprise that promiscuity went unchecked in Canudos. The bastard children were legion, and they did not carry the brand of their origin. . . . Their leader did not promote free love but he did tolerate it. (Cunha 2010, 157)
>
> In a large area around Canudos, ranches were destroyed, villages sacked, and cities attacked by storm. [After a raid on the town of Bom Conselho,] the criminals then returned with their spoils to the village [of Canudos,] where nobody paid the least attention to their destructive behavior. . . . Anything was permitted, as long as it contributed to the revenues of the community. (Cunha 2010, 159)

In the aforementioned testimonials referring to Rio, João do Rio and Luiz Edmundo spoke of the types of the *morro*, especially hustlers, washerwomen, sorceresses, and serenaders, who had particular lifestyles from which formal wage earning appeared absent. João do Rio (1908, 55) wondered, "Were those people workers? No." He saw the favela as a place of "indolent poverty" (54). Luiz Edmundo (1938, 249) described Morro de Santo Antônio as "a veritable village of misfortune, and a mortifying wound of human misery. Santo Antônio of the wretched!"

8. A danger to the social order of the whole region, all of the sertão, with a considerable risk of contagion: "The moral environment of the backlands favors contagion and the spread of mental pathology. The disorder, still local for now, could be the seed of a conflagration throughout the interior of the North" (Cunha 1985, 283).

At the beginning of the twentieth century, a time when the favelas were not yet numerous or very important to the city, the issue of contagion is not so evident. But it still existed, as one can see in the caricature in figure 2 in which Oswaldo Cruz is combing "lice" from a head representing Morro da Favella. Even if the theme of contagion was not explicit in the reports by early observers, it would be taken up again and amplified in the following period, when the favelas became a problem to be solved.

9. An embodiment of liberty as regarded land use, labor, customs, social practices, and the payment of taxes. Notwithstanding the backwardness and the perils of contagion Cunha criticized, he recognized the strength of Canudos's inhabitants and the value they placed on a space of freedom.

In the view of the first observers of the Rio favela, living in these locations was a choice, just as moving to Canudos depended on the free will of each individual. The inhabitants of the favela were connected to their community and did not want to leave it (Costallat 1924). This dimension of a *favelado* identity had been perceived by the earliest analysts and, much later, would be heavily valued by social scientists, as we will see in chapter 3.

Throughout this analogy, the respective representations appear forcefully structured by political concerns related to the consolidation of the young republic, the health of society, and Brazil's entry into modernity. The favela belonged to an older, barbarous world, from which it was necessary for Brazil to distance itself in order to attain civilization. Observers from a voyage much shorter than one to the Bahian backlands, journalists visiting the hills of Rio de Janeiro in the early decades of the twentieth century acted as witnesses, just as Euclides da Cunha had. And, as for Canudos, where it was already possible to see the duality of the backlands versus the coast (present in the discourse of *Os Sertões*), a duality could be found again, in the early images of Rio, transposed to an opposition of favela versus city.

The source image of the favela was thus already formed by the sharp, inquisitive gaze of the journalist-observer, "another world," much closer to the countryside, to the backlands, "far from the city," which one could only reach by way of the "bridge" built by the reporter or columnist, taking the reader to the top of the hill, where the reader, a member of the middle class or elite, did not dare go.[18] An exotic universe in the midst of poverty, once concentrated in the city center in tenements and other forms of collective housing, now stretched up into the hills — where it constituted a threat to the rest of the city.

The favela had been discovered . . . and the foundation had been laid for its transformation into a problem.

THE FAVELA AS PROBLEM

The discovery of the favela was soon followed by its designation as a problem to be solved. To the writings of journalists were soon added the voices of doctors and engineers, concerned about the future of the city and its population. What to do about the favela? Launched at the beginning of the century, the debate, by the 1920s, unleashed the first major campaign against this "aesthetic leprosy" (Mattos Pimenta 1926). The debate resumed in the 1930s in response to the Agache Plan for renewal and beautification of the city of Rio de Janeiro, followed by the Building Code of 1937.

In the early years of the century, housing for the poor became a central topic in regard to the future of the republic's capital. It was a topic heavily shaped by hygienist medical discourse and picked up by engineers. Luiz César de Queiroz Ribeiro (1997) has shown that the period 1890–1906 was characterized by an acute housing crisis: the population of Rio grew geometrically at an annual rate of 2.8 percent. Large building construction projects increased at an annual rate of 3.4 percent, but these properties were destined mostly for economic activities. As for the amount of housing, this only grew at a rate of 1 percent per year. The imbalance between housing construction and population growth brought a noticeable increase in household density, from 7.3 to 9.8 people per residence (Ribeiro 1997, 173).[19]

In 1905, in the midst of the Pereira Passos urban reform, the minister of justice and internal affairs, J. J. Seabra, appointed a commission charged with reporting on the problem of housing for the poor, naming civil engineer Everardo Backheuser to deal with its "technical sanitary" aspect. Backheuser had previously served as a municipal engineer. According to Backheuser (1906, 3–4), the task would entail "thousands of demolitions, in order to widen a number of streets, opening several streets, tearing down old ruined shacks, some of which still sheltered families, and shuttering others that were unhealthy, so unhealthy that they could not be sanitized. All of this had come to make poor housing — Rio's endemic pestilence — acute, disturbing, and formidable."[20]

In particular, it was the unsanitary collective housing that had captured the engineer's attention, since, in the matter of human habitation, there already were laws and international experience related to it. Concerned as he was with the issues of unhealthiness, epidemics, and contagion, Backheuser carried out a detailed study of tenements, boardinghouses, hostels, inns, and guest houses, indicating the legislation that regulated the construction and the use of these different kinds of housing in Brazil.[21]

Even though it held a less important place in the urban landscape, the favela did not escape the engineer's clinical eye. In his groundbreaking report, he specifically mentioned the favela, perhaps the first official record of its existence. And, once again, it was Morro da Favela that drew attention "for its originality and unexpectedness" (Backheuser 1906, 111). Three photographs allow the reader to see the favela: at a distance, in panorama, and up close, on a smaller scale — in which we see the shacks and their inhabitants apparently posing in front of their homes for the photographer.[22]

This illustrated document evoked the physical aspect of the location, with its poor dwellings:

Morro da Favella is steep, with escarpments; its hillsides with ravines are overlain with small shacks without sanitation or power, with nothing.

Imagine, in fact, *houses* (!) the height of a man, with floors of beaten earth and walls of woven laths plugged with mud, flattened kerosene cans side by side, boards from crates; with a roof of the same array of materials fixed to the framework of the covering by large stones as protection from the winds; poorly finished internal divisions, as partitions for the sole purpose of divisions to make better use of the space. This is a faint idea of what these dens are like, where, to complete indifference to the simplest notions of cleanliness are joined a nearly total lack of water for drinking and cooking. (Backheuser 1906, 111)

For his time, Backheuser was a sufficiently attentive observer of the social reality of the favela to have a detached perception of the current representations of its populations:

To there go the poorest, those in most need, those who, by paying with difficulty for a few feet of land, acquire the *right* to dig into the hillsides and plant four posts, the pillars of their *little palace*. The humble abodes spread over the hill, closer together at the bottom, more scattered as one goes up Church "Street" or Lookout "Street" — euphemisms by which are known the winding, narrow, and difficult-to-access paths to the clearing at the top of the hill.

Living there are not only the rowdies and criminals of the legend that Favella already has but also hardworking laborers whom either the scarcity or expense of proper lodging has cast out to these heights, where one enjoys relatively lower costs and a mild breeze that wafts continually, sweetening the roughness of the residences. (Backheuser 1906, 111; emphasis in original)

The inclusion of the favela in the roster of unhygienic housing had thus been forecast by Backheuser's report. The municipal government and its impetuous reformer, Pereira Passos, were ready to intervene. As Backheuser (1906, 111) wrote, "The illustrious Dr. Passos, the active, intelligent mayor of the city, already has his sights, as an astute administrator, on Favella, and soon measures will be taken, in accordance with municipal laws, to do away with these hovels."

In this way, the problematization of the favela preceded the spread of the phenomenon to the whole of the city; it happened when the process of favelization *had not yet become widespread* in the federal capital. As we have seen, this problematization depended heavily on a hygienist diagnosis applied to poverty and to the tenement, the latter being the source of the early representations of the favelas.

Just as in Europe (Topalov 1999), in Rio de Janeiro, reformer-engineers displayed a positivist view of science and of their social role. They were interested not only in technical problems but social ones as well. They carried within themselves the altruistic calling to serve the material development of the country, modernization, and Brazil's motto, "Ordem e progresso."[23]

Ever since the Empire, engineers and medical doctors had played an important role in municipal politics: Rio's Código de Posturas Municipais (Code of Municipal Orders) was based on suggestions by doctors contained in reports by the Comissão de Salubridade (Health Promotion Commission) of the Sociedade de Medicina e Cirurgia (Medicine and Surgery Society); the Clube de Engenharia (Engineering Club), founded in 1880, provided both names for the public boards and proposals to solve problems of the city's urbanization.[24] At the turn of the century, the Comissão de Saneamento do Rio de Janeiro (Rio de Janeiro Sanitation Commission), composed of engineers and medical doctors, was established in the Federal District. After the proclamation of the republic in 1889 and during the entire time that Rio de Janeiro remained the Federal District — that is, until 1959 — engineers and doctors governed the capital.[25]

For such professionals, the city of Rio de Janeiro was a privileged space of high symbolic value within which to demonstrate the national project. These professionals also displayed "the firm determination to go beyond the frontiers between their fields and devote themselves to the whole of society, with the goal of persuading its members to see the principles they envisioned as legitimate and necessary, as fundamental for building a modern society" (Herschmann, Kropf, and Nunes 1996, 8–9). These professionals, especially the engineers, believed that, in order to solve a city's problems, a competent administration was needed, one impervious to political pressure and based on the submission of the political to the technical. Administrations should be "uncompromised by personal or political interests and morally directed toward defense of the common welfare of the nation" (Kropf 1966, 148).

These principles of action oriented doctors' and engineers' procedures in defining the problem of the favela. The diagnosis applied to the tenements and to Morro da Favella was generalized to the universe of expanding favelas during the 1920s. In their studies of agents of epidemic outbreaks, hygienist doctors attributed contamination of the urban environment to the miasmas of the

Genesis of the Rio Favela

city. It seemed natural, then, for the favela to be represented as a place to combat sickness, contagious illness, and social pathology. For this, housing should be healthy, submitted to the rigor of the rules of hygiene, circulation of light and air, and a healthy atmosphere.

Believing that the environment was caused by human beings' physical and moral sickness, engineers and doctors offered technical proposals for treating these urban ills. And when they sought to identify the major problems as precisely and scientifically as possible, to identify technical solutions to make the city function well, they were, in fact, insisting on the need to organize, in a rational, controlled way, the entire set of urban elements: "The city, as a visible manifestation of the social whole, was repeatedly conceived as a machine, a mechanism, whose workings should be duly arranged and manipulated by the same leadership" (Kropf 1996, 108). According to this logic, the favelas were elements opposed to technical rationality and to the regulation of the city as a whole. Doing away with them would be a "natural" response.

José Augusto de Mattos Pimenta, an illustrious member of Rio's Rotary Club[26] and a great traveler, articulated these two views and synthesized them well in his writing, published mostly in the Federal District press. Presented sometimes as a doctor specializing in sanitation issues and other times as an engineer and a journalist, he was an important figure in Carioca affairs in the late 1920s. And yet he is poorly known and scarcely cited by current authors.[27] His record at the Rio Rotary Club, which he joined in 1925, indicated that he was a builder and real estate agent.[28] In 1937, he founded the Sindicato dos Corretores de Imóveis (Realtors Association), of which he was president until 1946. Moreover, the *Dicionário histórico brasileiro* highlights his activity as a journalist during the Vargas-led Revolution of 1930 and Constitutionalist Revolt of 1932 (Fundação Getúlio Vargas 2001).

At any rate, even though Mattos Pimenta was active in a variety of fields, his activity during 1926 and 1927 was directly connected with the favela. At that time, with the support of the local press and public officials, he undertook the first major campaign against the favelas, embedded in a broader project of modernization and beautification of Rio de Janeiro. More than any other figure of his time, Mattos Pimenta contributed to defining the favela as a problem, by combining hygienist medical discourse with progressive reformism and urbanism principles even more ambitious than those of Pereira Passos.

For two years this very well organized campaign occupied the pages of Rio's major newspapers—*O Globo, A Notícia, Jornal do Comércio, O Jornal, Correio da Manhã,* and *Jornal do Brasil*—presenting the image of the favela as "aesthetic leprosy." This analogy sums up perfectly the way Mattos Pimenta denounced poverty. In the Middle Ages, leprosy was considered the disease of the accursed, and even in the 1920s it was one of the worst contagious illnesses, disfiguring and leading to the segregation of its victims. For Mattos Pimenta (1926, 7–8), the favela required equally rigorous measures: "Even before the adoption [of the Plan for Growth-Renewal-Beautification of Rio de Janeiro], it is necessary to put up a prophylactic barrier against the infestation that is conquering the beautiful mountains of Rio de Janeiro, the scourge of the 'favelas'—the aesthetic leprosy that appeared on the hill there between the Brazil Central Railway and Avenida do Cais do Porto [Dockside Avenue] and that has been overflowing everywhere, first filling the newest neighborhoods with filth and misery, where nature was once most prodigious in its beauty."[29]

Mattos Pimenta projected onto the favela his sanitary reformist concerns, but he also displayed aesthetic and architectonic worries about "this masterpiece of nature that is Rio de Janeiro." Others had decried the favela as a lawless area, an antihygienic, unhealthy locale with concentrations of dangerous poor people. Mattos Pimenta (1926, 7–8) picked up this discourse: "Lacking any sort of policing, haphazardly constructed of scraps and flattened cans on free land of the National Trust, exempt from all taxes, strangers to any fiscal action, they are an excellent stimulus for indolence, an attractive lure for vagrants, a hideout for capoeira fighters, a refuge for petty thieves that carries insecurity and disquiet to the four corners of the city through the proliferation of robberies and thefts."

However, as I've just mentioned, Mattos Pimenta introduced a new theme, that of aesthetics, a concern for the beauty of the city as a whole. To defend Rio de Janeiro, he stressed the need to "care for its aesthetics, for its hygiene, and for its social order with the same care that God devoted to its charms."

According to Robert Pechman (1996, 354), during the 1920s, a new concept of urban planning began to be expressed that opposed the simple discrete actions proposed by hygiene and beautification projects. The purely technical view of urban problems—such as housing, sanitation, and circulation—gave way to a more systematic concept the city, which became the object of a new discipline with scientific ambitions: urbanism. Mattos Pimenta had spent many years in Europe, especially in Paris, where he had observed the development of this new field. He understood its prestige very well and appreciated the scale of the changes brought about by the baron Haussmann's reform in Paris.[30]

The campaign against the favela appears to have been successfully led and supported by the Rio Rotary Club, in its capacity as a professional association of the Rio business world. The campaign also innovated in regard to modes of communication, since part of Mattos Pimenta's strategy was to attack on several fronts. Among other things, he produced, with Rotary sponsorship, a ten-minute film titled *As favelas*, showing "the nightmarish spectacle witnessed during a stroll through the new favelas of Rio."[31] Mattos Pimenta knew that, at that time, few could climb the hills to see the favelas up close and from within. Castro Barreto, a medical doctor specializing in sanitation issues, was the first to furnish Mattos Pimenta with photographs of the favelas, especially pictures of children. *As favelas* was shown several times in 1926 and 1927, and it was even screened for then-president Washington Luiz.[32] We know nothing of the impact that this film had, though we can imagine that it had contributed noticeably to the "crusade against the ignominious shame of the favelas."[33]

After enlisting the press's aid in disseminating his ideas, Mattos Pimenta sought the support of the Departamento Nacional de Saúde Pública (National Public Health Department), along with its director, Clementino Fraga, Mayor Antônio Prado Júnior, and the chief of police. He had printed a prospectus that was distributed for free, "Casas populares" (Housing for the people), in which he promoted a solution to the favela problem and underscored three necessary measures for "public salvation": (1) an immediate halt to the construction of new shanties, thus blocking the growth of current favelas and the creation of new ones; (2) in order to enforce this, inspections to be carried out by employees of the Mayor's Office and the National Public Health Department to prevent clandestine, outlawed construction; and (3) a building program for workers housing and for shelters and communities for the disabled, the elderly, and abandoned children.

The Programa de Casas Populares (People's Housing Program) proposals that Mattos Pimenta developed in detail revealed his familiarity with practices of the real estate market. The Bank of Brazil and the construction companies were to sign a contract to open a line of credit with a mortgage guarantee and an obligation to build housing for the poor. The program should not burden the public coffers or promote payroll deductions. The purpose was to grant access to home ownership at payments equivalent to a monthly rent. Mattos Pimenta envisioned a plan with six-story buildings, each with 120 apartments: "Large apartment building construction and its sales system can be instituted in Brazil, with the advantage that they would be less expensive and would require less space than single-family houses—all in accordance with the modern principles of hygiene and comfort."[34] This proposal thus sought to replace favelas with large blocks of apartment buildings. According to its author, it would be possible, in fifteen years at a 9 percent annual interest rate, for favela residents to become owners of comfortable, solidly constructed residences, without the imposition of new, unbearable expenses, since "improvised, ignoble shacks for which one does not pay rent are rare, extremely rare."[35]

Whether directly related to this antifavela campaign or not, the truth is that, soon thereafter, in 1928 during the middle of Carnival, Cariocas witnessed the demolition of several hundred shacks by Mayor Antônio Prado Júnior, forcing their residents to search for other housing at their own expense (Conniff 1981, 33).[36] In contrast, Mattos Pimenta's plans to build low-cost housing for favela residents were never implemented.

Mattos Pimenta was not a reformer like the doctors and engineers mentioned earlier. Even though the few authors who have written about him call him a medical hygienist, it was his role as a real estate builder and agent that gave him a special importance among the Rio elite, an intellectual and economic importance heavily influenced by European ideas. Moreover, Mattos Pimenta personified the emergence of real estate capital.[37] In addition to being an important figure in urban development, he established the Bolsa Imobiliária do Rio de Janeiro — a real estate market association — at the moment that urban growth was beginning take shape thanks to the expanding supply of real property.[38] His activity, however, should not be seen as simply the result of a moral commitment or the desire for modernization displayed by social reformers. His contribution does serve as a testament to the mobilization of new economic agents dedicated to a new way of seeing urban development, one in which valuing their capital was the same as placing value on the city as a whole and not just on building new, modern neighborhoods. As a consequence, Mattos Pimenta's ideas about urbanism, favelas, and affordable housing contributed substantially to shaping elite representations. His groundbreaking proposals could not help but influence individuals and institutions that later took up the banners he had carried in the campaign against the favelas: the Agache Plan, the Building Code, and the BNH.

Immediately succeeding Mattos Pimenta as an important actor on the urban stage was Alfred Agache, a French urbanist, architect, and sociologist (Bruant 1994). He came to Rio for the first time in 1927, on the recommendation of Francisco Guimarães, Brazil's commercial attaché in France, and at the invitation of then-mayor Prado Júnior, to deliver three lectures that had great impact. He was then contracted by the Rio Mayor's Office to draw up the first growth, renewal, and beautification plan for the capital.[39]

Agache received special support from engineers associated with the municipal government (Godoy 1943), from the Engineering Club, and from the Rotary Club of Rio de Janeiro (Stuckenbruck 1996). As we have seen, in the years after its creation in 1922, the Rotary Club of Rio brought together important economic sectors of Rio society—Agache himself was from a family of powerful French industrialists in the textile sector with interests in Brazil.[40] The choice to put him in charge of a plan for the city of Rio caused three types of conflict, which took up whole newspaper columns and have been reported by several authors (Stuckenbruck 1996; L. Silva 1996; Pechman 1996).

The first conflict had to do, essentially, with the offer's extension to a European. Local architects—in a defensive corporatist position at a time when the profession was in the process of institutionalization—appealed to Brazilian professionals, arguing for a specifically Brazilian approach rather than the importation of foreign models (L. Silva 1996, 401–6), whereas Mattos Pimenta and other Francophile Rotarians found that the urbanism experience of Brazilian architects fell short of expectations.

The second conflict concerned Agache's appropriation of ideas, proposals, and work by Brazilian professionals; he was even accused of plagiarism of certain projects (L. Silva 1996, 405). However, Agache saw his role as that of a catalyzer, and he acknowledged having used a number of previous efforts, pointing out that the plan proposed and signed by him was "a joint, collaborative work and therefore, once again, was not a matter of inventing the parts but of condensing them and bringing them together in a single, methodical bloc, the summary of suggested and more or less manifested ideas that were in the air and that you, sirs, will recognize as your efforts as soon as you see them concretized in a single work, through images or the written word" (Agache 1930, 21).

Albuquerque Filho (cited in L. Silva 1996, 404) observed that the team that Agache directed consulted at least sixty-three studies, books, reports, and journals in addition to dozens of letters, maps, and photographs, and more than thirty plans, projects, and designs. "Likewise, five prior proposals were consulted and analyzed." In truth, a review of the original Agache Plan reveals the absence of a bibliography, of clarification as to the sources of the statistical data, and of precise references to authors or specialists who inspired his work. Instead, Agache stuck with the formula of a quite general acknowledgment: "I wish to address a collective thanks to all of the technical staff, artists, journalists, or mere enthusiasts of aesthetics who participated with me through their suggestions for desirable or possible changes to be introduced in the city. Those who have encouraged me, however, are too numerous for me to mention here individually" (Agache 1930, n.p.).

The third sort of conflict was connected to the urban plan put forth by Agache, in that one of the greatest problems was its choice of planning solution for the space created in the city center with the leveling of Morro do Castelo. That razing had occurred in 1922, during the term of Mayor Carlos Sampaio, "in the name of aeration and hygiene," and to prepare Rio for the commemoration that year of the centennial of Brazil's independence (M. Abreu 1987, 76).[41]

In spite of all of this, Agache executed an extremely ambitious proposal for the city.[42] He published a voluminous document whose quality was acknowledged by various specialists in the history of Brazilian urbanism. According to Margareth da Silva Pereira (1996, 369), it was "a formidable synthesis . . . that begins with a study of geography and history, evolves into an analysis of the social and economic indicators, continuing through a study of urban forms and outlines, in order to invent both physical interventions and legislative proposals that might govern the renewal, beautification, and growth of the city."

The favela does not go unnoticed by Agache's foreign eye — indeed, he was the first foreigner to write about it.[43] Le Corbusier had also been to Rio and had sketched these spaces (C. Santos et al. 1987). There are also reports of foreign intellectuals and artists who visited Rio de Janeiro at this time being taken by Brazilian friends to walk around and get acquainted with Morro da Favela. These visitors from abroad included French novelist and poet Blaise Cendrars, who traveled to Brazil several times between 1924 and 1929. According to Paola Berenstein-Jacques (2001a, 76), Cendrars even criticized the plans of the Mayor's Office, and implicitly the Agache Plan, as well as the utopian proposals of his friend Le Corbusier.

The favela seems to have made an impression on Alfred Agache, who had already mentioned it in his third lecture in late 1927, before being contracted to do the plan for Rio. In the lecture titled "Cidades-jardins e favellas" (Garden-cities and favelas), Agache approached the topic by stating only that "the favela is also a sort of satellite city, spontaneously formed, that chose to locate on the hilltops, and was composed of a somewhat nomadic population contrary to any rules of hygiene" (Agache 1930, 20). It was not until the document that presented Agache's plan that he refers to the favelas in any detail, devoting two pages to Morro de Santo Antônio (Agache 1930, 176–77) and another two to the problem of the favela in general, in the section "Elementos funccionaes do Plano Director" (Functional elements of the Master Plan; Agache 1930, 189–90). According to Armando Augusto de Godoy (1943, 79), the first time that Agache visited a favela, Morro da Providência, he was accompanied by engineers from the city. Two photographs recorded his visit (Zylberberg 1992, 32).

Mattos Pimenta's influence seems evident in Agache's observations and conclusions about the Rio favela. Note that (1) the campaign by the medical doctor turned real estate developer in favor of aesthetics was at its peak when

Agache landed in Rio; (2) Mattos Pimenta had also supported the decision of the Mayor's Office to contract Agache; (3) it was the Brazilian who delivered the Frenchman's welcoming speech; and (4) according Mattos Pimenta's daughter, the two became good friends.[44] It is thus possible to hypothesize that Mattos Pimenta had been Agache's main source of inspiration with regard to the favelas and, very likely, for other matters regarding the city of Rio. Speeches by the two are quite similar and refer to the same hygienist and aesthetic ideas. The modern concept of urban planning that had hygiene as a basic principle and beautification as a goal was common to both. The image of leprosy and the danger of contagion introduced by Mattos Pimenta is taken up again by Agache in his description of the favela: "As they are built without any of the precepts of hygiene, without plumbing, without sewers, without public sanitation service, without order, without normal materials, nothing ensures that the favelas do not constitute a permanent threat of fire and infectious epidemics for all of the districts that they infiltrate. Their *leprosy* sullies the beachfront neighborhoods and the districts most graciously endowed by nature, it strips the hills of their verdant adornment, and it corrodes the edges of the forests on the mountain ridges" (Agache 1930, 190; emphasis added).

At the same time, Agache is not content to see in the favela a contagious illness to be combatted, as Mattos Pimenta did. His work reveals a concern with understanding the causes of the phenomenon: "One could say that they are the result of certain measures in building regulation and the indifference shown by government officials regarding housing for the poor. In the face of the accumulated difficulties in getting a license to build — requirements and formalities that are only fulfilled after much time and many onerous fees — the poor worker becomes discouraged and joins the homeless in erecting shacks of flattened kerosene cans and wood from crates on the unoccupied slopes of the hills near the city, where no one collects taxes or demands a building permit" (Agache 1930, 189).

In fact, Agache seems to have been one of the first to notice that matters besides poverty, such as bureaucratic difficulties in accessing housing, also explained the plight of the favelas. It is possible to see how this early reflection, albeit summary, about the process by which these residential clusters came to be speaks to the sociological side of Agache's training, which had begun with social observation from a Leplaysian perspective.[45] His way of understanding the problem, of seeing the social, marks an advance over preceding observers in that he managed to detect the process of formation of social ties in the favelas, including the emergence of economic activities, in nearly sociological terms: "Gradually, small houses belonging to a poor, heterogeneous population arise, a principle of social organization is born, and the beginning of a sense of territorial ownership is seen. Entire families live side by side, create neighborhood ties, establish customs, and develop small businesses: stores, cantinas, tailor shops, and so forth" (Agache 1930, 189).

Agache also noticed the appearance of a real estate market, a rental market, which he described in the following terms: "Some of them, who had a successful business, improved their dwellings and rented them. They relocated and thus became small property capitalists who had suddenly settled on land that was not theirs and would be surprised if it was demonstrated to them that in no way could they claim rights of ownership" (Agache 1930, 189).

As for solutions, Agache advocated constructing housing for the poor and demolishing precarious dwellings, in accord with European social reformers from the late nineteenth century (Butler and Noisette 1983). He argued that such destruction was necessary "not only from the point of view of social order and safety but also from the point of view of general hygiene of the city, not to mention aesthetics"; demolition alone was not sufficient, however, as the same causes would produce the same effects, and he feared that if the favela residents "were only expelled, they would just settle elsewhere in the same conditions" (Agache 1930, 190). Thus in his Plan for Growth, Renewal, and Beautification, he proposed that housing be built for this population: "Inasmuch as the working-class garden-villas will be constructed in accordance with the data of the master plan, it would be appropriate to set aside a certain number of homes — simple and inexpensive, though hygienic and practical — for the relocation of the inhabitants of the favelas, a first stage in the training that will prepare them for a more normal, more comfortable life" (Agache 1930, 190).

Therefore, even if Agache repeated the proposed solutions already introduced by Backheuser[46] or Mattos Pimenta, he also innovated in his sociological perspective directed at the causes of the favelas' formation and at the development of social ties and economic activities in these neighborhoods. In fact, this contribution was undervalued, as was the whole of Agache's project, which, though officially approved, was set aside as a result of changes brought about by the Revolution of 1930.

ADMINISTERING AND CONTROLLING THE FAVELA

The Revolution of 1930, which led to the Getúlio Vargas dictatorship, opened a new chapter in representation of Brazilian poorer classes and thus of the favela. This revolution, spearheaded by the Tenentes, a set of junior army officers from the urban middle class who openly opposed the Old Republic and had rebelled against the central government in the 1920s. The Revolution in 1930 brought Vargas to power and ended the Old Republic, which dated from 1889 and was dominated by rural oligarchies that defended the interests of the agricultural export elite. The revolution opposed the pro-European orientation of the old elites and promoted a strongly nationalist climate, directed toward constructing and valuing Brazilian national identity and making anything foreign appear symbolically threatening. Many Brazilian scholars have written about Vargas, a controversial figure who has frequently elicited debates about his legacy:[47] Does Vargas represent regression or renewal, the reinforcement of oligarchic tradition or rupture with the past, continuity or change that opened the door for the interests of a new urban industrial order?

The Vargas years are divided into three subperiods: Between 1930 and 1934, he was the leader of the Revolution of 1930, under a banner of reform. From 1934 to 1937, he was president of Brazil under a constitutional regime, having been elected by indirect vote: "At that moment, a figure appears as head of a government committed to a liberal democratic project supported by the constitution of 1934, which even though it contained a chapter that was clearly interventionist in regard to social and economic order, affirmed the liberal principles embedded in the 1930 movement" (Diniz 1999, 23). The third subperiod dates from 1937, after a coup d'état that ended the democratic experiment of 1934–37 and installed an authoritarian government until 1945. This period of dictatorship was known as the Estado Novo (New State).

As many scholars have shown, the Vargas Republic strengthened the central state's capacity for intervention, persecuting communists and any other opponents of the regime. At the same time, it was a populist dictatorship that acknowledged and protected workers through laws regulating wage relations, modernized the educational system, and developed social protections, to an extent that Vargas has been considered the "father" of Brazilian social legislation. According to Angela de Castro Gomes (1999, 62), he projected an image of a guide and a "father of the poor"; his plan was to transform Brazil into an immense home and the state into a welfare state.

The Vargas regime continued the theme of hygienism that attributed the spread of numerous diseases to the unsanitary housing conditions of the poor. Vargas affirmed that home ownership and an adequate diet were legitimate aspirations of workers. For him, the family was the basic unit of grassroots politics, and housing was part of a larger issue (A. Gomes 1999, 62–63).[48]

Michael Conniff has studied the evolution of Rio's municipal politics in the period following the Revolution of 1930.[49] For the term 1931–36, Vargas appointed as mayor a doctor, Pedro Ernesto Baptista, soon known as "the doc-

Figure 5. Caricature illustrating the political clientelism of the 1930s
(from *Revista Careta*, no. 1527 [n.d., 1937], Eduardo Augusto de Brito e Cunha Archive).

tor of the poor." The beginnings of Rio's political clientelism developed the favelas during this period. Mayor Baptista's policies prioritized hospital and school construction. His approach to the social question was quite similar to progressive reformers of the early twentieth-century United States: that assisting the poor should be a public responsibility and should reduce the stigma of inferiority and dependency that often characterizes social welfare (Conniff 1981, 123).

Mayor Baptista's influence and actions in regard to favela residents were especially important in that he launched a new sort of relationship with them.[50] His extensive contacts with *favelados* between 1932 and 1934, intervening as a mediator in conflicts over land ownership, distributing the first public subsidies to the samba schools (most of which were based in favelas), and, in some cases, making decisions about the installation of public services. In 1934, for example, he organized an official rally in Mangueira favela to announce the opening of a public school. Such an act reveals a very particular political dimension — the fostering of clientelistic ties, insofar as votes were traded for favors. Baptista had more than 100 godchildren in the favelas of Rio and when he died in 1942, his funeral procession was accompanied by a considerable crowd, favela residents and samba school members walking side by side with limousines, displaying declarations in Baptista's honor (Conniff 1981, 107, 163).

Vargas removed Pedro Ernesto Baptista from office in 1936 out of fear of the mayor's growing popularity, but Baptista's activity had fit perfectly within the regime's populist politics and his activity continued after his term. The hygienist perspective that had accompanied previous discourse remained but with a new accent: the recognition of the fact of the favelas and need to improve the living conditions of their residents, a sharp contrast to the prior, sole solution of demolition.

This recognition took shape, in general terms, with the passing of the 1937 Building Code by the Rio Mayor's Office, directed by the new mayor, Father Olympio de Melo, also appointed by Vargas. This code followed three previous versions from 1924, 1926, and 1937 (Prefeitura da Cidade do Rio de Janeiro 1977, 85–86; Godoy 1943, 320–21; L. Silva 1996, 399–400).[51] The new code, which remained in effect until 1970, was drawn up, as were the previous ones, by a technical commission of municipal engineers, and it was part of efforts, albeit not very successful, to rationally organize the city. The intention was to give Rio the means to address new problems posed by urban growth, especially the beginnings of verticalization — the construction of taller building using reinforced concrete — and the issue of unhealthy neighborhoods. In regard to the latter point, this version of the code was innovative in its explicit attention to the phenomenon of the favela.

Chapter 15 of the 1937 Building Code, "Extinction of Antihygienic Residences," includes a section titled "Favelas" (107),[52] from which I cite article 349:

> Art. 349 — The formation of favelas, that is, of groups of two or more shacks regularly or irregularly arranged, built of improvised materials, and not in accord with the provisions of this decree, will absolutely not be permitted.

1. In the existing favelas it is absolutely forbidden to raise any new shacks, to carry out any construction on existing ones, or to do any other building.
2. The Office of the Mayor, through the Offices of Inspection and the Directorate of Engineering, and by any means within its reach, will see to the blocking of the formation of new favelas or the expansion or execution of construction in any existing ones, and will order to proceed summarily to demolish new shacks or those on which any building is carried out, as well as any construction done in the favelas.

   ·

7. When the Office of the Mayor finds that there is exploitation of the favela through charging of rent for homes or the lease or renting of land, the fines applied will be doubled. . . .
8. Construction or framing of shacks destined for habitation on lots, patios, or yards of buildings are subject to the provisions of this article.
9. The Office of the Mayor, as established in Title IV of Chapter 14 of this decree, will see to the extinction of the favelas and, to replace them, the provision of basic housing developments.

Right away, we see the continuity between the provisions of this article and the previous counsel of Mattos Pimenta and Agache: The code decreed the elimination of the favelas and their replacement with new housing in accordance with public health norms, and it proposed to block the expansion of favelas — which meant there was a possibility of maintaining them.[53] It is possible to interpret this ambiguity by observing that paragraph 9 associated the elimination of favelas with the transfer of residents, and the preceding paragraphs aimed to control the favelas until the new housing complexes could be built. The existence of the favelas was thus recognized by the code, and the details of its provisions revealed a broad understanding of that universe.

In this, the first official definition, two shacks were sufficient to constitute a favela (later, the definition in the censuses would consider a favela to have a minimum of fifty); a cluster of shacks could have an orderly placement or not; the construction was precarious; and the type of cluster developed was illegal ("not in accord with the provisions of this decree"). The extant favelas grew by extension—construction of new homes—or by densification—enlargement of existing homes. The favelas functioned in part as real estate markets: the volume of rents received (for both homes and land) was significant enough to call attention to itself. Finally, the favela arose not only from the invasion of vacant property but also from the process of favelization of built areas—through the occupation of gaps, patios, and yards belonging to already existing buildings.

In spite of its ambiguities, the 1937 Building Code seems have to initiated a new legal phase, just as Pedro Ernesto Baptista had inaugurated a new political period that, little by little, recognized and responded to the need to administer the favelas. With the need to administer came the need to understand.[54] As I have mentioned, one notices the outlines of a sociological approach to the *favelado* population in Agache's observations. But it is only in the 1940s that a concern for better understanding the territory and residents of the favelas would take shape.

UNDERSTANDING THE FAVELA FOR BETTER ADMINISTRATION AND CONTROL

To ensure sound administration and effective control, it was necessary to classify, measure, and quantify the object in question. Statistics were invented in European countries in the eighteenth century to better guide the actions of the state. However, in England and France, statistics only began to develop significantly in the nineteenth century. Gérard Leclerc (1979) and Alain Desrosières (1993) underscore the importance of statistical data to the strength of arguments in the nineteenth-century debate about social reform as well as the role of statistics as an instrument of power.

Official statistical data made their appearance in Brazil on the occasion of the first national census of 1872. Insofar as the Rio favelas are concerned, in the early 1940s, consideration started to go beyond an impressionistic view to gaining knowledge that would allow precise characterization of individuals, their families, and living conditions as well as classification of their circumstances and problems. The estimates of the *favelado* population available at the time needed to be replaced by exact figures.[55] In 1941, during the First Brazil-

Figure 6. "The 1937 Building Code Wants to Make Rio the Marvelous City" (from *Revista Careta*, 13 August 1938, Eduardo Augusto de Brito e Cunha Archive).

ian Urbanism Conference, "a complete study of the favelas" was requested "by means of which we can know the general and particular aspects of the problem" (Mariano Filho, Amarante, and Campelo 1941, 252).

The authors of this document, once again, were members of the Rio Rotary Club—physician José Mariano Filho, engineer Alberto Pires Amarante, and architect Américo Campelo. They made a list of information they believed would be necessary for a successful effort:

- Exact number of dwellings that make up each cluster
- Character and density of the formation
- Number of inhabitants
- Specific character of the dwellings
- Urban planning characterization of the occupied lands
- Occupations of men and women inhabitants
- Number of school-age children
- General sanitary conditions
- Area of the occupied land
- Photographic dossier
- Possibility of urbanization of each cluster
- Names of the owners of occupied lands

From this perspective came the first more systematic studies of Rio's favelas: the report by physician Victor Tavares de Moura published in 1943 under the title "Favelas do Distrito Federal"; and the final report for a social work professional program by Maria Hortência do Nascimento e Silva, published in 1942 under the title *Impressões de uma assistente social sobre o trabalho na favela* (Impressions of a social worker from work in a favela).[56] These two texts clearly indicate the beginning of a new phase that recognized the need for concrete data in order to more effectively manage poverty and its spaces. Moura's report even served as the basis for Mayor Henrique Dodsworth's actions and for the Proletarian Parks policy of Vargas's Estado Novo in 1941–43.

A preliminary study, "Esboço de um plano para estudo e solução do problema das favelas do Rio de Janeiro" (Outline of a plan for study of and solutions for the problem of favelas; 1940), was done by Moura at the request of the secretary-general for health and welfare of Rio de Janeiro, Jesuíno Carlos de Albuquerque.[57] Though a resident of Rio, Moura was a native of the Northeastern state of Pernambuco and brother-in-law of the state's governor, Agamenon Magalhães.[58] Magalhães had organized a Liga Social contra o Mucambo (Social League against the Mocambo; Pandolfi 1984; Melo 1985; Lira 1998). The *mocambo* (*mucambo* was an earlier spelling) was the equivalent of the favela shack in Recife, Pernambuco's capital. This league, in which Moura had directly participated, had been his source of inspiration (Moura 1940, 1). In the case of Recife, a Comissão de Recenseamento dos Mucambos (Commission for a Census of Mocambos; Lira 1998, 94) had been formed, and Moura cited the results of this survey: 45,581 *mocambos*, housing 164,837 people of all ages. In his report, he stressed the need for the collaboration of a statistician (Moura 1940, 7), and he recommended a detailed census of Rio's favelas, which, in his opinion, would be indispensable to setting public policies: "The success of the campaign will depend on the detail and criterion with which the census form is completed, for only with real, detailed information can one choose the road to follow toward a solution for a problem whose complexity I need not emphasize" (Moura 1940, 8).

For this census, Moura proposed a form prototype with various sorts of information to be collected: district, name of the favela, street name, name and address of the property owners (landowners, on the one hand, and owners of the dwellings, on the other), physical characteristics of the dwelling (materials, number of rooms, surface, general state), occupation status, value of the property, amount of rent for dwelling and for the land, type of use (residential, commercial, school, leisure, or mixed—revealing the existence already of a certain level of facilities in the favelas); place of birth, occupation, status, place of work, and income of the head of household and other active members of the family; the unemployed by sector of economic activity; the disabled; level of education; name, age, sex, and education level of children.[59]

We see that the arguments that Moura presented to justify the information to be collected reveal a detailed knowledge of the favelas' formation, making a distinction between those that were established by illegal invasion of public lands and those encouraged by the landowners themselves, where they could earn a significant profit without having to pay taxes (Moura 1940, 3). He gives as an example Morro da Favella, where on one side the shacks were on municipal property and on the other side they extended onto private land, noting that the latter areas were less populated since there "all the residents pay rent on the land or the dwelling, and if they do not, they are evicted, almost always violently" (Moura 1940, 10).

These plans were put into practice by the Comissão de Estudo do Problema das Favelas (Commission for the Study of the Problem of Favelas), whose creation Moura had recommended and whose fieldwork he was responsible for directing (Parisse 1969a, 65). Fourteen favelas were studied using his method. The report that presented these results was never published as a document, but it had considerable impact in the Rio press (Parisse 1969a, 68–69), especially in the newspapers supportive of the Vargas government. According to Leeds and Leeds (1978, 193), the report gave evidence, for the first time, of the complexity of the favela. Moura had pointed out the diversity among them, and the circumstances he described demystified the prevailing view of the time of the favelas as places of criminality, marginality, and social disorganization.

Maria Hortência do Nascimento e Silva's (1942) monograph is another landmark in the early days of favela research. Before the Vargas government, aid to the poor was almost exclusively private or religious, and it was organized according to practices and by institutions that dated from Brazil's colonial era.[60] In the 1930s, for the first time, the Rio Office of the Mayor began hiring social workers. To train these professionals, in 1937 the Instituto de Educação Social e Familiar (Institute for Social and Family Education, now the Department of Social Work) was founded at PUC.

Thus after the journalists, engineers, doctors, and urban planners, social workers appeared as a new type of agent in the history of knowledge about favelas. Once again, one sees a European influence: notwithstanding the Vargas government's nationalist orientation to social services, Brazil followed examples from the Old Country. Indeed, the French and Belgian schools of social work served as models for this new Brazilian institution (A. Lima 1987, 54–58). Two religious, one French, Fanny du Restu, and the other Italian, Jacinta Pietromarchi, were present at the birth of the aforementioned Social Institute, and the latter became its first director-in-chief.[61]

At the same time, the populist and clientelist orientation of social services, which had existed during Pedro Ernesto Baptista's time as mayor, continued after his term and was followed by these later social workers. As collaborators with municipal public servants, these social workers participated in a management of poverty that mixed social protection with social control of the poor.

By this time, the favelas seem to have become privileged fields of action in the new social services effort. Social workers were recognizing the importance of duly understanding the population in order to do their work effectively. It was in Largo da Memória, a favela in Leblon district, that Silva developed her research and verified the efforts of the municipal social services: "The first time that social services tried to solve the problem of Largo da Memória was in October 1940. The social worker in the Mayor's Office, Maria Luiza de Fontes Ferreira, a graduate of the Social Institute, was very interested in the issue of the favelas. She had the idea of building a social center in one of the structures there, well within the reach of favela residents. To ground her plan in concrete data, she carried out a detailed census of the residents of Largo da Memória with the aid of municipal employees" (M. H. N. Silva 1942, 43).

Figure 7. The favela of Largo da Memória before its destruction
(VT/MS/19390207, Social Medicine Series, Proletarian Parks
and Favelas Dossier, Victor Tavares de Moura Fund).

In this social center, Silva did the internship that would result in her monograph, a study that could be considered the first case study of a favela, even though it did not follow the guidelines later established by sociologists and anthropologists.[62] Although a final project for her course of study, the report is surprising, as it is, even today, an important source for reconstructing the history of research on the favela.[63]

Silva was the daughter of a wealthy family and a graduate of the best girls' religious school in Rio in the 1930s, the Colégio Sion, run by French religious and in which French was the language used. She pursued one of the few professional careers possible for a young woman at the time. In contrast with other observers who only occasionally visited the favelas, Silva commuted daily by trolley to Largo da Memória to carry out her work.[64] This favela, situated on a level piece of land in Rio's South Zone, was easily accessible by public transportation. Silva gave a detailed description of Largo da Memória, including plans of the various types of shacks, a description of the inhabitants' daily lives, and a discussion of exceptional cases, labeled "curious types," based on residents' accounts. She supplemented her fieldwork with statistical data from the Mayor's Office on a total of 1,619 people. Simple tables show the division of the population by sex, skin color, civil status, status of work, nationality, state of origin, age, date of the family's arrival in the favela, monthly salary, and trade. No fewer than thirty-six types of jobs were listed, from tailor to security guard.[65]

In addition, the monograph provided the first list of Rio's thirty-six major favelas (M. H. N. Silva 1942, 16–17); a typological outline—hillside favelas, favelas on flatlands, established favelas, recent favelas, favelas on municipal land, and favelas on private land (9–14); and a categorization of the state of the dwellings as "good, poor, and very poor" (23–27). Moreover, Silva described the activities of municipal social services in Largo da Memória, giving a better understanding of the content of social work done at the time. As regards the techniques used—dossiers, individual records of visits to the families, case diagnoses and proposed solutions—one sees strong similarity with the working methods of European social workers (Barret-Ducrocq 1991; Guerrand and Rupp 1978). The solutions implemented reveal the weight of clientelism, indicated by the frequency of letters of recommendation for jobs, physicians, hospitals, schools, and children's homes—services that the poor would have difficulty accessing without such referrals.

Even though Silva's monograph was an advance in detailed understanding of the favelas' social reality, it is also characterized by a rather moralistic point of view. Moreover, in spite of the field observations and data collection, her discourse is heavily structured by the representations of poverty prevalent at the beginning of the century (Valladares 1991). No doubt this was because of both her training as a social worker and her membership in a wealthier social class. She describes the favelas' place in the city in terms that resemble those of Mattos Pimenta: "In Rio, a city of color and exuberant festivity, the light that shines on this unmistakable and incomparable beauty makes the screech of the favela even more dissonant, standing out against the marvelous, refined tones of such bounty and grace. This is perhaps why our favelas seem more sordid and miserable than all others. A tremendous poverty is sheltered in those patched-up shacks, a shocking abandonment that pains the hearts of those who penetrate this world apart in which live fortune's outcasts" (M. H. N. Silva 1942, 7–8).

The value judgments and prejudices about people who are poor and Black, commonly associated with the favelas, show up even more evidently in chapter 3, in which she discusses the problem of the favela that "demands a definitive solution" (M. H. N. Silva 1942, 61). It is possible to detect a racist, perhaps even eugenicist orientation in the discourse, which, even though it recognized the consequences of slavery, not abolished in Brazil until 1888, attributed responsibility to the victims themselves:[66]

Child of a scourged race, our Black man—today's *malandro*—carries on his shoulders a morbid heritage too heavy for him to shake it off himself without help, living as he does in the same environment of poverty and privation. It is not his fault if, before him, his people suffered in the slave quarters and cured their ills with prayers and sorcery....

Is it surprising, therefore, that he would prefer to sit in his doorway, singing or fretting, rather than having the energy to overcome the inertia that binds him, the indolence that rules him, and resolutely set himself to work?

For him to manage to do this, it is necessary, before anything else, to cure him, to educate him, and, most of all, to give him a house where he can expect the minimum comfort required for the development of a normal life. (M. H. N. Silva 1942, 62–63)

Thus the practice of social services, including more regular visits to the favelas, more assiduous and intimate contacts with the families, contributed to the advancement of the discovery of the favela during the long phase that preceded that of the social sciences. At the same time, in spite of the firsthand collection of information, the interpretations of this information were conservative. These interpretations were shaped by the social workers' class origins and by the conservatism of the Catholic Church of the day, which was still basically structured according to a model of charity.

Also surprising was the social workers' alliance with the populist Vargas government, which maintained a different relationship with the poorer classes.[67] Both Moura's and Silva's studies were used in the development of Mayor Henrique Dodsworth's Proletarian Parks. This policy, promoted by a municipal commission of which Moura, then director of the Mayor's Office of Social Services, was the prime mover, became the first effective experiment in public housing construction for residents of Rio's favelas (Parisse 1969a; Leeds and Leeds 1978; Valla 1986; Medeiros 2002).

The three Proletarian Parks built between 1941 and 1944—Gávea (considered the model), Cajú, and Praia do Pinto—resettled between 7,000 and 8,000 people, a modest outcome if one considers that at the time the estimated population of favelas in the Federal District was 250,000 to 300,000, and that the goals set for this new policy had been much more ambitious (Parisse 1969a, 76).

The Proletarian Parks nonetheless marked a new stage in thinking about public action regarding the favelas (Burgos 1998). From Vargas's populist point

Figure 8. View of Provisional Proletarian Park no. 1, Gávea,
Rio de Janeiro (VT/MS/19390207, Social Medicine Series,
Proletarian Parks and Favelas Dossier, Victor Tavares de Moura Fund).

of view, it was no longer acceptable to intervene in the urban spaces considered problematic without also taking into account their populations. In the view of the new policy, it would no longer be sustainable to burn down irregularly occupied urban zones or just evict the poor, as had been done during Mayor Pereira Passos's term. The Vargas regime "assumed that many diseases in our cities were spread because of the poor hygienic conditions of low-income housing, which made the worker disaffected and dangerous. It also presumed that home ownership and adequate nourishment were legitimate aspirations of workers" (A. Gomes 1999, 62).

Here I pose the hypothesis that the Proletarian Parks can be considered a continuation of earlier proposals such as those of Mattos Pimenta and Agache, which were characterized by a strong concern for hygiene and aesthetics. Mattos Pimenta and Agache had stressed the importance of the struggle against the favela, and their proposals for resettlement of *favelados* were not taken up by the authorities of their day. With the populist Mayor Dodsworth, the perspective was different: the struggle against the favela had as its first objective improving the fortune of its inhabitants, who would in turn secure popular political support for the regime. Indeed, the name Proletarian Park was quite significant as it underscored the value placed on the workers, the *proletariat*.

These initiatives were not just mere provisional resettlement operations, however. They did not seek simply to remove residents from unhealthy places and provide them with new homes that met sanitation regulations. The objective was also to help residents and educate them so that they would change their practices and adopt a new way of life ensuring their physical and moral health. The Proletarian Parks were envisioned as provisional residences, transitional homes that with time would help those who lived there to integrate into urban life. These developments did include dispensaries, schools, social centers, sports facilities, daycare centers, and a police station. Social workers were mobilized to get to know the population to be resettled, accompany the process, and attend to their adaptation to the new way of living, under the social workers' strict control (N. Oliveira 1981, 47–50).

This was a policy surely inspired by transitional housing projects destined for the populations of *taudis* in France (Magri 1980). Moura, who had studied in France and Germany and had participated in various international conferences, likely knew of these European policies. The populist novelty of this experiment in Brazil lay in the political accommodation of the residents mobilized by the regime and controlled in their comings and goings. It was not by chance that the director of the Proletarian Park of Gávea gave a daily speech commenting on current events and educating the residents politically (Leeds and Leeds 1978, 195–97).

THE FIRST CENSUS AND OFFICIAL DATA

A new kind of understanding about the favela emerged in the late 1940s. The sort of knowledge, outlined first in Moura's pioneering work, now was reproduced by official, permanent organizations charged with data collection. This would illuminate previously unknown dimensions of the favela phenomenon, which would no longer be seen as just a problem of public health, urban order, aesthetics, and social services. A body of knowledge about the favelas' inhabitants would take shape regarding activity, employment, geographic origins, demographic characteristics, and so forth. However, this emergent official production of data and analyses, whose aim was to learn of the real extent and complexity of the favela phenomenon, was not accomplished without difficulty. It happened in two stages: a first census in 1948 that dealt only with the favelas in the Federal District and then the General Census of 1950, in which for the first time, the favelas were indicated as such.

Although Brazil had taken general censuses since the late nineteenth century, the Instituto Brasileiro de Geografia e Estatística (IBGE) was founded in

1938.[68] By virtue of Rio's status as the nation's capital, the Office of the Mayor also had a Departamento Municipal de Geografia e Estatística (Municipal Department of Geography and Statistics), but there were no precise data on the controversial universe that were the favelas. The survey taken during the 1920 census as well as the data from the Estatística Predial do Distrito Federal (Federal District Building Statistics) in 1933 only counted homes and businesses in some well-known favelas such as Morro da Favella and Morro do Salgueiro (A. Guimarães 1953, 253). There were no exact figures for favelas as a whole or their populations, only estimates of an alarmist nature.

The first favela was already fifty years old when the decision was taken to carry out a specific census of this type of neighborhood and its inhabitants. Defined as an *espaço provisório* (transitory space), Morro da Providência had not appeared with its real favela characteristics in the official censuses of 1920 and 1940. As I have noted, it was only in 1937 that the Building Code officially recognized the favela as a type of urban space within the territory of the Federal District.

Despite the calls for a complete, precise study, such as that proposed during the Primeiro Congresso Brasileiro de Urbanismo (First Brazilian Urbanism Conference), this measure only came about when government officials understood the importance of their own public administration plans of having trustworthy data on this form of habitation. This is what Alberto Passos Guimarães (1953, 256), then director of the Technical Division of the IBGE's National Census Service, noted: "Whatever the courses of action chosen to formulate the problems arising from the proliferation of groups of *favelados* may be, the success of the measures that could be put into practice will depend on the best understanding of the individual and social characteristics of these populations. This is why the Fourth General Census of Brazil has taken the initiative to refine the data of the demographic census referring to the favelas separately, thus providing to all concerned the basic elements about these groups of human beings."

We see that the arguments used here are practically the same as Moura's in 1940. However, although the results of Moura's report were widely commented on in the press of his time, his research seems to have been forgotten, since Guimarães, when describing the research prior to 1950, did not mention the survey that the former had performed for the Office of the Mayor. Guimarães (1953, 256) notes only research done in 1948 by the Fundação Leão XIII in two favelas, Morro de São Carlos and Morro do Jacarezinho, and the 1948 census.

In its desire to "extinguish the favelas or at least halt their development in the Federal District" (Prefeitura do Distrito Federal 1949, 6), the Rio Mayor's Office got ahead of the IBGE, having its Department of Geography and Statistics conduct its own First Census of Favelas of Rio, during the mayoral term of General Ângelo Mendes de Moraes.

Begun in the first weeks of 1947 and concluded in late March 1948, the census's date of publication is 1949. The first step was the inclusion of favelas as urban groupings, which allowed the identification of 119 of them at first. However, the research reduced this number to 105, counting therein a total population of 138,837 inhabitants, of whom 68,953 were male and 69,884 were female. These numbers were much lower than the alarmist estimates by the Rio press of between 400,000 and 600,000 residents. *Favelados* made up only 7 percent of the city's total population. The number of dwellings amounted to 34,528, or an average of 4.01 people per unit.

The official document in which the census results were published, *Censo das favelas: Aspectos gerais* (Census of favelas: General aspects; 1949), did not define "favela," nor did it indicate the exactly the principles used for identification. We do know that the reduction of the number of favelas from 119 to 105 resulted, on the one hand, from the exclusion of some units because the residents were also the landowners (thus revealing a criterion of definition) and, on the other hand, "from collapsing into a single unit those clusters set within the same topographic unit but with different names" (Prefeitura do Distrito Federal 1949, 7).

The document presented general tables grouped by districts and prepared based on data on the two principal aspects of each favela:

1. Dwellings according to their type and number of rooms, materials of roof covering, floor covering, type of sanitation, type of lighting, water supply, rent paid or not for both land and housing) and amount.
2. Population, classified by the following demographic characteristics: sex, age, place of birth, level of education, skin color, civil status, birth (registered or not), employment activity, zone of dwelling and zone of employment activity, declared wages or salary.

The results revealed an image of the favela populations quite different from the representations dominant up to that point. For example, two thirds of the inhabitants of favelas were from the Federal District (38 percent) or from the state of Rio de Janeiro (29 percent); the percentage arriving from the

Northeast comprised no more than 6 percent of the whole. Illiterate people over seven years of age constituted 53 percent of the inhabitants, not the great majority, as had been thought.

At the same time, the official document is truly surprising for the contrast between, on the one hand, the quality and interest of the information provided to the public for the first time and, on the other, its commentaries and interpretations, which expressed social and racial prejudices even more conservative and outdated than those presented by Silva (1942). A good example is the topic of "color" of the residents. First of all, results emerged that showed the most numerous group, at 36 percent, to be *mestiços* or *pardos*, followed by *negros* at 35 percent and *brancos* at 29 percent. These percentages contrasted with the weight of these same groups in the Federal District as a whole, according to the 1940 census: 17 percent, 11 percent, and 71 percent, respectively. The commentary that followed, far from contrasting these data with previous discourse, as one might expect, slid right into the most abject racial prejudice: "It is not surprising that *pretos* and *pardos* predominate in the favelas. Hereditarily backward, lacking any ambition, poorly adjusted to modern social demands, they supply the largest contingents of lower strata of the population in almost all urban areas" (Prefeitura do Distrito Federal 1949, 8).

From page 10 to page 19, the end of the document, a moral discourse prevails, full of clichés about and prejudices against the poor, even invoking the biology of race, with a eugenicist bias:

> The biological characteristics and capacities of a people are passed
> down through several generations and constitute a substratum
> on which its life is built. In the absence of biologically healthier
> human animals, no bounty of natural resources or improvement in
> institutional activity can ensure an increase in productivity. . . . The
> black man [*preto*], for example, as a rule, did not know how or was not
> able to take advantage of freedom gained or economic advancement.
> . . . Atavistic laziness was reborn in him, and the stagnation that
> weakens returned, fundamentally distinct from rest that reinvigorates.
> Or then — as with all individuals having primitive needs, lacking
> self-regard and respect for his own dignity — he deprives himself of
> all that is essential for maintaining a decent life and rather invests
> relatively high amounts in exotic apparel, in dance halls, and in
> groups of Carnival revelers, in the end spending everything left over
> after satisfying the strict necessities of a life on the edge of indigence.
> (Prefeitura do Distrito Federal 1949, 10–11)

The same discourse of moral judgment can be found in regard to hygiene and conditions of family life: "The consequences of this complex of negative conditions make themselves felt not only in the area of hygiene; the filth is aggravated by promiscuity, and the latter, which reinforces the action of other adverse factors, causes lamentable consequences for moral order" (Prefeitura do Distrito Federal 1949, 16–17).

The author or authors of this report, now armed with statistical data, considered themselves competent not only to analyze these data but also to separate the "deserving" from the "undeserving": "The high proportion of inhabitants of economically unproductive ages—notably children and adolescents, low levels of income and education, terrible conditions of hygiene, and the large number of natural liaisons all provide a propitious climate for development of factors in the disintegration of the human personality. The low number of legally constituted families in such a setting is worthy of admiration and, therefore, it is representatives of these who should first merit aid in any initiative that aims to rehabilitate the *favelados*" (Prefeitura do Distrito Federal 1949, 17–18).

That such conservative, archaic language would be published in an official document as late as 1949 might seem surprising, given the glorification of the folk encouraged during the Vargas era. In fact, however, the Vargas dictatorship had been toppled in 1945, and, as we have seen, for the Mayor's Office the purpose of the 1947 census was to justify a return to a policy of eradicating the favelas.

Moreover, at the time, Rio's mayor, whose name appears on the publication, was from the military—General Ângelo Mendes de Moraes—as was the director of the Municipal Department of Geography and Statistics, Major Durval de Magalhães Coelho. It is also surprising to find in this report racist and eugenic arguments four years after the end of World War II and the revelation of Nazi crimes committed in the name of this ideology. However, although the Vargas regime had joined the Allies in fighting Nazism, it shared some ideological sympathies with it, thanks to the spread of Nazi ideology in the Integralist Movement, Brazil's fascist nationalist movement founded in the 1930s (Trindade 1979).

Even if its official interpretation resembled earlier representations, publication of the favela census data still led to new knowledge production, and, as we will see, a number of authors were able to use these data to formulate new interpretations.

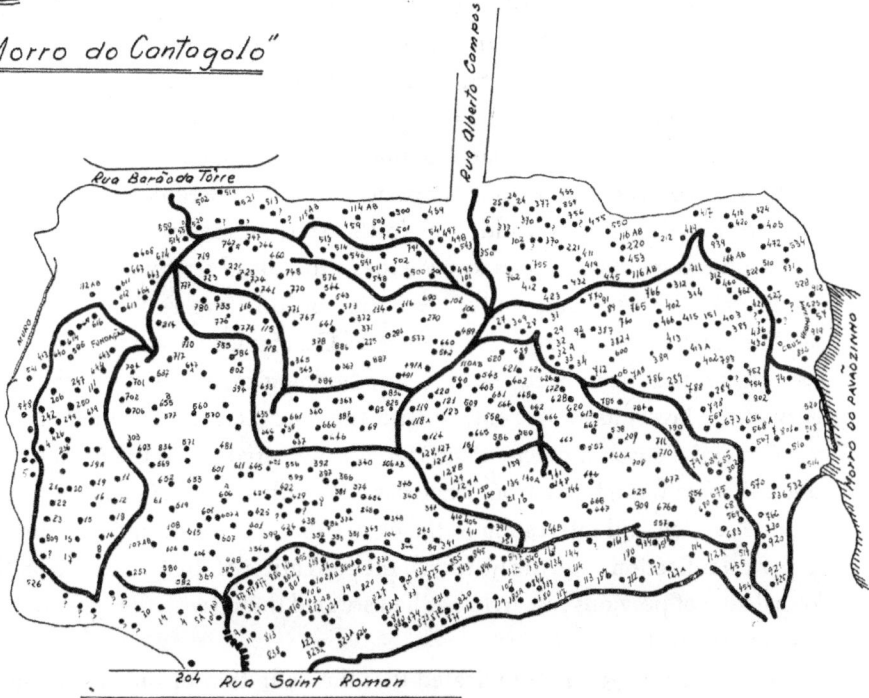

5° DISTRITO   12° CIRCUNSCRIÇÃO   COPACABANA

Acesso: Pela Rua Saint-Roman n° 204.

"Morro do Contagolo"

Figure 9. Map of the favela of Morro do Cantagalo prepared by the IBGE for use by census takers (from *Revista Brasileira de Estatística*, vol. 14, no. 55, July–September 1953).

THE GENERAL CENSUS OF 1950

The study of the favelas reached a new phase with the General Census of 1950. Executed by the IBGE under the auspices of the federal government, it recorded the same detailed data for the favelas as for the rest of the city. For the first time, the nation's demographic census not only provided knowledge about the favela populations and their living conditions but also compared these with those of the Federal District as a whole.

Without a doubt, the quality of the results of the 1950 census is due to Alberto Passos Guimarães, director of the Technical Division of the IBGE's National Census Service. A little studied figure, Guimarães, established the definition of favela that made the census possible and drafted the first official report presenting the results.[69] He was born in 1908 in the Northeastern state of Alagoas and died in Rio in 1993. Even though he had received no higher education, he belonged to a group of Alagoan intellectuals that included Aurélio Buarque de Holanda and Manuel Diegues Júnior.[70]

Before working at the IBGE, Guimarães had been responsible for the Serviço de Estatística da Rede Ferroviária Federal (Statistical Service of the Federal Railway) in Alagoas's capital, Maceió. At the IBGE he was influenced and trained by Italian demographer Giorgio Mortara. A member of the Partido Comunista Brasileiro (Brazilian Communist Party), Guimarães was known for his work on Rio's favelas and for publications on the economics and sociology of Brazil's agrarian world. The Northeastern origins of both Guimarães and Moura suggests that their knowledge of the social reality of that region's big cities informed a comparative perception of Rio's favelas.

The first notable innovative feature of Guimarães's presentation of the 1950 census was the importance of the methodological discussion of the category of the favela itself. In contrast with the 1948 Census of the Favelas, for the General Census, a precise definition was essential, given the need to distinguish what was a favela from what was not. In this regard, Guimarães's text is quite explicit and interesting to the extent that it is supported by a double historical reflection — on the history of the formation of the favelas and on the knowledge of previous research that had studied them (with the exception of Moura's report).

Guimarães (1953, 258) indicated that the definition of the favela had as its point of departure "the clusters that public consensus classifies as such whether they are located on hills or elsewhere." But this "consensus" was not sufficient, and a precise definition presupposed making its criteria explicit. Geographical location on a hill was no longer an exclusive criterion since we know that a number of favelas grew up on other types of terrain. The kind of housing — shacks, precarious construction — was not in and of itself a sufficient criterion since the author observed that this type of dwelling is found in numerous suburban neighborhoods that could not be considered favelas as a whole. Finally, the author highlighted that determining the boundaries of the favela was a methodological problem, often a quite complicated one. Guimarães summarized the process of defining neighborhoods recognized as favelas through the simultaneous use of five criteria, applied not to individual structures but to groups of buildings, that is, to clusters:

In this way, human clusters that possessed wholly or partially the following characteristics were included in the concept of the favela:

1. Minimum proportions: groups of buildings or residences comprised usually of more than fifty units.

2. Type of dwelling: predominance of poor houses or shacks of typical rustic appearance, made mainly of tin-plate or zinc-plate sheet metal, boards, or similar materials.
3. Legal status of occupation: construction lacking licenses or inspection, on property belonging to third parties or of unknown ownership.
4. Public improvements: total or partial absence of sanitation systems, electricity, telephone, and plumbing.
5. Urbanization: space not urbanized, lacking street layout, address numeration, or signage. (A. Guimarães 1953, 259)

Application of these criteria led the 1950 census to register 58 favelas rather than the 105 identified by the Office of the Mayor two years earlier. This significant difference could not have resulted from a real decrease in the number of favelas since there are no known cases of relocation or eradication of any of these clusters in the period in question. A possible hypothesis is that the difference is mostly due to the criterion of fifty buildings; the smaller favelas of the previous census were not considered in the later one. This is indirectly confirmed because, whereas the number of favelas decreased, the number of inhabitants increased, from 138,837 to 169,305. The smaller favelas no longer considered certainly had few total inhabitants, and those with more than fifty structures had seen their populations grow. It is quite likely also that the quality of the census-taking by the IBGE was superior to that of the Mayor's Office for the Census of Favelas. Despite the differences, however, we see that the order of magnitude is the same for the two censuses, much lower than the previous media estimates of between 400,000 and 600,000 *favelados*.

A more detailed introduction to the results afforded finer understanding of the diversity of Rio's favelas, especially in regard to their size and location. The most symbolic favela, Morro da Favella, by 1950 was far from the most populous, in thirteenth place, with only 4,567 inhabitants. The largest by far was Jacarezinho, with 18,424 residents, followed by Mangueira, with 8,949.

The list of favelas included an indication of administrative district, making it possible to compare among geographical zones. By that time, favelas were found in almost every district of the city, not just where their presence was most visible and most criticized—that is, the prettiest neighborhoods downtown and in the South Zone (especially Lagoa, Copacabana, and Gávea). In fact, this had already been demonstrated by the list and map that accompanied the 1948 Census of Favelas (Prefeitura do Distrito Federal 1949, 20).[71] The favela population has more or less the same importance in the North Zone (which has more poor and working-class neighborhoods) and the South Zone.

Nevertheless, the two largest favelas—Jacarezinho and Mangueira—are in the North Zone.

One curious datum in the 1950 census is the presence in the list of favelas of the Proletarian Park of Gávea. Conceived as a transitional solution for relocating *favelados*, eight years later it was considered a failure. What could have been an alternative became the equivalent of a favela.

As for the geographic origins of the residents, the results confirm the 1948 census, with additional details. Two-thirds of *favelados* had been born in the Federal District (38.6 percent) or in the state of Rio de Janeiro (27.5 percent). Of the remaining third, most came from the neighboring states of Minas Gerais (16.5 percent) and Espírito Santo (7.1 percent). The results also confirm that the migrants from the nine states of the Northeast are a minority (8.5 percent). At this time, there were no paved roads between Rio and Salvador, so ship was the only means of interregional transportation for the poorer classes.

Another novelty of the 1950 census was that this was a general national census and thus allowed for the first time a comparison between the favelas and the rest of the city. In his analysis of the results, Guimarães worked systematically on this comparison, observing, for example, that 56.5 percent of the Federal District's population was from the Federal District itself, as opposed to the 38.6 percent among the *favelados*. The latter population represented, in effect, a higher number of migrants than the rest of the city's population, even if they were mainly from the nearby region.

As for skin color, the orders of magnitude were the same, with slightly different results from those found in 1948: 32 percent *brancos*, 29 percent *mestiços*, and 38 percent *negros* in 1950, as opposed to 29 percent, 36 percent, and 35 percent, respectively, in 1948. The differences are not insignificant, but they could have resulted from differences in method of data recording, insofar as this variable was one of the least explicit.

With respect to the favela residents' activities, a comparison between the two censuses cannot be done. On the one hand, the categories of economic activity considered were different in the two censuses, and they were more detailed in 1950. On the other hand, the categories used in 1950 only considered people ten years old and older, in accordance with the definition of the criterion of economically active population, whereas the 1948 category included the population as a whole, without subtracting people under ten from the economically active population.

Guimarães (1953, 261) observed that the importance of processing and manufacturing industries is much greater among the *favelados* than it was for the population of the Federal District as a whole (23 percent versus 13 percent), whereas the importance of the service sector is rather similar (14 percent versus 12 percent). This led Guimarães (1953, 261) to conclude that the census revealed in the favelas "an active, predominantly working population, connected by way of their occupations to the major fields of economic activity functioning in the Federal District." Thus the earlier discourses about the laziness and idleness of favela residents as well as the analysis in the report from the Office of the Mayor's 1948 census were called into question. In the latter report, the category of economically inactive people was significant — 65 percent, or nearly two-thirds of the population. However, this category included children and adult women engaged in unpaid domestic activities, not just economically inactive adult men. Guimarães (1953, 261) is quite emphatic about this issue: "This, then, is not a population composed of 'marginals' but rather a group of people normally integrated into social life."

The IBGE representative also noted that this more detailed classification of the economically inactive "defined with greater precision in the Demographic Census of 1950 than in any other previous survey" yielded a greater understanding of the phenomenon (A. Guimarães 1953, 261). Indeed, among the population ten years of age and older, 48,103 people were classified as engaged in "unpaid domestic activities or scholastic learning activities," that is, homemakers or schoolchildren, against 11,130 classified as inactive. The weight of this truly inactive population is only slightly more in the favelas than in the population of the Federal District as a whole — 9 percent versus 7 percent, but Guimarães (1953, 261) adds that this difference is meaningful because "in the populations of a lower economic level, cases of partial or total disability are frequent and premature, either because of infirmity or other reasons."

Guimarães also stood out from his predecessors in the 1948 census who reiterated earlier racial prejudices. In his commentary on the relation between skin color and activity he analyzed in a much subtler way the connection between the social status of racial categories and the types of activity. Based on the results of the 1940 census determined by Giorgio Mortara, Guimarães (1953, 260) was not surprised to find that among the *favelados*, who are in lower income groups, there were higher proportions of *negros* and *mestiços*, who had less access to higher-skilled, higher-paying jobs.

The General Census of 1950 and Guimarães's 1953 report were landmarks in the history of the production of social representations of the Rio favela insofar as they defined the category. As we have seen, this census is distinguished from the 1948 Census of Favelas not only in the greater precision and pertinence of the categories used and the data produced but also in the quality of the interpretation, thanks to Guimarães, who made explicit the results' sociological importance and significance. After the publication of the report, the public image of Rio's favelas was never the same.

The 1950 census had an impact that went beyond Rio de Janeiro. In fact, since the category of favela had been introduced into the national census, it was possible to prove the existence of similar phenomena elsewhere, even if these went by other names, for example, the *mocambos* of Recife. The existence of spaces in other Brazilian cities that were comparable to the Rio favela, a reality previously hidden on the political plane, meant that they now became visible and measurable, thanks to these statistical categories. Guimarães's (1953, 254–55) report was explicit about the significance: "For this and other reasons, the favela is no longer a phenomenon apart, peculiar and exclusive to the Federal District, with unmistakable characteristics essentially different from other groupings of the poorer classes. Their populations are a parcel among a number of such that make up Brazilian society." The introduction of a category referring to collections of precarious dwellings into the Brazilian census — to this day found under the heading "subnormal cluster" — beginning with the case of Rio, contributed to the generalization of the word "favela," which progressively went from being a local term to a national category. What is more, in contrast to the other studies examined in this chapter, Guimarães's text is, most of all, analytical and methodological.

Guimarães (1953, 255–56) reminds us of the need for solutions to this social and urban planning problem:

> Should the favelas be urbanized or simply extinguished?
>
> Extinction of the favelas . . . would imply the settling of 60,000 families in various zones, the construction in short order of about 50,000 new houses for sale or rent at an affordable price, and it would require a solution to the problem of transportation, including expanding and making cheaper the current means of transport.
>
> Urbanizing the favelas might not be any less costly an undertaking, though it seems more in accord with the social and human sense of the matter. Who can guarantee, however, that once the favelas and their hillsides were urbanized that their current residents would remain there?[72]

This being said, the main concern was to assert the importance of an exact understanding of the phenomenon to formulate policies that were truly well adapted; at the same time, the report was discreet as to the choice of solutions. To repeat Guimarães's (1953, 256) vision for including the favelas in the census: "Regardless of the courses of action chosen to formulate the problems arising from the proliferation of groups of *favelados*, the success of the measures that could be put in practice will depend on the best understanding of the individual and social characteristics of these populations."

Thus arose a new stance toward intellectual work that added a contribution justified by scientific knowledge, a posture distinct from that of public policy, which was responsible for choosing solutions. This new stance should be emphasized in light of the intense political debate that reigned in the late 1940s and early 1950s about the fate of the favelas. Among the protagonists in this debate, the Catholic Church stood out. In defense of the favelas, it established the Fundação Leão XIII and, in 1955, the Cruzada São Sebastião (Saint Sebastian Crusade), an initiative of Dom Hélder Câmara.[73] At this same time, antifavela movements crystalized around journalist Carlos Lacerda, who began his "Batalha do Rio" in 1948.[74]

As we will see in the next chapter, the 1950 census contributed to the construction of new representations of the favela and to both the Church's and Lacerda's arguments. At the same time, thanks to an understanding of the phenomenon of the favela in its complexity, the census facilitated the entrance of the social sciences onto the stage.

In the 1950s, two works take up and explore the results of the 1950 census. *Favelas do Distrito Federal* (Favelas of the Federal District), by José Alípio Goulart, published in 1957 by the Ministry of Agriculture, was the first book devoted entirely to the favelas of Rio. Goulart revisited Guimarães's analyses, by way of journalistic observations that did not alter Guimarães's findings. Goulart placed value particularly on the data, which, as we know, called into question the contemporary view of the favelas as to their inhabitants' economic activity, migratory origins, and so forth. Goulart's stance seems, at the same time, less strictly scientific and more engaged in regard to solutions. He explicitly staked out a position in favor of the Fundação Leão XIII, whose data he also published, as well as data from the Cruzada São Sebastião.

The other notable work is *O negro no Rio de Janeiro* (The Black man in Rio de Janeiro), by sociologist Luiz Costa Pinto (1998), first published in 1953. This book does not deal specifically with the favela, but its chapter titled "Ecologia" (Ecology) analyzes the division of ethnic groups in the urban area of Rio de Janeiro and from this perspective deals with the favelas, supported by the newly available sociodemographic data.[75] For a better understanding of the favela from the point of view of race relations, Costa Pinto used the indicators of occupation and income level from the recent census and showed the interrelation among social stratification, ecological situation, and ethnic condition. Even though he does not cite Guimarães (he could not have read the report published the same year as his book) or Giorgio Mortara (who was Guimarães's inspiration), the conclusions are convergent.

Even if it was narrowly focused on race relations and presented results of a UNESCO study, Costa Pinto's book, as the first sociological work to treat the favelas, adopted the posture of social science research, of rigorous and nonreductive analysis. Costa Pinto kept cognitive procedure clearly separate from prescriptive procedure, in contrast with other contributions we have seen, in which impressionistic observations were inseparable from the solutions advocated. We must remember, however, that Costa Pinto analyzed only data that were secondary to those of the 1948 census. Mobilization of the social sciences for direct observation of the favelas still remained to be done. This mobilization would constitute a new phase, which we will consider in the next chapter.

CHAPTER TWO

THE SHIFT TO THE
SOCIAL SCIENCES

A new period of production of representations and knowledge about the favela began in the early 1950s and lasted until the end of the 1960s. Its two main
characteristics were its promotion of the favela's value as a community and its
launch of real field research using the methods of the social sciences. With respect to methodological approach, the actors in this phase took up and developed the discoveries from the end of the previous period, when the first censuses constituted the first systematic collection of data. In contrast, the view of
the favela as an element of society changed in a quite precise way.

This change appears to be connected to several convergent political
and economic factors. After the Second World War, in both Brazil and Latin
America as a whole, the resumption of economic growth accelerated urban
growth, and the influx of rural migrants into the cities also intensified the
growth of the favelas, which made the need for housing for the working class
more acute. This resumption took place in the political setting of developmentalism,[1] an idea characterized by the central role of the state in planning,
whether on the economic or territorial plane, an example of the latter being
the decision to build the new federal capital in Brasília, inaugurated in 1960.
In contrast to Vargas's policy, developmentalism was part of a global opening
in which development aid and international cooperation were subject to the
larger injunctions of international relations shaped by the Cold War. In order
to emerge from underdevelopment, the Brazilian elites turned to international
cooperation to reduce poverty, and foreign specialists were invited to propose
innovative solutions to Brazil's problems in the throes of development.

I will show that, insofar as the social sciences were brought to bear explicitly, they did so while complementing and prolonging political interventions
in the favela. Foreign specialists carrying out fieldwork to implement programs
rediscovered the favela and established important collaborations with Brazil-

ians. The most notable of these foreigners were Father Louis-Joseph Lebret, one of the founders of the French Catholic movement Économie et Humanisme, and the U.S. anthropologist Anthony Leeds, along with Peace Corps volunteers. Such actors, different as they were, had features in common: relating research to intervention, acting in parallel with the main Brazilian universities, and strongly valuing fieldwork. Thus in Brazil a unique "miscegenation" occurred between French influence and the Chicago School of sociology.

DOM HÉLDER CÂMARA, THE CATHOLIC CHURCH, AND THE RIO FAVELAS

In 1960, *O Estado de São Paulo*, the most important newspaper of the day,[2] published in two special supplements the SAGMACS study *Aspectos humanos da favela carioca* (Human aspects of the Rio Favela). It was republished that same year in installments by the Carioca daily *A Tribuna da Imprensa*. As numerous witnesses attest, this text had enormous political and media impact, as well as considerable influence on researchers — sociologists, anthropologists, architects, and geographers — who beginning in the mid-1960s and continuing into the 1970s engaged in fieldwork in the favelas. Parisse 1969a, 1970; Valladares 1978a; Leeds and Leeds 1978; and Valla 1986 are examples of work based explicitly on the findings of this study. According to Anthony Leeds, considered the greatest U.S. expert on favelas on the 1970s, "The SAGMACS study is still today the most important and the best report published on the favelas of Rio" (Leeds and Leeds 1978, 199).[3]

Two aspects of this publication seem rather surprising: on the one hand, that an important study of the favelas of Rio de Janeiro was published and financed by a São Paulo newspaper; and, on the other hand, that its main inspiration — the first one listed by the research team — was Father Louis-Joseph Lebret. Whereas the team members who performed the concrete research and wrote up the study were Brazilian, the person responsible for this operation, who gave it the greater part of its methodological orientation, was a French Dominican whose intervention in the debate on the solution to the favela problem was truly surprising. How does one explain that Lebret was responsible for the research, and that *O Estado de São Paulo* undertook this unusual venture of publishing an extensive research report in a newspaper?

The point of departure for such an initiative in Rio was the mobilization of the Catholic Church around the issue of the favelas that began in the 1940s. In fact, the Church was already present in these localities, whether because of the efforts of some parishes and certain religious groups or because of the

Fundação Leão XIII mentioned in the previous chapter. This foundation, created in 1947 through a partnership between the Archdiocese of Rio and the Office of the Mayor, was controversial from its beginnings. Founded by the conservative wing of the Church and other authorities in the same year that the Partida Comunista Brasileiro (PCB) was outlawed, one of its motives was to not leave the field open to the communists.[4] The communist threat seemed all the more important since the PCB, the third-strongest political force in the Federal District during the Constituent Assembly of 1945 after Getúlio Vargas's removal from office, come in first in the municipal election of 1947, winning a majority of the seats on the municipal council with a clear advantage over the second-place party, the Partido Trabalhista Brasileiro (PTB), which was linked to Vargas. These results greatly concerned the federal government and the upper levels of local administration (Parisse 1969a, 88; Pandolfi 1995, 146–47). Some sources and interviews with former communist militants confirmed the PCB's growing influence in the favelas. For example, Nísia Verônica Trindade Lima (1989) reviewed the published testimony by the communist leader Manoel Gomes (1980), completed using other interviews and analyzing the press coverage at the time.[5] I remember the influence of the "popular democratic committees" created by communists in several neighborhoods, with some subcommittees in several favelas, action that led to the rise of the Associação dos Favelados do Morro do Borel (Borel Favela Association) and afterward to the expansion into twelve other favelas through the creation of the União dos Trabalhadores Favelados (*Favelado* Workers Union) in 1954. This association mobilized the residents against several landowners, with later help from Antoine de Magarinos Torres, known as the "lawyer of the poor" (M. Gomes 1980).[6] Lima's research as well as interviews that I have been involved in more recently show that the communists developed aid work with medical doctors and professors in these favelas, especially in Morro do Borel and Morro do Turano.[7] They went as far as proposing changing the names of the favelas to Morro da Independência and Morro da Liberdade, respectively, but the older names prevailed.

The stated objectives of the Fundação Leão XIII consisted of ensuring "material and moral aid for the inhabitants of the hills and favelas of Rio de Janeiro," and providing "schools, dispensaries, childcare centers, maternity clinics, refectories, and housing blocks for the people" (Estatutos da Fundação [Founding Statutes], cited in Valla 1986, 47). The foundation's activity was inscribed in the new perspective offered by Mayor Pedro Ernesto Baptista (see previous chapter), which abandoned repression and moral condemnation and instead preached social education and integration.

Another initiative of the Catholic Church was the Cruzada São Sebastião, launched in 1955 by Dom Hélder Câmara, then auxiliary archbishop of Rio. Well known in the Catholic milieu in both Brazil and internationally, Dom Hélder successively held several key positions in the Brazilian Church. He was the secretary of the CNBB during the First Conference of Bishops of the Northeast in 1956, when agrarian reform was announced. As auxiliary archbishop, he took the side of the least favored, becoming known as "defender of the poor" (Marin 1995). Considered to have come from the left wing of the Church, Dom Hélder was, in the 1950s, the main person responsible for the campaign in defense of Rio's favelas. He took advantage of the Thirty-Sixth National Eucharistic Conference, held in Rio in 1955, to get the federal government's support for a new program of action.

The Cruzada's objectives were set out in Article 2 of the organization's statutes, "to promote, coordinate, and execute measures and arrangements destined to provide a rational, humane, Christian solution to the problem of favelas in Rio de Janeiro, . . . to marshal the financial resources necessary to ensure, in satisfactory conditions of hygiene, in comfort and safety, stable housing for the families living in favelas, [and] to collaborate in the integration of ex-*favelados* into the normal life of the neighborhood" (Parisse 1969a, 175–76).

These two competing initiatives launched by the Catholic Church in 1947 and 1955 performed different activities with different means of intervention (Rios, in Valla 1986, 63–65). On the one hand, the Fundação Leão XIII delivered material and moral aid to the population, especially through efforts in education and health (childcare centers, walk-in clinics, etc.) and by creating many social action centers in various favelas. On the other hand, the Cruzada São Sebastião promoted broad efforts to build new housing and infrastructure, which today we would call urban development of the favelas.

Dom Hélder got the Fundação Leão XIII to collaborate in two Cruzada São Sebastião actions: installation of running water and street lighting, and, with the help of residents in some favelas, public telephones. There was also collective management of the Conjunto São Sebastião, made up of seven properties, with a total of 790 residences, right in the South Zone in the district of Leblon, built for a significant number of the residents from the favela of Praia do Pinto, located nearby.[8]

The principle of community development, which inspired Dom Hélder's action, was based on the premise that success required stakeholder involvement. This new perspective spread throughout Brazil at the end of the 1940s and the beginning of the 1950s, through the coming together of various processes: the influence of the progressive French Church on the progressive Brazilian Church; the model of community development promoted by international organizations—such as the United Nations, UNESCO, and the Organization of American States—that were quite active in Brazil; the concern for this topic in schools of social work; and public efforts to train adults, especially in rural communities (Ammann 1997; Vidal 1996).[9]

Dom Hélder also believed in research and argued that a "rational solution" should be supported by good knowledge of the local situation. This was in accord with many of the social actors mentioned in chapter 1. In this, he assumed the pragmatic position defended by Lebret.

The Cruzada São Sebastião constituted a shift in the political representation of the favela. The recognition and promotion of the favelas' residents to the status of a community and, as a consequence, as potentially autonomous political subjects broke with both the purely negative view of an evil to be eradicated and the clientelistic, charity-based aid policy of the earlier period. The Crusade was also the first intervention to produce a quantitatively significant amount of permanent housing nearby for those from demolished favelas, as opposed to the Proletarian Parks, which were conceived of as transitional housing.

Within this new social construction of the favela, Lebret's contribution was important because of the study of Rio's favelas carried out by SAGMACS, with the support of Dom Hélder Câmara.[10]

FATHER LEBRET AND BRAZIL

Father Lebret was already well known in France for his role in founding the international movement Économie et Humanisme, as a researcher at the Centre National de la Recherche Scientifique (CNRS), and after 1954 for being in charge of the drafting of Pope Paul VI's encyclical *Populorum progressio*. He visited Brazil various times between 1947 and 1965. Several authors have emphasized that his trips to Brazil gave him a certain distance from the problems so far encountered in Économie et Humanisme. What is more, the Brazilian experience offered him "a movement in crisis in a new field of action" (Pelletier 1996, 29). According to José Arthur Rios (n.d.) and Francisco Whitaker Ferreira (1997, 134), these visits opened a "new field of action" in underdeveloped regions for Économie et Humanisme (Pelletier 1996, 303). According to Denis Pelletier, "In the genesis of the Catholic Third Worldism of Économie et Humanisme, Brazil served as a veritable field of experimentation." In 1957, "Lebret, who was now busy with his international activities, was no longer occupied with Économie et Humanisme. After 1950 he began to understand that development was the problem of the century" (Garreau 1997, 273) and that Brazil would be "after 1952, the laboratory of this change of direction, soon to be extended to Latin America as a whole" (Pelletier 1996, 292). The Institut de Recherche et de Formation en vue du Développement Harmonisé (IRFED), created in France in 1958, is testimony to Lebret's effort to train specialists in technical cooperation, with the intent of promoting harmonious development and a civilization in solidarity. Of the 591 students who attended IRFED between 1958 and 1963, 260 came from Latin America, many of these from Brazil (Rios n.d., 13).

To understand Lebret's impact on urban planners and the managerial elite in Brazil, well before his work in the favelas, it helps to recall some of the elements that characterized Brazil's sociopolitical situation in the late 1940s and to analyze the social networks that invited Lebret to come to Brazil and on which he relied to spread his ideas and methods.

Without doing a deeper analysis of this period, the point is that after the fall of the Vargas dictatorship in 1945,[11] political life in Brazil was increasing characterized by a growth in the number of communists and by the need for the Catholic Church to react to the ascension of Marxism. At that time, Christians and anticommunist elites sought a political project for a society in the throes of reconstruction. Lebret's approach, which proposed a humanist alternative in solidarity with the poor, seduced both Brazilian Catholic youth and a large portion of the elites searching for a way forward that was both anti-imperialist and anticommunist and that could drive social change and economic development. Lebret was invited to Brazil for the first time in 1947 by the Brazilian Dominicans who had frequented the La Tourette convent near Lyon, in which the Économie et Humanisme movement regularly held activities.[12] From May to September of that year, Lebret taught a course, General Introduction to Humane Economy,[13] at São Paulo's Escola Livre de Sociologia e Política (ELSP), which brought together a diverse audience including senior administrative staff, engineers, medical doctors, and members of the São Paulo Catholic elite. On the same occasion, thanks to the influential support of the Dominicans, he established permanent structures for introducing the thought of Économie et Humanisme. Thus in 1947 the planning office for SAGMACS was established, on the model of the Société pour l'Application du Graphisme et de la Mécanographie à l'Analyse (SAGMA), founded in France in 1946.[14]

From this first stay in Brazil, Lebret maintained personal and professional ties that would determine future visits and the spread of his ideas in Brazil. For example, Josué de Castro, a sociologist from Pernambuco, professor at the

UFRJ, and author of *Geopolítica da fome* (Geopolitics of hunger), would adopt Lebret's methods in a major nationwide study by the Vargas government's Comissão do Bem Estar Social (Social Welfare Commission) of living standards in Brazil's thirty-four largest cities.[15] As president of this commission, Castro selected Lebret as an adviser. When he was later named director of the Food and Agriculture Organization of the United Nations (FAO), Castro also opened its doors to his former adviser.

For the Church's part, the privileged relationship that formed between Lebret and Dom Hélder Câmara while the latter was auxiliary archbishop of Rio de Janeiro helped break down the resistance of the Brazilian senior clergy, who saw in the intellectual-priest's ideas more militancy than religious doctrine. It is also reported that it was Dom Hélder who attenuated Lebret's observations about the illegality of the Communist Party, which made him persona non grata in Brazil for a time. Moreover, Dom Hélder would also influence Lebret's view of the favelas.

The engineer Lucas Nogueira Garcez, who attended the course taught at the ELSP in 1947, participated in the first SAGMACS teams. When he was elected governor of the state of São Paulo, he continued the activities of the SAGMACS planning office, demonstrating the utility and efficacy of the method of analysis of regional development that Lebret professed. He also secured funding for an international conference on humane economics held during the festivities of the quadricentennial of the founding of the city of São Paulo. Participants in this conference included Pierre Monbeig, Alfred Sauvy, and a number of Latin Americans who later brought Lebret to Uruguay, Paraguay, and Chile. This symposium, therefore, was at the root of important contacts arranged with the Economic Commission for Latin America (ECLA) in Chile, then directed by Raúl Prebisch.[16]

Lebret's ideas also spread in Brazil through his spiritual influence on Catholic youth, especially the Juventude Universitária Católica (Catholic University Youth, JUC), which campaigned intensely during the 1950s to lift the country out of underdevelopment. Relationships that Lebret established with intellectuals — such as Alceu de Amoroso Lima, a writer, philosopher, and Catholic leader connected with both the managerial elite and Catholic activist groups — contributed to his insertion into Brazilian Catholic milieus. Many of Lebret's books were published in Portuguese: *Principes pour l'action* (France 1945; Brazil 1950, 2nd ed. 1952), *Appels au Seigneur* (France 1955; Brazil 1963), *Dimensions de la charité* (France 1958; Brazil 1959), *Suicide ou survie de l'Occident* (France 1958; Brazil 1960), *Manifeste pour une civilisation solidaire* (France 1959; Brazil 1960), and *Le drame du siècle* (France 1960; Brazil 1962). The speed with which these works were translated is testimony to both the spread of Lebret's ideas and his level of success with the public in Brazil.[17]

If it is true that Lebret was able to penetrate certain political settings, thanks to relationships with Lucas Garcez and Josué de Castro, it is also important to note that, from his earliest time in the country in the late 1940s, the Brazilian academy never opened its doors to him as it had to others, French or otherwise, who had a more academic profile. Note that the ELSP,[18] which had welcomed the priest, was not part of the Universidade de São Paulo (USP). Even USP's Faculdade de Filosofia, Ciências e Letras (College of Philosophy, Science, and Letters, FFCL), which had brought the likes of Fernand Braudel, Claude Lévi-Strauss, Pierre Monbeig, and Roger Bastide—whose presence played an important role in training Brazilian sociologists, anthropologists, and geographers—did not receive Lebret.[19]

Even in France, Lebret, who was neither a sociologist nor an anthropologist by training, did not belong to the academic world or share in the dominant sociological tradition, for which Durkheim was the most important point of reference.[20] Lebret was a naval engineer, a former student of the Brest Naval School, who had added to this training the vocation of a Dominican. His entry into the social sciences was part of a cultural and professional trajectory quite different from that of the French academy: instead of the Durkheimian tradition, he followed a sociological practice inherited from Frédéric Le Play and, more specifically his successor, Henri de Tourville.[21] At that time, these La Play and Tourville were not considered legitimate representatives of French sociology. In the eyes of the elitist USP, the work done by Économie et Humanisme, almost unknown in Brazil, did not correspond to the canonical sociology exported by France. And neither did Lebret.

So Lebret found his place in Brazil in another school, oriented toward a more empirical, more applied sociology than the theoretical one valued by USP. In fact, there was a big difference between the two São Paulo institutions where a student could get an education in the social sciences in the 1940s (Miceli 1989; Massi 1989; Limongi 1989): USP's FFCL, in which a generalist and essentially theoretical instruction predominated, and the ELSP, which had as a goal the training of research professionals endowed with administrative competencies. In the latter, the model of U.S. sociology quickly established itself. In contrast to USP, still very connected to the French tradition, the ELSP invited U.S. and German professors. The school's curriculum and the instruction offered were marked by the presence for eighteen years of U.S. sociologist Donald Pierson. Originally from the University of Chicago, this former student of Robert Park had chosen to study the relations between Blacks and whites in Bahia for his doctoral thesis, on Park's advice (Pierson 1942).

Seeking to transpose the didactic model of the Chicago School to São Paulo, Pierson succeeded in establishing a similar operation at the ESLP, one that promoted the value of empirical research, educating students for the professional practice of sociology, and rapidly disseminating the results.[22] From this perspective, Pierson criticized training based exclusively on the acquisition of sociological theory and gave priority to fieldwork and apprenticeship in different research techniques and methods. Faithful to the Chicago spirit, he rejected the idea of a separation between sociology and anthropology, with fieldwork itself being more important than debates about the autonomy or specificity of the disciplines. The journal *Sociologia*, founded by the ELSP in 1939, reveals in its issues of the following two decades a predominance of articles based on empirical research. Brazilians following the U.S. model devoted themselves to numerous community studies in several regions of Brazil.[23]

And so it was the ELSP, the institution associated with promoting the value of field research, that welcomed Lebret in 1947 to teach the four-month course on humane economics. We can imagine that, in addition to the interest in the political and theological ideas of Économie et Humanisme, this coming together could also be explained by a common conception of the role of research, the importance attributed to fieldwork, and the orientation toward professional training. We can also suppose that the ELSP would be more open than a traditional university, showing a greater receptivity to courses and seminars outside of the classical curriculum.

Lebret's visit to Brazil was funded by the Federação das Indústrias do Estado de São Paulo (FIESP),[24] which can be explained by the interest of certain members of the industrial elite in finding a new socioeconomic model. Convinced as they were of the utility of planning, they longed for a kind of progressivism and were interested in the innovative focus of social Catholicism based on scientific principles. One of these was the intellectual, industrialist, politician, and administrator Roberto Simonsen, who was then president of the ELSP and was a director of the Serviço Social da Indústria (SESI).[25]

Former students of USP's Escola Politécnica, who were already engaged in engineering careers, attended Lebret's course in 1947. They later went to work for SAGMACS, which would maintain its image as a pioneering institution for sixteen years (Lamparelli 1995). As a place for study and planning, SAGMACS introduced interdisciplinary practice and developed for the first time in Brazil research on urban organization and land use planning, producing the groundbreaking study *Estrutura urbana da aglomeração paulistana* (Urban structure of the São Paulo agglomeration), among others.[26] These studies were important for Lebret himself, who revisited elements of these in his *Manuel de l'enquêteur* (Researcher's handbook), published in 1952 in France, which included graphics taken from studies he had coordinated in São Paulo (Lebret 1952, 83–85).

Lebret's role in training a generation of urban planners in São Paulo in 1950–60 is unquestionable. In fact, most of these attended his second course in 1953 (Lamparelli 1995, 39). In this period, the Lebret method was already known thanks to the success of SAGMACS, which continued to employ and train on the job Brazilian urban planners and researchers. Many SAGMACS members were also affiliated with USP, where this second course was given. This marks Lebret's entry into USP, though in the Faculdade de Arquitetura e Urbanismo (College of Architecture and Urbanism, FAU), not in the Department of Sociology. Celso Monteiro Lamparelli (1995) and Francisco Whitaker Ferreira (1997), both architect-planners who benefited from their direct contact with Lebret, report that the experience of working at his side helped them acquire empirical research methodology that later grounded their work in more than just technocratically based urban planning.[27]

FATHER LEBRET DISCOVERS THE
FAVELAS OF RIO DE JANEIRO

Ever since his first time in Brazil, Lebret had been deeply aware of the country's strong contrasts and social inequality. In the late 1940s, Brazil was characterized by underdevelopment and its attendant extreme poverty, illiteracy, and hunger. The geographic contrast was apparent between the rural Northeast, backward and impoverished, and the Southeast, with its megalopolises and intense industrial development. As the main beneficiaries of federal resources, São Paulo and Rio de Janeiro had the highest urban growth rates in the country. The dualism was thus even more shocking within these two metropolises, where poverty and wealth lived side by side, with the life of the poor being extremely precarious.

From his arrival in Brazil in 1947, "the disturbing discovery of the favelas of São Paulo [had] plunged [Lebret] into the misfortunes of the Third World and the struggles for more humane development" (Houée 1997, 115). But it would be in Rio years later that Lebret would find himself directly involved with this issue. In fact, during his first stay in Brazil in the late 1940s, the favelas of São Paulo were not yet numerous. The estimate at the time held that there was a

The Shift to the Social Sciences

maximum of 50,000 *favelados* distributed in seven clusters (Meihy and Levine 1994, 22). In Rio de Janeiro, the favelas were more visible. As we saw in chapter 1, the 1949 census had counted in the favela clusters about 170,000 inhabitants, or 7 percent of the Federal District's population, and for several decades the favelas had been at the center of discourse about the city's future.[28]

Lebret visited the city of Rio during his first trip to Brazil, and he returned there regularly, staying in the Dominican convent in the district of Leme. After the late 1940s, the adjacent district of Copacabana started to become more densely populated thanks to vertical growth, and favelas increasingly occupied the hills nearby. It was said then that construction workers would use the refuse of the construction sites to build their own shacks. During this time, there was among the Dominicans in Leme a Frenchman, Father Secondi, who celebrated mass every Sunday near the convent in the chapel of Morro da Babilônia,[29] which served as the headquarters of the Cruzada pela Infância do Leme (Leme Crusade for Children), a social service of the parish. It appears that it was also Secondi who organized a group of young women to do social work on this hill and who was one of the first to show Lebret the world of the favelas.[30] Considering Lebret's interest in the poor, during evening meetings at the convent, Secondi surely told him about the social service the parish was doing and its impact among the needy *favelados*.

Dom Hélder Câmara was the other member of the religious who had an important if not determining role in fostering Lebret's interest in the favelas. Dom Hélder wished to carry out research to show the superiority of solutions he had professed for the problems of Rio's favelas. This was important because, as we saw in chapter 1, in 1948 the journalist Carlos Lacerda, former communist turned implacable anticommunist, was leading a campaign in the local press called "A Batalha do Rio" (The battle of Rio) that preached the return of the favelas to the countryside and at the same time demanded energetic intervention to expel residents from existing favelas and prevent the proliferation of new clusters. The favela of Praia do Pinto, the same one in which the Cruzada São Sebastião would concentrate its efforts, was a particular target of Lacerda's campaign.[31] Dom Hélder sought a study, developed and carried out with ample autonomy, away from the government's control and not passing directly through the Church, that could provide an indirect evaluation of the activity of the Crusade. In his eyes, SAGMACS held an ideal position to perform such a study, ensuring trustworthiness, solidity, and detail.

In 1947, while Lebret was in Brazil, Dom Hélder had already asked SAGMACS in São Paulo for a study of working-class housing.[32] After this experience, Dom Hélder had come to trust in Lebret's competence as well as in his ability to coordinate teams even outside France. Even though we do not know exactly when the two men met, the ties between them formed after this first collaboration were clearly very strong.[33] What is more, Lebret's theoretical political orientation was wholly compatible with that of Dom Hélder, who was a weighty ally during difficult moments of Lebret's residence in Brazil.[34]

One concern of this "third way" brought these two figures together. Based on a critique of the modern world, according to Isabelle Astier and Jean-François Laé (1991, 83), the Économie et Humanisme movement proposed the following:[35]

1. Elaboration of scientific knowledge of humane economy based on the city, the district, and local associations.
2. Construction of research instruments, both monographic and statistical supported by a nomenclature of social facts.
3. Affirmation of an ethic founded in the base community: family, professional group, neighborhood, and district.
4. Intention to play the role of intermediary between the bureaucratic state and a population without representation.

This "third way" aligned perfectly with the convictions of Dom Hélder and his closest collaborators. The favelas should have the right to political representation, no longer to be a mere space of administrative interventions (the position held by the believers in the favelas' elimination), so that they might become base communities, in which the family would be the basic unit and the neighborhood would guarantee social cohesion. What is more, the idea of community allowed isolated individuals to be associated with a group, a vision very close to that proposed by Économie et Humanisme: "Conceived in order to include and protect individuals within it, the [community] appears in a second stage as a form of collective representation. . . . The notion of community has everything [needed within it] to describe the levels of responsibility and the states of development of participatory democracy" (Astier and Laé 1991, 94).

The idea of serving as an intermediary between the bureaucratic state and the local population, in the interest of the latter, was one of the explicit objectives of the Crusade. This enabled it to negotiate with the Rio de Janeiro Tramway, Power, and Light Company (Light for short, the company that provided electricity to Rio) an authorization to install fifty-one electrical networks in various favelas. The intent was to counter the clientelistic practices of many state deputies and municipal councilmen who had long considered the favelas as their "electoral corrals."[36] Aside from the political implication, however,

The Shift to the Social Sciences

this church initiative led to the recognition of the fact of the favelas as well as a recognition of their inhabitants' right to the basic public apparatus. Positioning itself, at least in theory, outside of the political game, the left wing of the Church intended to play the role of substitute, defending the poor and, at the same time, helping with their political emancipation, whereas, at the same time, the traditional Church was in the habit of putting the poor under its tutelage through its numerous charitable activities. Victor Vincent Valla (1986) suggests that, in many favelas, the Fundação Leão XIII exercised control over residents through its social centers. SAGMACS came to the same conclusion, showing that the rise in 1951 of the first favela residents' association, the União de Defesa e Melhoramentos da Barreira do Vasco (Barreira do Vasco Defense and Improvement Union) resulted from mobilization against the activity of the Fundação Leão XIII (SAGMACS 1960, 2:33).

According to Dom Hélder, if, in the first stage, the local community should rely on an intermediary—in this case, the Cruzada São Sebastião— during negotiations with higher levels of administration, it should also develop on its own its capacity to negotiate. This goal of drawing out the residents' own representation was not far from the idea preached by the Économie et Humanisme movement of "drawing out from the population the natural leaders; that is, extract from the base of activist, socialist, or Catholic circles an elite that knew how to express itself" (Astier and Laé 1991, 95). Even in this, Lebret's thinking and Dom Hélder's proposals were close: since 1959, São Sebastião district had had a residents' association (Parisse 1969a, 183). This convergence of viewpoints led to an effective collaboration, confirmed with the passing of years, with the complicity and complementarity of a man of action (Dom Hélder) and a researcher in the service of action (Father Lebret).

As I noted in chapter 1, these ideas, which were quite innovative in the local context, met up with an emerging new global current. In fact, since 1956 the United Nations had been proposing to underdeveloped countries the route of community development, defined as the process by which the efforts of the people join with those of governmental authorities to integrate those communities into the life of the nation" (Ammann 1997, 32). As it was proposed and promoted by international organizations, this position was echoed in Brazil by schools of social work that educated the social workers whose primary targets were the neighborhoods and population of the favelas. In Rio de Janeiro, the School of Social Work at PUC had the responsibility of placing its students and alumni in agencies of the Office of the Mayor.

Insofar as they shared the same analysis of poverty and agreed on the topic of self-development and the quest for individual autonomy, Dom Hélder and

Father Lebret became soldiers in the same struggle. They intended to prove that the poor living in an urban setting, even if destitute, were capable of having a sense of community and were already giving proof of this. This community feeling would need to be encouraged and promoted, however. This in turn would require improving their living conditions and recognizing their full right to the city, facilitating for them the material means needed to live in it without being excluded and to serve as their own intermediaries. However, in order to lead such an action for the benefit of the poor, the *favelados* and their way of life better had to be better understood. For that, it was necessary to study them.

THE INTERESTS OF THE SAGMACS RESEARCH

In the late 1950s, when *O Estado de São Paulo*, then the most important newspaper in Brazil, decided to fund a study of the favelas of Rio, Lebret was considered more of an expert than a researcher, more of a consultant than an observer-analyst, but he was able to remain in Brazil long enough to do the fieldwork. During this period of his life, he resumed international activities: he was sent on missions, gave lectures, met important figures, and organized the creation of local teams that he would supervise from a distance. His main role during several trips to the Third World was to open doors: the "Lebret" seal was enough to guarantee the scientific credibility and practical interest of the studies he coordinated, to the extent that, during the 1960s, Lebret became a sort of myth in Latin America, dividing his time among Brazil, Chile, and Colombia, countries that witnessed the spread of the Économie et Humanisme movement through the founding of numerous planning offices.[37]

It is also possible that the work carried out in France on working-class housing, especially with tenements, by other members of Économie et Humanisme had been publicized in Brazil, thanks to Lebret.[38] The methodology of the work of this movement, insofar as it put forth research method guidelines for using socioeconomic statistics, involving human geography, monographs, maps, and so forth, corresponded to the demand found in Brazil.

Four planning offices, all called SAGMACS, were created in Brazil, with great impact, both because of the training of their technicians and because of the research performed (Whitaker Ferreira 1997).[39] The first was opened in the city of São Paulo in 1947, followed by the offices in Belo Horizonte and Recife (where certain studies were performed with Lebret's active participation).[40] The Rio office was the last to be established. In the 1950s, Rio was still the capital of Brazil, and the São Paulo SAGMACS needed a basis from which to approach the federal ministries. The Rio office functioned initially within this scope, and it only changed direction with the favela study sponsored by *O Estado de São Paulo*.

Before analyzing the elaboration of SAGMACS's research on the favelas, we should understand the paradox of a São Paulo newspaper funding a study of Rio de Janeiro. Though this might appear unimportant, a discussion of the matter will help clarify the study's purposes and the political context in which it was carried out.

On the one hand, let us return to the overall political context. In the second half of the 1950s, the construction of the new capital of Brasília mobilized all sectors of the Brazilian economy, all political groups and parties, and all the press and communication media. President Juscelino Kubitschek, the defender of the developmentalist project, was attacked by the União Democrática Nacional (UDN), the party of the conservative elites, and by *O Estado de São Paulo*. The newspaper tried to destabilize Kubitschek publicly, attacking in particular the building of the new capital, which it considered economically disastrous. Articles and editorials argued that it would be better to invest the millions uselessly spent on the Brasília project in the struggle against poverty in Rio de Janeiro. Indeed, this poverty kept increasing, threatening more and more the capital's wealthy districts. As we have seen, for some time the favelas had already constituted an important topic of political debate. Thus we can contemplate that a major scientific study of the favelas might furnish *O Estado de São Paulo* with solid arguments against the policy of decentralization of federal power, which Brasília represented.[41]

On the other hand, the strategy of *O Estado de São Paulo* could be analyzed through the lens of the existing competition between Brazil's two largest cities on both the economic and cultural planes, which had been exacerbated in the first half of the twentieth century. The São Paulo region's recognized economic primacy made Rio very zealous in protecting its role as the leader of the country's cultural development, in particular the image of the Cidade Maravilhosa (Marvelous City), the label given at the beginning of the century, an image that was the best guarantee for the development of its tourist industry. Thus, certainly, the dissemination of a study that highlighted the favelas and the question of poverty could only weaken Rio's position and strengthen that of São Paulo in this competition.

In fact, important political interests were at the root of the funding for this study, which at first glance, seemed like a mere scientific project, all the more so because this funding came from the Mesquita family, owners of the newspaper and known since the 1930s for their support of the arts and sciences.

When USP was being created, the Mesquitas financed the travel to and stay in Brazil of the French scholars who helped establish the university.[42] For the Mesquitas, funding a research project was not an exceptional act; it fit within the family tradition.

Finding a capable team was not hard. As we have seen, Lebret and SAGMACS enjoyed wide renown because of the planning studies completed for the state of São Paulo at the request of Governor Lucas Garcez, for the Belo Horizonte Mayor's Office, and for the government of the state of Pernambuco (whose capital is Recife).[43] Moreover, Lebret was well known in high-level administrative circles, thanks to his numerous relationships and networks. In spite of its direct ties to the Catholic movement Économie et Humanisme, SAGMACS was a research center that was lay in character.

At this time, there were few centers or teams, public or private, devoted to research in Brazil. The Brazilian university, we have seen, was concerned overall with the general and theoretical training of its students. In 1950s Rio de Janeiro, those who held the higher-level positions were intellectual essayists, writing literature "of a mixed genre of essay, composed at the confluence of history with economics, philosophy, or art, which is a very Brazilian form of investigation and discovery of Brazil" (Antonio Cândido, cited in M. Almeida 1989, 190). In São Paulo the tradition was no different, with the notable exception of the ELSP.[44] It is true that the IBGE, based in Rio de Janeiro, had existed since 1938, but the demographers and geographers at this institute, responsible for the censuses, were engaged in purely statistical analyses. The Faculdade Nacional de Filosofia (National College of Philosophy) of the Universidade do Brasil, founded in 1939, was entirely devoted to teaching, with the notable exception of Costa Pinto, who was engaged in international research projects, as I noted in chapter 1. The CLAPCS, which would be very important later, had just been created in 1957, as a UNESCO initiative.[45]

Thus the study of Rio de Janeiro's favelas was entrusted to SAGMACS. Lebret assumed his scientific responsibility ahead of *O Estado de São Paulo* and Dom Hélder Câmara, but it was the sociologist José Arthur Rios, already directing the SAGMACS office in Rio, who took on its effective coordination. The importance of Lebret's name as a "seal of approval" stands out in the introduction to the supplement published in the *O Estado de São Paulo*. On the first page, the composition of the research team is spelled out clearly: "The socioeconomic study of the Rio favelas sponsored by *O Estado* and presented here was directed by Father Louis-Joseph Lebret, with technical direction by José Arthur Rios, and had as a coordinator Carlos Alberto de Medina; the architect

Hélio Modesto collaborated in the portion concerning the urban planning of the Federal District" (SAGMACS 1960, vol. 1, "A equipe de pesquisa").

Who were the members of this Brazilian team, jointly responsible for the development of a representation of the favelas that ended up being asserted after the SAGMACS report?

Rios had studied law in Rio de Janeiro after earning a master of arts in sociology at Louisiana State University in the late 1940s. As a result, he was abroad during Lebret's first stay in Brazil in 1947. After his return from the United States in 1950, he used his U.S. training in directing surveys on the staff of the Serviço Social Rural (Rural Social Service) and the Serviço Especial de Saúde Pública (Public Health Special Service) in the interior of Brazil. It was then, as a rural sociologist, that he gained field experience, quite influenced by U.S. empiricism.[46] He had a Catholic background connected with the Dominicans, and he joined the Économie et Humanisme group established in Rio by Father Romeu Dale (Pelletier 1996, 298) before he even met Lebret during a trip to France. Indeed, Rios already knew about the course taught by Lebret in São Paulo in 1947, which he had not been able to attend. While on a trip to Europe, Rios spent a week at La Tourette, where he became familiar with Lebret's research method and work philosophy. Soon thereafter, he was invited to head the Rio office of SAGMACS.[47]

Carlos Alberto de Medina, the second author of the report mentioned, followed a different course from that of Rios. Having likewise had a legal education, he benefited from the generalist training offered by the faculty at the Faculdade Nacional de Filosofia of the Universidade do Brasil in Rio.[48] A student of Costa Pinto, he was later trained in research practice and ethnology by Kalervo Oberg, a Canadian anthropologist who spent a long time in Brazil at the ELSP, at the invitation of Donald Pierson.[49] Countless trips with Oberg, within the framework of a Brazil-U.S. agreement, for the Public Health Special Service, educated Medina in the practice of observation and in fieldwork. His relationship with Lebret, however, was more distant than Rios's. It was Rios who invited him to participate in the SAGMACS research. He had attended some lectures by Lebret, but Medina's contact with him had been limited to the preparatory meetings about the favela study when the Brazilian team discussed the development of the project.[50]

The third person named as responsible for the report, Hélio Modesto, was an architect. Coming from the Faculdade de Arquitetura (College of Architecture) of the Universidade do Brasil, he went on to spend two years in London at the School of Planning and Research of Regional Development. Thus, like

Medina, he belonged to Rios's circle, and he had not had any direct relationship with Lebret before the research project.[51]

Given its makeup, the coordinating team was interdisciplinary, experienced in research—especially in rural Brazil, thanks to Rios and Medina—and oriented toward empirical research. Its inspiration came from two main sources: on the one hand, Anglo-American social sciences and urban planning; on the other, the French sociological tradition. Convinced of the interest of an interdisciplinary project, Rios had also solicited geographers, chosen from among the best known in Rio, Lysia Bernardes, Nilo Bernardes, and Orlando Valverde, by virtue of their deep knowledge of the history of settlement of Carioca space. They were heirs of the French geographical tradition, and they strongly valued empirical studies.[52]

Research assistants who could be charged with empirical observation and fieldwork were hard to find. In 1950s Rio, students of the social sciences were both numerous and inexperienced. Rios was obliged to turn to the ELSP. Donald Pierson, who trained students in the practice of fieldwork according to the Chicago School model, suggested the names of young researchers educated in São Paulo. Some Rio social workers who had worked in favelas were contracted.[53] As we saw in the previous chapter, the social services of the Office of the Mayor, since the late 1930s, had daily contact with poorer populations. The social workers were used to circulating in the favelas, and their profession brought them into regular contact with various local networks.

HUMAN ASPECTS OF THE RIO FAVELA: THE SAGMACS REPORT

How was the SAGMACS research carried out? What were the report's main contributions?

The project took three years (1957–59). This was not just a simple study aiming for immediate results; rather, it was a deep effort that could yield new, concrete data. The research used observation combined with a secondary analysis of data, such as statistics available in official organizations, including the Fundação Leão XIII, reworked by the team. In the first phase, sixteen case studies were conducted; in the second phase, research through direct observation was concentrated in two favelas, extended later to seven.[54] In the introduction to the report, the authors wrote,

> The problem of the sociologist is not exactly to find the statistical mean of a group of attributes but rather to discover the typical forms that

the behavior of people in society takes. A mean is a number; a type is a compound of psychological and social traits that the sociologist has to construct based on repeated observations of the group and the living testimony that its members furnish. . . . Sociologists' methodological problem is generalization. They must gather sufficient data that can be considered typical. And they know that these traits, these patterns of behavior, can only be collected on the individual and through the individual. (SAGMACS 1960, 3)[55]

The methodological requirement was a characteristic of this work, as shown by the authors' indication of the limits—but also the advantages—of research founded on detailed case studies and not on a representative sample of the population. For this reason, the introduction sets out that "our conclusions are valid only for certain favelas and for certain aspects of the *favelados'* lives. . . . What is most important in research of this nature is not so much to exhaust units of the universe researched or the aspects analyzed but rather to give the interested reader the dominant lines of the social facts and processes" (SAGMACS 1960, 3).

Cartographic and visual representations were very important in this pioneering work. The researchers needed to make plans and sketches of the spaces occupied by the favelas that would allow them to situate the clusters based on aerial photos and with the help of consulting geographers. The proper subdivisions of the favelas' internal organization needed to be indicated to show the existence of differentiated zones. (The plans and sketches are in SAGMACS 1960, part 2, 17–20.)

The report is divided into two parts, a "general part," which introduces the research on the sixteen favelas, and the "specific part," which presents the seven favelas analyzed more systematically.

At the beginning of the general part, after the methodological preambles, the emphasis is on the social and economic factors at the root of the development of Rio's favelas. The report makes clear the phenomenon of Rio's urban growth in relation to the country's galloping urbanization as well as the roles a high birth rate and migration play in it. Next, the report analyzes changes in the city, especially the capitalist appropriation of urban land. The development of the labor market and its limited capacity to absorb the workforce, the variations in the cost of living and salaries, and high housing prices are all studied as factors that contributed to the development of the favelas. A fine demographic analysis, supported by statistical data from the 1950 general census and from the Statistical Yearbook of the Federal District, enables comparison of the fa-

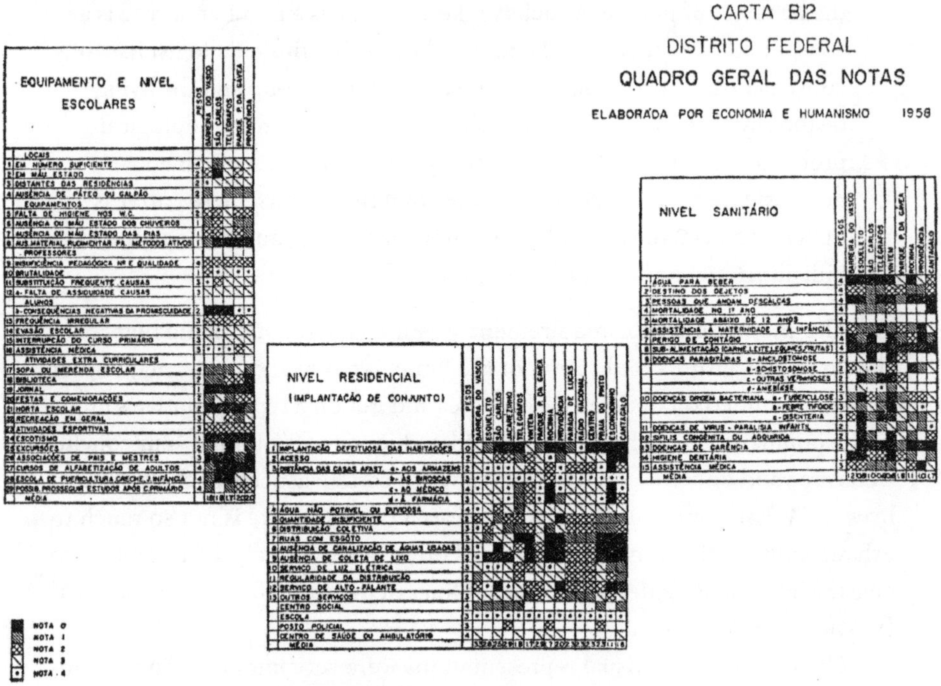

Figure 10. Tables of notes from SAGMACS favela research. The charts record (*left to right*) educational level and infrastructure, residential level (facilities), and level of sanitation (*Estado de São Paulo*, 13 April 1960).

velas' population with that of the Federal District as a whole. Various age pyramids and bar graphs display these differences according to age, skin color, sex, lines of work, religious affiliation, level of education, and geographic origin. In fact, this part of the report is a demographic study that, while relying on prior studies like that of Alberto Passos Guimarães, systematizes and analyzes the favela issue using new modes of presentation.

The second section of the general part analyzes the sixteen favelas studied. A set of summary charts presents the scores given to the different favelas for the categories of school facilities, sanitary level and facilities, and service facilities, which was the approach characteristic of the input from the Économie et Humanisme movement. Analysis of these summary charts reveals the differences among the favelas. The chapters that follow deal with the particular aspects such as dwellings, sanitary conditions, traditional medicine, education, forms of solidarity, leisure, delinquency, and religious life, studied primarily on the level of the family unit, the point of reference chosen by the researchers from among the units of the neighborhood.

The Shift to the Social Sciences

Finally, in the third section, "solutions" that have been proposed are introduced and analyzed, with the Cruzada São Sebastião occupying the center of the debate.

The specific part takes up in more detail topics such as family, education, and delinquency in the seven favelas that were researched more deeply. In addition, particular attention is given to the political life of the favelas: the demagogic and clientelistic practices developed there, with the electoral chiefs in charge of negotiating favors from the politicians in exchange for votes.

At the end of this specific part, signed by Modesto, is a sort of historical and urban planning analysis of urban evolution and growth of the city, of its various plans and the place of the favelas and working-class housing in the context of legislation. It is also a detailed presentation of successive regulations.

The report ends with a diagnosis: "The causes of the problem of the favelas in the Federal District, aside from nationwide socioeconomic ones, are direct consequences of the lack of direction of urban expansion, of bad land use, and of administrative disorganization" (43). With this diagnosis as a point of departure, the study concludes with a presentation of the possible short- and long-term solutions to the problems of the favelas and their inhabitants. Maps of the Federal District made by the SAGMACS team support these proposals. The report's appendix presents three of the questionnaires used in the research with students, teachers, and electoral chiefs.

ÉCONOMIE ET HUMANISME AND THE CHICAGO SCHOOL

The SAGMACS research and report suggest a strong similarity between the Économie et Humanisme approach to research, explicitly used in this study, and the concepts of the first Chicago School, the school of Robert Park, made up of sociologists and anthropologists. This similarity is not a coincidence, and it goes beyond Rios's visit with Pierson when the former went searching for researchers in São Paulo. For at least forty years now, interest in the Chicago School has been maintained outside the United States through a growing number of publications and translations.[56] The SAGMACS study of the Rio favelas is interesting because it reveals an unusual association not perceived until now.

Lebret did not experience the influence of U.S. empirical sociology, even though he was not separated from social research and practice. His generation was not familiar with the contributions of the Chicago School, although Maurice Halbwachs (1932) had acquainted French readers with the existence of the school and its work on the city.[57] The Chicago School was not given much consideration by the French pioneers of urban sociology. Paul-Henri

Chombart de Lauwe (1952, 40–41) referred to *The City* by Park and Ernest Burgess (1925). He maintained a dialogue about the debate about functional areas and the competition between the spatial schemes of Burgess and of Homer Hoyt, but he distanced himself critically from James Quinn's later theses about human ecology. In his *Manuel de l'enquêteur* (1952), Lebret, who was of the same generation as Chombart de Lauwe, referred to works by some U.S. researchers — such as Warner and Lunt 1946, Lynd and Lynd 1929, and even Thomas and Znaniecki 1927 — but he did not cite the work of Park, Burgess, or even William Foote Whyte (1943) in regard to urban research and participant observation. Moreover, he did not mention any of these works in the text in which he developed his methodological concepts.[58]

An examination of the research methods used by SAGMACS in Rio as well as the forms of presentation of the research clearly reveal the joint influence of the Économie et Humanisme movement and of the methodological principles professed by the Chicago School. It is true that several authors, especially Howard Becker, in his presentation to the colloquium "The Chicago School: Yesterday and Today" (1998),[59] rejected the idea that there was unity of thought and method in the school. Nevertheless, it is possible to clarify some of its conceptualizations or basic principles that coincide with the proposals of the Économie et Humanisme movement, such as the following:

The importance given to empirical research as the principal way to access the reality one wants to learn about. This is the basic principle found both in Park's idea of the city-as-laboratory, which underscores the importance of studying concrete reality to understand local phenomena and global society, and in the four volumes of Lebret's *Guide pratique de l'enquête sociale* (Practical guide to social research; 1952, 1955). Volume 3 of this guide, which is devoted to urban research, presents empirical studies as indispensable, suggesting an analysis of neighborhoods alongside analysis of the city itself.

The importance accorded to observation and understanding social processes more for identifying tendencies and types than for constructing typologies a priori. The two currents value the use of case studies, systematic, exhaustive observation in which semidirected interviews deepen what the observer's gaze has already perceived. This stance toward research is no doubt the one adopted by the Chicago sociologists in classic works such as Nels Anderson's *The Hobo* (1923), Clifford Shaw's *The Jack-Roller* (1930), and Paul Cressey's *Taxi-Dance Hall* (1932), which introduced participant observation, disseminated later by Whyte (1943) and Everett Hughes (1996).

In his handbook, Lebret devoted an entire chapter to data collection, calling attention to the existence of a psychology of the researcher. For him, "research is a trade that, like any other, is learned through experience" (66). As for the interviews, he stressed that they should never sound like an interrogation. He also surveyed various interview techniques (97–98). Lebret even suggested that researchers keep a diary and schedule weekly meetings with their research director to discuss the progress of their work (69).[60]

Simultaneous use of data coming out of the fieldwork, after a long period of observation that includes semidirected interviews, and use of available secondary sources, such as censuses and other statistical data. This posture rejects the opposition between qualitative and quantitative, in addition to affirming the heuristic character of both approaches and the combination of data and research practices from various sources. In prevailing representations, the Chicago tradition recommended qualitative investigation and case studies. Recently, however, it has become evident that students at that university were also introduced to quantitative approaches and were not unaware of the methods of social surveys (Platt 1996). At Chicago the students were "trained to use all the methods of investigation possible and not to hesitate to link them to their fieldwork" (Cefai 2000). Classic works such as Thomas and Znaniecki 1927 on Polish peasants based their analyses on an array of sources and combined various methods, using at the same time letters, archives, and a bibliography. Shaw's research on delinquency also shows how various approaches can be joined together. Relying on one life story, he wrote *The Jack-Roller* (1930) while at the same time conducting a study based on statistics about delinquency in different areas of Chicago (Shaw and McKay 1942). The *Local Community Fact Book*, produced by the University of Chicago's Department of Sociology, consulted before any study of Chicago, is simply an amply documented collection of statistical information from different government agencies. Many authors have even incorporated ecological analysis, descriptive statistics, and social psychology (Platt 1996).

For his part, Lebret insisted that all research should have as a point of departure the search for a "global vision" based on direct observation and interviews (Lebret 1952, 14), but he also underscored that all research in its second stage requires a statistical procedure that brings together classification, identification of types and classes, and the synthesis of the profiles of types or classes (15–21). According to Lebret, "It is necessary to distinguish between the monographic analysis of an individual, offered by its own structure, and the statistical analysis of a population or subpopulation, offered by the structure of a group of individuals or of groups coming from the same complex" (99).

The importance of the graphic representation of data: diagrams, charts, and maps. At Chicago, well before Park, the tradition of using maps had been inherited from the practice of Booth in England and from U.S. social services (Leclerc 1979).[61] Alongside the sociological approach, the spatial dimension was thought to have explanatory value for social processes. The paradigmatic example was Burgess's analysis of the growth and expansion of the city and its urban areas. In fact, according to Burgess (1925, 61), the method employed in Chicago studies of growth of cities was "to describe urban expansion in terms of extension, succession and concentration; to determine how expansion disturbs metabolism when disorganization is in excess of organization; and, finally, to define mobility and to propose it as a measure both of expansion and metabolism, susceptible to precise quantitative formulation, so that it may be regarded most literally as the pulse of the community." These different processes could and should be represented graphically.

For its part, Économie et Humanisme also advocated the use of mapping, especially as a technique to give a better synthesis of data and as to make the message more explicit for the recipient. Maps, pie charts, and Cartesian graphs, or polar graphs—techniques in which Lebret no doubt deployed his training as an engineer—were one of the strongest features of his work. In *Manuel de l'enquêteur*, many passages or even entire chapters highlight the importance and usefulness of graphs (Lebret 1952, 15–51): "Most statistical charts can be represented by one or several graphs. On its own, a number does not tell much. Its transcription into a graph . . . allows one to compare it with all the others at a glance and, in certain cases, to follow the evolution of a phenomenon or to compare several evolutions. A number is always static; a graph easily translates dynamism."

Interest in research oriented toward social action. The idea of socially engaged research was present from the beginning at the University of Chicago, and the Department of Sociology, led by Robert Park, put this concept into practice (Bulmer 1984). Some of the research was funded by public institutions, for example, the Institute for Juvenile Research of Chicago (Shaw and McKay 1942). The Local Community Research Committee, which financed several studies, reflected well the spirit of social reform that reigned at the University of Chicago, where it was believed that any research should lead to results capable of informing social action (Platt 1996).

In a very similar way, in *Manuel de l'enquêteur*, Lebret (1952, 12) placed value on "the synthetic view that follows analysis and affords intervention." Lebret could not conceive of an analysis that did not have an operational objective; this was his great success with Latin American planners and administrators who valued applied research. His assertion of the target audience for his research guides leaves no doubt: "The research guides for rural research and for urban research are intended first for those who need to see clearly in order to intervene politically, organizationally, socially, or culturally in the life of base communities, neighborhoods, municipalities, cantons, electoral districts, and states" (2). Lebret was more practical than academic, more a man devoted to planning and action than a classic man of the academy.[62]

The University of Chicago and Économie et Humanisme shared the ideal of social reform and of an activist practice of sociology, and both nourished research activity. In both settings, we can note, for example, the presence of social workers on the research teams, whether in the United States, France, or Brazil.

The centrality of the neighborhood in research and the necessary relationship between neighborhood and social intervention. The Chicago School always considered the neighborhood to be the basic unit, the point of departure for any investigation. These sociologists justified this position by viewing the neighborhood as a *community*, the basic unit of social life. They also justified it with a methodological perspective according to which "each particular element added to the mosaic contributes to making the whole picture comprehensible to us" (Becker 1966, vii). Analysis of the microsociological space is basic to understanding the macrosociological. In *Street Corner Society* (1943), Whyte clearly demonstrates how focus on a limited territorial unit can account for the more general processes of social organization, which are not necessarily perceptible when the observation is carried out in a larger geographical unit.

In the same way, for the Économie et Humanisme researchers who had done urban studies in France in the 1940s and 1950s, the neighborhood allowed for a rethinking of the city (Loew 1945). It suited them to examine the city's neighborhoods so they could detect the injustices connected with size of residences and with interneighborhood and intraurban mobility (Astier and Laé 1991, 85). For them, the neighborhood was also conceived foremost as a community, even though this conception might differ from that of the Chicago sociologists. For the Économie et Humanisme researcher, the neighborhood, a place of life as opposed to a place of work (for example, the factory), became a sort of "ideal community" that is desirable to preserve, for though it is true that the family, the basic unit, is the best guarantee of social ties and solidarity, it is threatened by modernization. Therefore, it is in the space of the community that one must intervene to ensure the development of a harmonious society. Solidarity is the basis of the social bond. "The community possesses an internal function and an external function. Conceived to integrate and protect the individuals within it, it also manifests as an intermediary form of collective representation in the same way as professional organizations and trade unions" (Astier and Laé 1991, 94).

Nevertheless, if we establish that there was a common belief in the importance of studying smaller units first, we can see different readings of the social realities of these urban units. For Économie et Humanisme, the construction of social identity is understood based on the class situation — thus the importance of the reference to the factory — and social intervention is perceived as the backdrop to trade union activity and to the labor movement. However, for the Chicago School, the integrative elements of the local community are cultural — ethnicity and national origin.

Valuing a multidisciplinary approach to social phenomena and recognizing the complementarity among disciplines. The University of Chicago's Department of Sociology was, until the 1940s, an exception in the U.S. context to the extent that it rejected any disciplinary monopoly in the analysis of social phenomena. Sociology laid claim to the philosophical pragmatism tradition of John Dewey and George Herbert Mead. Moreover, there was frequent use of biology and social psychology in the empirical studies produced by William Thomas (Bulmer 1984, 29). The Department of Sociology, which until 1929 also included anthropology, valued Park's past as a journalist[63] as well as Vivien Palmer's contribution from social work. The use of statistics and cartography, thanks to Burgess and William Ogburn, was likewise encouraged. This absence of rigid frontiers between the disciplines (Bulmer 1984, 38) was the result of Park's and Burgess's practice of contact and exchange with the university's other social science departments. The different research projects carried out through the Local Community Research Committee were testimony to this multidisciplinary tendency (Bulmer 1984, 125).

Because of his training as a naval engineer, no doubt, Lebret was also a partisan of treating social research as independent of any one discipline. A believer in both economics and sociology, he knew to use several methods before developing his own. It was after twenty years of self-taught practice of sociological and economic research that he came to synthesize what he recognized as the work of a team in a unified methodological understanding. In the bibliographical summary in supplement no. 6 of *Manuel de l'enquêteur* (Lebret 1952, 121–25), Lebret lists the French and foreign works useful for training researchers or research coordinators. For research guides, Lebret refers to Gaston Bardet, Charles Bettelheim, Chombart de Lauwe, and Pierre Deffontaines; for statistical and demographic analyses, he recommends the French Institut National de la Statistique et des Études Économiques (INSEE) and Alfred Sauvy;

The Shift to the Social Sciences

for sociology in general, almost all the references are to U.S. authors such as Robert Merton. Armand Cuvillier is the only French author cited, but Lebret does recommend *L'Année Sociologique* and *Cahiers Internationaux de Sociologie*. Other references, such as to Frédéric Le Play and his followers, are also present. Human geography is also amply represented; Lebret refers readers to Paul Vidal de la Blache, Max Sorre, Pierre George, and Jean-François Gravier.

Up to now, we have examined in detail the points of commonality between the Chicago School and the Économie et Humanisme movement. The SAGMACS study of the favelas of Rio de Janeiro was, in fact, an opportunity for the explicit encounter of the two perspectives. The account that Rios, the project's research director, gave was unambiguous: "My methodology was built on the intersection of Économie et Humanisme—that is, of Lebret's analytic, monographic methodology, inspired by Le Play—with the Chicago School. I made maps of favelas, seeking to define their internal zones, without a doubt, under the influence of the human ecology of the Chicago School. I am a crossroads."[64]

This hybridism already existed in the social sciences in Brazil. Ever since their development in the universities between 1930 and 1940, Brazilian sociology and anthropology had valued this double affiliation, as heirs to both French and U.S. sociology and anthropology.[65] The explicit vestige of this hybrid character appears in the very themes of the research. Some topics are clearly linked to the typical approach of Économie et Humanisme, such as housing, family, solidarities, school, or religion, while issues including delinquency or political processes (demagoguery, clientelism) were favored by the Chicago School.

RECEPTION AND CONSEQUENCES
OF THE SAGMACS STUDY

Because it was published in a daily newspaper with wide circulation, the SAGMACS report had an immediate impact on public opinion and political debates about the favela in 1960. That influence alone merits a historical study that has not yet been done.[66] The publication of the report also had an important effect on the academic world and some institutional political consequences, a summary of which follows.

In the twenty years after its publication, this report was often cited by authors studying the favelas. After the 1980s, it was gradually forgotten, no doubt because it had not been published as a book and thus was absent from university libraries. A major retrospective synthesis, *Um século de favela* (A century of the favela; Zaluar and Alvito 1998), did not even cite the study in its bibli-ography.

The SAGMACS document, in its results and methods, contributed much, as one can see in the works that refer to it in the period after its appearance. I therefore argue that this study deserves much more consideration, insofar as it set a real research agenda for the study of Rio's favelas that conditioned the work of subsequent generations of sociologists and other researchers.

The City, the anthology published by Park and Burgess in 1925, included a research agenda that might seem excessive at first sight. This foundational text was, indeed, written in a privileged university context as a guide to defining themes and questions to be broached in future research, both by faculty and students at the University of Chicago as well as those at other U.S. universities.[67] In no way was SAGMACS presented as research program proposal. Only a posteriori was it possible to see its role as an agenda for future generations of researchers, who were to favor the same themes and similar techniques, as we will see in chapter 3. The various topics tackled by SAGMACS to analyze the emergence and development of the favelas would be systematically met again in later studies: the relation to the country's process of urbanization, the relationship to the historical development of the city of Rio de Janeiro, the avatars of the housing market and politics, the neighborhood, religious life, traditional medicine, schools, and delinquency and criminality.

Finally the methodological procedure that combined analysis of available statistical data, observation, and case studies was a widely followed model. For example, SAGMACS's statistical approach was the first to compare census data from the favelas and their population with data from other neighborhoods and their inhabitants, an approach that would later be found in countless studies, whether of favelas or not.

But if SAGMACS blazed a trail in the topics approached and methods used, it also innovated in regard to certain results, though with a less certain legacy. The report described and analyzed the favelas as heterogeneous realities with a heterogeneous population. The document insisted on the differing origins of each of the favelas studied as well as on the importance of internal differentiations, a veritable "zoning" that, once identified, would allow consideration of the social and spatial differences inside the favela. Scholars who published later, such as Leeds (1969), Medina (1969), and Parisse (1969a; 1969c), developed this topic of diversity, as we will see below. Nevertheless, many others, including some current authors, have "forgotten" these analyses, privileging a unifying view over one of the specificity of the favela.[68]

The view of the favelas revealed in the SAGMACS report went against the myths already questioned in early censuses, especially the 1949 census that dealt specifically with Rio's favelas and the IBGE's general census of 1950. The favelas shown in this research did not constitute a world apart: their inhabitants were poor like other poor people, they too were victims of political clientelism. Favela residents found themselves in a political situation similar to that of other urban areas of the country, and they should not be thought of as having their own type of political behavior (SAGMACS 1960, 2:35).

What were the political consequences of this report? These issues, and the history of the SAGMACS research itself, can show the emergence of a new representation of the favelas. The political dimension of the favela issue, on which the report placed value, can be demonstrated by the invitation Rios received in 1960, that is, right after the completion of the study, to direct the Serviço Especial de Reabilitação das Favelas e Habitações Anti-higiênicas (SERFHA), a governmental organization created in Rio four years before to manage the favela problem. Afterward Rios assumed leadership of the Office of the Secretariat of Social Services, an agency created during an administrative reform by Governor Lacerda of the new state of Guanabara (the former Federal District) after the federal capital moved to Brasília in 1960.

Rios used the results of the SAGMACS study to develop his proposals (Leeds and Leeds 1978, 214). He thus considered the favelas to be poor neighborhoods needing urban development, that is, needing the same municipal services provided to other neighborhoods of the city. This was a proposal that sectors of the Catholic Church had been defending for many years, although from a more paternalistic perspective. The new political point of view that Rios introduced by a 1961 order (Machado da Silva 1967) requesting that favelas organize themselves in the residents' associations to allow better dialogue with administrative offices and service agencies, leading to a formal agreement signed between these associations and SERFHA, with the goal of countering the earlier clientelistic practices.

This political engagement by Rios, a researcher, was not viewed well by some; he was criticized as a manipulator in the framework of an alliance with the Right that was bound to control the population of the favelas with the help of the machinery of the state (Valla 1986, 175–98). Other researchers defended him, pointing out that Rios had spent little time in the Lacerda government because he had not accepted to serve Lacerda's electoral interests (Leeds and Leeds 1978). Lacerda had divided the city of Rio into twenty-three regiões administrativas (administrative regions, RAs). He integrated the favelas into these RAs in a way that turned them into zones of electoral clientele.

At the same time, the notoriety that Rios gained thanks to the SAGMCS study was not limited to political circles. He published several articles and so became known as "the professor of the favelas," meaning the person all researchers interested in 1960s favelas must consult. Up to the end of the decade, the headquarters of SAGMACS in Rio was a mandatory stop for all foreign researchers coming to Brazil to study the favela. Anthony Leeds, Lucien Parisse, and Janice Perlman passed through here, to name a few. With the passage of time and the death of Lebret in 1966, however, SAGMACS faded away, replaced by a new planning agency, which in turn also disappeared. Rios, who had joined the faculty at PUC, retired but continued occupying his office. It was he who wrote the entry for "favela" in the *Dicionário das ciências sociais*, published in 1987 by the Fundação Getúlio Vargas.

Rios made way for a new group of actors who would "discover" the favelas after the 1960s: the Peace Corps volunteers who were steered to the Third World during the Kennedy years, with the goal of international cooperation. During one of his trips to the United States, Rios was invited to participate in a training course for these young people determined to "disembark" in the favelas of Rio.

During the 1960s, international cooperation developed very intensely, and professionals from the United States became ever more present and active in Brazil. Experts from international organizations (Pearse 1957; Bonilla 1961) and from several universities in the United States began to be interested in Rio's favelas. Agencies in the United States, such as the Ford Foundation, supported American studies in the universities. Several intergovernmental agreements were established with the state of Guanabara. It was within this general context — in which Fidel Castro's communist Cuba was a model to be combatted — that the Peace Corps arrived in Brazil.

THE PEACE CORPS AND COMMUNITY DEVELOPMENT

The Peace Corps was created in the 1960s to mobilize young volunteers to help needy populations in rural and urban areas of underdeveloped countries. The advertising inviting U.S. citizens to participate in the Peace Corps clearly expounded the need for this aid and showed that the people of the United States should feel responsible. Promoting the idea of the Peace Corps as the "Human Care Package," one poster alluded to the practice by the nonprofit organization CARE of sending donor-funded packages to developing areas. The poster pictured an open crate with a young person sitting beside it. The text reads as follows:

There is a man somewhere who has nothing.

Maybe you would like to give him something.

Here are some suggestions:

Send him patience: He will appreciate it for the rest of his life.

Send him understanding. It is something he can use.

Send him kindness. It's something that'll never go out of style.

Send him the one thing only you can send him. Send him you.

("The Peace Corps, Washington D.C.," qtd. in E. Hoffman 1998, 131).

The Peace Corps, one of the most important Cold War initiatives of the Kennedy administration (F. Fischer 1998), symbolized a new form of relations between the United States and the Third World. Its declared objective was to promote better understanding between the United States and the rest of the world. As an official program of U.S. foreign policy, it professed a humanitarian ideal without hiding its goal of promoting a better image of the United States and its diplomacy, an image that had deteriorated during the Cold War. The Peace Corps could recreate the best of what the United States had to offer (E. Hoffman 1998, 23), and John Kennedy had perceived, quite rightly, that university students would be the best group to assume this role.[69]

In *All You Need Is Love* (1998), Elizabeth Cobbs Hoffman analyzes in detail the impact of this appeal in the United States. In addition to the role of the humanitarian ideal, the success in terms of young people recruited (in total, 94,023 worked around the world between 1961 and 1979) can doubtless be explained by the taste for adventure and the desire to see new things that this experience might satisfy. The destinations were always exotic, far-off places, where the challenges were misery and underdevelopment. The idea of becoming a "hero" (in the sense of one of the book's chapters, "The Hero's Adventure") excited the imagination of these young people, ready to change their lives for several years by renouncing the comfort and safety of their country of origin.

Numerous volunteers departed all over the globe, the first ones, deployed from 1961 on, had to be at least eighteen years old, be in good health, and have a bachelor's degree or its equivalent in professional experience. The term of service for a volunteer was twenty-seven months, of which three were devoted to training prior to departure on the mission. Candidates could not choose the location where they would exercise their duties; these were determined in accordance with the demands of the host country and the qualifications of the volunteer.

Learning to live among the poor was an important strategic objective characteristic of this new "crusade." Although clearly distinct from the European Catholic tradition, the missionary impulse of this "army" of lay volunteers was still evident. Sharing in the daily life of the village or neighborhood and participating in the community's problems made up the core of the aid. One had to live like the other to feel the other's hardships and show one's involvement and engagement.

The belief in the possibility of transforming people, and especially of improving their conditions, was clearly proclaimed: "The Peace Corps works in forty-six countries — not intending to change the world completely, but also not leaving without changing it some."[70] This goal implied total commitment; it was necessary to fulfill the mission, as a soldier would, ready to assume all necessary risks. It was expected that those sent to rural areas lacking sanitary facilities would know how to build wells, ditches, and latrines, and they would know a minimum of agricultural techniques. At the same time as mastering these skills, the volunteers should imbibe the culture of the region or country in order to manage culture shock. It was expected that engineering students would learn traditional techniques before considering introducing other more modern ones. Medical students were invited to specialize in tropical or local diseases before attempting to install infrastructure with a view to improve public health and hospital administration.[71]

The aid would be even more effective if the "missionaries" had the means to identify with the local population in any place they might be sent and to understand, from the inside, the problems to be overcome. The goal was to refuse to remain "outside" even though one might be a foreigner, to respect the local culture and traditions, and to accept as naturally as possible the culture shock experienced by every Peace Corps volunteer.[72] In the end, disorientation and culture shock were part of the inevitable and necessary experience. To help others, one had to live and feel like them and to penetrate their world and culture.

As I mentioned at the beginning of this chapter, in the 1960s and the 1970s, the theory of community development was considered by the majority international cooperation organizations to be the most appropriate perspective for any action with the poor and their communities, be they rural or urban. The objectives of the Peace Corps fit perfectly within this vision.

THE PEACE CORPS IN THE FAVELAS OF RIO

During the 1960s and the 1970s, at least 31,186 Peace Corps volunteers were sent to Latin America and the Caribbean. In the following decade, the number dropped to 8,851. As a consequence, the great moment for the Peace Corps in that region occurred during the earlier decades.[73] The total number sent to Brazil from 1961 to 1981 was about 6,000, destined especially for remote spots in the Northeast and the Center-West (C. Azevedo 1998).[74]

A certain number were sent to the urban Southeast, however. In Rio de Janeiro, the favelas were the privileged location for these volunteers.[75] Idealistic and full of goodwill, they believed they could help improve the living conditions of Brazil's urban poor. In the 1960s, there were about thirty of them, distributed to different favelas in Rio, considered the locale par excellence of concentration of poverty and indigence in the Marvelous City.[76]

While still in the United States during the three months of intensive training, all of the volunteers read *Child of the Dark* (1961)[77] and, no doubt, Oscar Lewis's *Five Families* (1959). Carolina's edited diary enjoyed great success in the United States, and the book in its numerous editions could be found in most of the country's libraries.[78] Written by a Black woman and single mother who could barely read and write, the diary was a cry against poverty and social injustice. Carolina lived in a favela in São Paulo, but her account would have been the same had she lived in a favela in Rio, which in both international literature and media was a symbol of the segregated spaces of Latin American cities in which a geographically, socially, and economically "marginal" population lived.

More than as an enclave of poverty, the favela described in the book appeared as a culturally differentiated microcosm in which anomie and individualism overcome the collective spirit. Without a regular income and living in extreme indigence, Carolina shared with others an impoverished space without any infrastructure. What is more, the favela is pictured as a pile of people completely lacking in any internal organization. There, the bonds of solidarity were seen as fragile if not absent. The legal status of the squatter settlement was aggravated by the image of total abandonment by the public sector. In Rio, the objective of the Peace Corps, defined on the basis of this type of representation, was to help the poor organize themselves and promote their own development.

The Peace Corps, as an international aid organization, maintained official ties with the Rio Mayor's Office. There were other intergovernmental agreements, such as with USAID, meant to help finance working-class housing through the Companhia de Habitação Popular do Estado da Guanabara (COHAB-GB).[79] The first volunteers were stationed in the favelas with the help of the Mayor's Office,[80] but their choices fell to only some of the 147 favelas surveyed by the latest census: Morro do Borel, Tuiuti, Salgueiro, Morro Azul,

Ruth Ferreira, Vigário Geral, Roquete Pinto, Morro do Estado, Rocinha, and, especially, Jacarezinho.

It appears that the Peace Corps did not choose Borel or Jacarezinho randomly. Borel, as we saw in chapter 1, was where the União dos Trabalhadores Favelados was organized. According to the census of 1960, Jacarezinho was the largest favela in the city. It was home to a significant working-class population, and a number of FAFEG activists lived there.

We do not know exactly how, but the volunteers managed to rent housing in these areas. In the 1960s, in Jacarezinho, there was talk of one Dona Filinha, who had gradually transformed her masonry home into a Peace Corps boardinghouse. The beginning of this transformation can be attributed to the legendary case of Peggy Dulany Rockefeller, who lived and worked in Rio as a young woman, whose fiancé was a Peace Corps volunteer in Jacarezinho,[81] and who had contributed to improvements on the house. Later, researchers would stay in this same residence in the favela.[82]

So what was the concrete content of the Peace Corps activity in the favelas? How did these young volunteers organize their community work? And, in the end, what was their contribution to this mechanism of aid to the poor? Answering these questions requires recourse to numerous sources of information, including interviews with and other accounts by the actors themselves and Brazilians who knew them,[83] and still others from my own field experience in a Rio favela.[84]

The Peace Corps volunteers who parachuted into the favelas had very limited knowledge of Rio de Janeiro and, in particular, of these poor neighborhoods. Even if they had had received specific training before leaving the United States, especially from lectures by professors and senior researchers who had worked in Brazil,[85] they lacked any means to confront a new reality unknown to most of them—the Third World. Culture shock was inevitable. In fact, the volunteers experienced a double uprooting: the difference between their country of origin and their country of deployment, and the distance between daily life in middle- and upper-class neighborhoods of a U.S. city and the Brazilian favela. In turn, the favela residents perceived the volunteers as strange, different, and outside the local context. Until then, the only, and rare, foreigners with whom they had shared their way of life had been Catholic nuns or priests whose presence had an understandable basis in the *favelados'* universe, in which Catholicism already had its place.[86]

The first need of the Peace Corps volunteers was to be accepted by the group. Once their presence in the favela was recognized, they had to establish a diagnosis, make a list of local priorities, and, finally, act. But how could they

The Shift to the Social Sciences

be accepted in the favela, which was unvisited, indeed avoided, by the Brazilian middle class, with the exception of a few artists and activists? How could one believe that a gringo, of his or her own free will, could do what a large majority of Brazilians would not dare or even care to do?

With some exceptions, these volunteers from the United States had considerable difficulty integrating themselves, finding a place in the favela, not to mention justifying their presence and usefulness in an environment considered a disinherited enclave of the Marvelous City. Lacking the training of an ethnologist, who knew perfectly well the importance of a good introduction in the field when one wants to carry out a participant observation, the members of the Peace Corps believed that they could meet their objectives simply by gaining the apparent confidence of some residents who had been turned into their interlocutors.[87] Thrilled when a family might accept them and invite them to share some moments of daily life, such as a Sunday chicken dinner, enraptured to hear them talk about their problems, or fascinated by the conversation of the men at the corner bars, they did not question the nature of the relationships thus established. In spite of this bedazzlement, however, the volunteers little by little learned the geography of the favela, became acquainted with its network of alleyways, discovered the history of its settlement, and learned the life stories of some of the families with whom they were in closest contact. For many, living in the favela seemed to be sufficient to formulate a diagnosis of the main problems they would have to face.

At the same time, the community development work that they believed they were conducting depended on the residents themselves and on their agreement as to the priorities of the actions to be carried out. Many residents knew that the Peace Corps volunteers regularly produced reports and maintained relations with the U.S. consulate, which often made them suspect.

As I mentioned earlier, several favelas already had quite active residents' associations, which had experience with accords with various government entities. Brazilian social workers had known the community development perspective since the 1950s and, within the scope of the municipal administration, had favored and even contributed to the formation of such associations, and they shared with members of the Catholic Church control of social assistance to the poor.[88] With the arrival of the Peace Corps, a new actor entered the field. We can easily imagine that this did not happen without some tension and competitive situations.

The Peace Corps volunteers learned of the existence of informal networks for furnishing water, of semilegal electrical networks, of social networks around the samba schools and religious centers. It was impossible to ignore the importance of strong connections among the favela leaders, certain politicians, and some representatives of municipal government. The density of these social networks left the volunteers stunned. Before their arrival, they had a very different idea of life in these neighborhoods, supposedly occupied only by migrants from rural areas. Carolina Maria de Jesus's story had led them to imagine that in the favelas of Rio, they would encounter a situation of anomie and absence of collective action by the residents. The reality was quite different, as some Peace Corps volunteers later attested (Morocco 1966; Silberstein 1969).

It was therefore necessary to take into account these networks, which revealed the existence of potential for collective engagement. In fact, the history of the favelas showed that the little infrastructure present was always the result of a combination of public investments from official organizations and the collective mobilization of the inhabitants in the form of a voluntary community work crew or *mutirão*.[89] This form of mutual aid, coming from the rural areas and strongly associated with the "culture of the poor," was considered by the residents to be a "natural" complement to the rare public works and urban development. From the 1940s on, the Fundação Leão XIII, supported by these forms of internal mobilization, had succeeded in installing partial running water systems and opening some public streets. For their part, the residents' associations had invoked the *mutirão* practice to show politicians and the government that the favelas could participate actively in any action driven by external assistance.

Almost all the Peace Corps volunteers were unaware of or, more likely, did not understand the complexity of the social setting and the networks of relationships that characterized "the favela issue." When they did manage to participate in some of the local groups and become accepted or when they managed to find there some collaborators, they often tried to rely on the practice of the *mutirão*. When they had not perceived the social structure of the favela and the different groups in states of conflict or competition,[90] the volunteers would involuntarily use as a point of reference the small groups into which they had been integrated, defending the special interests of this group. By helping some to the detriment of others, more or less consciously, they ended up taking a side in conflicts and disputes, making broader community action harder.

In spite of their good intentions and their spirit of cooperation, the Peace Corps volunteers faced numerous handicaps. Coming mainly from the social sciences, they had received university educations that did not furnish them with the needed technical skills. Moreover, they were very poorly acquainted with the functioning of Brazilian bureaucratic machinery. How, then, could they plan sanitation operations, or the installation of sewage systems, without

The Shift to the Social Sciences

having the minimal rudimentary knowledge of engineering or urban planning? How could they participate effectively in the regularization of land ownership if they did not know in detail Brazilian land law and the very complex differences in legal status of the various parts of the same favela? These elements explain in part the limits that such community development projects encountered. Observations by Norma Evenson (1973, 25), on a visit to Rio in 1966, confirmed the lack of success of action undertaken in certain favelas to mobilize residents around what volunteers perceived to be the main problem—the illegality of settlement and the absence of legal title to property: "A Peace Corps volunteer assigned to the Jacarezinho favela reported that he had once tried to instigate a movement among the inhabitants to obtain land titles, only to learn from the *favelados* that they had no desire to obtain ownership of their house plots. Many had resided in the favela as long as twenty years and were convinced that the government would make no attempt to remove them."

We can imagine that the reticence on the part of the *favelados* resulted from political caution that the young volunteers did not pick up on since, contrary to the explanation cited above, mobilization against expulsions and removals had been potent: FAFEG, founded in 1962, had released a statement against the removal of Pasmado favela in 1964, and it carried out a press campaign in 1968 whose slogan was "Urbanization yes, removal never!" It unleashed intense political repression and saw some of its principal leaders imprisoned in 1969 (Valladares 1978a, 29–30).

Moreover, the political circumstances in Brazil were not at all favorable for collaboration between activists and the volunteers from the United States, even if these young volunteers might seem sympathetic to the *favelados*. The Peace Corps was present at the time of the 1964 coup d'état, and it remained in the country during the harshest years of the military regime. Most Brazilians questioned the "good intentions" of the volunteers, often regarded as CIA agents. The content of their reports was suspect, as were their visits to the U.S. consulate in Rio. The Cuban Revolution and the Vietnam War did not help their image at all. In the Cariocas' view, these young gringos had come to Brazil mostly to avoid the Vietnam draft. The role of the Peace Corps in the Kennedy government's foreign policy was interpreted less as a U.S. overture to the Third World—the official justification analyzed by Elizabeth Cobbs Hoffman (1998) and Fritz Fischer (1998)—and more as a way to combat the advance of communism in Latin America, of which the Cuban Revolution was a symbol.

The young volunteers sent to the Brazilian favelas wound up opting for more modest objectives. Some concentrated their efforts on vaccination and disease prevention; others devoted themselves to teaching professional devel-

opment and English courses. Some gave up promoting community development, continuing to live in the favela but developing activities in other locations.[91] Finally, some took advantage of their situation as residents to observe
local life, collaborating notably with Anthony Leeds, who, in the second half
of the 1960s, turned Rio's favelas into his field for research.

Nowadays, the perception of the Peace Corps volunteers in the Rio favelas of the 1960s should not rest only on their lack of technical knowledge, or on
the political circumstances of the time, or on the interventions the volunteers
proposed. An analysis of their activities depends especially on the reading by
the Peace Corps as an institution of the favelas and of poverty at the time. The
idea of the "favela," in the singular, in the sense of a homogeneous community,
predominated and justified a line of universalist, ineffective action in the face
of the favelas' actual diversity. The staff in Washington also failed to see the difficulties in coming into and intervening in spaces as particular as the favelas.
The ignorance of the local sociopolitical reality among the Peace Corps volunteers was therefore obvious, in spite of the effort devoted to training in the
United States. Especially evident was the lack of understanding of a political
scene made up of numerous local and national actors — an ignorance typical
of a "missionary" point of view of social intervention.

ANTHONY LEEDS AND TRANSFORMING PEACE
CORPS VOLUNTEERS INTO OBSERVERS

Even if the Peace Corps volunteers sent into the favelas essentially failed as
agents of community development, some of them played important roles as
observers, thanks to the active presence of Anthony Leeds,[92] who knew how
to take advantage of the opportunity that all of these potential participant observers presented. This observer role was specific to the Peace Corps in Brazil. Publications about the Peace Corps do not mention such a practice in any
other country (Ridinger 1989; E. Hoffman 1998; F. Fischer 1998).

Thanks to Leeds's initiative, the results of these observations by the university students in the Peace Corps were presented at the Thirty-Seventh
International Conference of Americanists in Mar del Plata, Argentina, in 1966
(Hoenack 1966; E. Leeds 1966; Morocco 1966; Naro 1966; O'Neill 1966). Later
some of them found their field experiences to be of value in their scholarly activity (Silverstein 1969; E. Leeds 1972).

Anthony Leeds was born in New York in 1925 into a family of European
intellectuals and between 1947 and 1957 attended Columbia University, where
he earned his PhD. Like any urban anthropologist at the time, he was trained in

classical anthropology and in the Chicago School. According to Charles Sanjek (1994), his main influences were Alfred Kroeber and Karl Marx, in addition to the current of evolutionary ecology of U.S. anthropology, from which he had developed a personal orientation that was both materialist and behaviorist, particularly attentive to the ecological approach and to the question of power.

He spent two years, 1951–52, in the cacao-growing region of the state of Bahia, where he participated in a team from Columbia, advised by Charles Wagley and the Bahian anthropologist Thales de Azevedo. This led to the completion of field research that was the basis of his dissertation (A. Leeds 1957). This experience helped him to learn about Brazilian reality and become, in the eyes of his U.S. colleagues, a Brazilianist with an original reading of how Brazilian social structure functioned, of relations between elites and lower classes, of social mobility, and of interactions between localities and the structures of power.[93] In the 1960s, Leeds returned several times to Brazil, first as the head of the Urban Development Program of the Pan-American Union, then as a researcher sponsored by the Social Science Research Council, and later as a professor funded by the Ford Foundation.

Leeds decided to make the favelas of Rio his research field for the study of poverty in Latin America. He may have had an implicit division of labor with other Anglo-American Latin Americanists who worked on urban poverty and working-class housing: Oscar Lewis first devoted himself to Mexico and later to Puerto Rico and Cuba; William Mangin to Peru; John Turner to Peru and Chile; and Anthony Leeds to Brazil. At the same time, Leeds was very critical of Lewis (Leeds and Leeds 1978, 87–88). Based on his experience in Brazil, he questioned the thesis of the "culture of poverty" and the "theory of marginality" (discussed in the next chapter), seeking ever to broaden his work comparatively, with research on Peru and academic dialogue with Mangin, Turner, and José Mattos Mar.

Leeds quickly saw the importance of convincing some of the Peace Corps volunteers to become participant observers. The Peace Corps was an organization that he knew well since, between 1963 and 1972 as a professor at the University of Texas (one of the universities responsible for training future volunteers), he had contributed to the courses on Brazil and Latin America.

For their part, some of the young volunteers had studied sociology and anthropology. Once in the favelas, they saw that their community development work did not make sense. Meeting a professor of anthropology renowned in the United States who could help them find value in their placement in these favelas thanks to their privileged position as residents was, no doubt, an opportunity they could not pass up (Sanjek 1994).

Already living in the favela, speaking Portuguese, and having established a network of relationships (even if sometimes problematic), they represented a rich source of information for Leeds himself, who could gather data on many favelas in Rio. As the heir to a U.S. tradition in which case studies and field research were the favored tools of the ethnologist, he also knew his limits; that is, the impossibility of generalizing from only one case study. Indeed, Leeds himself criticized any work of microanthropology that limited itself to studying only one community without considering its place in the overall social process with its economic and political dimensions and without taking into account its character as a subgroup of a city and of national society (Leeds, in Sanjek 1994, 234).

Leeds had as an objective arriving at a global explanation of the phenomenon of the favela, with full awareness of the weightiness of this task: 147 had been catalogued during the 1960 census. One of Leeds's major articles (1969) has the explicit title "The Significant Variables Determining the Character of Squatter Settlements." To reach an acceptable level of generalization, to measure this complex and differentiated universe, it was necessary to study numerous cases in parallel. For this, Leeds needed many strategically placed observers. The Peace Corps volunteers could form exactly the needed network of qualified informants, since they had blazed the trail. So Leeds trained the volunteers to do the fieldwork he needed. He went to where they lived and advised his contacts, indicating the information that they should collect.[94]

Leeds himself lived first in the favela of Tuiuti and later in Jacarezinho, the largest favela according to the 1950 census, where the best known leader of the *favelado* movement lived, the president of FAFEG. He made this his permanent fieldwork site and lived there in 1967 with Elizabeth Plotkin, whom he married, returning there until 1969.[95]

In the manner of the Chicago School,[96] Leeds held a research and discussion seminar during his stays in Rio, notably in his Copacabana apartment in 1967–68. In his biographical essay "The Life of Anthony Leeds: Unity in Diversity," Timothy Sieber (1994, 11) stressed the importance of this seminar that informally brought together members of the Peace Corps, Brazilian and U.S. researchers, social workers, and favela residents who, as a group, discussed the conditions of life in the favelas.[97] According to Sieber, it was not just a matter of comparing data or interpretations, from the seminar also came strategies for local community development action or even its spread to other locations (ibid.). As a meeting place for a good portion of those interested in favelas in the 1960s, whether to study them or to conduct activities there, such seminars played in important role in the history of research on Rio's favelas. Without the informal team made up of Leeds and the Peace Corps volunteers, work on the favelas would not have been able to reach the broad audience that it did.

We cannot forget, however, that Leeds had also established important relationships with the Brazilian specialists of his generation: José Arthur Rios, whom Leeds himself credited for his first contacts with the favelas in 1961 when he went to Rio on behalf of the Pan-American Union (Leeds and Leeds 1978, 212); Hélio Modesto, the architect who participated in the SAGMACS study; and Roberto Cardoso de Oliveira, a Brazilian anthropologist who, in his capacity as the director of the new master's program at UFRJ's National Museum, would invite Leeds to introduce the foundations of urban anthropology there.[98]

CONVERGENCES AND CONTINUITIES

The period I have just described is the founding moment of research on the favelas of Rio de Janeiro. In fact, the major research was still very much connected to public policy concerns, but it was taking on new autonomy by way of the intellectual construction of its object and through the appropriate application of empirical research methods. The number of actors involved was still restricted, constituting a limited network, with interpersonal ties that extended from Lebret to Rios and from Rios to Leeds. At the same time, other figures were also important. Lucien Parisse, the young Dominican associated with Économie et Humanisme, who came to do his thesis on the Rio favelas in the late 1960s,[99] and Luiz Antonio Machado da Silva, who had begun his research in 1964 and later joined the Leeds seminar, were among those who would participate in the construction of Brazilian university research. Their works laid the foundation for the sociological and multidisciplinary research that would follow. Both the inaugural SAGMACS study and the ethnographic studies arising from the Peace Corps volunteers' participant observation made up the approaches that the Brazilian academy would develop on a greater scale.

Despite the diversity of these actors, their works converge neatly on several points:

1. An insistence on consideration of the favelas' place in the process of urban growth and the transformation of the city of Rio de Janeiro (SAGMACS 1960; Parisse 1969c, 1970; Leeds 1969).
2. The need to consider different levels of analysis, from macro (economic, sociological, and political) to local variables (Leeds 1969).
3. Rejection of the broadly established consensus, which sought to

stigmatize the favela and its inhabitants as "marginals" (SAGMACS 1960; Machado da Silva 1967; Leeds 1969: Silberstein 1969; Parisse 1970).

4. Value placed on analysis of the internal processes of the favela in order to learn the different strategies employed by residents, whether as individuals and families or as local networks (SAGMACS 1960; Morocco 1966; Machado da Silva 1967; Leeds 1969; Medina 1969).

5. The existence of a considerable economy in the favela, much broader than just its housing market (Leeds 1969).

These convergences do not negate the nuances in the points of view about internal organization of the favelas and the recommendations relative to the role of local organizations. Even though the authors declare themselves, without exception, to favor the formation and official recognition of the residents' associations, divergences among them remain.

A reading of the 1960 SAGMACS report leads us to believe that the favela residents already had organizational practices but that these were very dependent on demagogic politicians and their electoral chiefs (Medina 1964). If the *favelados* were already capable of organizing collectively, they remained dependent on intermediaries linked to public agencies or the Church.

Some deduced that, in order to ensure these organizations' independence from the circuits of political clientelism, it would be better for them to link directly and only to the Office of Social Services. This was the conclusion of Rios, who, after directing the SAGMACS study, became the secretary of the state of Guanabara's Office of Social Services and SERFHA, and thus was the main person responsible for the official accord signed in 1961 between the favela residents' associations and the state office.[100] The debate unleashed by this political and administrative measure connected to the obligation of a single association and to a tie of dependency with the administration raised two important questions: the first about the supposed homogeneity of the favelas' internal structure and the second about autonomy versus heteronomy of the forms of residents' organizations. These two questions had been masked by the representation of the favelas as a *community*, a representation shared by the clergy, social workers, and the municipal administration itself.

This new bond of administrative dependency was interpreted by Machado da Silva (1967) as a reinforcement of the favelas' internal differences in which it was necessary to recognize the presence of a "*favelado* bourgeoisie," which ensured its power by controlling local resources (such as water systems and electrical networks, precarious as these might be) and often through control of the residents' association as well. From Machado da Silva's point of view, there was no political autonomy of the favela in relation to the general policy toward the favelas.

For his part, Anthony Leeds defined the question of relations between local power in the favela and supralocal institutions as an important element of his problematic. Criticizing the Anglo-American notion of "community" widespread in anthropology, he proposed to replace it with the notion of "locality."

> The use of the term locality does not oblige us to postulate a minimum or maximum unit of organization as the community . . . nor to debate its ontological status. . . . It does not oblige us to suppose that the locality in which we live and do research is also a community. Usually, it is not. . . . Localities, as nodal points of interaction, are characterized by a highly complex network of various types of relationships. Kinship ties of the nuclear family and often of other close relatives are widely found in localities, especially in small ones. Close friendships tend to exist within a locality. Neighbors exist, by definition, within a locality. (Leeds and Leeds 1978, 32–33)

Again, according to Leeds, what contributes to the characterization of a locality is that it allows only the identification of dwelling places of the individuals—the fact of residence in a locality does not necessarily signify an individual's belonging to a local community (Leeds and Leeds 1978, 55). This concept is supported by a view of urban society as a complex system; it is impossible to understand one element in isolation without considering relationships with all of the other elements.

This holistic vision that Leeds developed was already present in Lebret, who insisted on a systemic vision, as we saw in the examination of the SAGMACS report. Leeds's proposal resulted from his field observations and from long-standing contacts in Rio's favelas established by him or by his informal group of observers. In addition to these nuances, we must stress valuing the social reality of the favelas. This value is linked to the political affirmation of the favelas' right to exist, to be accepted, and to receive needed improvements, just like any other residence of the poor in the greater urban area.

Because of the importance of the urban social problem that they represent, because of the visibility of the public policies concerning them, and because of the quality and effect of the research cited, in the late 1960s, Rio's favelas became a recognized object of interest for the social sciences. This interest is confirmed by issue 12 of the journal *América Latina*, published in 1969 by the CLAPCS, whose headquarters, as I have noted, was in Rio de Janeiro.[101] This special issue, introduced by the Brazilian anthropologist Manuel Diegues Júnior (1969, 6), indicated to the Brazilian and international academic public that it was now possible "to posit the favela as a topic that the social sciences can study and analyze."[102] In fact, at the time of this issue's publication, not only had researchers from the United States and France "discovered" the favela as an object of study but some Brazilian academics also were beginning to see it as an area of interest for the social sciences that went beyond the question of public policy, which up to that moment had been considered central.[103]

From my point of view, this special issue of *América Latina* was a symbolic milestone in the incorporation of the favela into the scholarly agenda, not just the political agenda. From this moment on, the favela was truly ripe for becoming an object of academic interest.

CHAPTER THREE

THE FAVELA OF THE
SOCIAL SCIENCES

A new phase in the representations and knowledge of Rio's favelas came after 1970 with the development of graduate studies in Brazilian universities. There is clear continuity with the preceding period: as urban anthropology became part of the recently established master's program in anthropology at the National Museum, a number of master's students chose favelas as their object of study or used them to debate more general questions such as urban poverty and the daily practices of populations in the cities. From the 1970s to the present, writing and research proliferated, the simultaneous result of an explicit university agenda, the need for planning, and a policy of scholarship fomenting research that paid ongoing attention to urban poverty or themes directly associated with it. The favela became a fashionable topic, including for the NGOs increasingly mobilized for intervention in this type of working-class neighborhood. Thus the vast corpus of what I refer to here as "the favela of the social sciences" should not be reduced to academic production in the narrow sense; it should be understood in its broader meaning to include institutional production of research and reports that address a specific social demand, both technical and political.

This moment exhibited three characteristics: (1) the recognition of the favela as a topic that the social sciences should study; (2) attempts to conceptualize this object of study based on theorizing about urban poverty and the debate about housing for the poor; and (3) the consolidation and generalization of points of "dogma," especially resulting from academic research studies and findings.

This production is embedded in the evolution of a Brazil that lived through the harsh military regime (1964–84), then returned to democracy, and today espouses, simultaneously and contradictorily, both participatory democracy and economic neoliberalism. With a rate of urban population growth of 66 percent in 1980 and 81 percent in 2000, by 1997 Brazil had the eighth-largest economy in the world, while remaining a leader in social inequality (World Bank 2013). The exploding size of megacities ("metropolization"), even more spectacular than mere urban growth, challenges any planning and accentuates the visibility of social problems in large cities. The urban poverty that accompanies this growth and presents itself as a social issue is a topic of reflection in the academy but also for all those who try to combat it.

Many methodological approaches have been developed to study favelas, taking on different forms according to the authors' disciplines. Classic fieldwork has evolved through university teaching of participant observation and qualitative methods. Institutions specializing in planning created databases and performed surveys, while in 1991–92 the Rio Mayor's Office put together a registry of favelas as a technical instrument, available to public agencies interested in working in these neighborhoods. Finally, techniques for sampling and identification using aerial photography have been refined, and modern cartography has developed with information technology such as geographic information systems.

In continuity with the period analyzed in the previous chapter, the process of placing value on the favela, begun especially by the Catholic Church, got a further boost. Now, however, it was the Brazilian academy that took the initiative and set the tone. The technical and scientific knowledge that oriented or at least justified public policies cast these clusters as a specific fact of the Brazilian urban world, especially in the large cities. Finally, the last years of the twentieth century witnessed the official recognition of the favelas' existence by the government through the constitution of 1988, the Estatuto da Cidade (City Statute) of 2001, and urban adverse possession (squatters' rights). The Programa Favela-Bairro (Favela to Neighborhood Program) proved that eradication and removal were public policies of the past, with all agreeing on the necessity of integrating the favelas into the urban fabric.

By virtue of the volume of the production and the number of people involved, the approach of this chapter differs noticeably from the first two. We must move from a sociology of individual actors to a sociology of collective ones. Those responsible for the set of reflections on the favela are no longer small networks of easily identifiable researchers. Nowadays, favelas are studied as much by anthropologists, sociologists, architects, and geographers as by numerous specialists in law, history, public health, social medicine, and political science. In universities that are increasingly compartmentalized, these researchers practice the most varied approaches and methods. Research has also become an activity of NGOs who fiercely defend the banner of action research.

New networks proliferate. Favelas are observed and researched by countless interested parties. As Alberto Rodríguez et al. (1972) described, regarding the *barriadas* of Lima, the residents have gone "from being invaders to the invaded."

To understand the social representation of the favela at present, one must consider the recent evolution of the Brazilian university. Three elements of the sociopolitical situation at this time are especially important: (1) the development of the Brazilian university from 1970 on; (2) the increasing attention given in Latin American intellectual milieux to the phenomenon of urban poverty and its recognition as the most important component of the social question; (3) the enormous wave of removals in Rio de Janeiro financed by the BNH in tandem with a pilot experiment in favela urbanization directed by a local agency, the Companhia de Desenvolvimento de Comunidades (CODESCO).

THE UNIVERSITY AS A PRODUCER OF RESEARCH

The first graduate courses in social sciences in Rio de Janeiro were given at UFRJ's National Museum. This graduate program in anthropology offered, in addition to classical training, courses focused on indigenous groups and the peasantry, the program's priority themes. At the same time, under the influence of Anthony Leeds, the graduate program included the city as one of its areas of work. In 1968, during one of his stays in Brazil studying favelas, Leeds established relationships with several Brazilian academics of his generation. Among these was Roberto Cardoso de Oliveira, who had become the director of the National Museum's new master's program and who asked Leeds to come back to Rio for the second semester of 1969 to teach two courses: Urban Anthropology and Urban Ecology.[1]

These master's courses in social anthropology, held at the CLAPCS headquarters, included among their students Luiz Antonio Machado da Silva, Gisélia Grabois, and Carlos Nelson Ferreira dos Santos, who at that time were already doing research on favelas. Yvonne Maggie and Gilberto Velho also attended Leeds's courses; they would meet again at the University of Texas. On his return to Brazil, Velho assumed the chair in urban anthropology at the National Museum. Some years later, he published Anthony and Elizabeth Leeds's (1978) book, giving Brazilian readers access to their research findings on the favelas of Rio and the *barriadas* of Lima.

There is clear continuity between these master's seminars in 1969 and the informal meetings that Leeds regularly led during his previous stay in Rio, also attended by the Peace Corps volunteers, as I mentioned in chapter 2. One of these volunteers stayed in Brazil after his term with the Peace Corps was over and was admitted to the National Museum graduate program where he was enrolled in Leeds's courses.[2]

Leeds's contribution during the beginnings of urban anthropology at UFRJ can be evaluated both for the content of his courses and for the methodology they proposed, from the same point of view as the work he conducted with the Peace Corps volunteers. Leeds saw urban anthropology as the application of theories in circulation, stimulating observation of the way of life in the city and the neighborhood, in addition to insisting on the links between social stratification and place of residence. Velho (1972) stressed Leeds's importance as an adviser. He identified his ethnographic work done in an apartment building for Leeds's course as the origin for his research on the middle class of Copacabana district. The many theses and dissertations about favelas or having favelas as their site of research produced beginning in the early 1970s are testimony to Leeds's motivation and influence. These include those of Gisélia Grabois (1973), Maria Julia Goldwasser (1975), Ana Margareth Heye (1979), Carlos Nelson Ferreira dos Santos (dissertation defended in 1979 and published in 1981), Jane Souto Oliveira (1980), Patricia Birman (1980), and Lygia Segala (1991). Even though only some of them were enrolled in Leeds's courses, his mark is present in the work of all these Brazilian anthropologists.

At the same time, Leeds's influence on the nascent urban anthropology is not sufficient to explain the rapidly growing importance of academic work in the social sciences on the favela from the late 1960s on. It was Brazilian universities as a whole that were mainly responsible for the proliferation of research and writing on the Rio favelas in the last several decades, works that have contributed to shaping the social representations of these urban spaces and their inhabitants, whereas in previous periods, as we have seen, such representations resulted from political debates and the production of journalists and other practitioners of the liberal professions.

To understand this process, first one needs to consider the complex institutional structure connected to the development of graduate studies in the social sciences, to the extent that such research is very much linked to the execution of theses and dissertations. To begin with, since the 1950s, there had been an important movement in Brazilian universities, especially in São Paulo and Rio de Janeiro, in which intellectuals and academics had already brought to light an extensive scholarly production,[3] and some of these scholars had already been recognized by international institutions such as UNESCO or by important U.S. universities.[4] As I discussed in chapter 2, since 1941, the ELSP

The Favela of the Social Sciences

in São Paulo already had a graduate program, directed by Donald Pierson, that was inspired by the Chicago School.[5]

In the mid-1950s, higher education reform started to be debated, stressing the growing need to (1) provide full-time education for professors and students, (2) develop training geared to research, (3) offer scholarships to students, (4) organize research teams, and (5) give universities the means and facilities necessary for contributing to the progress of Brazilian society through the development of basic and applied research (O. Velho 1983).[6] The creation of the Universidade de Brasília in the 1960s, based on a model of excellence, was a sign of the value placed on scholarly development in a country that intended to face the future and that had the goal of building a great modern nation.

It was in this context, then, that graduate programs in the social sciences progressively matured. The first one had been created in the early 1940s at USP based on a quite traditional model, without required specific courses for graduate students in the dissertation phase. The number of dissertations defended in anthropology, sociology, and political science was still small— about two per year between 1945 and 1965 (Lamounier 1981, cited in O. Velho 1983, 246), and most of these were defended abroad, mainly in France and the United States.[7] Beginning in the 1970s, though, the graduate programs began to expand. The master's program at UFRJ's National Museum was created in 1968, with others launched the following year at Instituto Universitário Pesquisas do Rio de Janeiro (IUPERJ) and the Universidade Federal de Minas Gerais (UFMG). Doctoral programs were then instituted at the universities above and at others in the South and the Southeast: at the Universidade de Campinas (UNICAMP) and the Universidade Federal do Rio Grande do Sul (UFRGS), and even later, at major universities in the Northeast: at the Universidade Federal de Pernambuco (UFPE) and the Universidade Federal da Bahia (UFBA).

This expansion of doctoral programs in the social sciences and other fields in Brazil, paradoxically, coincided with the military dictatorship. This is somewhat surprising at first glance, compared to what the military did to universities when it was in power in other countries in Latin America, such as in Argentina, where the institutions were completely destroyed. This development can only be explained by special characteristics of the Brazilian military dictatorship.

Privileging higher education was, in fact, an explicit strategy of the regime that held power from 1964 to 1984, as that education was mainly concerned with training educators and technical professionals. Within two decades, this policy resulted in the establishment of graduate programs in thirteen states and the Federal District. By 1994, there were fifty-four graduate departments in the social sciences, with twenty-seven in sociology, thirteen in political science, and fourteen in anthropology (Vianna, Carvalho, and Melo 1995, 32).

The Brazilian military valued the model of the U.S. universities, in which the PhD was considered central in all scholarly fields and applied research was recognized as necessary for economic development. The expansion of graduate programs in Brazil was not only viewed positively, it was encouraged. At the same time, while insisting on the importance of developing high-level scholarly and technical training, the military government did not neglect a political and ideological purge of the Brazilian academy, in which sociologists, especially those identified with Marxist ideas or connected to the Communist Party, were closely watched. In the social sciences, the dictatorship's support for graduate education was directed especially to anthropology and political science, disciplines seen as less suspect by the military. We can also suppose that the model of the specialized researcher-professor invested in research activity inspired by the U.S. model was more acceptable to the military government than the generalist intellectual disposed to intervene in public debate on society's great questions. For academics, professionalization also was a means of self-preservation against governmental repression. Many who were excluded from the university could partially resume their professional activity through private research and study centers, of which the Centro Brasileiro de Análises e Pesquisas (CEBRAP) is an exemplary case.

Thus, beginning in the 1970s, public universities continuously received significant aid, which made possible a potential increase in teaching on the doctoral and university research level. In the context of this new policy of scholarship, the Financiadora de Estudos e Projetos (FINEP) was created. FINEP was responsible for administering the Fundo Nacional para o Desenvolvimento Científico e Tecnológico (National Fund for the Development of Scholarly and Technological Development). Support for universities took the form of financing master's and doctoral programs, funding for development of integrated programs of empirical research, and reinforcement of public agencies. The Coordenação de Aperfeiçoamento do Pessoal do Ensino Superior (CAPES) and the Conselho Nacional de Pesquisa (CNPq), which expanded their activities, increased the number of scholarships for study in-country and abroad.[8]

After the return to democracy, marked by the election of Tancredo Neves as president in 1985, the university population continued to grow noticeably. With the development of the labor market for graduates of higher education, doctoral programs spread not only to other regions of the country but also beyond the main metropolitan areas, including in the states of São Paulo and Rio de Janeiro, where a considerable number of private universities arose alongside the public ones.

Various foreign entities — first among them the Ford Foundation — joined in this reinforcement of research and doctoral studies in Brazil. They took on a significant role during the first twenty years of institutional growth, first in São Paulo and Rio de Janeiro and later during the decentralization of higher education begun in the 1970s (Figueiredo 1988).[9]

The institutionalization of the social sciences was evident after the creation in 1977 of the Associação Nacional de Pós-graduação e Pesquisa em Ciências Sociais (ANPOCS), which had the dual function of organizing scholarly debate and of coordinating programs and politico-institutional representation.[10] ANPOCS, which began with fourteen research centers and graduate programs, now includes 106 — sixty-four research centers and forty-two graduate programs in sociology, anthropology, and political science spread around the country. At the same time, the research centers and graduate programs oriented toward urban studies (urban and regional planning, urbanism and architecture, geography, economics, public administration, and so forth) also had an organization, the Associação Nacional de Pós-graduação e Pesquisa em Planejamento Urbano e Regional (ANPUR), formed in 1983 with five programs and bringing together centers active in the urban studies mentioned above.

Urban research, which up the 1950s was conducted only by geographers,[11] benefited from the national policy of institutionalization. The social sciences encouraged studies of the city within the scope of graduate programs in sociology, political science, anthropology, history, and economics. At the same time, governmental agencies directly connected to planning especially contributed to research in urban planning and urbanism, and financed, directly or indirectly, projects conducted by universities: the Instituto de Pesquisa Econômica Aplicada (IPEA), linked to the Ministry of Planning, specialized in the urban labor market and interregional and interurban migration; the BNH, housing, water supply, and sanitation; the Serviço Federal de Habitação e Urbanismo (SERFHAU), local planning; and the Conselho Nacional do Desenvolvimento Urbano (CNDU), topics related to metropolitan areas and urban systems. All of these agencies required academic specialists, and they signed contracts for studies and research with these academics and their universities.

In 1995, urban research was concentrated in Brazilian universities: 50 percent in the graduate programs and 14 percent in the university research centers (Valladares and Coelho 1995, 93–94). In 1992, the metropolis of Rio de

Janeiro alone had ten graduate programs, where urban issues had their place in programs in anthropology, sociology, political science, history, geography, urban planning, architecture, urbanism—and even in social medicine, public health, and social work programs (Valladares and Sant'Anna 1992). By 2001, there were nineteen programs, including new doctoral programs in urban law and social work.

Dissertation production is another indicator of the importance of the Brazilian university structure. The first survey of dissertations on urban Brazil during the period 1940–88 counted 1,001, of which 905, or 90 percent, were defended in Brazilian universities (Valladares, Sant'Anna, and Caillaux 1991). The production capacity of Brazilian universities was confirmed in a second survey of dissertations devoted solely to Rio de Janeiro. Between 1960 and 1990, 239 of a total of 265 dissertations collected, or again 90 percent, were defended in Brazilian universities (Valladares and Sant'Anna 1992). Of the 623 researchers active in Brazil, as catalogued by URBANDATA-Brasil, 288 or 46 percent worked in Rio de Janeiro, of which 61 percent belonged to university institutions (Sant'Anna and Lima Júnior 2001).

These cursory indicators show the importance and speed with which the scholarly potential of the Brazilian academy developed in the thirty years since its institutionalization. The current university context contrasts strongly with that of the 1950s, when Brazil was considered a typical Third World country, as described in *Geografia da fome* (Castro 1946; *The Geography of Hunger*, 1952) and *Os dois Brasis* (The two Brazils; Lambert 1959). That is, it was a country divided between the rich and peasants where a third of the population was illiterate.

POVERTY AND TERRITORY: THE CONSTRUCTION
OF SOCIAL MARGINALITY

In this institutional context, the theme of urban poverty was affirmed as one of the main areas of social science research. This affirmation was based on the convergence of three processes: the elaboration of the debate on poverty in studies regarding the country's modernization, Brazil's demographic curve, and internationalization of the Latin American discussion of these issues.

It is true that urban poverty had been a concern of Brazilian elites since the nineteenth century.[12] As I have demonstrated, debates conducted in Europe during the nineteenth century resounded considerably in Brazil (Valladares 1991).[13] As in England, the idea of labor as a central element of the organization of social life was, in Brazil, a key to understanding the predominating concepts

The Favela of the Social Sciences

in public dealings with the problem of poverty. Imposing a work ethic and repressing idleness constituted the dual challenge of emerging public policies. In the Brazilian debates, given that issues of indigence and poverty were connected to the situation of the labor market, social representations stressed the image of the vagrant, and idleness was underscored to explain certain individuals' lack of occupation. By virtue of its very recent past as a regime supported by slavery, considerable effort was needed for the Brazilian nation to impose this work ethic on a population that did not put faith in labor as part of human dignity.

These conceptions from the beginning of the nineteenth century, which associated poverty with the refusal of people to sell labor and with difficulty in respecting the rules of wage-earning, the conviction grew that poverty was a matter of personal responsibility: individuals were poor because of their moral weaknesses. The image of the poor as "dangerous classes" thus came to dominate the social imaginary of the "lettered classes," and it justified early public interventions against the urban territory of the poor of the time, the tenements in the city center.

As we saw in chapter 1, the discourse about poverty took another direction under the populist regime of Getúlio Vargas, who sought to banish the stigma of slavery and impose a new, positive vision of the poor by attaching value to the figure of the worker. In an attempt to build the bases of a welfare state, Vargas's regime instituted the minimum wage, which went into force in 1940 and was followed by a set of social laws (L. Vianna 1976). Even though this legislation only protected workers who were part of the formal labor market and did not include the large masses of men and women outside the formal wage sectors, Vargas used these laws to build his image as "father of the poor."

This change in perspective paralleled another gradually established representation of the causes of poverty: the idea that objective impositions, external to individuals, could lead them to a situation of poverty, thus relativizing the importance of personal responsibility at the same time that it justified the need for some social policy measures. At the same time, the development of political clientelism and the populist regime little by little transformed the masses of urban poor into an object of attention for the political machine and the government. Instead of "dangerous" they became "manipulable."

These poor urban masses also became more numerous. Brazil's demographic evolution was spectacular between 1959 and 1980: in thirty years the country's population went from predominantly rural to mostly urban. According to the 1950 census, 64 percent of the population still lived in the country; as of the 1980 census, 68 percent of the population lived in cities and towns.

The resulting urban growth was explosive. The population of cities and towns multiplied by a factor of 4.2 between these years—mainly through growth of the favelas, of subdivisions on the urban periphery lacking in infrastructure, and the expansion of tenements, giving the phenomenon of urban poverty an unprecedented breadth.

Demographic analyses of the process of urbanization in Latin America, including Brazil, between 1950 and 1960 stressed the exceptional nature of this process, especially compared to the European experience,[14] such that it came to be known as "overurbanization." A result of the random migratory flows and very high rates of population growth, overurbanization made urban poverty highly visible. Geographers underscored the disequilibrium caused by the anarchical growth of the large metropolises within the urban networks of each country and the urban primacy over space in the large cities. Economists stressed that modern sectors and traditional sectors of the economy were out of step with each other, unable to handle the ever-growing supply of low-skilled labor. Underemployment, a consequence of overurbanization, was soon seen as the major cause of poverty, and between 1960 and 1970 this became a favorite topic for reflection and research in Latin America, especially in Brazil (Morse 1965).[15]

A considerable literature of clear Marxist orientation concerning modernization and social marginality in Latin America was produced. This production highlighted the deficiencies in the dynamic of economic development, which was unable to create enough jobs to absorb the population growth and satisfy the needs of migrants arriving in the cities, who had been expelled from the countryside as a result of the transformations in rural labor (Cardoso and Reyna 1967). Several categories were then used to refer to these urban masses who had not been integrated into the new industrial urban society: "relative overpopulation," "reserve army of industrial labor," and "marginal mass" (Nun 1969).[16]

To conceptualize these marginal masses, abandoned by the formal economy, the theory of marginality developed in Latin America, combining approaches as diverse as functionalism, culturalism, and Marxism. The success of this theory lies in its ability to overcome purely economic approaches through reference to two other dimensions of society: the spatial and sociocultural. At the same time, even if "marginality" was given a range of meanings to refer to the most diverse situations and social groups (Kowarick 1975), its contributions had the merit of proposing a global reading of the phenomenon, thus offering an analytical framework for the social space of urban poverty in Latin

America capable of inspiring numerous research projects and urban policy operations (Mangin 1967).[17]

Social marginality found its territorial expression in the *barrios marginales*, a Spanish phrase that refers to the same sort of urban spaces as the favelas, seen by Latin American specialists as the most typical manifestation of nonintegration of broad segments of urban society (Vekemans and Venegas 1966).[18] Indeed, it is in the big metropolises that the unbalances become most visible insofar as urban space is a translation of sociospatial segregation and of the problem of insertion faced by growing successive waves of populations coming from the rural world.

The displacement of marginality from the field of economics to the areas of urban social space and of culture suggests a certain continuity with the processes of urban ecology, and, in particular, the affirmation of the existence of a "culture of poverty." The idea of a culture of poverty articulated with the theory of marginality under the influence of U.S. anthropologist Oscar Lewis, whose fieldwork on the *vecindades* (large tenements in the downtown areas of Mexico City) was the basis of his best-seller *Five Families* (1959).[19] According to his model of interpretation, the residents of poor neighborhoods who were of rural origin had adopted a specific way of life, characterized by values and behaviors different from the dominant culture. This "subculture," produced and reproduced by them, would explain their reactions, through specific cultural traits, to the social situations they confronted. This culture of poverty would be passed from one generation to another, thus maintaining a vicious cycle that might guarantee survival for the poor in a modern society. According to Lewis, such a way of life ends up giving rise to a syndrome specific to poor populations, in which is manifest a spirit of resignation, of fatalism in facing the future,[20] as well as a certain joie de vivre that makes the conditions of life more bearable.[21]

FROM THE FAVELA AS A PROBLEM TO
THE FAVELA AS A SOLUTION

From the 1960s, the discussion of theses of social marginality applied to the Brazilian case led to an explicit critique of the theory of marginality. At the same time, even if these theses reinforced dominant representations of a dichotomy in society marked by the opposition of city and favela, as illustrated by Carolina Maria de Jesus's memoir,[22] for many who worked on Rio's favelas, their populations were not marginal and isolated; rather, they were integrated into the city in different ways. For example, Anthony Leeds had come to this conclusion in his essay "Brazil and the Myth of Urban Rurality: Urban Experience, Work and Values in 'Squatments' of Rio de Janeiro and Lima."[23] Leeds relied not only on his own fieldwork and the work of his informal team in Rio (see chapter 2) but also on his multiple visits to the *barriadas* of Lima and the work of Turner (1969) and Mangin (1967). He shared with these authors the belief that these poorer neighborhoods, which had been seen as enclaves, were actually highly integrated into urban life through involvement with markets of labor, politics, and culture (the last especially during Carnival).

Several years later, Janice Perlman synthesized this Latin American debate in her dissertation, published in English and later in Portuguese.[24] *The Myth of Marginality* (1976; *O mito da marginalidade*, 1977) was quite successful and still today is better known and more often cited in Brazil and the United States than Anthony Leeds's numerous works. But it is important to stress that its critique of the theory of marginality was neither original nor pioneering, in the United States or Brazil. U.S. historian Julio César Pino, who published several essays on the favelas of Rio in the late 1990s, is incisive: "Perlman's book is usually assumed to be the first to revise the study of the favela, but in fact it was neither the first nor the most original of such treatments" (Pino 1996, 451n6). Moreover, when the book was published in Portuguese in Brazil, it was similarly criticized by Gilberto Velho for its lack of originality. Velho (1977, 322) cited U.S. and Brazilian authors (e.g., A. Leeds and Machado da Silva), "who for some time had already competently and effectively carried out this demystification in relation to the favelas of Rio de Janeiro." Ruben George Oliven (1978) criticized Perlman's view of the poor and her affirmation that "in short, *they have the aspirations of the bourgeoisie, the perseverance of pioneers, and the values of patriots*" (Perlman 1976, 243; emphasis in original). Oliven (1978, 35) reminds us that "the danger in exaggeratedly emphasizing the good qualities of the poor is that this perspective takes as a given that they need to be defined and their virtues proven. . . . Perlman winds up situating herself within the liberal perspective of demonstrating that the *favelados* are no different from the rest of the population without, at the same time, having studied other groups with which they might be compared." In 1971 Machado da Silva had already done a study of metropolitan manual labor markets and marginality, treating the debate among Fernando Henrique Cardoso, José Luiz Reyna, José Nun, and Aníbal Quijano. His work was the first to provide a critical account in Portuguese of the thought and theses on marginality in Latin America.

As we saw in chapters 1 and 2, new questioning of the traditional representations of *favelados*—prolonged in a way by the theory of marginality—began with the publication of the results of the 1950 census (A. Guimarães 1953) and continued with the SAGMACS study. Even though these efforts — followed by Medina 1964, 1969; Parisse 1969a, 1969b, 1969c; A. Leeds 1969; and Machado da Silva 1967, 1969 — had found a certain intellectual audience, they were not enough to affect the representations that structured the collective imaginary of the elites and change public policy. In the 1960s and 1970s the perception of *favelados* as the result of a process marked by social marginality was widely dominant. It served as ideological justification for the antifavela operation undertaken by Governor Carlos Lacerda (1962–65) and continued by Governors Francisco Negrão de Lima (1966–71) and Antônio de Pádua Chagas Freitas (1971–74). In twelve years, eighty favelas were affected, 26,193 precarious homes were destroyed, and 139,218 people were removed (Valladares 1978a, 39). This was the most important intervention against the favelas that Rio de Janeiro had ever known. It was an operation whose "success" had been made possible by the federal government. Without the resources coming from the central government and the BNH, the scale of the operation would have been much more modest.[25]

This view of the favela-as-a-problem corresponded perfectly to the urban planning measures taken by Brazil's authoritarian regime, which, like its counterparts in other Latin American countries, followed a policy of destroying illegal neighborhoods. The logic behind such policies blamed economic and social ills on the milieu and saw the favela "problem" exclusively from the point of view of housing. During the 1960s several Latin American states invested in grand projects of conventional social housing, which entailed removing the inhabitants of "marginal" neighborhoods (Gilbert and Ward 1985, 12–13).

Gradually, several factors contributed to a renewed questioning of the view of the favela as a problem, with massive relocation of residents to housing projects as the solution. In international architectural circles, a critique developed of the distance between blueprint and reality, a distance solidified by training in schools of architecture that privileged design, formal research, and theories of urbanism without considering urban reality and life in the neighborhoods. Authors who placed value on "the street" and "the neighborhood" as the locus of social ties and important practices of urban life, such as Jane Jacobs and Herbert Gans in the United States, impelled a trend opposed to the urbanism of large planning projects that were in denial of "the city," such as those of Le Corbusier and the Athens Charter.

Among specialists in housing policy — academics and public policy staff — these traditional solutions were approached with a different sort of questioning. English-language researchers were the first to study the role of these poor areas in the urbanization of cities and in the urban and economic development of various Latin American countries (Mangin 1967; Turner 1969). After several stays in Peru in 1958–64, John Turner was surprised at the people's self-help initiative (in Rodríguez et al. 1995, 233). Calling attention to such poor neighborhoods and to the building of dwellings by the residents, they questioned certain elements of the paradigm of marginality and of Lewis's ideas. Indeed, this was an object of debate in the U.S. academy, which tended to universalize his concept of the culture of poverty.[26]

In the second half of the 1960s, Turner waged a campaign in the *Journal of the American Institute of Planners* against the traditional view that the problem of housing for the poor should be solved by transferring them to new, industrially built residences. As a consultant for the United Nations, he had visited many Third World countries and had always sought to make their leaders understand the drawbacks of large housing projects. In his book *Housing by People* (1976), he suggested considering residents as agents, responsible for their own housing. Turner had been in Brazil and sought out agency officials responsible for the removal policy, with whom he argued for a policy that would give the interested parties the freedom to build, as opposed to imposing on them a single, one-size-fits-all model of public housing.

Based on their own research and on the results of fieldwork by a number of researchers in several Latin American countries, Mangin and Turner stressed two points: (1) contrary to what was supposed, these "marginal" neighborhoods did not reproduce in the city the way of life of rural communities, nor did they provide evidence of the birth of a new culture, a sort of urban ruralism; and (2) these neighborhoods constituted an effective popular response to housing shortages in large, rapidly urbanizing metropolises. In fact, the subtitle of Mangin's 1967 article, "Latin American Squatter Settlements: A Problem and a Solution," was quite explicit. These authors emphasized that such neighborhoods contributed to the national economy, thanks to the residents' investments in their dwellings, the small businesses established there, and the neighborhoods' role as a pool of inexpensive labor. Moreover, Turner (1969) insisted on the "trampoline" effect that these neighborhoods can have, giving families with low or irregular incomes first a way to survive and later a chance at some social mobility, even on a small scale.

In Brazil, another factor that led many to question traditional representations and solutions was the results of the early housing policies themselves. In Rio de Janeiro, the policy of removal had unexpected effects (Valladares 1978a). On the one hand, the relocation operations led to an increase in the

The Favela of the Social Sciences

population of favelas not threatened with removal. This growth was due, in part, to the return of *favelados* who had been moved earlier but had not managed to stay in the housing blocks. They passed their homes on and returned to the favela.[27] On the other hand, these policies were built on economic schemes that proved unviable. That is because these were policies of access to property ownership, not of rental public housing. The loans paid by the relocated families should have been reinvested in construction of new housing to guarantee continuity of the process. However, many of the families could not make the payments, or paid irregularly, or went broke, such that the financial balance of the projects was compromised.

The change in perspective can also be explained by pressure from the grassroots, from the residents and their organizations that had always opposed removal, favoring instead legal status for their neighborhoods and the installation of public services, as in other parts of the city. In Rio particularly this pressure was not recent but followed a history of local mobilization — recall the earlier examples of the União dos Trabalhadores Favelados and of FAFEG, whose slogan "Urbanization yes, removal never!" still echoed in the ears of local and military authorities at the end of the 1960s.

These various factors led progressively to a new policy of public intervention that was shaped by a more positive view of the favela. The circumstances under which this view emerged were deeply ambiguous. In the second half of the 1960s, during the term of Mayor Negrão de Lima and the early years of the military dictatorship, a time when most authorities held firmly antifavela views, CODESCO, a public agency, was founded with the mission of maintaining the favelas, restoring facilities, and facilitating greater access to infrastructure and public services.

As we have seen, the idea of urbanizing the favelas aligned with an old proposal presented at various times and defended by parties as varied as the Catholic Church, the Communist Party, politicians linked to the clientelism of "water tap politics," and favela residents' associations. In a way, the rise of CODESCO was a concrete manifestation of these urbanization policy proposals.

The creation of CODESCO was interpreted as an act of political skill. According to Carlos dos Santos (1981, 57), "The governor [of the state of Guanabara] was urged to found a company to satisfy his earlier commitment to the *favelados*, as an honorable solution to the impositions of federal housing policy." The objective was to win acceptance of an authoritarian housing policy that would make Rio de Janeiro, the Brazilian city with the most favelas, an example for the whole country.[28]

The military regime ended up accepting CODESCO, to demonstrate that it could direct a diversified policy: on the one hand, a few pilot experiments with favela urbanization; on the other, the grandiose removal project developed by the Coordenação de Habitação de Interesse Social da Área Metropolitana do Grande Rio (CHISAM), a federal agency established at this same time. Thus the dictatorship could assert that it was capable of allowing a certain kind of pluralism.

However, the peaceful coexistence of the two institutions did not last long: CODESCO was only tolerated during its first phase of activity (1968–71); some even considered that this was an attempt to prove, by way of a hoped-for failure, that urbanizing the favelas was an illusory, impossible goal (C. N. F. dos Santos 1981, 80).

The CODESCO project sought to keep residents in the favelas, organize their participation in the reconstruction of neighborhood spaces, ensure the installation of infrastructure (water, sewer, and electricity), furnish families with small loans to improve their homes' construction, and make land settlement official by selling individual lots to residents (Machado da Silva and Santos 1969).

I will not analyze CODESCO in detail here or evaluate its real impact; several other authors have already done this.[29] Instead, I will focus on the change in perspective that the project made manifest among certain public policy actors, academics, and other specialists associated with it: the view of the favela as a solution rather than a problem, a perspective found as early as the analyses of Mangin (1967) and Turner (1969).

If the favela could be seen as a solution, this was thanks in large part to recognition of the value of "popular know-how" and the participation of the "voice of the people" beginning in the 1960s. The Catholic Church contributed heavily to this shift in values in Latin America—the 1960s was the decade of Second Vatican Council, the Basic Ecclesial Communities, and of the "preferential option for the poor" voiced by liberation theology. This perspective spread among young professionals who participated in the People's Pastorals as permanent and attending aids in the 1960s and 1970s.[30] According to Ana Maria Doimo (1995, 74–76), the idea of "the people as a subject" was present from the beginning of the 1970s in the discourse of many important social actors, including "the Catholic Church, especially its progressive sectors; the ecumenical movements, particularly those with a secular profile, connected with the ethics of social commitment; segments of the academic intelligentsia, mainly those who founded independent research centers in response to the purging of the universities at the request of the military regime; and groups on the left, broken by the dictatorship but soon disenchanted by violent models of transformative action."

Community development programs inspired by social work, such as those funded by the Alliance for Progress (see chapter 2), returned with the growth of anti-imperialism, and new European trends also gained favor, such as the "philosophy of praxis" and Marxist interpretations of society and especially the city.

It was, no doubt, the desire for "action in solidarity," nourished by respect for the "know-how of the people," that led a group of Rio architects interested in the favelas, known as Quadra, to become FAFEG advisers and participate actively in the CODESCO program in the favela of Brás de Pina.[31] Articles by Carlos dos Santos bear titles that reveal Quadra's discontent and his generation's willingness to take positions different from those of architects with more traditional points of view and practices:[32] "Estarão as pranchetas mudando de rumo?" (Might the blueprints be changing direction?; C. N. F. dos Santos 1978) and "Como projetar de baixo para cima uma experiência em favela" (How to plan an experiment in a favela from the bottom up; C. N. F. dos Santos 1980a). CODESCO contracted with this group, which became responsible for a pioneering experiment, in which architects and residents together redesigned neighborhoods and houses in a process of mutual apprenticeship in which the residents' freedom of choice was respected.[33]

In the 1980s, the theme of popular participation returned to the center of thinking among sociologists on the Brazilian left, as Doimo (1995) has pointed out. In the national meetings of ANPOCS, one of the most active working groups in 1980, 1981, and 1982 was Movimentos Sociais Urbanos (Urban Social Movements).[34] A conception of passive participation shifted to one founded on recognition of the "active capacity of the people," shared by a majority of Brazilian sociologists (Doimo 1995, 75). Often this conception was more activist than sociological; as Renato Boschi (1987) observed in his review of studies of urban social movements in Brazil, a majority of the analyses that considered such collective movements to be key elements of the country's political change in the 1980s were marked by ideological bias.

Santos's 1981 study of the CODESCO intervention in Brás de Pina is interesting in that, in addition to offering a detailed analysis of the process of spatial restructuring of a favela, it furnished a less ideological view of popular participation. Santos provided a reading that is neither romantic nor utopian about the various actors, including the local population and the residents' association. In the manner of participant observation, his study showed the coexistence of various sorts of demands and rejections, of different alliances and internal conflicts, in which the state could be a "friend" or an "enemy," depending on the interests in play.[35]

I also treated this complex game of negotiation and exchange among government agencies by lower-and midlevel public servants and the world of the "people" in *Passa-se uma casa* (Valladares 1978a), published several years earlier and centered on an analysis of favela residents' participation in the removal process undertaken during the military dictatorship. In this book, I analyzed residents' responses to an imposed operation contrary to their demands and interests. Through participant observation, it was possible to identify many informal mechanisms developed throughout the process — from the time of the announcement of the favela relocation to the opening of the new housing complex, with the families settled in their new homes and a new way of life imposed on these former *favelados*, now mortgage-holders (Valladares 1978a, 47–81). Familiar social ties were undone and new ones formed. Unexpected new practices arose and became for some the "new normal." All of this happened in a setting in which public employees (social workers and high- and low-level officials) and various representatives of the population (directors of residents' associations and other local organizations as well as the residents themselves in all of their diversity) mixed and mingled through their exchange of services.

The argument of *Passa-se uma casa* both contested the traditional readings of these relationships as purely hierarchical and questioned the interpretation of the residents' social response to the removal as an urban social movement (cf. Castells 1980). I preferred the model of the free rider, which stresses personal interest and advantages that can be gained from a given situation. The practice of the *jeitinho brasileiro*[36] also contributed to the formal and informal mechanisms and means for obtaining benefits. If the participation of the *favelados* was active and creative, it was also recognized as more individual than collective, each person trying to collect certain private advantages, suggesting that a utilitarian ideology and individualistic ethics were stronger than an orientation toward collective action.

This demystification of popular participation was not sustained, and the process of valuing the favela that had been under way gained strength both in scholarly thought and among planners and specialists in public agencies. This evaluation, as we have seen, brought together two types of argument: (1) those regarding the favela's objective urban advantages for its residents (access to housing, flexibility of investment in do-it-yourself construction according to fluctuations in resources, and proximity to places of work and public ser-

The Favela of the Social Sciences

vices) — in spite of construction's being inferior to technical guidelines and despite deficient infrastructure; and (2) those about the *favelados'* capacity for participation and for collective action in contributing to improved technical and social solutions. Despite CODESCO's short life span and the political context of the military dictatorship, this view of the favela as a participatory solution increasingly became a common point of reference for public policy actors,[37] as it was also a model in the university milieu.

THE EVOLUTION OF SCHOLARLY
PRODUCTION ON RIO'S FAVELAS

Beginning in the 1970s, reflection on Rio's favelas took on a new dimension thanks to the development of graduate studies. Representation of the favelas would be increasingly shaped by contributions of university research. The change was qualitative, in light of the agents and their types of work, but it has also been quantitative, given the large number of theses and dissertations, articles, reports, and books produced in the last forty years.

We should take stock here of this production as a whole, in order to define its characteristics, rather than follow the classic procedure of literature review in the social sciences, which considers periodization of scholarly production, the paradigms that orient the authors, delimitation of the field and of its main topics of research, the major works produced, and the topics to be developed — a procedure that colleagues and I have used in previous bibliographic reviews about housing in Brazil (Valladares and Figueiredo 1981), about urban poverty and the labor market (Coelho and Valladares 1982), and about early childhood in Brazil (Alvim and Valladares 1988).[38]

The corpus is made up of a total of 838 texts about the favelas of Rio de Janeiro, gathered from research by URBANDATA-Brasil, including publications through 2002.[39] In 2003, I published with Lídia Medeiros an analytical bibliography with 668 references covering the period 1906–2000 (Valladares and Medeiros 2003), a work that is almost certainly the most complete bibliography on the subject.[40] Forty-six different libraries in Rio de Janeiro, as well as Brazilian, U.S., and French internet-accessible databases, were consulted. The corpus includes articles from Brazilian and foreign periodicals (37.8 percent), dissertations (20.4 percent), research reports (11.9 percent), books (13.7 percent), unpublished presentations in colloquia (9.6 percent), conference annals (4.2 percent), and other documents (2.1 percent).[41] The following analysis is based on the data extracted from this bibliographic corpus.[42] The

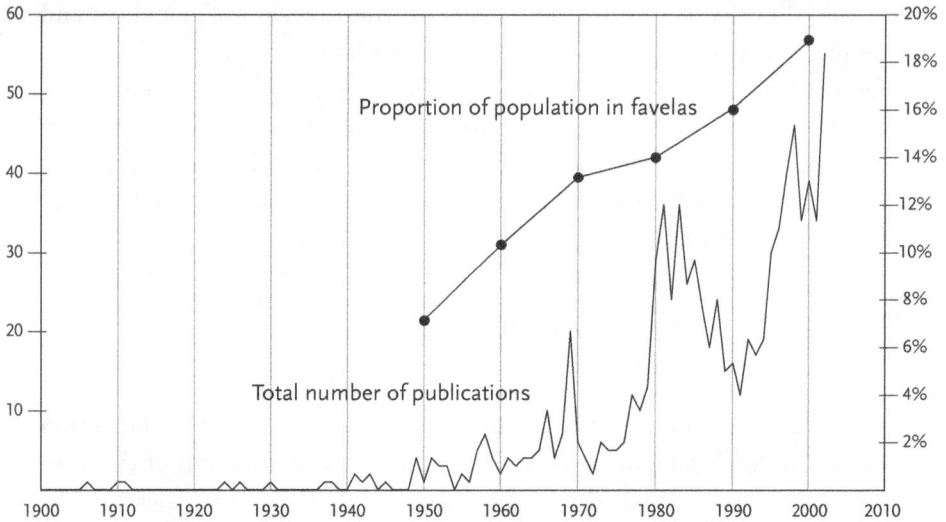

Graph 1. Number of publications on the favelas of Rio de Janeiro,
by year of publication, and the proportion of Rio's population
living in favelas, 1900–2002 (URBANDATA-Brasil, 2004).

distribution of publications by year enables a preliminary reading of the evolution of the production as a whole: graph 1 shows three periods, which correspond approximately to chapters 1, 2, and 3, respectively.

The small number of publications recorded up to the 1940s demonstrates
that scholarly thought was still in its formative stage. As I noted in chapter 1,
these publications were limited to essays and impressions and reports from
visits.

The second period begins in the late 1940s and runs through the mid-
1960s. As we have seen, the censuses of 1949 and 1950 brought the first significant increase in the number of scientific studies.

The third period begins in the mid-1960s. It is marked by a large increase in
the number of publications and alone accounts for 90 percent of all of the texts.
At the same time, this period is marked by considerable fluctuations. We can
see three subperiods of progress: the late 1960s, the first half of the 1980s, and
the second half of the 1990s. The first and second subperiods were followed by
quite noticeable declines.

During the 1960s, the studies started to become more systematic.[43] This
phase was related to the discovery of fieldwork by the early U.S. and Brazilian
researchers. The culminating point of this subperiod in graph 1 corresponds

The Favela of the Social Sciences

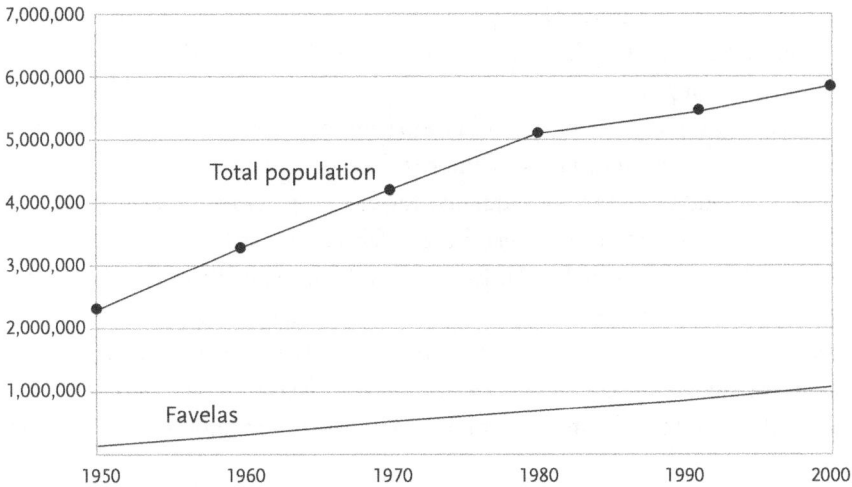

Graph 2. Population of Rio de Janeiro:
municipality and favelas, 1950–2000 (IBGE censuses).

to the publication of the aforementioned special issue of the journal *América Latina* in 1969, which represented the consolidation of this research topic by the social sciences.

The later fluctuations can be explained with several arguments. One of these consists of relating the intensification of research (and consequently of publications) to the intensification of the favelization process itself. Basically, the intensity of the urban social problem is what mobilized researchers. The growth of the two phenomena is undeniably concomitant. Between 1950 and 2000, a period that witnessed a large growth in publications, the population of Rio's favelas grew from 7 percent of Rio's total population to 18.7 percent.[44] Nevertheless, if the annual number of publications fluctuated significantly, the same was not the case with the favela population. As we see in graph 2, the growth in the favela population is quite constant throughout the period 1950–2000, without the explosion seen in the number of publications (graph 1). Late in this period, however, we can see an upturn in the growth rate in the favela population, while the growth rate in the population of the municipality as a whole declines. Contrary to the frequent argument that favelization resumed in the 1990s, we can see that the rate increase began in the 1980s. It is true that fluctuations could occur between censuses, which are taken every ten years. Indeed, the 1996 tally showed a deceleration of the growth rate in the first half of the 1990s (1.54 percent), followed by an acceleration in the second half of the decade (a rate of 3.5 percent; see Cezar 2002, 11, quadro 2). These are, nevertheless, rather limited trends compared to the sharp fluctuations in the numbers of publications.

When the results of the 1991 and 2000 censuses were published, the Pereira Passos Institute noted that 85 of the 545 favelas identified had appeared between 1980 and 1991. As a consequence, the visibility of the new favelas, related to their location, could have also been a factor that stimulated researchers. The new favelas identified had arisen within the municipality of Rio, contrary to the belief that they would only appear in the distant periphery of the urban area.[45] These new clusters were appearing in the city's zones of expansion, such as Jacarepaguá and Barra da Tijuca, which witnessed the expansion of favelas in parallel with that of gated communities for the upper middle class (Ribeiro 1997).

A final argument for the "objective" factors that stimulated the interest in the favelas was the evolution of poverty. According to Sonia Rocha (1994, 126), the proportion of the poor within the metropolitan area of Rio de Janeiro had grown significantly between 1981 and 1990, from 27 percent to 32 percent, while the average for all metropolitan areas in Brazil had dipped slightly, from 29.1 percent to 28.9 percent.[46] Thus this increase in poverty in Rio, measured in the early 1990s, along with its increased visibility, could have contributed to the intensification of research on the favelas.

These "objective" factors, however, do not constitute a convincing explanation, whether because the argument does not hold up (since, in fact, there was no "resumption of growth" of the favelas but rather a continuous growth) or because the increase in the poor population, per se, is insufficient to explain the development of research on favelas. Indeed, one must go beyond these factors to understand the fluctuations in the research agenda. If one distinguishes processes outside the academy from ones within it, other explanations emerge.

The effects of politics and the "conjuntura" (moment) also suggest the reason for the variations observed. Interest in the study of the favela appears to be linked to urban public policies dealing with the favela, which varied in intensity and orientation over time. This explanation accounts for the increase in the number of publications in the 1970s. The antifavela policies of mayors Carlos Lacerda, Negrão de Lima, and Chagas Freitas, the last two with the support of the BNH, were massive and widely covered in the media. They also provoked debates, critiques, and opposition. The 1980s, when publications clearly decreased, was a period without any expansive public policies after the time of the removals. Finally, the sharp upswing in the 1990s corresponds to a new, ambitious public policy launched in 1993, again with heavy media influ-

The Favela of the Social Sciences

ence. This was the Programa Favela-Bairro, which resumed and considerably expanded CODESCO's pioneering experiment with favela urbanization. This mode of intervention became an unquestionable touchstone for public policy.

The return of the favela to the research agenda in this latest period can be explained, first, as an effect or policies to stimulate research through funding, especially by government agencies such as FINEP and the Caixa Econômica Federal (Federal Savings Bank). Two years after the announcement of the Programa Favela-Bairro in 1993, several research centers and graduate programs were charged with performing about fifteen studies within the research development framework of the Sistema de Avaliação do Programa Favela-Bairro (Programa Favela-Bairro Evaluation System). In 1994, the Rio Mayor's Office, with support from the Instituto de Arquitetos do Brasil (IAB), held a public competition to choose the proposals to be implemented in the first nineteen favelas identified by the new program. Competing planning offices presented methodological proposals with the intent, not simply of providing technical solutions but of "transforming the favelas into true working-class neighborhoods and seeking the means to promote integration of the two distinct faces of the Brazilian urban world: the formal city and the informal city" (Duarte, Silva, and Brasileiro 1996, 13).

About 100 professionals, professors, and researchers responded to these various calls and received funding for their research or study activities. Their teams, which also included graduate students, used established social science methods: case studies with semistructured interviews, participant observation, sample survey research, and interviews with various social actors and representatives of the local population. The fifteen initial proposals spawned numerous theses and dissertations, books, articles, and conference presentations, all feeding the flow of publications on Rio's favelas. In this sense we can assert that in the 1990s, the favela came back into fashion in institutional and academic publications thanks to the stimulus of public policies, especially the Programa Favela-Bairro.

A second element of the political circumstances that followed this course was the research carried out for various NGOs, which often combined research and action. With the support of multilateral cooperation agencies, such as the World Bank and the Ford Foundation, countless NGOs arose in Rio beginning in the 1970s.[47] As Leilah Landim (1998, 69) has indicated, these NGOs have been quite connected to the university world: in addition to programs of cooperation with academic institutions, many of their activists are also university students and teachers, and many students do internships with NGOs or participate in other of NGO activities. The NGOs often have a presence on the Web,[48] and they publish books, magazines, manuals, and documentation of activism — often bordering on academic publications. What is more, NGOs have made the favelas a priority, establishing a presence in these areas, to the detriment of other impoverished spaces in the city. The NGOs' production has been substantial and makes up a sizeable portion of the bibliography about favelas in Rio de Janeiro.

This university mobilization around programs linked to public policies, along with the political-academic activities of the NGOs, cannot be solely explained by the availability of funding. The strong tradition of Brazilian intellectuals' involvement with politics is another element that has stimulated the large amount of academic production about Rio's favelas. In Brazil, the intellectual and political fields have had important overlaps and interactions. As Daniel Pécaut (1990, 6) has stated, Brazilian intellectuals are more politically engaged than their European counterparts: "For a long time now, they have put themselves in service of knowledge about the national reality and the formation of Brazilian society." In the last thirty years, since the return to democracy, specialists in the social sciences have contributed, as researchers and as citizens, to thinking about the changes and challenges in Brazilian society. In their dual role, they have participated actively in political parties, labor unions, and NGOs, but they have also contributed through going and coming between academic and professional positions, sometimes even holding offices in public agencies and in local, state, and federal government.

This activity outside the university that researchers have been involved in is accompanied by processes within the academic setting. The resumption of interest in the favelas has likewise resulted from the inclusion on the social science research agenda on two topics of great relevance: violence and social exclusion. Although the participation of the poor, as seen from the perspective of social movements, was a research priority in the 1970s and 1980s in Brazil (Valladares and Coelho 1995, 88–90), urban violence came to the foreground in the 1990s, as Alba Zaluar (1999), and Roberto Kant de Lima, Michel Misse, and Ana Paula Mendes Miranda (2000) have shown in their descriptions of violence, crime, and public safety in Brazil, and especially in Rio.

Over the last thirty years, the populations of the large Brazilian cities have been affected by a great sense of insecurity. In 1984, the Globo television network, in partnership with the Instituto Brasileiro de Opinião Pública e Estatística (IBOPE), distributed questionnaires throughout the entire Rio metropolitan area for its O Rio contra o Crime (Rio against Crime) campaign.[49] This very process demonstrated how important this phenomenon already was to the population. From then on, the press and communications media in gen-

The Favela of the Social Sciences

eral have insisted on disseminating information and images about acts of violence both individual and collective. Various sorts of crimes—kidnappings,
massacres, *arrastões* or criminal dragnets by organized bands that terrorized
beachgoers in Copacabana and Ipanema—appeared regularly in newspaper
headlines and television newscasts.

This information, which intensified in the 1990s, led one to imagine that
violence had increased to the point that public authorities were no longer
in control. In 1993, events such as the police massacres of street children at
Candelária Church downtown and of residents of Vigário Geral favela led
to outcries against police brutality by both domestic NGOs and international
agencies promoting human rights. More recently, the press and media have
published information about police involvement in corruption, kidnapping,
and drug trafficking.

Continuing its tradition of sensitivity to and engagement with sociopolitical conditions, the academy got intensely involved in the debate about explanations for the diverse forms that criminality and violence took in Brazilian cities
in the late twentieth century. According to Zaluar (1999), the poor figure in the
scholarly literature as both protagonists of violence and its most frequent victims. A number of important joint efforts (e.g., Soares 1996; Velho and Alvito
1996) analyzed the role of poverty and social inequalities in contributing to increased violence in its various forms. Machado da Silva (1994, 150) argued that
a violent sociability developed among youth; that is, violence became a new
form of sociability to serve their interests. This interpretation would explain
the spread and acceptance of violence by a large portion of the poor. Indeed, an
essay collection edited by Hermano Vianna (1997) attested to the importance
that Brazilian researchers attributed to the topic of violence among the young,
especially in Rio de Janeiro, where the favelas were increasingly identified as
the prime territory of drug trafficking and also of the site of the *bailes funk*. The
baile funk dance parties have been very popular among the young of all classes,
including the working-class *galeras* (posses, crews, cliques) classified by their
group identification and collective stances.

The book *Cidade partida* (Divided city) was written by journalist Zuenir
Ventura, who visited the favela of Vigário Geral for a month after the police
massacre of twenty-one of its residents in 1993. Ventura (1994, 12) affirmed an
image of a world to which "the republic has not arrived." As the book's title suggests, he described a veritable sociospatial apartheid between the world of the
favelas and the rest of the city of Rio de Janeiro.

This idea of a social apartheid, advanced by economist and statesman
Cristovam Buarque (1993), quickly spread in Brazilian sociological thought,

based on a thesis of a duality and polarization of favela versus "asphalt."[50] In spite of the return to a democratic regime, economic inequality, the distance between rich and poor, continued to grow. Efforts by the wealthy to maintain their privileges became increasingly vigorous, and social abandonment by the state ever more apparent. The poorer classes, left to their fate and excluded from any project of social transformation, witnessed the privatization of urban space and a segregation that was previously unknown. In scholarly analyses, exclusion as the key to understanding came to be used by nearly all studies of poverty and, by extension, of studies of the favelas and their inhabitants. The favelas thus acquired a new social dynamic, characterized in particular by drug traffickers' growing role in financing local services, in residents' associations, and in local life in general. In such representations, favelas come to be viewed as the locus of modern social exclusion par excellence. To the traditional deprecating images of the favela and its population during the era of the theory of marginality had now been added a new stigma linked to the negative social and political consequences of globalization (Fausto Neto 1995). Ideas about social fragmentation became dominant in the new intellectual dynamic, in which the contribution of NGO research helped bring together the notions of social exclusion and partial or incomplete citizenship.

DISCIPLINES AND THE FIELD OF RESEARCH

These changes and the resulting representations noted above have progressively broadened the academic areas involved in the study of the favelas. Today, few disciplines are not involved in this field of research, given that the favelas have been legitimated by the social sciences and by the media as the locus par excellence of poverty. Graph 3 shows the distribution of the whole of recorded publications according to the disciplines of their authors.

Twenty-nine different disciplines were registered.[51] Urban sociology (19 percent), urban planning and architecture (18 percent), and urban anthropology (14 percent) were the most frequent and accounted for over half (51 percent) of the total corpus. Urban geography and social work come next, with a combined percentage of 13 percent. The 9 percent related to "institutional production" is comprised of official publications produced or contracted by various planning agencies: censuses, official analyses or results, research on populations linked to various public policies, technical reports with proposals, and so forth. This category also includes publications from NGOs without identified authors. These last reports and studies have been increasingly numerous, and one cannot neglect their contribution to this category.

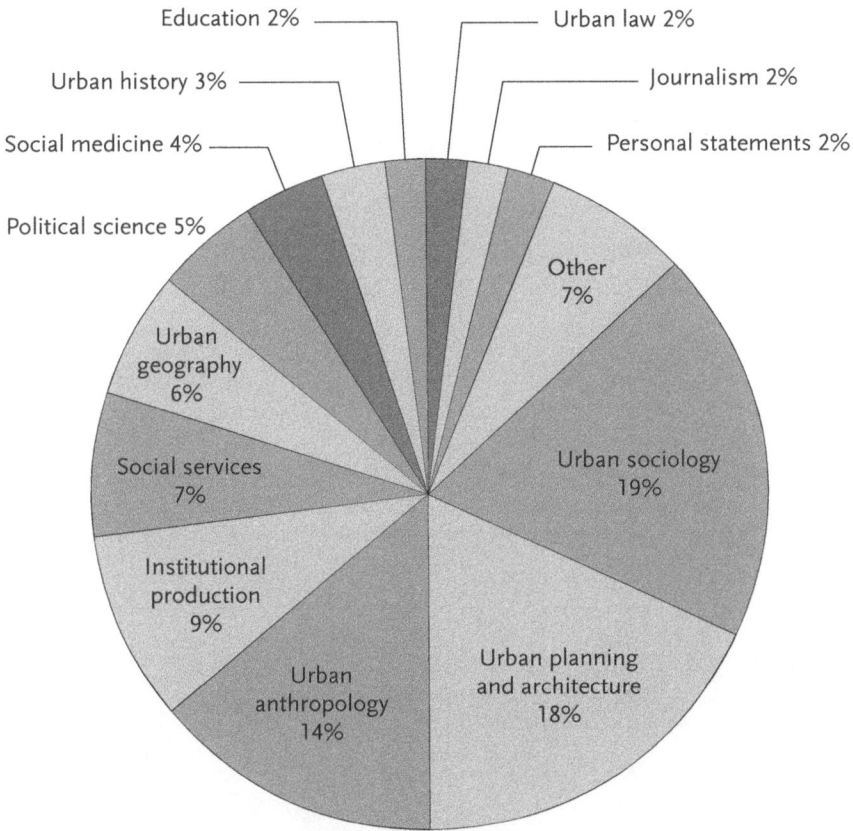

Education 2%

Urban law 2%

Urban history 3%

Journalism 2%

Social medicine 4%

Personal statements 2%

Political science 5%

Other
7%

Urban
geography
6%

Urban sociology
19%

Social services
7%

Institutional
production
9%

Urban planning
and architecture
18%

Urban
anthropology
14%

Graph 3. Publications on the favelas of Rio de Janeiro,
by author discipline (URBANDATA-Brasil, 2004).

In addition to the disciplines indicated in the graph, we find collected in
the category of "others" the following disciplines: psychology and psychiatry,
engineering, public administration, demography, economics, philosophy, social communication, cinema studies, public safety, social development, nurs-
ing, statistics, art history, theology, and geology.

Clearly, as this long list shows, the favela has become an object of interest
for researchers from numerous, diverse disciplines. At the same time, however, this breadth leads one to wonder if the interest in the favela and its residents have become diluted or lost and if, little by little, the favela might have
become instead merely the stage for investigating very diverse topics: violence,
housing, associations, education, political behavior, sports, religion, and so
forth. In other words, has the favela become the location of research, rather
than its object?

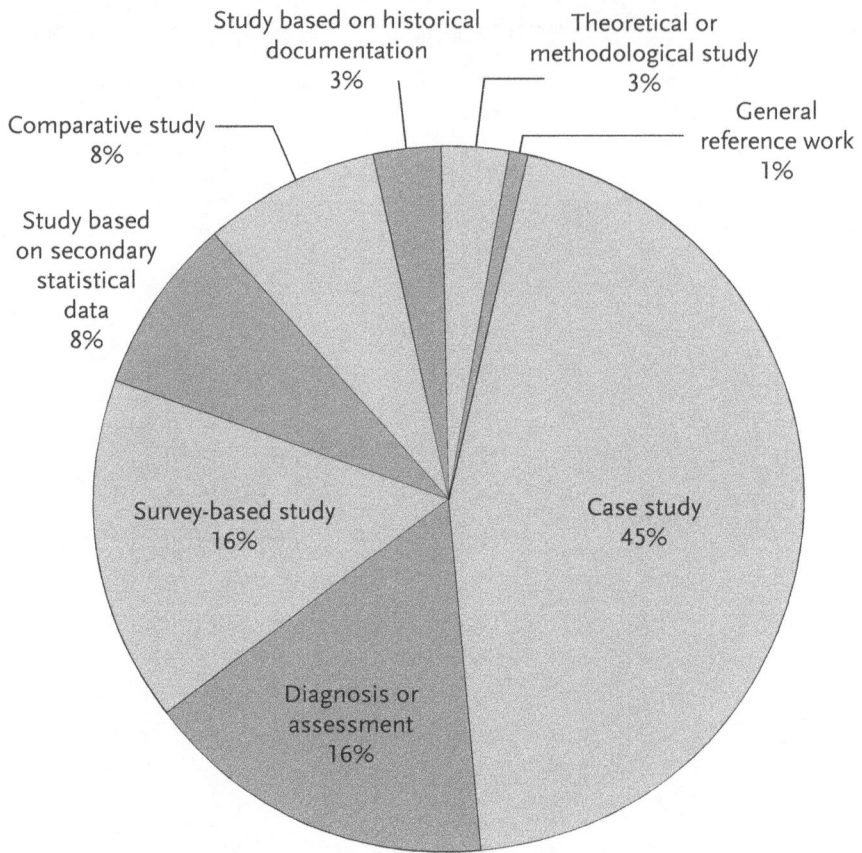

Graph 4. Publications on the favelas of Rio de Janeiro,
by mode of research (URBANDATA-Brasil, 2004).

A glance at the approaches and types of research will help define and demonstrate the error in this perception. Graph 4 — which considers only the texts in which it is possible to identify the type of research performed and excludes personal testimonials and institutional production — is quite enlightening.[52]

Case studies account for well over a third of the total (45 percent), which seems meaningful as an indication of the value of the favela as field for empirical study. The massive recourse to this methodological approach is related to the important contribution of anthropologists (14 percent of the distribution by discipline) and sociologists (19 percent).[53] At the same time, since we know that not all sociological analyses use this approach, it is clear that it is practiced by other disciplines. The fact that 20.4 percent of the total production was

The Favela of the Social Sciences

comprised of dissertations, among which predominate monographs, whatever the discipline, certainly contributed to the weight of case studies.

The second and third types of research were diagnostic studies (16 percent) and sample survey research (16 percent). In the first instance, the percentage can be explained by the weight of institutional production by both public agencies and NGOs, which need to learn about social and spatial characteristics or about the likely effects of their actions before intervening. The percentage of survey research is indicative of the difficulties in obtaining a representative sample of the favela population, in light of the irregularity of these areas.

Moreover, note the lower percentages for research based on secondary statistical data or on data series (8 percent) as well as for comparative studies (8 percent).[54] These low percentages can be explained by the lack of a tradition of comparative research in Brazil in the case of the latter, and, in the case of the former, the insufficient statistical training of researchers and the difficulty most of them encounter in accessing data. Not even the existence of the Cadastro de Favelas, created in 1981 (now the Sistema de Assentamentos de Baixa Renda; SABREN), or the fact that, since the 1950 census, the IBGE had distinguished "subnormal clusters" (favelas) from the other census categories, had stimulated researchers to intensively use such sources.

Even though case studies were the privileged research methodology, of a total of 752 favelas,[55] only some of them attracted such attention. There seems to have been a "preference" in the academic and institutional worlds for certain favelas or complexes of favelas. Graph 5 shows which cases attracted the most scholarly attention.[56]

Of a total of 752 favelas surveyed by SABREN in 2002, only 19 significantly attracted the attention of researchers (with 15 or more publications). These 19 favelas account for 416 publications, or 43 percent of the total.[57] Rocinha, the subject of 82 publications, is clearly the most studied; Complexo da Maré (a complex of several favelas) is the focus of 75 published studies; Jacarezinho, Santa Marta, Praia do Pinto, and Conjunto Habitacional Cidade de Deus (City of God Housing Complex, considered a favela by several authors) are among those that have between 20 and 40 publications. At the other extreme of the scale, we find 189 favelas that only yielded one publication each, 44 yielded two, and 20 yielded three.

The list of the 19 most-studied favelas may lead us to hypothesize as to the reasons for their "success" among researchers. Why some and not others? Six hypotheses seem most likely.

The first is proximity to universities: this is the case with Rocinha, near

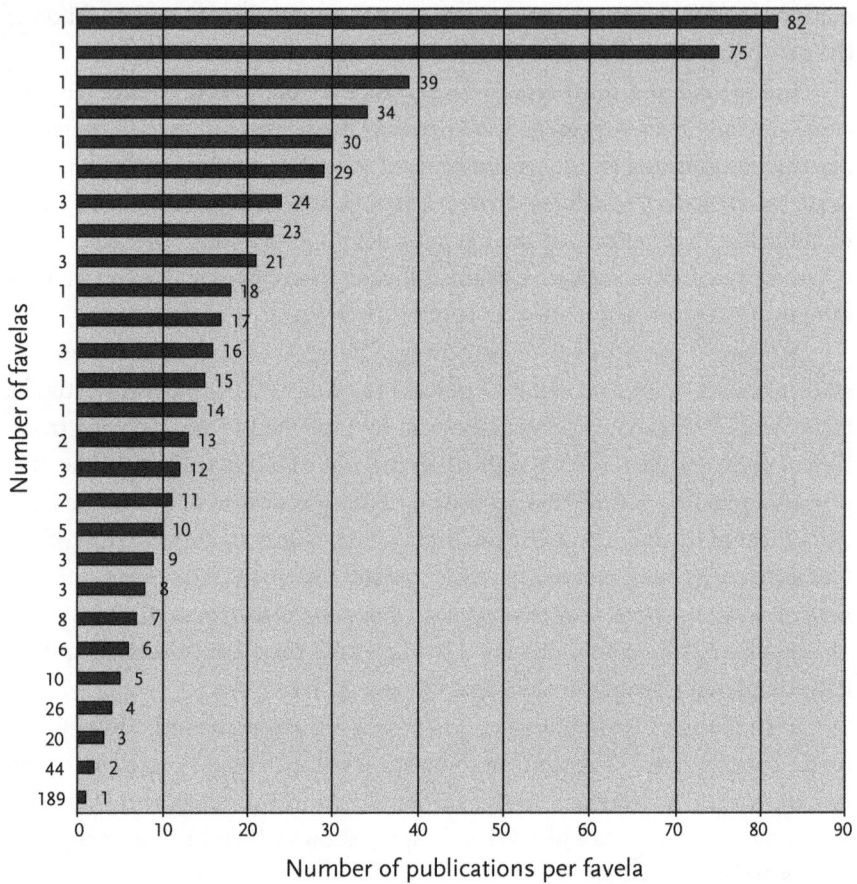

Graph 5. Number of publications on the favelas of
Rio de Janeiro, per favela (URBANDATA-Brasil, 2004).

PUC; Complexo da Maré (including Nova Holanda), close to the UFRJ campus on Ilha do Fundão and to the Oswaldo Cruz Foundation School of Public Health. When working on a thesis, dissertation, or other research, having a favela nearby is like having a social laboratory next door, facilitating access to social networks and participation in community volunteer work, often promoted by the university itself.

The second hypothesis is that these favelas had been the target of public policies: this is the case with Praia do Pinto and Catacumba, both demolished by the CHISAM removal program; Cidade de Deus, a housing complex to which residents of several favelas were relocated; Brás de Pina and Mata Machado, paradigmatic cases of favela urbanization promoted by CODESCO in the 1960s and 1970s; Pavão-Pavãozinho and Cantagalo, experiments by Gover-

The Favela of the Social Sciences

nor Leonel Brizola's program Cada Família um Lote (A Lot for Every Family); Serrinha and Mangueira, considered exemplary cases of the Programa Favela-Bairro; and Complexo da Maré, an area of Projeto Rio activity.

The third hypothesis is negative publicity because of violence of drug trafficking. Examples include Cidade de Deus, Santa Marta, Vigário Geral, Parque Acari, Nova Holanda, and Morro do Borel, favelas that bear the stigma of violence and criminality and are associated with histories of massacres and confrontations among gangs.

The fourth concerns notoriety connected to political conflicts or mobilization of associations. Jacarezinho and Morro do Borel were traditional favelas in which the labor movement was important and where several groups of leaders lived. They were symbols of resistance and struggle by residents. This is also the case with Vidigal, where the Favela Pastoral had an important role.

The fifth is connected to effects of cultural activity, reflecting the traditional image of the favela as the center of samba, *mulatas*, and *malandros*. This is the case with Mangueira and Morro do Salgueiro, whose samba schools are among the most famous in the country, and with Morro da Babilônia, known not only for its samba but also as the setting for Marcel Camus's 1959 film *Black Orpheus*; and of Santa Marta, which represents the ideal aesthetic of the favela space and was one of the locations for Michael Jackson's video "They Don't Care about Us."

Finally, the sixth hypothesis is a snowball effect resulting from the favelas' notoriety and the ease of access to the favela networks through NGOs active in these spaces, especially Rocinha, where Viva Rio has a number of ongoing activities,[58] and Complexo da Maré, home to the headquarters of the Centro de Estudos e Ações Solidárias da Maré (CEASM), the largest NGO originating in Rio de Janeiro.[59]

Curiously, Morro da Favella / Morro da Providência, the archetype of this sort of neighborhood, has inspired only sixteen publications.

DOGMAS

At first glance, a detailed examination of the literature on favelas produced by the academy and other institutions over the last forty years reveals an increase in the range of disciplines, methods, topics, and (to a lesser extent) favelas studied. I will not attempt to inventory here all of the topics and themes that researchers have approached; for this, I refer readers to *Pensando as favelas do Rio de Janeiro, 1906–2000* (Thinking about the favelas of Rio de Janeiro, 1906–2000; Valladares and Medeiros 2003).

However, on further reading of this body of literature, one can see the convergence of some basic features attributed to the Rio favela. Often these characteristics are merely presuppositions that are not discussed in the course of the research; sometimes these are included at the beginning in the definition of the object of study or the discussion of choice of method.

In spite of the nuances, the existence of a consensus around a few features of the favela has seemed so evident that we have to consider these characteristics to be veritable "dogmas," undebated but shared among a majority of researchers, that in one way or another constitute the implicit bases of their fieldwork. Rather than the multiplicity of themes and topics that inspire studies of the favelas, it is the smaller number of dogmas that we should investigate.

The first point of dogma deals with the specificity of the favela. Because of its particular history and its mode of growth, which differs from that of other neighborhoods, the favela has always been considered a singular, specific space. Urban researchers in general and geographers in particular have underscored the peculiar way the favela has occupied urban space, outside "regularity" and urban norms, without well-defined streets and with few or no collective services or facilities (V. Lopes 1955; Pearse 1961; Parisse 1970; Cavallieri 1986). From the start, this different style of occupation of built space identified the favela.

A priori, architects and urban planners have attached importance to differences arising from an unusual human habitat, urbanism, and aesthetic removed from rational architectonic or urbanistic models and standards (Drummont 1981; Guimarães and Cavalcanti 1984; Casé 1996; Berenstein-Jacques 2001a, 2001b). Official agencies have justified a specific approach to the favelas, with the incessant reminder for decades that this form of land use was not in accord with norms, that the favela was "irregular" and illegal, and that specific procedures had to be found to remedy the situation (Bronstein 1982; Poggiese 1985; E. Fernandes 2001).

Jurists have stressed the legal pluralism present in the favelas, where relative autonomy has resulted from the collective illegality of the dwellings (B. Santos 1977). Some *favelados* enjoy squatters' rights (Conn 1968). The land settlement situation, although varying from case to case, is still specific to favelas and generates conflicts between occupiers and landowners (E. Carvalho 1991). The Estatuto da Cidade (City Statute) and this particular urban adverse possession are new formulas for attempts at regularization of informal settlements (E. Fernandes 2001).

Demographic indicators have been used to show that, in these urban spaces, the population is younger, the migrants more numerous, the per-unit housing density higher, and the growth rate greater than for the city as a whole (Goulart 1957; Parisse 1969a). The urban quality of life in the favelas is clearly inferior to the average (IPLAN-RIO 1997). Finally, the census categories set by the IBGE crystalize these differences: for the IBGE, a favela is a "subnormal cluster" of at least fifty dwellings.[60]

Works by sociologists and anthropologists tend to conclude with the affirmation of this specificity to the extent that they refer to the "culture of the favela." A good example is the collection *Um século de favela*, edited by Zaluar and Alvito (1998) and published on the occasion of the favela's centenary. Of the twelve contributions, five deal with violence—crime, fear, drugs, and delinquency; four deal with popular culture—samba, Carnival, capoeira, and *bailes funk* and funk groups; and only three deal with political change and social structure.

The academy has been insisting that the favela, once the cradle of samba (Oliveira and Marcier 1998), is today the kingdom of funk and rap (O. Cunha 1996; H. Vianna 1977; Oliveira 1997; Cechetto 1997). In earlier times, it was the headquarters of the *jogo do bicho*, the parallel animal/numbers lottery; now it is the turf of Rio's drug traffickers (Ventura 1994; E. Guimarães 1998; A. Barbosa 1998; Deccache-Maia 1999). It is a fertile ground for the spread of various forms of popular religiosity, including Umbanda (Birman 1980) and more recently evangelical sects (Ventura 1994; O. Cunha 1996; Alvito 2001). It is a place where even politics appears in a different form on the heels of development of special relations with residents' associations. Once captive of mechanisms of political clientelism, residents' associations are now under the control of the narcotraffickers who have assumed the roles of the absent state (Centro de Defesa dos Direitos Humanos Bento Rubião 1994).

To summarize, all affirm the strong identity of these spaces, characterized not only by their particular geography and their illegal settlement status but also by the residents' obstinacy in remaining there[61] and by a way of daily life that ensures their identity. The typical social trajectory of young *favelados* is failure in school and, because of the attraction of power and money, entry into the "movement" (Zaluar 1985; A. Barbosa 1998; E. Guimarães 1998).[62] Thus the favela is believed to condition the behavior of its inhabitants, in a reboot of the deterministic hygienist or ecologist postulate that the milieu determines human behavior.[63]

The second point of dogma corresponds to another widely shared idea about the favela, one that concerns its territory and the social characterization of its inhabitants: the favela is the locus of poverty, the land of the poor. This is an especially potent idea, one that the social sciences have picked up from previous representations. The idea of a place of the poor, a place that is theirs alone, is long-standing, from the time of Mayor Pereira Passos's destruction of the *cortiços* on Avenida Central in 1904–10, which forced these populations to ascend into the hills or move to the suburbs. As we saw in chapter 1, the history of the growth of the favelas is the history of invasion by the poor — poor migrants and poor soldiers.

The theory of marginality, the first key to interpretation used by social scientists, also held the favela to be the habitat, the place of the poor (Perlman 1976). The 1970s and 1980s, when the theory of marginality was critiqued, saw a shift in perspective from the favela-as-problem to the favela-as-solution for housing for the poorer classes (C. N. F. dos Santos 1981; Brasileiro et al. 1982). Throughout, the idea of the favela as a space for the urban poor persists.

In the favela, the poor are "at home." Insofar as they form a city within the city — an illegal city within the legal city — the residents delineate their territory, a veritable enclave, where the mark of identity is omnipresent. Viewed as such, the favela is thought to have its own economy, its intramural laws, its own particular codes developed therein, abandoned as *favelados* to their own fate by the government. As a territory of partition, the favela is thought to be the very symbol of sociospatial segregation of the large Brazilian metropolises, especially Rio de Janeiro. In *Cidade partida*, journalist Zuenir Ventura presents a convincing synthesis of this territorialization of poverty, the urban translation of social exclusion.

Choosing the favela as the privileged territory for the study of poverty and social inequality, researchers have not hesitated when it comes to studying the poor — they go straight to the favelas. Thus they reveal their adherence to this dogma, and, at the same time, they contribute to fortifying it. Students and research assistants are sent to the favela because the premise is unquestionable: the favela is where the poor live; it is the space of the poor par excellence. Thus transformed into a *field*, the favela is where all of the phenomena associated with poverty and the universe of the poor are studied: violence, religion, health, politics, activity of associations, the informal sector, music, women, children, youth, school dropouts, and everything else. As the "territory of poverty," the favela has come to symbolize the territory of social problems, through an association of physical space with social fabric.

In fact, the term *favelado*, originally a resident of a favela — that is, of a certain place — came to refer, pejoratively, to anyone whose social "place" is characterized by poverty or illegality. In this view, the resident of a favela belongs to the world not only of the poor but also of social problems. With the increasing spread of the image of the favela as an enclave, both poverty-engendering

The Favela of the Social Sciences

poverty and poverty-engendering problems are reaffirmed. Could it be that we are faced with a vicious circle of stigmatization?

The third point of dogma affirms the unity of the favela, whether in scientific analysis or on the political plane. We think of the favela in the singular, whether in scholarly literature, fiction, or action. Even if we recognize it as a multifaceted reality, we get swept up in the habit of reducing a plural universe to a single category. The dominant social representation recognizes or treats the favela as a singular type and not in its diversity.

It is true that studies and official data distinguish among favelas of older or recent settlement; among those small, midsize, or large; among those consolidated or precarious; among those on hilly or flat land; among those in the North Zone, the City Center, the South Zone, the West Zone, or the metropolitan periphery (IPLAN-RIO 1983a). It is understood that this is a quite varied universe, geographically and demographically. Curiously, at the same time, the sociological differences are denied.

To speak of the favela in the singular has important implications; for example, when we adopt homogeneity as a premise and fail to attend to diversity, the internal differences in the world of the favelas automatically become secondary. The diversity, the plurality, of social relations and situations become invisible. The systematic evocation of an ideal type or an archetype recurs in the discourse about the favela (Préteceille and Valladares 2000). Thus *the* favela is, obligatorily, on a hill, illegally occupied, outside the law, underdeveloped, and filled with the city's poor. Under this generic denomination, the term "favela" encompasses phenomena with very different geographic, demographic, and urbanistic features.

This dogma has important methodological consequences, including frequent recourse to statistical comparison of favelas as a whole with the rest of the city. The SAGMACS study began this practice, though it was accompanied by case studies attentive to the differences among the favelas. Many researchers, however, have reproduced the procedures without considering the differences among the favelas. If one compares the favelas as a whole to the rest of the city, the differences among the favelas are not considered, nor are those differences that demarcate social spaces within them, when, in fact, differences within and among favelas cannot be ignored (Préteceille and Valladares 1999, 2000). Moreover, the differences in "the rest of the city" are not considered, even though they are considerable — for example, between the South Zone (especially Copacabana, Ipanema, Leblon, and Barra da Tijuca) and the working-class neighborhoods of the periphery (Préteceille and Ribeiro 1999; Ribeiro 2000). Thus the methodological choice that compared the favela with the nonfavela led Luiz César de Queiroz Ribeiro and Luciana Lago (2000) to conclude that there was a dualization in the city of Rio de Janeiro, because of a growing distance between the favelas and the rest of the city, attributed to the accentuation of social exclusion concentrated in the favelas. Meanwhile, a more detailed study of changes in social segregation showed that it was the wealthier neighborhoods that were distancing themselves from the average of the others, with favelas showing developments quite close to the other working- and middle-class neighborhoods, whose evolution also was not homogeneous (Préteceille and Ribeiro 1999; Ribeiro 2000).

The Favela of the Social Sciences

CHAPTER FOUR

CONCLUSION

The Favela, the Web, and the Census — A Disconcerting Reality

Today the constructed, coherent vision of the favelas, a result of articulation of the three dogmas I discussed in chapter 3, collides with an emergent complex and disconcerting reality, one resistant to reductive categorization. This reality can be clearly detected through various channels.

WWW.ROCINHA.COM.BR: WHAT SPECIFICITY?

Rio's favelas have become part of a virtual reality. Examples include the numerous websites for NGOs, social assistance or welfare programs, news outlets, samba schools, tourist agencies that operate in favelas, and even hostels. The target audience for these sites includes more than simply domestic internet surfers. A number of the sites have pages in English, French, or German, with photographs and videos, allowing the world outside access to the world of the favelas. Today the favela represents a much more diverse reality than that of the favela at its birth that I discussed in chapter 1.

By 1999 the TV Rocinha (TV-ROC) website was announced from the top of a five-story building in Rocinha, visible to all who passed through the Dois Irmãos Tunnel, which links the elegant districts of São Conrado and Barra da Tijuca to Leblon, Ipanema, and Copacabana in Rio's South Zone. One had only to click in one's browser to access information about the location and history of Rocinha, about projects under way, and about other initiatives. Also available were articles from the local newspaper *Correio da Zona Sul*. This site, created in 1997 as an initiative of TV-ROC, the cable television provider for the favela, clearly announced: "Rocinha is a veritable melting pot. Everything that you could imagine happens here. There are people to talk with and institutions to visit. All of this online, edited to take you to complete information about Rocinha and other needy communities in Brazil today."

A monthly cable subscription, providing access to forty-two channels, cost R$25.00 plus R$50.00 to join (2005 prices; approximately $10.00 and $20.00 respectively). Intended exclusively for Rocinha residents, TV-ROC reached 30,000 homes, whose families' monthly income ranged between R$800.00 and R$1,000.00. The minimum monthly wage in Brazil in 2005 was R$260.00 (slightly more than $100.00).

If cable television gave Rocinha residents access to images and events from an increasingly globalized world, the TV-ROC website informed the world about Rocinha and its people and activities. In 1999, the TV-ROC website counted about 1,500 visitors per month, of whom a majority were from the United States. That same year, TV-ROC posted the results of a survey it conducted with class C and D consumers (corresponding, broadly, to the working poor): the powdered detergent used by most was the international brand Omo and the most popular brands for television sets—97 percent of those surveyed—were Phillips and Sony.

In addition to cable television, other features reveal the integration of this vast built space into local, national, and global economic and commercial circuits. On entering Rocinha, one may be surprised to see a McDonald's franchise, open day and night, which in April 2000 had the highest ice cream sales in Rio de Janeiro; three branches of the photographic supply store De Plá, three points of sale for cellular telephones—Nokia and other brands; a profusion of video clubs; bank branches; and a post office. One also finds modern bakeries, pizza home delivery, a wine store, private parking, and so on. International NGOs have also established activities there. They offer computer courses for young people and others; and Viva-Cred finances local merchants without requiring the usual collateral needed for traditional bank loans.[1]

The typical profile of the local businessperson was studied by the Serviço Brasileiro de Apoio às Micro e Pequenas Empresas (SEBRAE): he or she is between thirty and forty years of age, has a secondary school education, and set up business with his or her own resources (605 of the cases) or with the help of family members (10 percent). To coordinate local commercial interests, an Associação Comercial e Industrial do Bairro (Neighborhood Chamber of Commerce and Industry) was established. That major credit cards—Visa, Credicard, American Express—are accepted attests to the purchasing power of the local population in domestic and international consumer markets.

Private medical services and clinics, including a center for medical tests such as ultrasound echography, preoperative prevention, clinical analysis laboratories, dentists, and specialists such as gynecologists receive patients in the favela. There is even a veterinarian. Law offices specializing in penal and labor law are here. In Rocinha, the eight real estate agencies negotiate rentals for residential and commercial use, the largest of which was managing 1,500 contracts. The crucial problem of transportation is solved by a private bus line (with 120 buses) and by *moto-táxis* (about 200, of the two-wheeled motorcycle or scooter sort, serving Rocinha from seven stands).[2] A telephone taxi company has headquarters there, with service to all of Rio's South Zone neighborhoods. A local entrepreneur also had the idea of creating a school bus service for families wanting to ensure the safety of their children in transit to public schools.

The discovery of the favela by the professional tourism sector seems to have been a sign of integration into the market economy: Rocinha is visited by around 2,000 tourists per month.[3] For $30.00 (in 2005 prices), a jeep will pick up visitors at the hotel and take them on a three-hour tour with an English-, French-, or Spanish-speaking guide, first by vehicle, then on foot. For the tourists to visit daycare centers, schools, or residents' associations, they must make a donation directly to the site visited. The success of this new activity puts it on the same level as an excursion to Tijuca Forest, Corcovado, or Santa Teresa. More recently, another group has started to exploit this source of social tourism. A plan to train local guides, all residents, took shape in a Tourism Workshop. The trainees learn English and the geography and history of Rocinha, the better to show tourists this area that does not match the dominant image of a bastion of the drug trade. The guides show tourists where they can take pictures, and take them to places that sell local crafts.

Tourism initiatives have multiplied, and this list could be greatly extended.[4] The fact is that the favelas cannot be reduced simply to the habitat of Rio's poor. They have also become a great marketplace, which for some of the social actors is a synonym for "business." The land and the homes are among the primary goods that give rise to energetic development of production and commercial activity. On land that was not theirs, many residents have managed to build their own home, along with a second, perhaps a third, and maybe even a fourth, to rent or sell. Indeed, it is possible to sell one's roof slab as if were a vacant lot. Thus real estate transactions have created a market parallel to the one run by the city's clerks and notaries. Alongside this very busy real estate rental and sales market has developed an enormous market for modern services to meet the increasingly diverse demands of a public that consumes products directly or indirectly linked to globalization. Among these "modern" consumer goods, illicit drugs claim the most attention, mainly because of the violent practices associated with the trade. But drug sales are directed mostly to outside the favela, thus one cannot reduce the favela economy to the drug economy. Many other economic activities have arisen there, perhaps less spectacular than the communications media discussed earlier, but in their economic structures, they are still engines of change and signifiers of transformation.

In the face of this development and the reality of daily life (of which Rocinha is only one example; other favelas, such as Parque União and Morro do Timbau in Complexo da Maré, as well as Vidigal, Borel, and Complexo do Alemão, also show similar characteristics), it is hard to make an analysis work that is based on the dogmas I outlined in chapter 3. Of what specificity are we speaking? Where, exactly, does the rupture with the city lie? Is it possible to think of a local entrepreneur as poor? The social differences between this supposed "poor" businessperson and his or her unemployed neighbor stand in the way of any possible amalgamation that allows one to think of the favelas' population as a single social category. Abject poverty is not, or at least no longer is, a general or immediately perceivable characteristic. The precariousness of the structures and facilities has to be relativized.

THE CENSUS AS A REVEALER OF DIVERSITY

Census data also call into question the excessively homogenizing view of the favelas. The data are revealing: no homogeneity, no favela specificity, no unity among them, and, in the case of the larger ones, no unity within them. Studies we conducted after the 1991 census (Préteceille and Valladares 1999, 2000) demonstrated that, contrary to the dominant view, favelas showed evident signs of heterogeneity in their physical, spatial, and social reality, to the point that it became impossible to align them within a unique, distinct category. Among the total of 10,542 census sectors in the Rio de Janeiro Metropolitan Area, the 1,291 sectors (12 percent of the whole) considered favela sectors by the IBGE were compared to all of the nonfavela sectors, based on a tripartite typology: urban infrastructure (water, sewer, and trash collection), settlement (of buildings and of land), and educational level and income of the head of household. The study discovered that, even though the favelas were more present in certain frequency distribution ranges in the three typological dimensions, the favelas were also found in reasonable proportions in all other ranges, except for the highest.

The supposed homogeneity of Rio's favelas was not confirmed in any of the three dimensions — infrastructure, status of settlement, or social status. As for specificity, some indeed have distinct characteristics with respect to urban infrastructure, but a good portion of the favela sectors are distributed similarly to many nonfavela sectors. As concerns abject poverty and the lowest range of social and urban indicators, the study showed that these, in fact, characterize a part of the space of the favela but only a part. Conditions of abject poverty are also a feature of significant number of nonfavela sectors, such as parcels in the urban periphery, poor districts, and so forth. There is no doubt that the number of favelas outside the municipality of Rio de Janeiro were underestimated, as a result of the absence of registration in the remaining municipalities in the metropolitan area. As I have noted, only the Rio municipality's Pereira Passos Institute (formerly IPLAN-RIO) has been carrying out a systematic survey in this regard. Moreover, the distinction between favela and nonfavela is much harder to make in the poor parts of the periphery. If we are to speak of a hypothesis of the favelas' identity, we should prefer a version more limited to their violent contrast with the middle- and upper-class neighborhoods that are nearby or even adjacent, rather than other characteristics. What stands out, then, is physical proximity alongside social distance.[5] Today, however, even this identification presents problems. The IBGE definition of the favela as a "subnormal cluster" nowadays would exclude a large part of the territory of Rocinha and of other favelas.

IN WHOSE INTEREST IS THE PERMANENCE OF DOGMAS?

Why could it be, then, that recent changes, more than evident and confirmed by recent censuses, have not shaken these dogmas? How does one explain the resistance of their defenders? Is there some interest in having them persist? At what point might their persistence in the collective imagination bring benefits to the favelas and their inhabitants?

It is true that social tourism depends on an exotic image; it is true that journalists, the media, and writers prefer this rather fascinating view of a universe — marginal, different, with local particularities. It is also possible that other social groups have an interest in the image of the favela not changing so soon.

Those responsible for public policies. Those responsible for public policies have always maintained the specificity of the world of the favela. Very different programs, from the removal of favelas and their residents to the urbanization of the favelas, have begun with the same premise: illegally occupied spaces, outside the norms and underdeveloped, must be the object of special measures. If this were not so, how would one justify a specific policy for these spaces? How does one legitimate a whole arsenal of technical instruments and procedures, specialized legislation, alternative measures, and "solutions" that, at different times, have been developed by different agencies?

What argument would be better than the specificity of the favela to justify a large-scale policy? It would be much more "appropriate" to work with one category, "the favela," with reference to consensual standards based on simple, shared criteria and definitions. Even though there are differences among and within favelas, and given that the government is not unaware of this, it is always more effective to have in view a homogeneous target to which special ad hoc programs, able to solve well-identified social problems and uncontested by either the base or the politicians, will apply exactly. From this comes the interest in a uniform postulate about the favela, from which it is possible to quickly and easily deduce the homogeneity of its inhabitants, privileging their dominant characteristics. The permanence of the expression "low-income population," used from the time of the BNH (established in 1964) up to the time of the Programa Favela-Bairro, attests to this tendency. Despite the favela residents' different manners of participation in the labor market (as wage earners, self-employed, or workers in the informal sector), whether they received regular or occasional, low or middle income; whether they paid rent or were property owners; whether they were illiterate or college graduates, they would always be assimilated into one group: "the poor." However, do the political and operational objectives justify the construction of a unitary group, as a "whole"?

Associations, NGOs, and the map of poverty. Public officials and technical staff are not the only ones who think of the favela as the specific territory of poverty. Despite a long history that has alternated between opposition to and cooperation with government, residents' associations have used the same argument of specificity. In order to qualify the collection of residents that they represent, the directors of these associations use the term "community," which shows the desire to replace the term "favela" — considered pejorative — with a positive idea. The use of "community" legitimates their own status as representatives invested by the collection of residents, but it also hides all the differences and conflicts among diverse spaces and inhabitants. The notion of community presupposes the idea of unity, which has not always been a feature of these associations or of the territories they represent. Thus it masks the diversity of social situations and the multiplicity of interests present in a structure more often atomized than communal.

Let us not forget that, in Rio's political tradition, aid to the poor has yielded votes, and that the residents' associations have always played a role in this game, as *A favela e o demagogo* (The favela and the demagogue; Medina

Conclusion

1964) and *Voto e máquina política* (Vote and political machine; Diniz 1982) have clearly shown. Politicians continue to use the clientelistic *bica d'água* (water tap) tradition, in which votes are traded for benefits to a person or to the whole neighborhood. Even the more recent Programa Favela-Bairro did not escape this practice.

When the residents' associations reaffirm the specificity of the areas they represent, they, in their role as mediators, are underscoring the residents' precarious status in regard to the legal status of their land tenure, of their city services, and of their citizenship. To ensure the assistance that evidently they need, the associations ceaselessly project the image of "needy community." The favelas are always lacking in everything because they are fragmentary, unfinished spaces, dependent on aid from public agencies and others, to which they must resort. That said, one cannot help but wonder if association leaders' insistence on "need," which is part of the game in defense of their interests, does not end up being reinforced by the practices of the residents. Proof of this is that the residents often invest last in improvements to the external appearance of their homes, prolonging the perception that they are precarious dwellings, whereas the comfort of the interior has progressed considerably.[6]

NGOs are also part of this cast of social actors that offer to the collective imaginary this representation of the favela and participate actively in its maintenance. Much closer to "the poor" than many other institutions, since their headquarters or branches operate in the favela itself, they pick up the discourse of the residents' associations, continuing to insist on the notion of "community" and its connotations of unity, solidarity, and cohesion. Often these organizations have specific clienteles—women, children, youth, Black residents, and so forth—and particular domains of activity, but they always highlight a more global vision that emphasizes the excluded, the victims of violence, female heads of households, for example, as segments of poverty. A globalizing discourse that opposes "the poor" to everyone else can only continue to produce a view of uniformity.

Even though the NGOs themselves constitute a heterogeneous group, in that they are not all defined by the same beliefs or ideologies, or by the same target population, all of them use a discourse of poverty to justify their existence.[7] In the case of foreign organizations, especially from European and North American countries that want to help the Third World, this discourse is an indispensable resource for ensuring flow of funding necessary for the continuation of their work. To the extent that they represent socially engaged civil society and fulfill partnership agreements with Brazilian governments, without a doubt, the NGOs provide important services to "communities in need." But in so doing, they reinforce a reductive representation of the favela as a place of poverty and a specific social space.

The importance attributed to the identification of the favelas with the question of urban poverty ended up becoming a double-edged sword regarding the defense of the less fortunate. The representation of the favelas as the space of the poor par excellence, although it has brought to favelas some benefits, has also cast a shadow on other sectors of the city, quite numerous and perhaps even needier, that are lacking in public investment, such as irregular subdivisions, poor suburbs, or certain degraded areas closer to the central districts.

In April 1999, the Pereira Passos Institute registered 604 favelas as well as 783 irregular subdivisions and 508 housing complexes. In the absence of a specific indication of these last two categories in the census, we do not know the numbers of their populations or residences, but we can see that their weight is considerable.

And researchers? A systematic review of the literature clearly shows that a majority of researchers accept these dogmas, though there are exceptions (Valladares and Medeiros 2003). Scholars, however, should be the first to reject such reductive views. Even if these representations have certain beneficial effects within an activist logic in support of residents' demands, they also can conceal or codify social problems, which is much less beneficial.

The reasons why these dogmas persist seem to be attributable to four stances. The first is based on an analysis of Brazil's academic history. As Pécaut has noted, generations of Brazilian intellectuals have been convinced of their responsibility to make social problems evident by critiquing the functioning of the state and suggesting solutions. At an early stage, a broad field of research was precisely identified and described. However, the search for regularities, similarities, and specificities led to the construction of a set, circumscribed, operational domain, and once this categorization was established, it became very difficult to break with it.

The dual participation of many Brazilian researchers in academics and activism certainly explains the difficulty that many experience in establishing nuances, especially when addressing a public that prefers simplified or simple-minded versions characteristic of both politics and the media. The researcher is therefore led to simplify to meet their demands.

Generally, it is hard to question oneself, and it is harder still to deconstruct a category or system of categorization that one had a role in constructing. Thus dismantlement is a risky operation that one often does not dare undertake.

The second reason for the persistence of these dogmas is pragmatism: re-

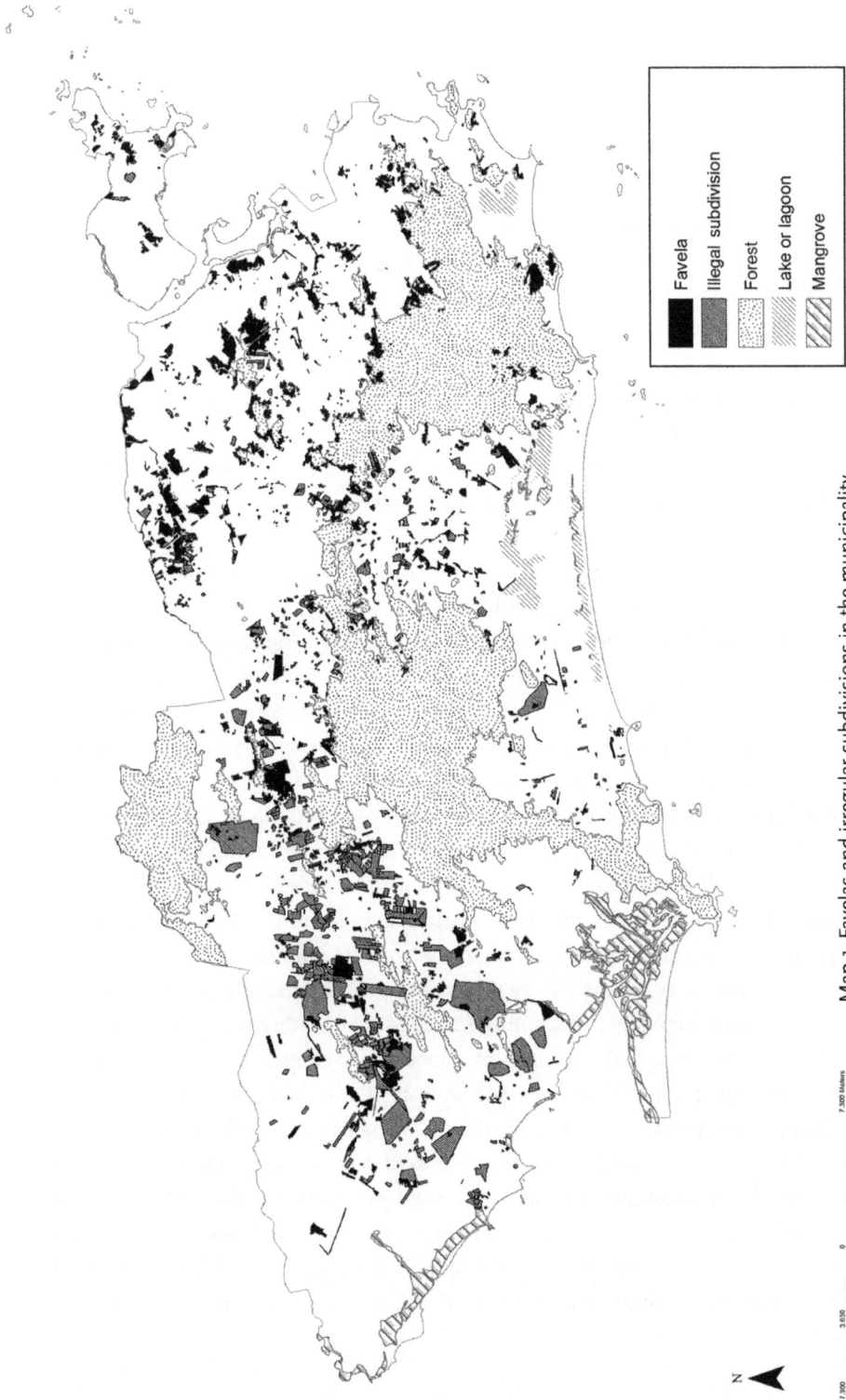

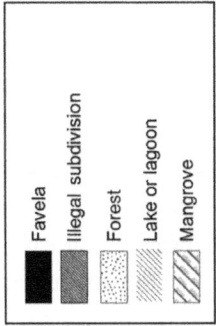

Map 1. Favelas and irregular subdivisions in the municipality of Rio de Janeiro, 2012 (Pereira Passos Institute).

■	Favela
▦	Illegal subdivision
⋰	Forest
	Lake or lagoon
▨	Mangrove

Mapmaker: Ísis Martins - IPP/DIC

N

7.300   3.650   0   7.300 Meters

searching the favela is good business. Researchers agree that it is much easier to obtain funding when the sponsor shares one's categories of perception and analysis. Once we have taken into account the reductive position of the funding agencies, we can understand why so many proposals are based on postulates accepted by those who fund the work. However, one has to bear in mind the structuring (and tranquilizing) nature of these dogmas. The researcher who navigates familiar waters runs little risk of running aground. Working with tested categories facilitates the repetition and accumulation of data. There will always be time to debate them later.

Finally, researchers are often professors and, to get a message across to students, it is sometimes more effective to simplify it. As a field of investigation, the favela seems to many professors a privileged site, especially for their students' monographs. It is the most economical way to "expatriate" middle-class master's and doctoral students, and it is also a way to confront them with "difference" and help them carry out their first field experiences in the familiar. The monographs that match the current sort are a way of collecting plenty of data without having to establish comparisons that might destabilize the thinking and investigation of the neophyte researcher.

The third reason poses the question of ideology. In Brazil, the tradition of engaged sociology necessarily places value on studies about categories of the "popular," citizenship, social exclusion, inequalities, and everything that has to do with "community." An analysis of dogmas enables one, by means of the proposed categories, to stress positively the specificity of the favelas and to show the "communities" of the favelas as locations for developing a different culture, with its own resources, values, and codes. In short, studying the favelas and believing in the dogmas is a "politically correct" procedure that brings two dimensions together—the intellectual (studying something that is different and valuing it) and the activist (helping those who are stigmatized).

The fourth reason is fed by international academic competition. The favela, as constructed by the dogmas is a relatively easy theoretical "instrument" to sell in international comparisons since it perfectly both matches and reinforces the current dominant perception of the dualizing phenomena induced by the processes of globalization—a dualization of urban metropolises, of societies, and of the present. In urban sociology, more precisely in the sociology of social segregation, the favela matches a certain reading of reality that is both original, since it is defined in a precise local context, and a "product for export." By seeming evident, the category "favela" constructed by the dogmas is even more seductive, to the extent that it appears usable in other contexts, even some very different ones.

And what about the future? From "PhD in favela" to "PhD from the favela." Questioning the dogmas is an obligatory step toward a real renewal in studies not only about favelas but about poverty, urban segregation, and the consequences of urbanization. This reflection may also be influenced by the rise of a new type of actor: a person from the favela who holds a college degree. An issue of *Veja* magazine published in October 1999 shows on the cover a resident of Maré who had just defended his doctoral dissertation in social sciences at PUC.[8] In his dissertation, about young *favelados* who had had access to higher education, Jailson de Souza e Silva analyzed the trajectory and life stories of eleven favela residents who had earned advanced degrees and had begun careers while continuing to live in the favela. Thus there might be another career open to *favelados* besides drug trafficking, as I have observed in a study of children and youths in Rocinha (Valladares 1991).

This trajectory of these residents, though it is certainly atypical, presents a new question for the social sciences in Brazil: the need to develop a sociology of social mobility, to this day underrepresented in the research.[9] Development of this thematic area would allow us to abandon the category constructed by the dogmas and would let the complex process of social differentiation taking place in Brazil, including in the favelas, emerge clearly. It is possible to be poor and not live in a favela, and it is possible to reside in a favela and believe in a chance for upward social mobility.

If we stop confusing the social processes observed in the favela with the social processes caused by the favela, we will be able to understand phenomena that, although they indeed appear in favelas, are also manifest in other places. In other words, to the extent that certain problems are no longer studied exclusively in the favelas, they will take on another dimension. My proposal is that the favelas no longer be the field systematically used for the most diverse questions concerning poverty. This is the only way we will cease to confuse the favela with poverty.

EPILOGUE

This book was written during the late 1990s and early 2000s, based on thirty years of research on favelas and an extensive bibliography covering the twentieth century. There is little to add regarding the historical analysis of the debates and the production of representations of the favela beyond the additional references mentioned in the previous chapters. But a lot has happened over the last decade, in terms of public policies as well as academic production; therefore, it is worth providing the reader with an update about those recent developments.

Due to the absence of a comprehensive bibliography such as the one I had built with URBANDATA for previous periods, I shall only present here a selection of what I think are the most representative academic publications and themes being debated, leaving aside the detailed description of recent public policies, for which there is an extensive literature, and the systematic analysis of media representations, a production that has become so important and diverse that it would require a specific research program.

Favelas may be more than a century old, but they have continued to expand, and did so quite substantially during the first decade of the twenty-first century. In the municipality of Rio de Janeiro, from 2000 to 2010, the number of favelas grew from 752 to 1,022, and their population from 1.1 to 1.4 million, a 27 percent increase, while the rest of the city only grew 4 percent. Outside the municipality, in the rest of the metropolitan area, the population in favelas doubled, but from a modest figure in 2000, thus the bulk of the increase took place within Rio.

This expansion of favelas was not evenly distributed, and it is changing the traditional pattern of the historical favelas mainly concentrated near the center of the city and the affluent neighborhoods south of the center and along the beaches. Already in the previous period major favelas like the Complexo da

Maré or the Complexo do Alemão developed in the city's North Zone. During the first decade of the twenty-first century, the greatest expansion took place again in the North Zone, but above all in the western and northwestern parts, in neighborhoods like Jacarepaguá, Barra da Tijuca, Guaratiba, Campo Grande, and Santa Cruz (Cavallieri and Vial 2012).

The academic production on favelas has also continued to grow considerably. Most of it comes from young authors, who form a new generation of specialists. As in the previous period, they come from many disciplines; I see contributions from sociologists, anthropologists, geographers, planners, historians, architects, lawyers, social workers, and journalists. A new type of contribution is coming from favela inhabitants writing about their own experience (e.g., Dudu de Morro Agudo 2010; Júnior 2011; Fiell 2011; Torquato da Silva 2012; E. S. Silva 2012; Andarilho 2014). Testimonies from *favelados* have been published by Dulce Pandolfi and Mário Grynspan (2003). There are also essays by actors engaged in the new public policies, especially those regarding security, such as the heads of the police and the armed forces who reflect about their practice (M. Duarte 2012; Beltrame 2014; R. Rodrigues 2014). Some of the recent academic seminars have been organized with the participation of the police force (Cano, Borges, and Ribeiro 2012).

As in the previous period, the vast majority of favela studies are qualitative case studies, with few comparative studies or quantitative studies. Many of these contributions, whether from "old" or "new" researchers, continue to focus on a limited number of favelas: Complexo do Alemão (Alves, Evanson, and Moura 2013; C. Machado 2013), Cantagalo (Castro et al. 2011; Moraes 2011), Santa Marta (Cunha and Mello 2012; Fleury 2012; Freire-Medeiros, Vilarouca, and Menezes 2012; Menezes 2015), Manguinhos (Fernandes and Costa 2009; Gutierrez et al. 2010; Cavalcanti 2013), Morro da Providência (Menezes 2009; A. Rodrigues 2012), Pavão-Pavãozinho (Moraes 2011), Rio das Pedras (Paiva and Burgos 2009; Telles 2009; L. Farias 2002), Borel (M. C. A. Silva 2013; M. B. Carvalho 2014), Maré (P. Lopes 2011; C. Mattos 2006, 2014), Acari (Dias 2009; C. Cunha 2015), Rocinha (Leitão 2009; Letalien 2009), and Cidade de Deus (Tommasi 2014).

A few favelas not studied previously have been subjects of publications, like those of Parque Royal (A. F. Magalhães 2013), Pereirão (L. Rocha 2013), Morro dos Macacos (Piccolo 2006), and Batan (Mendonça 2014).

None of the new or rapidly expanding favelas in the western and northwestern parts of the city have been considered by this new literature, with one exception, Vila Autódromo in Jacarepaguá (A. A. Magalhães 2013), which has drawn attention because it is a new case of demolition, related to the redevelopment of the area for the Olympic Games, and because of active social movements against the demolition.

The above remarks are based on my identification of academic publications since 2000, which could not be as systematic as our URBANDATA survey (Valladares and Medeiros 2003). I was able, however, do a more limited systematic search of the UERJ database for master's and doctoral dissertations. Between 2000 and 2014, it showed 50 new cases of fieldwork in favelas. Only 12 were presented in the Department of Social Sciences; the others were presented in the Departments of Psychology and Social Psychology (12), Social Communication–Journalism (5), Geography (5), Social Medicine (4), Social Service (4), Public Policy (2), Law (2), Education (2), History (1), and Arts (1). The favelas most studied were Mangueira (9), which is next to UERJ and is home to a university NGO; Maré (6); Rocinha (5); and Complexo do Alemão (3). These works dealt with a variety of subjects: youth association with violence and way of life, public policies associated with violence and the Unidades de Polícia Pacificadora (UPPs), and public policies associated with community nurseries. It is worth mentioning that public policies have been discussed by different disciplines, including social work, psychology, social medicine, history, geography, law, and social communication–journalism. It is also noticeable that 33 of those 50 dissertations were defended from 2010 onward, two years after the first UPP was established.

This partial survey confirms my analysis in chapter 3. Case studies constitute the majority of studies, they tend to focus on a limited sample of favelas, and new public policies regarding favelas have a stimulating effect on the academic production.

The most prominent theme in the last period has been, indeed, that of violence and public security policy, not only UPPs (Machado da Silva 2008; Leite and Machado da Silva 2013) but also urban violence more generally (Bill and Athayde 2006; Leite 2009; Perlman 2010; Alves, Evanson, and Moura 2013; J. Farias 2014), and the issue of the *milicias* (illicit militias; Cano and Duarte 2012). Violence is a theme that had already been present in the study of favelas since the end of the 1980s and the increasing power of drug-dealing gangs (Zaluar 1989, 1999, 2004). Luke Dowdney (2003) has published a map of Rio's favelas according to the dominant gang controlling them, the main gangs being Comando Vermelho, Comando Vermelho Jovem, Terceiro Comando, and Amigos dos Amigos. Because the police were absent from those areas, because the physical structure of the favelas made them easier for the gangs to control, and because several were located near affluent areas where many drug customers came from, drug dealers made them into strongholds with heavy weapons and a tight control of social life. This situation was also the result of the passivity of public authorities, partly due to corruption (not only of the police: drug dealers are known to have funded the campaigns of several politicians). Drug dealing flourished, as did violent street crime, due to the proliferation of guns. Confrontations between gangs and the police produced more and more casualties. The prejudice against *favelados* tends to liken them to bandits.

In 2008, the government of the state of Rio de Janeiro launched the UPP program, establishing special police stations inside favelas to reconquer those territories from the armed power of drug dealers and develop a new form of neighborhood policing that would keep the dealers out and build new trust with the resident population.[1] The strategy of pacification includes a first stage of military occupation, a second one of installation of a permanent police force, and a third one that aims to establish a dialogue among social actors and convey their demands to authorities—this being done by the associated program UPP Social (now called Rio+Social). Unlike previous public interventions against drug gangs, when the police went into the favela, caught or killed a few dealers, and then went back down to their stations, the UPP policy aimed to establish a permanent police presence. Because the police have been recognized as brutal and corrupt, a specially trained new type of police was supposed to be deployed in the UPPs. Unlike with previous policies, all this should work through a partnership between the federal government, the state of Rio, the municipality of Rio, local business associations, and the various civil society social actors.

As of March 2016, there were UPPs in thirty-eight favelas. The policy has attracted a lot of attention from the media—the military occupation of Complexo do Alemão with armored tanks and heavy weapons was filmed by TV Globo like a Hollywood war movie—and from scholars in the social sciences.

In 2010 Machado da Silva wrote a provocative article that was posted on several sites. He pointed out positive aspects of UPPs: they constitute an innovative form of crime repression; they have had generally good results in that respect; the arbitrariness and violence of police vis-à-vis residents, although not yet eliminated, are more limited in favelas where there are UPPs; their presence has improved the inhabitants' feeling of security; the media, by insisting on the goals of UPPs, has created an expectation of security for all sectors of the city's population.

But Machado da Silva also argued that a public policy should not be evaluated as just "good" or "bad." More precise analytical methods of evaluation are needed, with various criteria that should include democracy. He pointed out particularly that it would be very difficult, considering the history of the military police, to inculcate in them respect for and a civilized relationship with the local residents. He noted that the UPPs diminished the power of the existent residents' associations and gave a strong role to the chief of the UPP without any local control, thus transforming the responsibility for repression of crime into a political responsibility. He also noted that the establishment of a UPP in one favela might just cause drug dealers to migrate to other favelas.

Machado da Silva's critical questioning started a controversy, particularly with those who enthusiastically supported the new policy. Further events seemed to validate his negative predictions. There were increasing numbers of reports of corruption of police members, of violence against inhabitants, and of invasions of homes without a warrant. There were several cases of torture and assassination, some ending with the arrest of police officers and officials, and in one case even the head of a UPP. This is the famous case of Amarildo, a mason from Rocinha who disappeared in 2013 after being taken by the UPP police; a strong mobilization followed, with a campaign on Facebook and other social networks, *Onde está o Amarildo?* (Where is Amarildo?). The head of the UPP and twelve policemen were convicted of torture and assassination in February 2016.

After campaigning for several years in favor of the UPPs and underrepresenting their problems, Rio's daily *O Globo* gradually changed its position and now regularly publishes accounts of such police misconduct and crime. The return of drug trafficking and drug dealers has also been reported in most favelas. UPP Social, which was supposed to accompany the UPPs with social projects and public and private funding to stimulate "social inclusion" and decrease the attractiveness of criminal activities for the young, seems to have failed with time (Fleury 2012).

If these events tend to validate Machado da Silva's concerns, other contributions have yielded a different evaluation of the changes. One example is a study of the impacts of UPPs on crime by Ignacio Cano, Doriam Borges, and Eduardo Ribeiro (2012). It shows that in the favelas with UPPs, lethal violence decreased considerably, including that caused by the police, which went down to almost zero. The same decrease was experienced in areas surrounding favelas with UPPs. Other researchers have shown that lethal crime also decreased in parallel in the city as a whole (Rocha and Borges 2014).

Another example is research undertaken by the Instituto de Estudos da Religião (ISER) in different favelas of Rio, Batan, Borel, Providência, and Tabajaras, in the years 2010 and 2011 to look at practices and perceptions in everyday life (Rodrigues and Siqueira 2012). There were major positive conclusions:

residents evaluated very positively the (almost) permanent ceasefire and the continuous presence of the police; they experienced positive changes in the attitude of the police; they valued positively also the greater liberty to move in and out of the favela as well as to receive visits from outside. But other aspects were not so positive: the UPP Social, which, together with the UPP, was meant to be the center of a network of institutions, private and public, did not work well; there were too many partners and limited results. The results also show that the situation differs from one favela with UPPs to the other, and that this diversity should be considered to avoid hasty generalizations.

One question was posed by observers and inhabitants: Would UPPs survive after the Olympic Games? The UPP policy was part of preparations for the 2014 World Cup and 2016 Olympic Games, in order to ensure that they could take place safely. But there had been previous experiences in Rio when the military or police occupied favelas to guarantee the success of major international events, only to abandon them shortly afterward. The present economic situation in Brazil and in Rio and the massive corruption exposed by Operação Lava Jato (Operation Car Wash, the inquiry into the Petrobras scandal) are a disaster for the public budget, the state of Rio is bankrupt, and public education and public health services are half-paralyzed by spending cuts. Favela residents had a terrible fear of drug lords returning to take power in favelas with the possible demise of UPPs, previous episodes having led to bloody retaliation by the gangs. They were right: the collapse of public policies in Rio has paralyzed the police, in UPPs and elsewhere. The drug dealers have retaken control of most favelas where they had business, with a vengeance and heavy weapons, and favela residents now live in the midst of a war: there are daily confrontations between police and drug dealers, as well as between the different gangs competing to expand their dominion, taking advantage of the weakness of public authorities. On 1 February 2018, *O Globo* counted a total of 640 gun fights in Rio during the first month of 2018 alone, many of them in favelas, where every day people die as collateral damage of those confrontations. Recently, the authorities in charge of security for the state of Rio de Janeiro have declared that they may cut the number of UPPs by half.

Although violence and UPPs have become the major topic of discussion, other public policies continue to attract some attention, particularly those related to efforts to urbanize favelas, that is, to provide them with infrastructure and public services more similar to those in "normal" urban areas. In that respect, Rio de Janeiro has become a laboratory of public policies (Gonçalves 2013). The removal policy (1962–74, namely by CHISAM) was followed by Pro-Morar (which implemented Projeto Rio in 1979), the program of electrification of favelas (which started in 1979), the Projeto Mutirão (a self-help program in 1982). Then in 1983 came the program Cada Família um Lote, together with Proface (a program to provide water to favela households), a program of CEDAE, the state of Rio de Janeiro's energy and sanitation regulating agency. Considerable discussion of land regularization and the constitution of 1988, followed by the Estatuto da Cidade in 2001, opened up the possibility of redefining the sociojuridical status of favelas and changing the social function of land ownership (Gonçalves 2013), reorienting public policies away from the removal of favelas. A series of local policies followed in Rio, namely Favela-Bairro, Bairrinho, Morar Carioca, Pouso, and so on.

The most recent initiative from the federal government is the Programa de Aceleração do Crescimento (PAC) launched in 2007 (Cavalcanti 2013).[2] Quite a number of favelas benefited from the PAC, particularly Complexo do Alemão, Morro do Borel, and Manguinhos (in Rio's North Zone) as well as Rocinha, Cantagalo, Morro da Babilônia, Chapeu Mangueira, and Santa Marta (in the South Zone). These favelas received a lot of funding, especially for infrastructure and services. In the Complexo do Alemão, a cable car serving seven favelas was built as well as a *unidade de pronto atendimento* (UPA) urgent care center and some social housing. In Morro do Borel, a favela known for its strong *favelado* movement, there was a general urbanization process with the building of public spaces, paving of streets, building of a sewage system, and so forth. In Manguinhos, a favela known for its violence, a large square was inaugurated, with a UPA, a big, modern library, and a metro station (Cavalcanti 2013). In Rocinha, the biggest favela in the South Zone, the investments went to a sports center, a pedestrian bridge across the highway (designed by Oscar Niemeyer), a health center, a new area totally restructured with social housing, an ecological park, and a modern library. In other favelas of the South Zone, Morro do Cantagalo gained a modern elevator with direct access to the Praça General Osório metro station, together with a system of paved staircases and social housing. In Morro da Babilônia and Morro do Chapeu Mangueira, the same type of staircases and social housing were built. In Santa Marta, the first favela to have a UPP, an elevator was built together with social housing, and garbage removal was organized for a part of the favela.

The PAC projects (and the previous programs, such as Favela-Bairro) have brought improvements to the everyday life of inhabitants of those favelas, all the more so because in most cases the PAC was accompanied by a UPP. However, it has been argued that the recipient favelas were mostly those whose improvements contributed to wider urban improvements needed for the World Cup and the Olympics. Favelas further from the strategic areas received little

Figure 11. View of Rocinha, showing public works of the
Growth Acceleration Program, 2011 (Photo by Licia Valladares).

or no improvement, and the lack of basic urban infrastructure in areas of rapid, uncontrolled urban expansion is having very negative consequences, such the present epidemics of dengue, zika, and chikungunya in areas where the lack of sewage and garbage disposal leads to the proliferation of mosquitoes.

Some negative effects also have been noted in recipient favelas, such as the increase in rents and housing prices. Although the discussions of "gentrification" in favelas such as Vidigal and Santa Marta seem excessive, it is the case that these price increases are pushing the poorest residents out of those favelas.

We should note that throughout these programs, the issue of land regularization was not touched and remains an unsolved problem, maintaining a precarious status for favelas and their inhabitants. Some authors have also argued that the policy of consolidation is only partial, and that the rhetoric and practice of removal remain a significant element of public policies regarding favelas (A. A. Magalhães 2013).

Public institutions are not the only actors contributing to the changes in living conditions in the favelas. NGOs, already quite numerous and active in the previous period, have multiplied and diversified their activities (Pandolfi and Grynspan 2000). Several NGOs are of great importance, especially Viva

Rio and its subsidiary Viva Favela, Observatório de Favelas and Redes (both in Maré, originating from CEASM), AfroReggae, Central Única de Favelas (CUFA), Agência de Notícias das Favelas, and Nós do Morro.[3] I have already mentioned some in chapter 3 that date back to the 1990s.

Most of these NGOs and their projects are Brazilian and seek to rehabilitate the image of the favelas. They are led by public figures who come from the favelas — many of them with university degrees or attending university who appear in the press and the media now and then (see the recent book published by Luís Erlanger, *José Júnior no fio da navalha* [José Júnior on the razor's edge], 2015). Some of the NGOs have grown nationally and internationally; most of their websites are well designed; some publish news on the favelas through local journalism (C. Ramalho 2007); some have bulletins, printed or online, telling about local events and publishing advertisements for jobs and courses. Some NGOs have had books written about them (Platt and Neate 2008; A. Fernandes 2014). Some do research (*Guia de ruas Maré* 2012; Barbosa and Dias 2013). Most of them receive funding from Petrobras (at least they did until the recent corruption scandal of which the Brazilian oil company is at the center), the Secretariat of Culture of Rio de Janeiro, or the federal government. Some are also sponsored by banks and private companies.

Some favelas promote festivals and shows (Day of the Favela, Fight Festival between Favelas with boxing and jujitsu), specialized courses to improve access to universities (E. S. Silva 2006), digital culture, new technologies in social media, photography, and cinema. Some NGOs specialize in education, human rights, and culture: the Observatório maintains an exhibition of original works by modern artists; AfroReggae has a band that plays in various countries, with the slogan "Culture is my weapon"; and others focus on health and sports.

The projects of the NGOs are not the only ones in the favelas. Other projects are usually the initiative of a few people from outside the favelas who work as volunteers and eventually become a permanent NGO. They propose activities such as music (popular, classical, modern, jazz), education (courses to prepare for enrollment in universities, English and French courses, how to become a model, etc.), dance (classical, modern, traditional — such as capoeira and samba — and innovative dance as the *dança do passinho*), sports (surfing, boxing, jujitsu, other martial arts), theater, photography, and so on. Such projects have replaced ones that trained secretaries, manicurists, hairdressers, and the like, all professions that used to be associated with *favelados*.

A word must be said about a U.S. NGO that is very active on the internet both in Brazil and the United States, Catalytic Communities. It started in

Rio in Santa Marta. Its programs "include training favela leaders in communications and strategy, developing strategic forums and networks to bring visibility to community solutions and perspective . . . and advocacy campaigns."[4] Through its monthly digest, *Rio on Watch*, the U.S. audience is informed about what is going on in the favelas of Rio, reporting news in the Rio media and international media. Brazilian articles are translated into English, with the intent of "ending the stigma around favelas by producing thoughtful and nuanced coverage about them, ultimately influencing the discourse, policies, and initiatives around informal settlements around the world."

Academic production on favelas has also considered a wide variety of other themes. Some authors have studied of the history of favelas (Knauss and Brum 2012), updating it to the present (Gonçalves 2010; Amoroso 2011; A. F. Magalhães 2013). Others have discussed the problems of youth (P. Lopes 2011; A. Cardoso 2014; Rocha and Borges 2014) and the role of public schools (Paiva and Burgos 2009; Telles 2009), while still others focus on issues related to religion, like the relationship between drug trafficking and the evangelical churches (C. Machado 2015; C. Cunha 2015). Some have studied tourism, a recent and active sector of the economy in some favelas, and one that expanded with the UPPs (Freire-Medeiros 2007, 2013).

There is an increasing interest in the discussion of culture in the favelas, largely linked to the many NGOs and projects focusing on culture, or creation of museums in the favelas (Menezes 2009; Moraes 2011). As Sonia Fleury (2012, 198–99) points out, "There is a flourishing local cultural activity going on, resulting from the initiative of the residents themselves and of artists, academics, and civic associations." An example is the recent publication by the Observatório de Favelas, *Solos culturais* (Cultural solos; Barbosa and Dias 2013). The project, a partnership of the Observatório with the Secretariat of Culture of the state of Rio de Janeiro, was financed by Petrobras. It involved many residents of favelas acting as cultural producers in Cidade de Deus, Complexo do Alemão, Complexo da Penha, Manguinhos, and Rocinha, looking at groups devoted to samba, capoeira, choro, forró, funk, hip-hop, painting, graffiti, photography, video, and so forth. According to its authors, "Favelas make culture flourish in Rio. On its corners, and in its streets and public spaces." The authors argue that favelas are fertile ground for cultural creation. The publication also includes an inventory of artistic and cultural practices and a study of the habits and cultural practices of youth in the five favelas.

Researchers also study the government's paradigm of "integration" into the "formal city" (Gomes et al. 2006; Velloso et al. 2012) and questions of informality and land regularization (E. Fernandes 1999, 2001; Abramo 2002;

Donovan 2007). Regarding integration, the newest theme seems to be related to the promotion of entrepreneurship in the favelas. Lia Rocha (2014) states that entrepreneurship is fundamental in the process of transformation of the younger generation of *favelados* from "potential bandits" to "capable workers to join the labor market." She based her study on a pool of NGOs that in 2008 were working on a National Program of First Employment.

A different argument is put forward by Marilia Pastuk (2013), who believes the favela should be seen as an "opportunity," through entrepreneurship. She argues, based on a study of Complexo do Jacarezinho, Complexo do Alemão, Cantagalo-Pavão-Pavãozinho, Rocinha, Borel, and Manguinhos, that opportunities exist in the areas of culture, education, sports and leisure, health, tourism, and the like. She points out the programs and institutions that should lead such efforts, always quoting the government institutions that helped in the project, namely, the Pereira Passos Institute, the Banco Nacional de Desenvolvimento Econômico e Social (BNDES), PAC, and the Secretariat of Social Work and Human Rights of the state of Rio de Janeiro. Her project illustrates the government's idea of "social and economic inclusion."

Have these new analyses and representations of favelas confirmed or changed the predominant views discussed for the previous period? I have shown that they coalesced around three dogmas shared by most actors, from academics to NGOs to politicians to journalists: the specificity of the favela, the favela as the space of poverty, and the unity of the favela.

The first dogma, the specificity of the favela, seems particularly resistant. For social sciences production, this is largely due to a tradition of research design by case studies, at best comparing favelas but never challenging the dogma by comparing them with the situation and social practices in other types of urban areas: clandestine or peripheral housing developments, slums of the city center, various types of working class areas, and so on. Typically, cultural practices studied only in the favelas become practices *of* the favela instead of practices *in* the favela, ones that could be similar elsewhere—or different, which would prove the point instead of simply taking it for granted. Only a few studies compare favela with nonfavela families (Sant'Anna 2012).

The second dogma, the favela as the space of poverty, is also resistant but less so. One side of the equation—that the favelas are the typical space of the poor and that if you want to study poverty in the city, you go to favelas—is unchallenged in spite of the statistical evidence that there are more poor people in Rio outside favelas than inside them. But on the other side of the coin—that favelas are the place of the poor *only*—the dogma begins to shatter. The recognition that the social structure of the favela is more complex, that there are social inequalities within the favela, that there are various forms of social mobility through university degrees (Conceição 2011), entrepreneurship, NGOs, and so forth, is beginning to expand, although it still only a minority of the research contributions.

The third dogma, that of the unity of the favela, is also being partly shattered. One side, the belief in an internal unity, is resisting strongly, with the generalization of the designation of favelas as "communities." But some recognition of internal inequalities and different social interests has tended to progress. And there is definitely wider acknowledgment, on the other side, of the diversity *between* favelas. This is partly because of the cumulative effects of public policies improving a number of favelas while leaving others with much weaker infrastructure and services, like the more recent ones in the northwest of the municipality of Rio or in peripheral municipalities such as São Gonçalo or Nova Iguaçu that receive less public investment and more drug dealers expelled from their traditional strongholds by UPPs.

I have wondered whether the new widespread insistence on violence was building up a new dogma. But I realized that the convergence on its importance was accompanied by many divergent views about the nature and causes of violence among academics, NGOs, journalists, and even public policy actors.

I have discussed here the changes in representations mostly through academic production. I have the feeling—without being able to substantiate it with a rigorous survey—that parallel changes are taking place in the media, which are representing the favelas in more diversified ways, from news about crime and confrontations between drug dealers and the police to fiction, telenovelas, discussion of culture, economic news, and so on. The prejudices and stigmatization are still there, but *favelados* are customers and favelas are a marketable product, nationally and internationally.

A Chronology of the Rio Favela

Year	Political and institutional events	Urban political institutions in Rio de Janeiro	Representations in the media and other publications
1880		Creation of the Clube dos Engenheiros, an organization concerned with the future of Rio.	
1888	Abolition of slavery.		
1889	Proclamation of the Republic by Marshal Deodoro da Fonseca.		
1891	Promulgation of the first Republican Constitution; president: Marshal Floriano Peixoto.		Founding of the Rio-based newspaper *Jornal do Brasil*.
1893		The war on tenements, symbolized by the destruction of Cabeça de Porco.	
1894	Election of Prudente de Morais, first civilian president.		
1896			First edition of *O cortiço* by Aluísio de Azevedo (published in English as *The Slum*, 2000).

Year	Political and institutional events	Urban political institutions in Rio de Janeiro	Representations in the media and other publications
1897	The Canudos War: The Republican army kills the rebels in the backlands of the state of Bahia. Soldiers return from the war and settle in Rio on Morro da Providência.		The newspaper *O Estado de São Paulo* publishes reporting on the Canudos War. Morro da Providência comes to be known as Morro da Favella.
1901			Founding of the Rio-based newspaper *Correio da Manhã*.
1902	Election of Rodrigues Alves as president. The new president names engineer Pereira Passos mayor of the Federal District (1902–6).		Publication of the first edition of *Os Sertões* by Euclides da Cunha (published in English as *Backlands: The Canudos Campaign* in 2010).
1903	Oswaldo Cruz, a doctor specializing in hygiene, coordinates federal public health services (1903–9).		
1904	The Vaccine Revolt, a protest against the public health measures planned by Pereira Passos and Oswaldo Cruz.	Pereira Passos's urban reform reshapes the city center of Rio.	
1905		Opening of Avenida Central, a symbol of modern Rio.	
1906	Marshal Souza Aguiar is named mayor of the Federal District (1906–9) and continues Pereira Passos's public works.		Publication of the report *Habitações populares*, edited by the engineer Everardo Backheuser, containing photos of Morro da Favella.

A Chronology of the Rio Favela

Year	Political and institutional events	Urban political institutions in Rio de Janeiro	Representations in the media and other publications
1907			Two caricatures are published in the press about the "sanitizing" of Morro da Favella.
1908	The National Exposition is held in Rio.		The writer Coelho Neto characterizes the city of Rio as "A Cidade Maravilhosa." Journalist and man-about-town João do Rio describes a visit to Morro de Santo Antônio.
1917	Brazil declares war on Germany.		
1920			The word *Favella* goes from being a singular proper noun to a singular or collective common noun, *favela*. (The loss of the double l was a result of the 1911 Orthographic Reform.)
1921		Creation of the Instituto Brasileiro de Arquitetos, forerunner of the present IAB.	
1922	Establishment of the Rotary Club in Brazil, with Rotary do Rio the first chapter. Establishment of the PBC.	Demolition of Morro do Castelo, opening up space in the city center.	The painting *Morro da Favella*, by Brazilian artist Tarsila do Amaral. The Week of Modern Art in São Paulo takes stands against European artistic models.
1924			Journalist Benjamin Costallat publishes the *crônica* (narrative essay) "A favela que eu vi" (The favela I saw).

Year	Political and institutional events	Urban political institutions in Rio de Janeiro	Representations in the media and other publications
1925			Founding of the Rio newspaper *O Globo*.
1926	Prado Júnior is named mayor of Rio (1926–30).	Prado Júnior delegates command of the urbanization Plano do Rio to Alfred Agache.	Mattos Pimenta, with the support of the Rotary Club, launches a campaign against the favelas. The Rotary Club supports Agache's Plano do Rio.
1927			Urban planner Alfred Agache is photographed in Morro da Favela.
1928			Composer José Barbosa da Silva, "Sinhô," introduces the favela into popular music.
1929			Architect and planner Le Corbusier draws design sketches of the favelas.
1930	Getúlio Vargas becomes leader of the provisional government after the Revolution of 1930.	Agache presents the urban development plan for the city of Rio. Remodeling of the patio of the Escola Nacional de Belas Artes.	Agache describes the favela as leprosy that threatens the body of the city.
1931	Medical doctor Pedro Ernesto is named *interventor* for the Federal District.		Brazilian painter Cândido Portinari paints *Favella*, now in the collection of the Museum of Modern Art in New York.
1932	Founding of the Instituto Católico de Estudos Superiores, precursor of PUC.	Creation of the first commission for the Plano do Rio.	

Year	Political and institutional events	Urban political institutions in Rio de Janeiro	Representations in the media and other publications
1933	Founding of the ELSP in São Paulo. The PADF wins the elections. Pedro Ernesto defends the *favelados*.		
1934	The new constitution creates the Justiça do Trabalho (Labor Court System). The minimum wage is included in the constitution. Establishment of the FFCL at USP.		First feature-length film about the Rio favelas, by Humberto Mauro: *Favelas dos meus amores* (Favelas of My Loves). Publication of the novel *O bota-abaixo: Crônica de 1904* (The demolition: A chronicle of 1904), by José Vieira, inspired by the Pereira Passos reforms.
1935	Founding of the Universidade do Distrito Federal by Anísio Teixeira. Pedro Ernesto is elected to a five-year term as mayor of Rio. Attempted communist revolution.		Publication of the novel *Salgueiro* by Lúcio Cardoso. First official parade of the samba schools.
1936	Pedro Ernesto is sent to prison. Federal minimum wage law signed.	Creation of the degree in urbanism at the Universidade do Distrito Federal.	

Year	Political and institutional events	Urban political institutions in Rio de Janeiro	Representations in the media and other publications
1937	Following a coup d'état, Getúlio Vargas establishes the Estado Novo, dissolves Congress and the political parties, and proclaims a new constitution. Vargas names Henrique Dodsworth as *interventor* for the Federal District (1937–45). Vargas names Agamenon Magalhães as *interventor* for Pernambuco.	Creation of the second commission for the Plano do Rio. The construction code is promulgated. Creation of the Instituto Social, the social work school at PUC.	
1938	Creation of the IBGE.		Journalist Luís Edmundo describes the Morro de Santo Antônio in *O Rio de Janeiro do meu tempo* (Rio de Janeiro of my time).
1939	Creation of the Faculdade Nacional de Filosofia of the Universidade do Distrito Federal, on the model of USP.	Agamenon Magalhães creates the Liga Social contra o Mocambo (Social League against the Favela) in Pernambuco.	
1940	First application of the minimum wage.		Medical doctor Victor Tavares de Moura produces his preliminary study of Rio's favelas.
1941		Creation of a commission to study problems of hygiene in regard to the favelas. Demolition of Morro de Santo Antônio, opening up space in the city center.	First Brazilian conference on urbanism; the issue of the favela is discussed.

Year	Political and institutional events	Urban political institutions in Rio de Janeiro	Representations in the media and other publications
1942	Brazil declares war against the Axis. Law freezing rents. Death of Pedro Ernesto; *Favelados* and samba school members attend his funeral.	Start of the Proletariat Parks (1942–44) by mayor Henrique Dodsworth; the first park is set aside for the relocation of the residents of Largo da Memória.	Publication of the thesis of social worker Maria Hortência do Nascimento e Silva on the Largo da Memória favela.
1943	Promulgation of the Consolidação das Leis do Trabalho (CLT; Consolidation of the Labor Laws), which recalls social legislation of fascist inspiration.		
1944		Opening of Avenida Presidente Vargas.	
1945	Elections transform the favelas into a voting bloc. Vargas is deposed and general elections follow; General Eurico Gaspar Dutra is elected president.	Creation of the Office of Urban Planning of the Office of the Mayor of Rio de Janeiro.	
1946	New constitution enacted.	Creation of the Housing Department of the Mayor's Office. Creation of the Department of Social Services, directed by Victor Tavares de Moura. Opening of Avenida Brasil.	Publication of the novel *Favela* by Eloy Pontes.

Year	Political and institutional events	Urban political institutions in Rio de Janeiro	Representations in the media and other publications
1947	The PCB performs well in elections and is outlawed. Creation of the Fundação da Casa Popular (Affordable Housing Foundation), a federal agency that is a predecessor of the BNH.	Creation of the Fundação Leão XIII by the Catholic Church Creation of a federal commission for the suppression of favelas.	Father Lebret gives a three-month course at the ELSP.
1948	First census of the favelas by the Mayor's Office of the Federal District.		Journalist Carlos Lacerda launches the Batalha do Rio contra as Favelas in the press.
1949			Publication of the results of the favela census by the Mayor's Office of the Federal District.
1950	Getúlio Vargas is elected president with 49 percent of the vote.		First general census in which the IBGE defines favelas as a national category.
1951			Founding of the popular newspaper A Notícia, directed by Chagas Freitas.
1952		The Mayor's Office of the Federal District creates the Favela Rehabilitation Service.	
1953		Creation of a new municipal commission on the problem of the favelas.	Sociologist Costa Pinto publishes his book O negro no Rio de Janeiro (The black man in Rio de Janeiro).

A Chronology of the Rio Favela

Year	Political and institutional events	Urban political institutions in Rio de Janeiro	Representations in the media and other publications
1954	Getúlio Vargas commits suicide.	Creation of the União dos Trabalhadores Favelados (*Favelado* Workers Union).	
1955	Juscelino Kubitschek is elected president. Thirty-Sixth International Eucharistic Conference in Brazil.	Launch of the Cruzada de São Sebastião by Dom Hélder Câmara.	
1956		Creation of SERFHA.	
1957	Creation in Rio of CLAPCS, an initiative of UNESCO.	First congress of Rio *favelados*.	
1958			French filmmaker Marcel Camus shoots *Orfeu negro* (released in English as *Black Orpheus*) in Morro da Babilônia.
1960	Inauguration of Brasília, which becomes the new capital of Brazil. The former Federal District becomes the state of Guanabara (GB) until its unification with the state of Rio de Janeiro (1960–74). Carlos Lacerda is elected governor of the new state of Guanabara (1960–65).	Arthur Rios becomes director of SERFHA.	*Estado de Sao Paulo* publishes "Aspectos humanos das favelas cariocas" by SAGMACS. Publication of the testimonial by Carolina Maria de Jesus, *Quarto de despejo* (published in English as *Child of the Dark* in 1962) Census of the favelas of Guanabara and general census of Brazil.

Year	Political and institutional events	Urban political institutions in Rio de Janeiro	Representations in the media and other publications
1961	Jânio Quadros is elected president; resigns that same year; Vice President João Goulart becomes president. Acordo do Fundo do Trigo (Wheat Fund Accord) for favelas signed between Brazil and the United States.		
1962		Lacerda creates COHAB-GB with mixed capital. The Fundação Leão XIII becomes a public agency and is absorbed by COHAB-GB.	
1963		Lacerda signs accord with USAID to finance the removal of favelas; work begins on removals. Lacerda creates CEE for *favelados*.	The Seminar on Housing and Urban Reform promotes a national housing policy.
1964	Coup d'état that begins the military dictatorship, which lasts until 1985. Creation of the BNH.	Creation of BEMDOC, a program of cooperation with the United States for community development; the first Peace Corps volunteers move into favelas. First congress of favelas.	
1965	Negrão de Lima elected governor of the state of Guanabara (1966–70). Growth of the Máquina Chaguista (the Chaguist Machine), led by Chagas Freitas (1965–75).	Doxiadis Associates delivers a plan for urban development to Governor Negrão de Lima. The Organic Law of Municipalities imposes a master plan for municipalities.	

Year	Political and institutional events	Urban political institutions in Rio de Janeiro	Representations in the media and other publications
1966		Creation of SERFHAU.	Several Peace Corps volunteers present information of the Thirty-Seventh International Congress of Americanists.
1967	General Costa e Silva takes office as president (1967–69). A new constitution goes into effect. Creation of FINEP.	Creation of CODESCO, which seeks to urbanize the favelas.	
1968	The Fifth Institutional Act (AI-5) restricts the civil liberties stipulated in 1967 Constitution.	Creation of CHISAM, the federal agency charged with removing *favelados*. FAFEG Congress.	The national graduate education policy takes off.
1969	General Emílio Garrastazu Médici takes office as president (1969–74). The Eighth Institutional Act suspends elections. A new constitution goes into effect.		Publication of no. 12 of the CLAPCS journal, *América Latina*, dedicated to the favela. Anthony Leeds's course at the National Museum.
1970	Chagas Freitas elected governor of the state of Guanabara (1970–74).		
1974	General Ernesto Geisel takes office as president (1974–78).		
1975	Creation of the new state of Rio de Janeiro, merging the states of Guanabara and Rio de Janeiro.		

Year	Political and institutional events	Urban political institutions in Rio de Janeiro	Representations in the media and other publications
1976		Creation of the Favela Pastoral.	
1977	Creation of ANPOCS.		
1978	First election after state merger.		
1979	Creation of the Pro-Morar program by the BNH. Political amnesty in Brazil and a return to basic freedoms.	Creation of the SMDS. Launch of Projeto Rio in the favela of Maré. Light launches an electrification program for the favelas. Creation of the RIOPLAN Foundation, which later becomes IPLAN-RIO.	Carlos Drummond de Andrade publishes the poem "Favelas."
1980	Creation of the PT. Pope Paul VI visits the favela of Vidigal during his trip to Rio.		
1981		IPLAN-RIO creates the Registry of Favelas. Meeting of FAFEG.	
1983	Beginning of Leonel Brizola's first term as governor of Rio (1983–87).	Brizola creates the program Cada Família um Lote (A Lot for Every Family) to regularize land ownership in the favelas after a number of collective land invasions. CEDAE creates a program of water and sanitation for the favelas.	
1984	Campaign for the return to direct elections, Diretas Já!		First campaign against violence in Rio by TV Globo, *O Rio contra o crime.*

Year	Political and institutional events	Urban political institutions in Rio de Janeiro	Representations in the media and other publications
1985	Election of Tancredo Neves as president; end of the dictatorship.		
1987	Benedita da Silva, a Black *favelada*, elected federal deputy for the PT.		
1988	A new constitution grants fiscal autonomy to the municipalities. Marcelo Alencar elected mayor of Rio (1988–92); creates Rio-Cidade and prepares for the ECO 92 Conference.		
1990	Fernando Collor elected president.		
1991	Beginning of Leonel Brizola's second term as governor of Rio (1991–94).		
1992	Impeachment of Fernando Collor. UN's International Conference ECO-92 in Rio. César Maia elected mayor of Rio (1992–96).		
1993	Massacre abetted by the police in the favela of Vigário Geral. National campaign of Ação da Cidadania contra a Fome, a Miséria e pela Vida (Citizens' Action against Hunger and Poverty and for Life).	First formulation of the Favela-Bairro Program by the Rio Mayor's Office.	Creation of the NGO Viva Rio, directed by leaders of the NGOS IBASE and ISER.

Year	Political and institutional events	Urban political institutions in Rio de Janeiro	Representations in the media and other publications
1994	Launch of the Plano Real with the goal of stabilizing the economy, affected by high inflation.	Creation of Secretaria Municipal de Habitação (Municipal Housing Secretariat), responsible for the Favela-Bairro Program.	Publication of the book by journalist Zuenir Ventura, *Cidade partida* (Divided city).

1995	Fernando Henrique Cardoso elected president.
	    International Bank for Reconstruction and Development (IBRD) finances the Favela-Bairro Program.
	    The federal government creates the Comunidade Solidária (Community in Solidarity) program.
		Beginning of Favela-Bairro programs activities in nineteen favelas.	Creation of Center for Digital Inclusion (CDI), an NGO that establishes computer science schools in the favelas.

1996	Luis Paulo Conde elected mayor of Rio (1996–2000).		Michael Jackson films part of his music video "They Don't Care about Us" in Morro Dona Marta.
1997			Creation of the first homegrown favela NGO, CEASM, in Maré. Cable TV station TV-ROC, founded by Argentine businessmen, is established in Rocinha.
1998	Anthony Garotinho elected governor of the state of Rio de Janeiro. Names anthropologist Luiz Eduardo Soares undersecretary of public safety and coordinator of public safety, justice, and citizenship.	IPLAN-RIO becomes the Pereira Passos Municipal Institute for Urbanism.	

A Chronology of the Rio Favela

Year	Political and institutional events	Urban political institutions in Rio de Janeiro	Representations in the media and other publications
1999			João Moreira Salles films *Notícias de uma guerra particular* (News from a personal war) in Morro Dona Marta. Brazilian filmmaker Carlos Diegues shoots a new version of the play *Orfeu da Conceição*, *Orfeu* (cf. *Orfeu negro* [*Black Orpheus*]). The Doctors of Rio appear on the cover of *Veja Rio*. TV-ROC creates the website www .rocinha.com.
2000			CEASM conducts a census in the Complexo da Maré ahead of Brazil's general census that same year.
2001			Casa da Cidadania (Citizenship House) creates the website www .anf.ed.br of the Agência de Notícias das Favelas (Favela News Agency).

Notes

INTRODUCTION

1. See data from the Sistema de Assentamentos de Baixa Renda (SABREN) of the Instituto Pereira Passos, Municipality of Rio de Janeiro. In 2000 the Instituto Brasileiro de Geografia e Estatística (IBGE) noted the existence of 681 favelas. The 752 favelas registered by SABREN correspond to an increase of 71 favelas. These existed but had not been registered in 2000 and thus were reported by the press as new in 2002.

2. The Doxiadis Plan for automobile transportation was also part of the project to transform Rio de Janeiro.

3. In 1948, then journalist Lacerda had led a campaign in the press known as the "Batalha do Rio" (Battle of Rio).

4. This first school must be distinguished from the Second Chicago School, whose most influential authors were Herbert Blumer and Everett Hughes, the main founders of the current of symbolic internationalism. The collection *A Second Chicago School?* (1995), edited by Gary Fine, shows the continuity and differences between these two generations of Chicago sociologists and anthropologists.

5. A little later, these favelas became part of the Companhia de Desenvolvimento de Comunidades (CODESCO) program for the recuperation of favelas. CODESCO was created by Lacerda's successor Governor Francisco Negrão de Lima, "to satisfy his promises to the *favelados*, as an honorable way out of the impositions of federal housing policy" (C. N. Santos 1981, 57).

6. Emblematic of Carioca (Rio) culture are the *escolas de samba* (samba "schools") that produce the thematic Carnival parades, the religiosity of Afro-Brazilian religions and popular Catholicism, the illegal but tolerated animal/numbers game, and the lifestyle of the *malandro* (or hustler) viewed romantically or as an antihero. (Translator's note.)

7. In the chapter "Origens e desenvolvimento da pesquisa" (Origins and development of the research) in the book *Passa-se uma casa* (Passing by a house; Valladares 1978a), I relate the trajectory of the fieldwork. At that time, the population of Rocinha was 45,000, making it the second-largest favela in the state of Guanabara.

8. See the report *Favela e religião: Um estudo de caso* (Favela and religion: A case study; Medina and Valladares 1968).

9. The CNBB research program was funded by the German foundation Adveniat.

1. This chapter is a quite expanded version of my article "A gênese da favela carioca: A produção anterior às ciências sociais" (The genesis of the Rio favela: Production before the social sciences; Valladares 2000b). About the time that article was published and since, a number of authors have written on the history of favelas, including Zaluar and Alvito 1998; M. L. Silva 2003; and Gonçalves 2013.

2. In the period covered by this chapter, the late nineteenth century, Rio de Janeiro was the capital of Brazil, and its city limits were the same as the borders of the Federal District. Citations follow the orthography of the original.

3. Cf. Parisse 1969; Leeds and Leeds 1978; Valla 1986; and Burgos 1998.

4. See note from the translator.

5. This view of the *cortiços* of Rio de Janeiro seems similar to the diagnosis of the industrial cities of Europe, especially English slums (Engels 1969; Barret-Ducrocq 1991; Carré and Révauger 1995).

6. See Backheuser 1906, 105–6. The *cortiço* was defined by municipal regulation "as a construction prohibited by the Mayor's Office. It is a collective dwelling generally made up of rooms made of wood or light construction, sometimes installed behind buildings or one on top of another, with verandas and stairways with difficult access, without a kitchen, with or without a patio, service area, or corridor, and with common sanitary and laundry facilities. A *cortiço* might also be a building of old construction, in which are built clandestine divisions of wood (construction prohibited by the Mayor's Office), forming unfurnished rooms or cubicles, that often extended to the attics, ceilings, basements, kitchens, pantries, bathrooms, and so forth, generally inhabited by poor persons and with the name of 'casa de cômodos [boardinghouse]' with no address, where also there are laundry and sanitary facilities, whether inside internal or external, that are insufficient, and without bathrooms or kitchens."

7. Benchimol 1990.

8. M. Abreu 1994b, 40. This article also includes on the previous page a map that indicates the favelas built between 1891 and 1930. The author opted for *Correio da Manhã* because this periodical gave attention to so-called popular causes. He complemented the research with information from archives and other press outlets.

9. This Mangueira is not the same as the well-known Mangueira favela; it was located on the Botafogo side of the hill at the Túnel Velho (Old Tunnel).

10. See the Pereira Passos Institute's registry of favelas, officially called the Sistema de Assentamentos de Baixa Renda (SABREN) and the article by Lysia Bernardes (1958) on Ponta do Caju.

11. The medical doctor and public health official Oswaldo Cruz was the main person responsible for the Sanitarist Campaign during the Pereira Passos government. With respect to the Vaccine Revolt, see especially J. M. de Carvalho 1987. On Osvaldo Cruz, see Fundação Oswaldo Cruz 2003.

12. Various caricatures appeared in newspapers and magazines of the time. The one reproduced here is only the most widely circulated. See also "Saneamento dos morros" (Sanitation of the Hills), published in *Jornal do Brasil* on 14 April 1907.

13. The debate about poverty and housing for the poor at the turn of the century has been analyzed by J. M. de Carvalho 1987; Valladares 1991; and Chalhoub 1996.

14. One must bear in mind that the canonical work *Os Sertões: Campanha de Canudos*

by Euclides da Cunha (1902, published as *Backlands: The Canudos Campaign*, 2010, from which citations in English are taken) had a foundational role in Brazilian social and political thinking in the first three decades of the twentieth century. *Os Sertões* centered on the hostile space of the *sertão* or semiarid backlands of Northeast Brazil and, at the same time, on the *sertanejo*, the inhabitant of the region. The book was a wake-up call for the Brazilian political elite, who until then had focused on the coastal regions of the country and on "civilization," where European influence flourished, especially in Rio and São Paulo. A true epic of modern times in Brazil, the work narrates the federal government's campaigns against the town of Canudos (1896–97) and analyzed its mysterious main character, Antônio Conselheiro (the Counselor). A charismatic religious leader, he was responsible for the fierce resistance of Canudos's population, which defeated four army expeditions sent by the Republican government, which had only recently been constituted and felt it was threatened by these "savages." Thus Canudos, a remote, unknown settlement in the hinterlands of the state of Bahia, first made the newspaper headline of the day. After the publication of *Os Sertões*, the story of Canudos became a legend.

15. According to the *Novo Aurélio* (A. Ferreira 1999) (the Brazilian equivalent of *Webster's*), "Favela-branca [white favela]" is a "small tree of the family Leguminosae (*Enterolobium ellipticum*), with whitish-yellow sessile flowers with a monopetalous corolla, arranged in capitula; whose fruit is a leathery, curved pod with several seeds. It is a source of an attractive, heavy hardwood, good for woodworking." Cunha defined the favela plant thus: "The favelas, still without a scientific name and unknown to scholars, but only too well known to greenhorns, are possibly members of a future genus *Cauterium* of leguminous plants. They possess in their leaves cells elongated into fuzz, which are a notable tool for condensation, absorption, and defense. On the one hand, their skin, as it grows cold at night with a great drop in temperature, will in spite of the dryness of the air collect tiny drops of dew. And on the other hand, whoever touches it has touched a fiery sheet of constant flame" (E. Cunha 2010, 38).

16. In Hochman 1998b, 218. "The Avenue" here refers to Avenida Central, now Avenida Rio Branco, built by Pereira Passos during Rio's urban renewal, between 1903 and 1906.

17. The essay "A palavra é: Favela" (The word is: Favela; Oliveira and Marcier 1998, 110–14) count 125 songs written on the theme. The authors suggest that the favela is not just a space of the poor but also one of samba. In the musical representations, the favela appears both as an image of the noncity and as the locus of urban marginality, as well as, after 1960, a social issue.

18. In chapter 1 of Joaquim Maria Machado de Assis's novel *Esaú e Jacó* (Esau and Jacob; 1904) two of the characters, Natividade and Perpétua, climb Morro de Santo Antônio in search of a seer known as Cabocla. (A *caboclo* or *cabocla* is a person of mixed indigenous and European descent and, by extension, a *sertanejo*. Translator's note.)

19. For information on the housing crisis, especially in the last decades of the nineteenth century, see Damazio 1996, which provides a social picture of Rio at the turn of the nineteenth to twentieth centuries.

20. Backheuser's report is available in Brazil's National Library. The analytical bibliography in Valladares and Medeiros 2003 shows that this report initiated reflection on the favelas of Rio de Janeiro.

21. Backheuser's legislation and other work has been studied, notably by Lia Carvalho (1986).

22. These are, no doubt, the first published photographs of Favella. The best known, by photographer Augusto Malta, date from the 1920s and are reproduced in Zylberberg 1992.

23. "Order and Progress," the motto of positivist origin, emblazoned to this day on the Brazilian flag. See Herschmann and Pereira 1994, 45: "These intellectuals, bearers of specialized technical knowledge, claimed responsibility for social organization, and their discourse took shape in the basic norms of Brazilian society."

24. With regard to the power of medical doctors and engineers in Rio de Janeiro, see Herschmann, Kropf, and Nunes 1996, which focuses on the years 1870–1937. Stuckenbruck 1996 also shows how a social concern that permeated the discourse of engineering resonated widely in the urbanism practiced in Brazil beginning in 1920. On the Clube de Engenharia, see M. A. R. de Carvalho 1985.

25. Pereira Passos (1903–6), Paulo de Frontin (January–July 1919), Carlos Sampaio (1920–22), and Alaor Prata (1922–26) were engineers. The exception is Antônio Prado Júnior (1926–30), a São Paulo industrialist. About these mayors and their respective terms, see Stuckenbruck 1996. The doctors who were mayors include Barata Ribeiro (1892–93), Francisco Furquim Werneck de Almeida (1895–97), Pedro Ernesto (1931–35), and Henrique Dodsworth (1937–45); the last two were appointed by Getúlio Vargas.

26. The Rotary Club of Rio de Janeiro, founded in 1922 and inspired by the Rotary Club of Chicago, was the first Rotary chapter in Brazil. Cf. Reis and Aragão 1993, 7, which offered a historical account of the club on the seventieth anniversary of its founding. In addition to its philanthropic activities, especially in education (for example, libraries), the Rio Rotary Club also functioned as a venue for discussions and a pressure group in economic settings dealing with urban problems, such as flooding, water supply, urban renewal, and the preservation of historic monuments. Maragareth Pereira (1996a) has written about the diffusion of the U.S. model in Brazilian urbanism discourse, stressing the role of the Rio Rotary Club.

27. I have found references to Mattos Pimenta only in the following sources: M. Abreu 1994; Pechman 1996; L. Silva 1996; and Stuckenbruck 1996. Only Maurício de Almeida Abreu writes specifically about Mattos Pimenta and the favela. The other authors discuss him mostly in connection with contracting the urban planner Alfred Agache to carry out the Plano de Extensão-Remodelação-Embelezamento do Rio de Janeiro (Plan for Growth-Renewal-Beautification of Rio de Janeiro). The main authors who have reconstructed the history of governmental policy toward the favela curiously did not mention this figure (Parisse 1969a; A. Leeds 1969; Valla 1986). Nor is there any mention of Mattos Pimenta in the 1960 SAGMACS study.

28. This record, found while doing research at the Rio Rotary Club itself, removed all doubt as to Mattos Pimenta's primary occupation. I also conducted an interview with his daughter, Wanda de Mattos Pimenta Pompéia, in which she confirmed that her father had been connected with the real estate market; indeed, he was one of the most important realtors at that time.

29. A speech delivered at a luncheon at the Rio Rotary Club on 12 November 1926, under the title "As favellas," published in Correio da Manhã and O Jornal, both dated 18 November 1926. This speech is reproduced in its entirety in Para a remodelação do Rio de Janeiro (Toward the remodeling of Rio de Janeiro; Mattos Pimenta 1926).

30. Mattos Pimenta's substantial knowledge of European cities and even French legislation is apparent in his writings. See the notable speech he gave at a Rio Rotary Club

luncheon on 29 October 1926, published in *Notícias Rotárias*, 12 November 1926, under the title "O remodelamento do Rio de Janeiro" (The remodeling of Rio de Janeiro).

31. See the speech titled "As favellas" (Mattos Pimenta 1926); see note 29.

32. According to research on newspapers of the time (*O Globo*, 11 March 1927; *Jornal do Commercio*, 12 March 1927; and *A Notícia*, 11 March 1927), the first screening of the film seems to have taken place in the Hotel Glória in Rio on 12 November 1926, as part of a campaign on behalf of the aforementioned Rio "remodeling" or renewal plan advanced by the Brazilian trade attaché in France, Francisco Guimarães. The same newspapers also reported that it had been shown to President Luiz in the Theatro Capitólio of Petrópolis on 13 March 1927. There are also reports that the film was screened at the famous Cinema Odeon in downtown Rio (Stuckenbruck 1996).

33. See "Pela belleza e hygiene da nossa cidade; façam-se casas baratas ao alcance da bolsa da gente pobre! Uma voz de propaganda e de enthusiasmo. O que se deve ao Dr. Mattos Pimenta" (For the beauty and hygiene of our city; let there be built inexpensive homes within reach of the pocketbooks of the poor! A voice of promotion and enthusiasm. What we owe to Dr. Mattos Pimenta); *O Globo*, 15 August 1927.

34. A copy of the contract proposal is found in "As casas populares — um projecto do engenheiro Mattos Pimenta para resolver a crise de habitações" (Houses for the poor — Engineer Mattos Pimentas's proposal to solve the housing crisis), *O Jornal*, 9 December 1926.

35. Ibid.

36. Coincidentally, the favela entered the popular songbook in 1928 in an explicit reference to the demolition of shanties (Oliveira and Mercier 1998, 65–66).

37. Mattos Pimenta left the practice of medicine when he returned to Brazil from France in 1918, after World War I, during which he had served as a captain and doctor. He was also director of the Companhia Construtora do Brasil (Construction Company of Brazil), a post he held until 1926 (Fundação Getúlio Vargas 1984).

38. Luiz César de Queiroz Ribeiro (1997, 183–98) analyzed the expansion of the Federal District in 1920–33.

39. See note 27. Vera Rezende (1982) presented four plans for the city of Rio de Janeiro: Agache, Doxiadis, Pub Rio, and Pit Metrô.

40. Interview with Catherine Bruant in 2000.

41. On the history and iconography of the leveling of Morro do Castelo, see Santos and Nonato 2000.

42. According to Michael Conniff (1981, 33), "The Agache plan was European in that it assumed full powers to remake the entire city; it was the heir of Haussmann's designs for Paris."

43. Le Corbusier visited Rio in the same period as Agache, but after him. My research shows that, of all the foreign visitors of the time, Agache was the only one to leave a mark on the thinking about the favelas of Rio. Paola Berenstein-Jacques (2001a), who studied the influence of the favelas on the Brazilian modernists of the 1920s, suggested that it was they who turned the favela into a national symbol. Famous modernist painters such as Tarsila do Amaral, Emiliano Di Cavalcanti, Lasar Segall, and Cândido Portinari painted Rio's favelas on various occasions.

44. Interview with Wanda de Mattos Pimenta Pompéia, daughter of Mattos Pimenta, 1998.

45. According to Catherine Bruant (1994), Agache belongs to the lineage of Frédéric Le Play, as member of the Section d'Hygiène Urbaine et Rurale of the Musée Social in Paris. He was connected to Edmond Demolins, creator of the École des Roches. He was also a member of the International Society for the Social Sciences, and he had published *Les Études Sociales*.

46. Backheuser was one of the first to present specific proposals to build housing for the poor explicitly inspired by European reformist thinking. In his report, he even wrote about the villas built in Rio de Janeiro since 1890 by Arthur Sauer, incorporator of the Companhia de Saneamento (Sanitation Company), that nevertheless only benefited 5,102 people of the 61,060 envisioned (Backheuser 1906, 89).

47. For a synthesis of these debates, see L. Oliveira 1978 and Diniz 1999.

48. According to Angela de Castro Gomes (1999, 62), "The regime assumed that the many diseases propagated in our cities were because of the bad hygiene conditions in homes of the poor, which made the workers disaffected and lazy."

49. Brazilian historians have studied Pedro Ernesto Baptista recently as well; see Sarmento 2001.

50. Conniff (1981, 101–2) mentions Father Olympio de Melo as one of Mayor Baptista's principal aids, and Father Melo was a linchpin in the mayor's clientelist politics. According to Conniff, the priest was a very popular in the working-class neighborhoods of Rio in the 1930s, and he was also the treasurer of the PADF, founded by Baptista.

51. The 1926 text was a basis, with some modifications, of the Agache Plan (Godoy 1943, 321).

52. Page numbers refer to the fourth edition of the 1937 code, published in 1964 under the direction of A. C. Brandão.

53. Conn's pioneering 1986 work contains the most complete discussion of the 1937 Building Code and of the *favelados*' rights of tenure. However, what discussion among engineers might have led to this code is not known.

54. Anthony Leeds and Elizabeth Leeds (1978, 191–92) state that the code itself can be read as the first formal policy related to the favela, with purely administrative measures.

55. Agache (1930, 190) estimated the number of inhabitants of Rio's favelas at 200,000, duplicating Mattos Pimenta's estimate "of more than 100,000 persons" ("Pela belleza e hygiene da nossa cidade," *O Globo*, 15 August 1927).

56. Moura's debut in public administration came in 1937 as head of Rio's Albergue da Boa Vontade (Goodwill Shelter) a halfway house for the needy and immigrants. For more about the Albergue da Boa Vontade and Moura's activity, see Medeiros 2002.

57. An unpublished typescript, part of the archive donated by Maria Coeli de Moura, available at the Archive and Documentation Department of the Casa de Oswaldo Cruz / FioCruz, a IUPERJ / Casa de Oswaldo Cruz project, coordinated by the author.

58. Vargas appointed Magalhães, a strong ally, as Pernambuco's *interventor* (the Estado Novo equivalent of state governor) in 1937.

59. The form that the Commission for the Study of the Problem of Favelas Census Service used is dated 1941 and is available at the Casa de Oswaldo Cruz / FioCruz Archive and Documentation Department.

60. Moncorvo Filho 1926 and Russell-Wood 1968 have offered an overview of aid to poor children during the colonial era and the nineteenth century. Irma Rizzini (1993) and Irene Rizzini (1997) took up the topic of aid to poor children in Brazil from a historical perspective. Leilah Landim (1993) has analyzed Brazilian philanthropy.

61. Fanny du Restu and Jacinta Pietromarchi belonged to the Congregation of the Heart of Mary. They were received by the minister of education and health and even by Vargas himself (A. Lima 1987, 54–55).

62. Lídia Medeiros (2002, 99) points out that other social work students in the 1950s and 1960s discussed in their final monographs the function of visiting social workers as well as the social services implemented in the favelas and the Proletarian Parks by the Mayor's Office and by the Fundação Leão XIII. This foundation, established in 1947, is also discussed in chapter 2.

63. Several authors refer to this work—among them Parisse 1969a; Leeds and Leeds 1978; and Valla 1986—but this monograph has still not received the detailed analysis it deserves.

64. Interview with Maria Hortência do Nascimento e Silva in 1998, not long before her death.

65. Even though Maria Hortência do Nascimento e Silva (1942) cites only the Office of the Mayor as the source, these data certainly come from Moura's research.

66. José Tavares de Lira (1999) has demonstrated this same sort of eugenic orientation in the speeches about the poor and the *mocambos* of Recife in the decades that followed Abolition.

67. Historians and sociologists have still not dealt adequately with the history and role of social workers in Brazil. Two published studies are A. Lima 1987 and Jamur 1990.

68. Italian demographer Giorgio Mortara was the person mainly responsible for the training of the IBGE's first technical staff. A complete, detailed history of the IBGE from 1938 to 1998 can be found in R. Almeida 2002.

69. A. Guimarães 1953. Information here about Alberto Passos Guimarães is from an interview with his son, Alberto Passos Guimarães Filho, from a list of his publications for IBGE, and from an interview with Luiz Nogueira Barros, who worked on his biography in 2000.

70. Diegues Júnior, who had been a student of Gilberto Freyre, in the 1960s became director of UNESCO's Centro Latino Americano de Pesquisas em Ciências Sociais (CLAPCS) in Rio.

71. The 1948 Census of Favelas included the first map of favelas in the Federal District that I know of.

72. This proved to be a prescient observation, as we shall see in the analysis of the removal policies of the Lacerda, Negrão de Lima, and Chagas Freitas administrations; that is, the return to the favela was a direct consequence of governmental actions (Valladares 1978).

73. For more on the Cruzada São Sebastião, see chapter 2. Saint Sebastian is the patron saint of Rio de Janeiro, and the canonical name of the Rio archdiocese in Portuguese is Arquidiocese de São Sebastião do Rio de Janeiro. (Translator's note.)

74. On the Batalha do Rio, see M. L. da Silva 2001 and 2003.

75. Because Costa Pinto's work preceded the 1950 census, he used the 1948 Census of Favelas, which, as has been shown, yielded results similar to the 1950 census but fundamentally differed from the 1948 census in its interpretations.

1. The apogee of Brazilian developmentalism under democratic regimes was during the presidency of Juscelino Kubitschek de Oliveira, 1956–60.

2. This is the same newspaper that sent Euclides da Cunha as a war correspondent to the Canudos conflict in 1897.

3. It is a pity that the study carried out by SAGMACS, under the direction of sociologist José Arthur Rios, has been forgotten by most recent authors, who only cite it indirectly through the writing of Lucien Parisse (1969a, 1970), Anthony and Elizabeth Leeds (1978), or Victor Valla (1986). More recently, Marco Antônio da Silva Mello et al. published *Favelas cariocas: Ontem e hoje* (Rio favelas: Yesterday and today; 2012), a collection of essays from a 2010 colloquium on the SAGMACS study. It includes a CD of "Aspectos humanos da favela carioca." The anthology also includes an essay by Rios (2012), in which he analyzed the study and contributed remembrances about SAGMACS and the publication.

4. See SAGMACS (1960, 28): "It is necessary to go up into the hills before the communists descend upon them."

5. Manoel Gomes's (1980) book has a preface by Luiz Carlos Prestes.

6. Interview with Luiz Werneck Vianna. Both Gomes and Magarinos Torres were communists.

7. We interviewed three former militants who confirmed work in popular education developed in several favelas: Nadia Abreu Teixeira (Peralva), Henrique Miranda, and Momi Seljan.

8. Detailed analyses of the Cruzada São Sebastião were done by Lucien Parisse (1969a, 175–90) and more recently by Bart Slob (2002) and Soraya Simões (2010).

9. One of the agents for education in the rural milieu was José Arthur Rios, who had published the book *Educação dos grupos* (Education of groups) in 1957. This is the same sociologist that Father Lebret later put in charge of the SAGMACS study.

10. According to an interview with Carlos Alberto de Medina, of the SAGMACS team.

11. Vargas's Estado Novo regime lasted from 1937 to 1945. See chapter 1.

12. The invitation came from Romeu Dale, then prior of São Paulo. He had been at La Tourette, where he became friends with Lebret, according to the document "Introduction générale à l´économie humaine" (Lebret 1947).

13. The typewritten four-volume text "Introduction générale à l'économie humaine" is in the library of the Dominican Convent in Rio de Janeiro.

14. Denis Pelletier (1996, 298) points out that, in the beginning, SAGMACS was subsidized by the Jockey Club of São Paulo, conceived of as a social research laboratory at which the Dominicans were not officially present. Among the founding members were the former director of the Escola Politécnica de São Paulo and the secretary general of Catholic Action of São Paulo.

15. This would have been during Getúlio Vargas's elected term as president, 1951–54.

16. ECLA was established by the United Nations in 1948. In 1984, its scope was expanded to include the Caribbean, now as the Economic Commission for Latin America and the Caribbean (ECLAC). The organization is often known by its acronym in Spanish and Portuguese, CEPAL, for Comisión Económica para América Latina y el Caribe / Comissão Econômica para a América Latina e o Caribe (CEPAL, "About ECLAC," http://

www.cepal.org/en/about, accessed 21 June 2017). In 1950–70, ECLA played an important role in the development of Latin American economic and social thought.

17. The editorial success of the book *Princípios para a ação* (Principles for action, already in its seventh edition in 1959) shows the considerable audience for Lebret's thought, bearing in mind that in the 1950s Brazil was considered an illiterate country.

18. On the history of the ELSP during its formative years, 1933–53, see Kantor, Maciel, and Simões 2001.

19. On the history of the Brazilian university during the first half of the twentieth century, see Miceli 1989, particularly the contribution by Fernanda Massi (1989) on the role of French and U.S. social scientists in Brazil. USP especially was developed with the help of French professors such as Fernand Braudel in 1935 and 1948, Claude Lévi-Strauss in 1935, Pierre Deffontaines in 1934, Pierre Monbeig in 1935–46, François Perroux in 1936, Roger Bastide in 1941–54, and Georges Gurvitch in 1947–48.

20. Even though Lévi-Strauss and Bastide had opposed Durkheimian thought in the course of their scientific careers, one cannot deny the impact of Durkheim on their training. This is how they were perceived in Brazil (Massi 1989).

21. On Le Play's legacy, see Pelletier 1996, 131–36.

22. On Donald Pierson and the relation between the Chicago School and Brazilian sociology, see Vila Nova 1998 and Corrêa 1987.

23. The history of anthropology in Brazil has been studied by several Brazilian authors. See especially Melatti 1984; Durham and Cardoso 1961; and Peirano 1995.

24. Interview with Celso Lamparelli, who was a student of Father Lebret.

25. SESI is a nationwide network founded to promote the training and welfare of industrial workers. Portal da Indústria, "O que é o SESI," http://www.portaldaindustria.com.br/sesi/institucional/o-que-e-o-sesi/, accessed 22 June 2017. (Translator's note.)

26. Leme and Lamparelli (2001) underscored Lebret's pioneering contribution to urban planning studies in São Paulo and described in detail its methodology.

27. Lamparelli (1995, 9) distinguishes (1) U.S.-style urban planning, which poses a model of the bourgeois city able to respond to the interests of property owners and economic growth through restructuring the physical bases of a capitalist metropolis, and (2) planning directed at development that gives priority to improving the living conditions of the entire population and that comes from knowledge of the real city, of its dynamics, needs, and potential.

28. According to Taschner 1997, it was not until the 1970s that the favelas began to attract the attention of officials in the São Paulo municipal government.

29. It was in Morro da Babilônia that Marcel Camus filmed *Black Orpheus* (1959).

30. Interview with Adriane Macedo, who participated in the Leme Crusade for Children's social work in the late 1940s.

31. On the "Batalha do Rio," see Parisse (1969, 113–20), whose analysis was based on newspapers of the time (May 1948). Maria Laís Pereira da Silva (2000, 2003) has also researched this topic.

32. The results of this research were published in the journal *Économie et Humanisme* and in Portuguese in the *Revista do Arquivo* (Lebret 1951).

33. Pelletier (1996) stressed the friendship between Dom Hélder and Father Lebret. In the introduction to his book, Paul Houée (1997) mentions the words uttered by Dom Hélder during his visit to the tomb of Father Lebret.

34. Father Lebret had trouble with the Church during his first stay in Brazil: "Correspondence between Father Tauzin, Dominican Vice Provincial in Brazil, and Father Nicolas in Toulouse also attests to the hostility expressed by the archbishop of São Paulo toward the Dominicans in general and toward Father Lebret in particular, after latter's episode in 1947" (Pelletier 1996, 300).

35. This article by Astier and Laé analyzes the social research of Économie et Humanisme in France in 1940–50 and presents the group's basic principles.

36. Carlos Alberto de Medina (1964, 73–101) was one of the first authors to call attention to the presence and pathways of demagoguery in the favelas.

37. It was in an interview with Michel Marié that we learned of the "Lebret myth" in Latin America. According to Marié, other planning offices inspired by Father Lebret were established in several Latin American countries, such as the Compagnie d'Études Industrielles et d'Aménagement du Territoire (CINAM).

38. Texts, for example, by Jacques Loew (1945) on the stevedores of Marseille, and by Michel Quoist (1952) on the working-class neighborhoods of Rouen.

39. Among the works important for planners who participated in the studies conducted in the SAGMACS offices was the *Guide pratique de l'enquête sociale*. Pelletier 1996, 305–10, gives a synthesis of the research done during the years 1952–54 by the São Paulo and Recife teams. I recall that the archbishop of Recife at the time — Dom Hélder Câmara — supported SAGMACS-Recife.

40. According to Leme and Lamparelli 2001.

41. This is the hypothesis defended by Rios, introduced in N. Lima 1989 and reaffirmed in an interview with Rios.

42. It is worthwhile drawing a parallel between the founding of USP and that of the University of Chicago. Both have in common being supported financially by local patrons of the arts and sciences. These philanthropists saw a university as essential to role of the large modern city as both national pioneer and standard of excellence. On the origins of the University of Chicago, see Bulmer 1986; on the origins of USP, see Miceli 1989.

43. For a list of publications on urban and regional planning produced by SAGMACS, see Pelletier 1996, 465–66.

44. On the differences between the processes of institutionalization of the social sciences in Rio de Janeiro and São Paulo, see Miceli 1989.

45. The same Costa Pinto was later appointed by UNESCO as the first director of CLAPCS. For the history of this research center, see L. Oliveira 1995, 268–300.

46. The U.S. sociologist Linn Smith, who studied rural Brazil, was his main interlocutor.

47. Interview with Rios.

48. Interview with Medina.

49. In his testimony, collected by Mariza Corrêa (1987), Pierson twice mentions Kalervo Oberg, his colleague at the Smithsonian Institution, pointing out that Oberg had not only been a professor at the ELSP but also a researcher in the interior of Brazil, to which Brazilian students and scholars accompanied him regularly (pp. 58, 71).

50. After having worked on the SAGMACS research, Medina joined CLAPCS.

51. There is little information about Modesto, who had already passed away when I began this research. After working on the SAGMACS project, he held several positions of responsibility at urban planning agencies in the state of Guanabara.

52. Among the French geographers who most influenced the training of Brazilian

geographers, one stands out: Pierre Deffontaines, who after a time in São Paulo established himself in Rio (M. Abreu 1994; M. Ferreira 2000). The geographers who collaborated on the SAGMACS report did so at the high point of French influence on Brazilian geography. Lysia Bernardes had written an article in 1958 on Ponta do Caju, an area settled early and already partly favelized in the nineteenth century. In an interview, Rios referred to the geographers associated with the SAGMACS project as "the bouquet of French-trained geographers."

53. Interview with Rios.

54. Among the favelas studied were Morro da Providência, Carlos, Esqueleto, Jacarezinho, Barreira do Vasco, Vila do Vintém, Radio Nacional/Parada de Lucas, Vila Proletária da Penha, Cordovil, Telégrafos, Morro do Bom Sucesso, Escondidinho, Praia do Pinto, Rocinha, Cantagalo, and Parque Proletário da Gávea, which by that time had become a favela. The two favelas in which the first detailed studies were done were Barreira do Vasco, where the Fundação Leão XIII had been active for many years (Aragão 1949), and Parque Proletário da Gávea. The second round of detailed studies looked at Rocinha, Jacarezinho, Cantagalo, Mangueira, Praia do Pinto, and Morro de São Carlos, where the Fundação Leão XIII had also been active.

55. We see here an implicit reference to Max Weber. He is not cited because the report was published in a daily newspaper without the tradition of bibliographic references that an academic publication would observe. About the report, see Mello et al. 2012, which includes the report on CD.

56. On the production of the Chicago School in French, see Valladares and Lima 2000.

57. Maurice Halbwachs, a visiting professor at the University of Chicago, in 1932 wrote the article "Chicago, expérience ethnique," republished in Grafmeyer and Joseph 1984.

58. Manuel Castells (1968) presented a critique of the Chicago School, especially regarding the community studies, to justify his Marxist approach to urban studies. Nicolas Herpin (1973) was one of the first in France to recover the Chicago School, but the French translation of the classic texts by the school's founders first appeared in Grafmeyer and Joseph 1979.

59. A Franco-American colloquium organized by Jean-Michel Chapoulie and Paul Tripier at the Université de Versailles–Saint-Quentin-en-Yvelines in April 1998.

60. In fact, Lebret's suggestions regarding fieldwork are not as precise and detailed as Palmer's instructions to the Chicago students in 1928 (Bulmer 1984; Platt 1996), but they are very similar in their pragmatism.

61. As Gérard Leclerc (1979, 66–67) has observed, the method of exposition based on cartography, following the technique of European statistics, influenced the Chicago School's works on urban ecology after 1920.

62. Interview with Michel Marié.

63. Yves Grafmeyer and Isaac Joseph (1984, 8) insisted on Park's experience as a journalist, maintaining that there no epistemological rupture in the passage from journalism to sociology: "The task of the sociologist is to add to the vision of the journalist an instrument to improve the image, like a microscope or magnifying glass."

64. Interview with Rios. Rios had experience with both perspectives: he received a master's degree in sociology in the United States and he had connections with the Dominicans in Rio and in France.

65. The two-volume history of the social sciences in Brazil edited by Sérgio Miceli

(1989, 1995) and Guy Martinière's (1982) book detail the French influence. As for the U.S. influence on the social sciences in Brazil, see Marcos Chor Maio's (1997) study of the UNESCO project.

66. The only analysis of SAGMACS was published in Valla 1986, which offered a detailed critique of the content but without saying anything about the study's impact.

67. The particular, exceptional conditions of the University of Chicago in the first decades of the twentieth century are emphasized by all of those who have studied the origins of the school (e.g., Bulmer 1986; Chapoulie 2001).

68. Valladares 2000a offers a critique of this dual view, advanced by most of the authors currently studying the favelas.

69. Elizabeth Cobbs Hoffman (1998, 11) quotes presidential candidate John Kennedy's speech before 10,000 University of Michigan students in 1960: "How many of you are willing to spend ten years in Africa or Latin America or Asia, working for the United States and working for freedom? How many of you who are going to be doctors are willing to spend your days in Ghana; technicians or engineers, how many of you are willing to work in the foreign service and spend your lives traveling around the world?" It is easy to imagine the impact of Kennedy's speech on these students.

70. Advertisement for the Peace Corps published in the *New York Times* in 1964, qtd. in E. Hoffman 1998, 124.

71. E. Hoffman 1998, 133, provides data on the early years of the Peace Corps: in 1961–65 more than half of the volunteers worked as primary and secondary school teachers, 30 percent in community development, and 20 percent in activities connected to agriculture, health, public works, and administration. According to Hoffman, these percentages did not change much in the following decades.

72. "Culture shock was another way of promoting cultural relativism and thus the ideal of universal respect" (E. Hoffman 1998, 134).

73. As Elizabeth Cobbs Hoffman (1998, 263–64) points out, these numbers refer to volunteers in several countries classified as "Inter-America": Anguilla, Antigua and Barbuda, Argentina, Barbados, Belize, Bolivia, Brazil, Chile, Colombia, Costa Rica, Dominica, Dominican Republic, Ecuador, El Salvador, Granada and Cariacou, Guatemala, Guyana, Haiti, Honduras, Jamaica, Montserrat, Nicaragua, Panama, Paraguay, Peru, Saint Kitts and Nevis, Saint Lucia, Saint Vincent–Granada, Suriname, Turks and Caicos Islands, Uruguay, and Venezuela.

74. The Peace Corps ceased operating in Brazil in 1981. See C. Azevedo 2002 about the Peace Corps volunteers in Brazil.

75. The only extant work on the Peace Corps activity in Rio's favelas is Valladares 2002b, on which the present analysis is based.

76. Elizabeth Leeds offered this estimate in an interview with me when she was working for the Ford Foundation in Rio. The author of several studies of Rio's favelas, she first came to the city in the 1960s as a Peace Corps volunteer. She worked on public health and community development in the favelas of Tuiuti and Jacarezinho. She married the anthropologist Anthony Leeds, with whom she collaborated on various research projects and publications.

77. According to Robert Levine, the Peace Corps volunteers had already learned about the diary from their courses training them to work in favelas and other poor and isolated neighborhoods in Brazil (Meihy and Levine 1996, 16).

78. The diary was originally published in Portuguese in 1960 as *Quarto de despejo* (Junk

Room). Carolina Maria de Jesus collected trash and recyclables as a source of income and resources for the residents. (Translator's note.) On the impact of the book in the United States, see Meihy and Levine 1996, 13–19.

79. The agreement between USAID and the government of the state of Guanabara covered several sectors: construction of working-class housing (Vila Kennedy, Vila Aliança, and Vila Esperança) for residents of favelas that had been removed, financing for an urban development pilot project for a favela (Brás de Pina), and construction of a public health center (Leeds and Leeds 1978).

80. Elizabeth Leeds shared that the group to which she belonged was dependent on the São Cristóvão RA. The health center where she came to work with the Peace Corps served as her bridge to the favela of Tuiuti. In my interview with her, she said that most of the volunteers in Rio opted to live in the favelas.

81. Synergos, "Synergos Founder and Chair: Peggy Dulany," http://www.synergos.org /bios/pdulany.htm, accessed 10 July 2017. (Translator's note.)

82. Interview with Jane Souto de Oliveira, who, years later, also lived in Dona Filinha's boardinghouse.

83. For example, Luiz Antonio Machado da Silva.

84. When I began my fieldwork in Rocinha in 1967, a couple from the Peace Corps already lived there, having rented one of the best masonry homes there at the time. They taught at PUC and tried to promote community development, without success. Since I remained in Rocinha after their return to the United States, I could see better the traces of their passing and the impression they left on the residents (Valladares unpublished field diary).

85. As I mentioned earlier, José Arthur Rios participated in one of the Peace Corps training courses in the United States. Anthony Leeds also helped train volunteers through his university courses in the United States even before he studied favelas, as he had spent time in the cacao region the state of Bahia for his doctoral dissertation.

86. During my fieldwork in Rocinha in 1967, the only other foreigners that I met were three Italian nuns who lived in a rather poor shack, unlike the U.S. couple (Valladares unpublished field diary).

87. The volunteers from the United States had probably not read William Foote Whyte and the famous methodological appendix to *Street Corner Society* (1943), only published from the 1955 edition on.

88. Social workers had a tradition in this field: the Office of Social Services and the Fundação Leão XIII organized professional development courses for young people and adults, offered medical aid in the social centers, and played the role of intermediaries between the local population and the municipal government.

89. Several authors have written about collective work of the *mutirão*. The classic sources are Maricato 1979 and Bonduki and Rolnik 1979. See also Valladares and Figueiredo 1981; Sachs 1985; and Bisilliat 1995.

90. For an analysis of favelas' internal structures and the role of voluntary associations, see Medina 1969 and Valladares 1977.

91. This was the case of the Peace Corps couple whom we met in Rocinha. Faced with the difficulty of moving their project forward, they turned their attention exclusively to teaching activities at PUC.

92. Information on Anthony Leeds comes from various sources: interviews with his widow Elizabeth Leeds, with Gilberto Velho, who published the only book in Portuguese

by Leeds and Leeds (1978), and with Luiz Antonio Machado da Silva, who knew Leeds from the time of his arrival in Brazil; personal contact with Leeds during his stays in Brazil in 1960 and 1970; and the book about Anthony Leeds edited by Roger Sanjek (1994).

93. His dissertation (A. Leeds 1957) was never published. His 1964 article, "Brazilian Careers and Social Structure," written with the collaboration Carolina Bori of São Paulo, had a great impact among the U.S. scholarly community.

94. Interview with Luiz Antonio Machado da Silva.

95. The Portuguese sociologist Boaventura Santos has questioned the image of Leeds and the Peace Corps volunteers in the story of his work in Jacarezinho in 1970: "One day a friend introduced to me to a person who knew a lot about the favelas and the Americans. Without waiting for my questions, he held forth about the favela, its geographical location, the types of houses and shacks, the residents' professions, and so forth. It was a fluent discourse, using popular scientific language, that showed he had a technical knowledge of the community. I was surprised, and I had no doubt that he wanted to impress me. The speech ended with this startling sentence: 'You're here to do research in the favela, right? The Americans wrote their books on my back.' I couldn't help laughing. But my friend told me later that, true or false, it was said that this person had earned a lot of money doing interviews with the American sociologists" (B. Santos 1988, 59).

96. Bulmer 1984 reports that the backbone of the graduate course at the University of Chicago was a research seminar in which each doctoral student shared in a group the progress of their research, its results, and its difficulties.

97. In this seminar, which I attended, there were a several Peace Corps volunteers, Brazilian researchers who were studying favelas at the time, including Luiz Antonio Machado da Silva and the architect Carlos Nelson Ferreira dos Santos, who worked with the CODESCO favela urbanization program, and some students from the United States who were doing their doctoral research, such as Diana Brown, Lawrence Salmen, and Janice Perlman.

98. Interview with Gilberto Velho.

99. I met Lucien Parisse in person in the 1960s, but I was not able to interview him for this book. I do not know his exact connection with Father Lebret or the reasons he chose the favelas of Rio for his thesis in geography at the Université de Strasbourg—the first French thesis on this subject (Pires-Saboia 2000). Both were Dominicans staying in Rio at the Leme Convent, though at different times. Parisse's work differs from that of the U.S. scholars: his task was to do a synthesis, gathering the available data on the favelas of Rio—their growth and their place within the process of urbanization in Rio. He published several works (see bibliography).

100. The text of this accord is found in Leeds and Leeds 1978, 248–50.

101. This journal was one of the few sociology periodicals in Brazil at the time. It published articles in Portuguese, Spanish, English, and French, which gave it an international character. For their part, sociologists in São Paulo had at their disposal the journal *Sociologia*, published by the ELSP.

102. Diegues Júnior was the director of the CLAPCS at the time. The articles that appeared in issue 12 were signed by two U.S. scholars (A. Leeds 1969; Silberstein 1969), two Frenchmen (Parisse 1969c; Bombart 1969), and two Brazilians (Medina 1969; Machado da Silva 1969).

103. Already by 1964, Luiz Antonio Machado da Silva, Ana Judith, and social worker Ledy Olinda Firme were participating in action research in cooperation with the United

States, through Brasil–Estados Unidos Movimento de Desenvolvimento e Organização de Comunidades (Brazil-U.S. Movement for Development and Community Organization).

CHAPTER 3

1. Information on Leeds's time at the National Museum is from an interview with Gilberto Velho, who also provided the syllabi of the two courses taught by the U.S. anthropologist.

2. This was Paul Silberstein, who published in the special issue of the journal *América Latina* dedicated to the favela.

3. Analyzing the intellectual settings frequented by the French scholars Jacques Lambert, Pierre Monbeig, and Roger Bastide, Maria Queiroz (1990) insists on USP's high quality even before 1940. Moreover, by the end of the 1950s, USP included among its faculty Florestan Fernandes, Oracy Nogueira, Luiz Pereira, and Antonio Cândido.

4. For example, the UNESCO project, conducted by Columbia University in partnership with the state of Bahia, with a broad research program in anthropology and sociology (Wagley, Azevedo, and Costa Pinto 1950). See also Maio 1997.

5. Fernando Limongi (1989) mentions that, in addition to Donald Pierson, this program included two German sociologists: Herbert Baldus and Emilio Willems. On the ELSP, see also the testimonials in Kantor, Maciel, and Simões 2001.

6. According to O. Velho, such proposals had been sent to CAPES. See also the proposals for anthropology in Durham and Cardoso 1961, analyzed by Christina de Rezenda Rubim (1997).

7. There were exceptions: sociologist (and later president) Fernando Henrique Cardoso defended his doctoral dissertation at USP in 1962.

8. A detailed analysis of the expansion of master's and doctoral programs in the area of sociology appears in Martins et al. 2002.

9. Marcus Figueiredo (1988) studied the funding of the social sciences in Brazil between 1966 and 1985, especially by the Ford Foundation and FINEP.

10. Before ANPOCS, there had been an association of geographers, established in the 1930s, and an association of anthropologists, created in the 1950s. For a general history of geography and of the geographers of the IBGE, see Almeida 2002.

11. For the development of geography and its contribution to urban studies in Brazil, see Abreu 1994. In A. Carlos 1994, various contributors analyze the contributions of geography to the understanding of Recife, Brasília, São Paulo, and the state of Minas Gerais.

12. The history of thought on urban poverty in Brazil and its differing registers have been studied by several authors, including Machado da Silva 1971; Kowarick 1975, 1987; H. Hoffman 1977; Coelho and Valladares 1982; and Valladares 1991.

13. The literature by European authors on questions of indigence and work, from the Middle Ages to the nineteenth century, is quite extensive. The discussion of the modern wage-earning relationship, beginning with the English Poor Laws, is treated in Polanyi 1980; Castel 1994; Topalov 1994; and Thomas 1997, among other sources.

14. As Denis Fassin (1996, 57–58) has shown, the demographic excess could not be exported as it could from Europe in the nineteenth century. Fassin points out that, moreover, Latin American countries did not have at their disposal a social policy capable of dealing with the urban masses.

15. Richard Morse (1965, 1971) wrote two classic reviews of the urban research literature in Latin America, showing the debates and the interest in Latin American studies that mobilized scholars in the 1960s and 1970s.

16. According to José Nun (1969), "relative overpopulation" refers to the unemployed and underemployed, the "reserve army of industrial labor" to workers whom capital may come to incorporate, and the "marginal mass" to those who will never have a place in the labor market because of the obstacles to economic development resulting from the dependency of Third World countries.

17. We are not dealing here with the contributions to and the critique of the theory of marginality, such as Perlman 1976. We are only underscoring its influence on research on the Rio favela.

18. It was at the Centro para el Desarrollo Económico y Social de América Latina (DESAL), the Chilean Catholic research institute, that the notion of marginality was developed in Latin America in the first place. At the same time, we know that in 1961, Peruvian scholar José Mattos Mar, studying the *barriadas* of Lima, was already interrogating the relationships between migration and urbanization, and their role in integration into urban life.

19. Lewis was in Mexico for the first time in 1943, doing fieldwork in the town of Tepoztlán, studied previously by his dissertation director at the University of Chicago, Robert Redfield. His research in Mexico City began in 1947. His first book, *Five Families: Mexican Case Studies in the Culture of Poverty* (1959), has been reprinted many times in paperback. It was in this work that he proposed the culture of poverty as a key to understanding. However, it was his article "The Culture of Poverty" (1966) that popularized the term.

20. There is a tendency among a number of authors (Perlman 1976; Fassin 1996) to evoke only the "negative" characteristics of the culture of poverty—that is, the gregariousness, alcoholism, frequent recourse to violence, strong predisposition to authoritarianism, machismo, precocious sexual initiation, tendency toward matriarchy, a preference for the present, fatalism, and so forth.

21. In the introduction to *The Children of Sanchez* (Lewis 1961, xii), one reads: "Certainly the lives of the poor are not dull. The stories in this volume reveal a world of violence and death, of suffering and deprivation, of infidelity and broken homes, of delinquency, corruption, and police brutality, and of the cruelty of the poor to the poor. These stories also reveal an intensity of feeling and human warmth, a strong sense of individuality, a capacity for gaiety, a hope for a better life, a desire for understanding and love, a readiness to share the little they possess, and the courage to carry on in the face of many unresolved problems."

22. On Carolina Maria de Jesus's views, see Vogt 1983.

23. This article was presented for the first time in 1967 at a conference in the United States and published in Portuguese in Leeds and Leeds 1978.

24. With a preface by former president Fernando Henrique Cardoso.

25. During the Lacerda government, it was basically USAID that financed COHAB-GB. The removal of favelas only became "spectacular" with the advent of CHISAM, a federal government organization. On the policy of removal, see Grabois 1973. On the reaction of residents to removal, see Valladares 1978a.

26. At the beginning of *Five Families*, Lewis (1959, 1) claims, "My purpose has been to contribute to our understanding of the culture of poverty in contemporary Mexico and,

insofar as the poor throughout the world have something in common, to lower-class life in general. This book has grown out of my conviction that anthropologists have a new function in the modern world: to serve as students and reporters of the great mass of peasants and urban dwellers of the underdeveloped countries."

27. Valladares 1978a analyzes the informal process that led residents of the housing blocks to return to the favelas, culminating in the passing on of residences, a process that also involved the value of this transfer.

28. Rio was the Brazilian city with the largest number of favelas. In São Paulo, favela expansion did not occur until the 1970s (Taschner 1978; Véras and Taschner 1990).

29. For a detailed analysis of CODESCO's activity in the favela of Brás de Pina, treating it as a paradigmatic case of favela urbanization, see Blank 1980 and C. N. Santos 1981.

30. For example, the Federação dos Órgãos para Assistência Social e Educacional (FASE) was established in 1961. During 1965–68, this NGO was an agency for projects geared to training teams to give technical assistance to Basic Ecclesial Communities (Doimo 1995).

31. Carlos Nelson Ferreira dos Santos (1981, 43) gives the reasons for this engagement: "We came to the conclusion that we had had enough of so much talk about reality without going there to see it where it was. We decided that we needed concrete action, practice in areas related to our empirical professional field: the city and its housing problems. This could serve as raw material on which to base our knowledge, which, because of the well-known gaps in university education, was very incomplete."

32. Other architects in this group were Rogério Aroeira Neves, Sylvia Lavenère-Wanderley, Sueli de Azevedo, and Fernando Casério de Almeida.

33. A detailed ethnography of the various stages of participation in Brás de Pina appears in C. N. Santos 1981, 32–85.

34. For a complete list of conference presentations in these years, see Boschi 1987, 177–78.

35. Santos was a participant observer given his dual role as an architect during the Brás de Pina urbanization process and as an anthropologist working on his master's thesis at the National Museum. In his article "Como e quando pode um arquiteto virar antropólogo?" (How and When Can an Architect Become an Anthropologist?), Santos (1980b) described his "transformation" and the effects of his new perspective that had come from his training in anthropology.

36. The *jeitinho brasileiro*, the Brazilian way or manner of working things out, has been discussed by Lívia Barbosa (1992, 79–80). In this social drama, Barbosa distinguished the following characteristics of the *jeitinho*: (1) use of bargaining and argumentation; (2) origination in an egalitarian premise, accessible to everyone in society; (3) dependence not on deeper societal ties but rather on individual attributes; (4) possibility of beginning and ending anonymously, in spite of being a recognized practice; (5) explicit understanding as an element of social identity; and (6) encouragement of diffuse positive reciprocity.

37. For example, the *mutirão* (work crew) of the Secretaria Municipal de Desenvolvimento Social (SMDS) in 1979. See chapter 2.

38. The *Revista Brasileira de Informação Bibliográfica em Ciências Sociais*, launched in 1977 and specializing in thematic reviews, has published 82 volumes as of 2017.

39. The database URBANDATA-Brasil records the following features of each publication: author, title, date and place of publication, publisher, type of document (periodical article, dissertation, book, research report) as well as information about

the type of research carried out (case study, sample survey research, secondary source analysis, diagnosis or assessment, comparative study, historical study), discipline(s) of the author(s), location studied, and thematic areas classified according to twenty-six thematic areas. An abstract accompanies each publication, with each word of the abstract serving as a keyword.

40. Before Valladares and Medeiros 2003, there had only been the following bibliographies: Parisse 1969b and the rather incomplete Pino 2000. Leeds and Leeds's expected contribution, a bibliography of Latin American housing settlement types, has never been published.

41. URBANDATA-Brasil does not record articles in newspapers or weekly publications, except for special supplements, such as the SAGMACS report (1960). Nor does it list internal institutional technical reports.

42. The lengthy task of reading and collecting texts was done by the URBANDATA-Brasil team. Researcher Lídia Medeiros directed CNPq and FAPERJ fellows in the five years before the original publication of the present book.

43. The time passed between the start of research and the publication of results is at least two years; this can be five years or more in the case of dissertations. The large number of publications in the second half of the 1960s can thus correspond to research begun in the first half of that decade.

44. According to Paulo Bastos Cezar (2002), who analyzed the IBGE data most recently available then.

45. Santos (1977) was the first to detect the march of the favelas to the periphery of the metropolitan area of Rio de Janeiro. In a later article, based on data from the Instituto de Planejamento Municipal of the Rio Mayor's Office (IPLAN-RIO), we discussed the return of the favela to the municipality of Rio de Janeiro, both through the densification of the existing ones and through the creation of new clusters (Valladares and Ribeiro 1994). Adauto Lúcio Cardoso (1997) has reminded us that the information on favelization in the peripheral municipalities of the Rio de Janeiro Metropolitan Area is not very trustworthy, and that the official statistics underestimate the phenomenon. The Registry of Favelas is now in the Pereira Passos Institute's multimedia Sistema de Assentamentos de Baixa Renda (SABREN), and it only records the favelas in the municipality of Rio de Janeiro. Cardoso has also suggested that the population of the favelas might have increased in all of Rio's Metropolitan Area.

46. Rocha calculated the poverty line based on the price of the *cesta básica*, a monthly cost of living estimate based on the cost essential food, personal hygiene, and cleaning products for a family.

47. Examples of these include the Instituto Brasileiro de Análises Sociais e Econômicas (IBASE), created in 1981, which led the Campanha contra a Fome, Miséria e pela Vida (Campaign against Hunger and Poverty and for Life); and the Instituto de Estudos da Religião (ISER), founded in the 1970s and from which sprang in 1993 the NGO Viva Rio (Long Live Rio), which today hosts the Portal Viva Favela, created in 2001. For more about Viva Rio and Viva Favela, see Sorj 2003.

48. Examples of these websites include Portal Viva Favela (www.vivafavela.com.br) and Observatório de Favelas (www.observatoriodefavelas.ed.br).

49. This campaign was analyzed in Zaluar 1989 and later in Soares and Carneiro 1996.

50. An analysis of the "favela/asphalt" image is found in Leite 2000.

51. The discipline indicated is the discipline of the author. When a text has two or more authors from different disciplines, all were recorded. Moreover, texts signed by institutions without the name of a personal author were classified as Institutional Production, without considering the discipline.

52. This graph refers to 385 publications.

53. It is worth noting that Brazilian researchers, with rare exceptions, do not include a methodological and epistemological reflection on fieldwork in their publications, in contrast to works by French scholars, such as Mauger 1991; Schwartz 1993b; Olivier de Sardin 1995; Kaufmann 1996; Laplantine 1996; Pinçon and Pinçon-Charlot 1997; Beaud and Weber 1997; and Memmi 1999.

54. In the category of comparative studies, we considered works that had as an empirical basis more than one case, even if this was a matter of two separate case studies. These could refer to comparison between two favelas, comparison of a favela with another poor neighborhood, or comparison of Rio favelas with those in other cities.

55. Cf. data from SABREN.

56. For this graph, only publications that dealt with clearly identified favelas, based on case studies, were considered.

57. In the cases in which a publication refers to more than one favela, the two or more were considered in the calculation for the graph.

58. The Viva Rio website (www.vivario.ed.br) contains information about the NGO's programs, including Viva Favela, which has its own site (www.vivafavela.com.br).

59. CEASM has split into two NGOs: Observatório de Favelas (Favela Observatory) and Redes da Maré (Maré Networks). See epilogue.

60. The IBGE's definition is analyzed in chapter 1. Cezar (2002, 1) reaffirmed that, for the IBGE, these were "subnormal clusters of more than fifty housing units, arranged in a disorderly and dense manner, on land that belongs to third parties, and lacking in essential public services. These are opposed to normal sectors, which, by omission, constitute the formal city. In this, we cannot observe categories of sociological content. The IBGE uses this division more for purposes of organizing the task of data collection in the field."

61. A stance brought into mainstream in the 1960s through the famous musical revue *Opinião*, which featured favela musician Zé Kéti, middle-class bossa nova star Nara Leão, and Northeasterner João do Vale. As the theme song stated, "Podem me prender / Podem me bater / Podem até me deixar sem comer / Mas eu não mudo de opinião / Aqui do morro eu não saio não" (They may beat me / They may leave me hungry / But I won't change my mind / I won't leave the *morro*, no way).

62. In the language of the drug traffickers, "o movimento" (the movement) carries a positive connotation regarding the activities of the trade.

63. The image of the favela conveyed by contemporary Brazilian cinema also reinforces that environment conditions a person (Bentes 1999).

CHAPTER 4

1. Viva-Cred is an extension of financial assistance provided by the NGO Viva Rio. The small business financing comes from the International Bank for Reconstruction and Development (IBRD).

2. The moto-taxis serve residents circulating both within and outside the favela. See

"Cruzando a Rocinha em duas rodas," *Jornal do Brasil*, 25 December 1999, or the video "Moto-taxi Ride through a Rio Favela," *BBC News*, 12 June 2014, http://www.bbc.com /news/av/world-latin-america-27737837/moto-taxi-ride-through-a-rio-favela.

3. See "Rocinha terá guia turístico," *Jornal do Brasil*, 10 April 2000.

4. There are tour operators who prefer vans to open jeeps. For an overview of tourism in Rocinha and other favelas, see Freire-Medeiros 2013.

5. As Jean-Claude Chamboredon and Madeleine Lemaire (1970) stated regarding housing projects in France.

6. Considering the ease of consumer credit that has been quite widespread in recent years.

7. See the work by Landim (1993, 1998) that discusses this universe of militancy, charity, and assistance developing in Rio and elsewhere in Brazil.

8. This dissertation was published as a book under the title *Por que uns e não outros? Caminhada de jovens pobres para a universidade* (Why some and not others? The journey of poor young people to university; Souza e Silva, 1999, 2003). The impact of the discovery of successful university students in the favela was doubtless fundamental to the development of CEASM, an NGO directed by "favela PhDs."

9. Studies of social mobility in the favelas are very rare. There are, however, studies about social mobility on Brazil in general, notably E. Silva 1988 and Scalon 1999.

EPILOGUE

1. See the official website, http://www.upprj.com.
2. See the official website, http://www.pac.gov.br.
3. Most of these organizations have a web presence.
4. See the official website, http://catcomm.org.

Bibliography

Abramo, Pedro. "Uma teoria econômica da favela: Quatro notas sobre o mercado imobiliário informal em favelas e a mobilidade residencial dos pobres." *Cadernos IPPUR*, Rio de Janeiro, vol. 16, no. 2, pp. 103–34, August–December 2002.

———, ed. *A cidade da informalidade: O desafio das cidades latino-americanas.* Rio de Janeiro: Livraria Sette Letras, Fundação de Amparo à Pesquisa do Estado do Rio de Janeiro, 2003.

Abreu, Maurício de Almeida. *Evolução urbana do Rio de Janeiro.* Rio de Janeiro: Zahar / IPLAN-RIO, 1987.

Abreu, Maurício de Almeida, and Lilian Fessler Vaz. "Sobre a origem das favelas." Paper presented at IV Encontro Nacional da ANPUR, Salvador, 1991.

———. "Estudo geográfico da cidade no Brasil: Evolução e avaliação (contribuição à história do pensamento geográfico brasileiro)." *Revista Brasileira de Geografia*, Rio de Janeiro, vol. 56, no. 1/4, pp. 2–122, December–January 1994a.

———. "Reconstruindo uma história esquecida: Origem e expansão inicial das favelas do Rio." *Espaço e Debates*, São Paulo, vol. 14, no. 37, pp. 34–46, 1994b.

Abreu, Regina. *O enigma de "Os Sertões."* Rio de Janeiro: Fundação Nacional de Artes / Rocco, 1998.

Agache, Alfred. *Cidade do Rio de Janeiro: Extensão—remodelação—embelezamento.* Rio de Janeiro: Prefeitura do Distrito Federal; Paris: Foyer Brésilien, 1930.

Almeida, Cícero Antônio F. de. *Canudos, imagens da guerra: Os últimos dias da Guerra de Canudos pelo fotógrafo expedicionário Flávio de Barros.* Rio de Janeiro: Museu da República, Lacerda, 1997.

Almeida, Maria Hermínia Tavares de. "Dilemas da institucionalização das ciências sociais no Rio de Janeiro." In Sérgio Miceli, ed., *História das ciências sociais no Rio de Janeiro.* São Paulo: Vértice (Editora Revista dos Tribunais), IDESP, vol. 1, 1989. pp. 188–216.

Almeida, Roberto Schmidt de. "A geografia e os geógrafos do IBGE no período 1938–1998." PhD diss., Universidade Federal do Rio de Janeiro, 2002.

Alves, Maria Helena Moreira, Philip Evanson, and Fernando Moura. *Vivendo no fogo cruzado: Moradores de favela, traficantes de droga e violência policial no Rio de Janeiro.* São Paulo: Editora da Universidade Estadual Paulista, 2013.

Alvim, Rosilene, and Licia do Prado Valladares. "Infância e sociedade no Brasil: Uma análise de literatura." *Boletim Informativo e Bibliográfico de Ciências Sociais*, Rio de Janeiro, no. 26, pp. 3–37, 1988.

Alvito, Marcos. *As cores de Acari: Uma favela carioca*. Rio de Janeiro: Fundação Getúlio Vargas, 2001.

Ammann, Safira. *Ideologia de desenvolvimento de comunidade no Brasil*. São Paulo: Cortez, 1997.

Amoroso, Mauro. *Nunca é tarde para ser feliz? A imagem das favelas pelas lentes do Correio da Manha*. Curitiba: CRV, 2011.

Andarilho, Jessé. *Fiel*. Rio de Janeiro: Objetiva, 2014.

Anderson, Nels. *The Hobo: The Sociology of the Homeless Man*. Chicago: University of Chicago Press, 1923.

Aragão, Maria Luiza Muniz de. "Favela: Vivem ou vegetam as 1.111 famílias da Barreira do Vasco?" *Serviço Social*, no. 54, pp. 65–75, 1949.

Astier, Isabelle, and Jean-François Laé. "La notion de communauté dans les enquêtes sociales sur l'habitat en France." *Genèses*, no. 5 (Dossier "Observer, Classer, Administrer"), pp. 81–106, September 1991.

Azevedo, Aluízio. *O cortiço*. São Paulo: Martins, 1890.

Azevedo, Cecília. "O sentido da missão no imaginário político norte-americano." *Revista de História Regional*, São Paulo, vol. 3, no. 2, 1998.

———. "As contradições e os limites da 'americanização' da América Latina." Paper presented at XIII Congresso de História Econômica, Associação Internacional de História Econômica, Buenos Aires, 2002.

Backheuser, Everardo. "Habitações populares." In *Relatório apresentado ao Exmº. Sr. Dr. J.J. Seabra, Ministro da Justiça e Negócios Interiores*. Rio de Janeiro: Imprensa Nacional, 1906.

Barbosa, Antônio Carlos Rafael. *Um abraço para todos os amigos: Algumas considerações sobre o tráfico de drogas no Rio de Janeiro*. Niterói: Editora da Universidade Federal Fluminense, 1998.

Barbosa, Jorge Luiz, and Caio Gonçalves Dias, eds. *Solos culturais*. Rio de Janeiro: Observatório de Favelas, 2013.

Barbosa, Lívia. *O jeitinho brasileiro: A arte de ser mais igual que os outros*. 2nd ed. Rio de Janeiro: Campos, 1992.

Barcellos, Caco. *Abusado: O dono do Morro Santa Marta*. Rio de Janeiro: Record, 2003.

Barret-Ducrocq, Françoise. *Pauvreté, charité et morale à Londres au XIXe siècle: Une sainte violence*. Paris: La Découverte, 1991.

Beaud, Stéphane, and Florence Weber. *Guide de l'enquête de terrain: Produire et analyser des données ethnographiques*. Paris: La Découverte, 1997.

Becker, Howard. Introduction to Clifford Shaw, *The Jack-Roller: A Delinquent Boy's Own Story*. Chicago: University of Chicago Press, 1966. pp. v–viii.

———. "Whose Side Are We On?" In *Sociological Work*. Chicago: Aldine, 1970. pp. 123–34.

Beltrame, José Mariano. *Todo dia é segunda-feira*. Rio de Janeiro: Sextante, 2014.

Benchimol, Jaime Larry. *Pereira Passos, um Haussmann tropical: A renovação urbana da cidade do Rio de Janeiro no início do século XX*. Rio de Janeiro: Secretaria Municipal de Cultura, Turismo e Esporte, Coleção Biblioteca Carioca, 1990.

Bentes, Ivana. "The Sertão and the Favela in Contemporary Brazilian Film." In João Luiz Vieira, ed., *Cinema Novo and Beyond*. New York: Museum of Modern Art, 1999.

Berenstein-Jacques, Paola. *Les favelas de Rio: Un enjeu culturel*. Paris: L'Harmattan, 2001a.

————. *Estética da Ginga: A arquitetura das favelas através da obra de Hélio Oiticica*. Rio de Janeiro: Casa da Palavra / RIOARTE, 2001b.

Bernardes, Lysia Maria Cavalcanti. "Pescadores da Ponta do Caju: Aspectos da contribuição de portugueses e espanhóis para o desenvolvimento da pesca na Guanabara." *Revista Brasileira da Geografia*, vol. 20, no. 2, pp. 49–69, April–June 1958.

Bertaux, Daniel. *Biography and Society: The Life History Approach to the Transformation of Sociological Practice*. Beverly Hills, Calif.: Sage, 1981. pp. 29–45.

Bill, M. V., and Celso Athayde. *Falcão: Meninos do tráfico*. Rio de Janeiro: Objetiva, 2006.

Birman, Patricia. "Feitiço, carrego e olho grande, os males do Brasil são: Estudo de um centro umbandista numa favela do Rio de Janeiro." M.A. thesis, Universidade Federal do Rio de Janeiro, 1980.

————. "Favela é comunidade?" In Luiz Antonio Machado da Silva, ed., *Vida sob cerco: Violência e rotina nas favelas do Rio de Janeiro*. Rio de Janeiro: Nova Fronteira, 2008. pp. 99–114.

Bisilliat, Jeanne. *La construction populaire au Brésil: Une expérience à São Paulo*. Paris: Karthala, L'Orstom, 1995.

Blank, Gilda. "Brás de Pina: Experiência de urbanização de favela." In Licia Valladares, ed., *Habitação em questão*. Rio de Janeiro: Zahar, 1980. pp. 93–124.

Bloch, Sérgio, Inês Garçoni, and Marcos Pinto. *Guia gastronômico das favelas do Rio*. Rio de Janeiro: Arte Ensaio, 2012.

Bombart, Jean-Pierre. "Les cultes protestants dans une favela de Rio de Janeiro." *América Latina*, Rio de Janeiro, vol. 12, no. 3, pp. 137–59, July–September 1969.

Bonduki, Nabil, and Raquel Rolnik. "Periferia da Grande São Paulo: Reprodução do espaço como expediente de reprodução da força de trabalho." In Ermínia Maricato, ed., *A produção da casa (e da cidade) no Brasil industrial*. São Paulo: Alfa-Omega, 1979. pp. 117–54.

Bonilla, Frank. "Rio's Favelas: The Rural Slum within the City." American Universities Field Staff Report. *East Coast South America Series*, Rio de Janeiro, vol. 8, no. 3, pp. 1–15, 1961.

Boschi, Renato. *A arte da associação: Política de base e democracia no Brasil*. São Paulo: Vértice (Editora Revista dos Tribunais); Rio de Janeiro: Instituto Universitário de Pesquisas do Rio de Janeiro, 1987.

Boschi, Renato, and Licia do Prado Valladares. "Movimentos associativos de camadas populares urbanas: Análise comparativa de seis casos." In Renato Boschi, ed., *Movimentos coletivos no Brasil urbano*. Rio de Janeiro: Zahar, 1982. pp. 103–43.

Boschi, Renato, and Licia do Prado Valladares. "Problemas teóricos na análise de movimentos sociais: comunidade, ação coletiva e o papel do Estado." *Espaço e Debates*, São Paulo, no. 8, pp. 64–77, 1983.

Bourdieu, Pierre, ed. *La misère du monde*. Paris: Seuil, 1993.

Bourdieu, Pierre, Jean-Claude Chamboredon, and Jean-Claude Passeron. *Le métier de sociologue: Préalables épistémologiques*. 1968. Paris: Mouton, 1980.

Brandão, Alonso Caldas. *Código de obras e legislação complementar: Decreto 6.000 de 1-7-1937*. 4th ed. 2 vols. Coleção de Códigos e Leis Vigentes. Rio de Janeiro: A. Coelho Branco Filho, 1964.

Brasileiro, Ana Maria, Karen Giffen, E. Shluger, and M. A. Ungaretti. "Extending Municipal Services by Building on Local Initiatives: A Project in the Favelas of Rio de Janeiro." *Assignment Children: UNICEF*, no. 57/58, pp. 67–100, 1982.

Bresciani, Maria Stella. *Londres e Paris no século XIX: O espetáculo da pobreza.* 2nd ed. São Paulo: Brasiliense, 1984.

Bretas, Marcos Luiz. *A guerra das ruas: Povo e polícia na cidade do Rio de Janeiro.* Rio de Janeiro: Arquivo Nacional, 1997.

Britto, Ana Lúcia Nogueira de Paiva. "Les modes de gestion des services d'eau et d'assainissement à Rio de Janeiro (1975–1986): Logique technico-sectorielle nationale vs. logiques politiques locales." PhD diss., Université de Paris XII, 1995.

Bronstein, Olga. "De cima para baixo ou de baixo para cima? Considerações em torno da oferta de um serviço público nas favelas do Rio de Janeiro." Paper presented at VI Encontro Nacional da Associação Nacional de Pós-graduação e Pesquisa em Ciências Sociais, Friburgo, 1982.

Brown, Diana. "Macumba and Umbanda in Brasil." PhD diss., Columbia University, 1972.

Bruant, Catherine. "Donat Alfred Agache (1875–1959): L'architecte et le sociologue." *Études Sociales* (Revue de la Société d'Économie et de Science Sociales), no. 122, pp. 23–61, 1994.

———. "Un architecte à 'l'école d'énergie': Donat Alfred Agache, du voyage à l'engagement colonial." *Revue du Monde Musulman et de la Méditerranée / Figures de l'Orientalisme en Architecture,* nos. 73–74, Aix-en-Provence: EDISUD, pp. 99–117, 1996.

Buarque, Cristovam. *O que apartação: O aparelho social no Brasil.* São Paulo: Brasiliense, 1993.

Bulmer, Martin. *The Chicago School of Sociology: Institutionalization, Diversity and the Rise of Sociological Research.* 1984. Reprint, Chicago: University of Chicago Press, 1986.

Burgess, Ernest W. "The Growth of a City: An Introduction to a Research Project." In Robert Park and Ernest W. Burgess, eds., *The City.* Chicago: University of Chicago Press, 1925.

Burgos, Marcelo Baumann. "Dos parques proletários ao Favela-Bairro: As políticas públicas nas favelas do Rio de Janeiro." In Marcos Alvito and Alba Zaluar, eds., *Um século de favela.* Rio de Janeiro: Fundação Getúlio Vargas, 1998. pp. 25–60.

———. "Cidade, territórios e cidadania." *Dados,* vol. 41, no. 1, pp. 189–222, 2005.

Butler, Rémy, and Patrice Noisette. *Le logement social en France, 1815–1981: De la cité ouvrière au grand ensemble.* Paris: La Découverte / Maspero, 1983.

Cano, Ignacio, Doriam Borges, and Eduardo Ribeiro, eds. *Os donos do morro: Uma avaliação exploratória do impacto das UPPs no Rio de Janeiro.* São Paulo: Forum Brasileiro de Segurança Publica; Rio de Janeiro: LAV, Universidade do Estado do Rio de Janeiro, 2012.

Cano, Ignacio, and Thais Duarte, eds. *No sapatinho: A evolução das milícias no Rio de Janeiro (2008–2011).* Rio de Janeiro: Fundação Heinrich Boll, 2012.

Cardoso, Adalberto, ed. *Juventudes na cidade: Violência, cultura, religião, escola.* Rio de Janeiro: Azougue, 2014.

Cardoso, Adauto Lúcio. "Em torno da cidade partida: Dualização, segregação e produção do espaço no Rio de Janeiro." Paper presented at VII Encontro Nacional da ANPUR, Recife, 1997. In *Anais ANPUR,* vol. 2. pp. 1314–33.

Cardoso, Fernando Henrique, and José Luís Reyna. "Industrialização, estrutura ocupacional e estratificação social na América Latina." *Dados,* Rio de Janeiro, vol. 2, no. 3, pp. 4–31, 1967.

Carlos, Ana Fani Alessandri, ed. *Os caminhos da reflexão sobre a cidade e o urbano.* São Paulo: Editora da Universidade de São Paulo, 1994.

Carlos, José. *O Rio de Janeiro de J. Carlos*. Ed. Cassio Loredano; text by Zuenir Ventura. Rio de Janeiro: Lacerda, 1987.

Carré, J., and J. P. Révauger, eds. *Écrire la pauvreté: Les enquêtes sociales britanniques aux XIXe et XXe siècles*. Paris: L'Harmattan, 1995.

Carvalho, Eduardo. *O negócio da terra: A questão fundiária e a justiça*. Rio de Janeiro: Universidade Federal do Rio de Janeiro, 1991.

Carvalho, José Murilo de. *Os bestializados: O Rio de Janeiro e a República que não foi*. São Paulo: Companhia das Letras, 1987.

Carvalho, Lia de Aquino. *Contribuição ao estudo das habitações populares: Rio de Janeiro, 1886–1906*. Rio de Janeiro: Prefeitura da Cidade do Rio de Janeiro, Secretaria Municipal de Cultura, Coleção Biblioteca Carioca, 1986.

Carvalho, Maria Alice Rezende de. *Quatro vezes cidade*. Rio de Janeiro: 7Letras, 1985.

Carvalho, Monique B. "Os dilemas da 'pacificação': Práticas de controle e disciplinarização na 'gestão da paz' em uma favela do Rio de Janeiro." PhD diss., Universidade do Estado do Rio de Janeiro, 2014.

Casé, Paulo. *Favela: Uma exegese a partir da Mangueira*. Rio de Janeiro: Relume-Dumará-Prefeitura, 1996.

Castel, Robert. *Les métamorphoses de la question sociale: Une chronique du salariat*. Paris: Fayard, 1994.

Castells, Manuel. "Y a-t-il une sociologie urbaine?" *Revue Sociologie du Travail*, vol. 10, no. 1, pp. 72–90, 1968.

———. *Cidade, democracia e socialismo*. Rio de Janeiro: Paz e Terra, 1980.

Castro, Josué de. *Geografia da fome: O dilema brasileiro*. Rio de Janeiro: Civilização Brasileira, 2001.

Castro, Paulo R. de, et al. *Galo cantou! A conquista da propriedade pelos moradores do Cantagalo*. Rio de Janeiro: Record, 2011.

Cavalcanti, Mariana. "Do barraco à casa: Tempo, espaço e valor(es) em uma favela consolidada." *Revista Brasileira de Ciências Sociais*, vol. 24, no. 69, February 2009.

———. "A espera, em ruínas: Urbanismo, estética e política no Rio de Janeiro da 'PACificação.'" *Dilemas, Revista de Estudos de Conflito e Controle Social*, vol. 6, no. 2, pp. 191–228, April–May–June 2013.

Cavallieri, Paulo Fernando. "Favelas cariocas: Mudanças na infra-estrutura." In *4 estudos*. Rio de Janeiro: IPLAN-RIO, 1986. pp. 19–35.

Cavallieri, Paulo Fernando, and Adriana Vial. *Favelas na cidade do Rio de Janeiro: O quadro populacional com base no censo 2010*. Rio de Janeiro: Instituto Pereira Passos, Coleção Estudos Cariocas, May 2012.

Cechetto, Fátima. "As galeras funk cariocas: Entre o lúdico e o violento." In Hermano Vianna, ed., *Galeras cariocas*. Rio de Janeiro: Editora da Universidade Federal do Rio de Janeiro, 1997. pp. 95–118.

Cefai, Daniel. "Combining Methods in Field Studies: A Few Things We Learn from Chicago Sociology." In *CD-ROM: Social Science Methodology in the New Millennium / Colloque de l'International Sociological Association*. Cologne: Jorge Blasius. 2000.

Centro de Defesa dos Direitos Humanos Bento Rubião. *Favelas e as organizações comunitárias*. Petrópolis: Vozes, 1994.

Cezar, Paulo Bastos. "Evolução da população de favelas na cidade do Rio de Janeiro: Uma reflexão sobre os dados mais recentes." Estudos da Cidade, Prefeitura da Cidade

do Rio de Janeiro: Armazém de Dados da Prefeitura. February 2002. http://www
.armazemdedados.rio.rj.gov.br.

Chalhoub, Sidney. *Cidade febril: Cortiços e epidemias na Corte Imperial*. São Paulo:
Companhia das Letras, 1996.

Chamboredon, Jean-Claude, and Madeleine Lemaire. "Proximité spatiale et distance
sociale: Les grands ensembles et leur peuplement." *Revue Française de Sociologie*, vol. 11,
pp. 3–33, 1970.

Chapoulie, Jean-Michel. *La tradition sociologique de Chicago, 1892–1961*. Paris: Seuil, 2001.

Chombart de Lauwe, Paul-Henri. *Paris et l'agglomération parisienne*. Vol. 1, *L'espace social
dans une grande cité*, Paris: Presses Universitaires de France, 1952.

Clifford, James. "Notes on (Field) Notes." In Roger Sanjek, ed., *Fieldnotes: The Makings of
Anthropology*. Ithaca, N.Y.: Cornell University Press, 1990. pp. 44–70.

Coelho, Magda, and Licia do Prado Valladares. "Pobreza urbana e mercado de trabalho:
Uma análise bibliográfica." *Boletim Informativo e Bibliográfico de Ciências Sociais*, Rio de
Janeiro, no. 14, 2nd semester, pp. 5–28, 1982.

Compans, Rose. "A cidade contra a favela." *Revista Brasileira de Estudos Urbanos e
Regionais*, vol. 9, no. 1, pp. 83–99, May 2007.

Conceição, Wellington da Silva. "Trajetórias de jovens de origem popular rumo à carreira
acadêmica: Mobilidade social, identidades e conflitos." M.A. thesis, Universidade do
Estado do Rio de Janeiro, 2011.

Conn, Stephen. "The 'Squatters' Rights of Favelados." *Ciências Econômicas e Sociais*, São
Paulo, vol. 3, no. 2, pp. 50–142, December 1968.

Conniff, Michael. *Urban Politics in Brazil: The Rise of Populism, 1925–1945*. Pittsburgh:
University of Pittsburgh Press, 1981.

Copans, Jean. *L'enquête ethnologique de terrain*. Collection 128. Paris: Nathan, 1999.

Corrêa, Mariza, ed. *História da antropologia no Brasil: Testemunho, Emilio Willems e Donald
Pierson*. Campinas: UNICAMP, 1987.

Costallat, Benjamim. "A favela que eu vi." In *Mistérios do Rio*. Rio de Janeiro: Prefeitura
Municipal da Cidade do Rio de Janeiro, Secretaria Municipal de Cultura, 1995.

Costa Pinto, Luiz Aguiar, ed. *O negro no Rio de Janeiro: Relações de raça numa sociedade
em mudança*. São Paulo: Companhia Editora Nacional, 1953. Reprint, Rio de Janeiro:
Editora da Universidade Federal do Rio de Janeiro, 1998.

Coulon, Alain. *L'École de Chicago*. 1992. Paris: Presses Universitaires de France, 1994.

Cressey, Paul G. *The Taxi-Dance Hall: A Sociological Study in Commercialized Recreation
and City Life*. Chicago: University of Chicago Press, 1932.

Cunha, Christina Vital da. *Oração de traficante*. Rio de Janeiro: Garamond Universitária;
Fundação de Amparo à Pesquisa do Estado do Rio de Janeiro, 2015.

Cunha, Euclides da. *Edição crítica de "Os Sertões."* Ed. Walnice Nogueira Galvão. São Paulo:
Brasiliense, 1985.

———. *Backlands: The Canudos Campaign*. Translated by Elizabeth Lowe. New York:
Penguin, 2010.

———. *Diário de uma expedição*. Ed. Walnice Nogueira Galvão. 1st ed. Introduction
by Gilberto Freire. Rio de Janeiro: Livraria José Olympio, Coleção Documentos
Brasileiros, 1939; São Paulo: Companhia das Letras, Coleção Retratos do Brasil, 2000.

———. *Os Sertões: Campanha de Canudos*. Edition, preface, chronology, notes, and
indexes by Leopoldo M. Bernucci. São Paulo: Ateliê, Imprensa Oficial do Estado,
Arquivo do Estado, 2001.

Cunha, Neiva Vieira da, and Marco Antônio da Silva Mello. "Novos conflitos na cidade: A UPP e o processo de urbanização na favela." *Dilemas, Revista de Estudos de Conflito e Controle Social*, vol. 4, no. 3, pp. 371–401, July–August–September 2011.

———. "A UPP e o processo de urbanização na favela Santa Marta: Notas de campo." In Marco Antônio da Silva Mello, Luiz Antonio Machado da Silva, Letícia de Luna Freire, and Soraya Silveira Simões, eds., *Favelas cariocas: Ontem e hoje*. Rio de Janeiro: Garamond, 2012. pp. 433–74.

Cunha, Olívia Maria Gomes da. "Cinco vezes favela: Uma reflexão." In Gilberto Velho and Marcos Alvito, eds., *Cidadania e violência*. Rio de Janeiro: Editora da Universidade Federal do Rio de Janeiro, Fundação Getúlio Vargas, 1996. pp. 188–217.

DaMatta, Roberto. "O ofício do etnólogo, ou como ter 'anthropological blues.'" In Edson de Oliveira Nunes, ed., *A aventura sociológica*. Rio de Janeiro: Zahar, 1978.

———. *Carnavais, malandros e heróis: Para uma sociologia do dilema brasileiro*. 5th ed. Rio de Janeiro: Rocco, 2000.

Damazio, Sylvia F. *Retrato social do Rio de Janeiro na virada do século*. Rio de Janeiro: Editora da Universidade do Estado do Rio de Janeiro, 1996.

Davidovitch, Fany. "Programa Favela-Bairro e tendências de restauração da metrópole: O caso do Rio de Janeiro." Paper presented at VII Encontro Nacional da ANPUR, 1997, Recife. *Anais ANPUR*, vol. 2. pp. 1473–83.

———. "Repensando a favela: Tendências e questões." Paper presented at XXIII Encontro Anual da ANPOCS, Caxambu, 1999.

Davis, Mike. *Planet of Slums*. New York: Verso, 2007.

Deccache-Maia, Eliane. "Esporte e juventude no Borel." *Estudos Históricos*, Rio de Janeiro, vol. 13, no. 23, pp. 192–206, 1999.

Depaule, Jean-Charles, and Christian Topalov. "La ville à travers ses mots." *Enquête*, no. 4. pp. 247–66, 1996.

de Soto, Hernando. *Economia subterrânea: Uma análise da realidade peruana*. Rio de Janeiro: Globo, 1987.

Desrosières, Alain. *La politique des grands nombres: Histoire de la raison statistique*. Paris: La Découverte, 1993.

Dias, Amanda. "Du Moukhayyam à la favela: Une étude comparative entre un camp de réfugiés palestiniens au Liban et une favela carioca." PhD diss., École des Hautes Études en Sciences Sociales and Universidade do Estado do Rio de Janeiro, 2009.

Diegues Júnior, Manuel. "Apresentação." *América Latina*, Rio de Janeiro, vol. 12, no. 3, pp. 3–6, July–September 1969.

Diniz, Eli. *Voto e máquina política: Patronagem e clientelismo no Rio de Janeiro*. Rio de Janeiro: Paz e Terra, 1982.

———. "Engenharia institucional e políticas públicas: Dos conselhos técnicos às câmaras setoriais." In Dulce Pandolfi, ed., *Repensando o Estado Novo*. Rio de Janeiro: Fundação Getúlio Vargas, 1999. pp. 21–38.

Doimo, Ana Maria. *A vez e a voz popular: Movimentos sociais e participação política no Brasil pós 70*. Rio de Janeiro: Relume Dumará, 1995.

Donovan, Michel Geiger. "At the Doors of Legality: Planners, *Favelados*, and the Titling of Urban Brazil." PhD diss., University of California, Berkeley, 2007.

Dowdney, Luke. *Crianças do tráfico: Um estudo de caso de crianças em violência armada organizada no Rio de Janeiro*. Rio de Janeiro, 7Letras, 2003.

Drummont, Didier. *Architectes des favelas*. Paris: Dunod, 1981.

Duarte, Cristiane R. de Siqueira, Oswaldo Luiz Silva, and Alice Brasileiro, eds. *Favela, um bairro: Propostas metodológicas para a intervenção pública em favelas do Rio de Janeiro*. São Paulo: Grupo de Pesquisas HABITAT / Pro-Editores, 1996.

Duarte, Mário Sérgio. *Liberdade para o Alemão: O resgate de Canudos*. Rio de Janeiro: Ciência Moderna, 2012.

Dudu do Morro Agudo. *Enraizados: Os híbridos glocais*. Rio de Janeiro: Aeroplano, 2010.

Durham, Eunice, and Ruth Cardoso. "O ensino da antropologia no Brasil." *Revista de Antropologia da USP*, São Paulo, vol. 9, no. 1–2, pp. 91–107, July–December 1961.

Edmundo, Luiz. *O Rio de Janeiro do meu tempo*. Rio de Janeiro: Imprensa Nacional, 1938.

Engels, Frederick. *The Condition of the Working Class in England: From Personal Observation and Authentic Sources*. Introduction by Eric Hobsbawm. London: Panther, 1969.

Erlanger, Luís. *José Júnior: No fio da navalha*. Rio de Janeiro: Record, 2015.

Eufrásio, Mário A. *Estrutura urbana e ecologia humana: A escola de sociologia de Chicago (1915–1940)*. São Paulo: Editora 34, 1999.

Evenson, Norma. *Two Brazilian Capitals: Architecture and Urbanism in Rio de Janeiro and Brasília*. New Haven, Conn.: Yale University Press, 1973.

Falcão, Edgar de Cerqueira. *Oswaldo Cruz: Monumento histórico*, vol. 1, *A incompreensão da época*. São Paulo: Brasília Documenta, 1971.

Faria, Vilmar. "Desenvolvimento, urbanização e mudanças na estrutura do emprego: A experiência brasileira nos últimos trinta anos." In Bernardo Sorj and Maria Hermínia Almeida, eds., *Sociedade política no Brasil pós-64*. São Paulo: Brasiliense, 1983. pp. 118–63.

Farias, Juliana. "Governo de Mortes: Uma etnografia da gestão de populações de favelas no Rio de Janeiro." PhD diss., Universidade Federal do Rio de Janeiro, 2014.

Farias, Luiz Kleber. "A representação de interesses em favelas: Vida e morte da Associação de Comércio e Indústria de Rio das Pedras." In Marcelo Baumann Burgos, ed., *A utopia da comunidade: Rio das Pedras, uma favela carioca*. São Paulo: Loyola, 2002. pp. 135–48.

Fassin, Didier. "Exclusion, *underclass, marginalidad*: Figures contemporaines de la pauvreté urbaine en France, aux États-Unis et en Amérique Latine." *Revue Française de Sociologie*, vol. 37, pp. 37–75, 1996.

Fausto Neto, Ana Maria Quiroga. "Violência e dominação: As favelas voltam à cena." *Revista Sociedade e Estado*, vol. 10, no. 2, pp. 417–38, July–December 1995.

Fernandes, André. *Perseguindo um sonho: A história da fundação da primeira agência de noticias das favelas do mundo*. Rio de Janeiro: ANF, 2014.

Fernandes, Edésio. "A regularização de favelas no Brasil: Problemas e perspectivas." In Nelson Saule Júnior, ed., *Direito à cidade: Trilhas legais para o direito às cidades sustentáveis*. São Paulo: Polis, 1999. pp. 127–56.

———. "Perspectivas para a renovação das políticas de legalização de favelas no Brasil." *Cadernos IPPUR*, Rio de Janeiro, vol. 15, no. 1, January–July 2001.

Fernandes, Ruben César. *Privado porém público: Terceiro setor na América Latina*. 2nd ed. Rio de Janeiro: Relume-Dumará / CIVICUS, 1994.

Fernandes, Tânia Maria, and Renato Gama-Rosa Costa. *Histórias de pessoas e lugares: Memórias das comunidades de Manguinhos*. Rio de Janeiro: Fiocruz, 2009.

Ferreira, Aurélio Buarque de Holanda. *Novo Aurélio século XXI: O dicionário da língua portuguesa*. 3rd ed. Rio de Janeiro: Nova Fronteira, 1999.

Ferreira, Marieta de Moraes. "Diario personal, autobiografía y fuentes de Pierre Deffontaines: Historia, antropología y fuentes orales." Barcelona, no. 24, pp. 95–106, 2000.

Fundação Getúlio Vargas (FGV) / Centro de Pesquisa e Documentação de História Contemporânea do Brasil (CPDOC). *Dicionário histórico biográfico brasileiro, 1930–1983*, ed. Israel Beloch and Alzira Alves de Abreu. 1984. Rio de Janeiro: Forense Universitária, FGV/CPDOC, Financiadora de Inovação e Pesquisa, 2001.

Fiell, Repper. *Da favela para as favelas: História e experiência do Repper Fiell*. Rio de Janeiro: Coletivo Visão da Favela Brasil, 2011.

Figueiredo, Marcus. "O financiamento das ciências sociais: A estratégia de fomento da Fundação Ford e da FINEP." *Boletim Informativo e Bibliográfico de Ciências Sociais*, Rio de Janeiro, no. 26, pp. 38–55, 1988.

Fine, Gary Alan, ed. *A Second Chicago School? The Development of a Postwar American Sociology*. Chicago: University of Chicago Press, 1995.

Fischer, Brodwyn. *A Poverty of Rights: Citizenship and Inequality in Twentieth-Century Rio de Janeiro*. Stanford, Calif.: Stanford University Press, 2008.

Fischer, Fritz. *Making Them Like Us: Peace Corps Volunteers in the 1960s*. Washington, D.C.: Smithsonian Institution Press, 1998.

Fleury, Sonia. "Militarização do social como estratégia de integração: O caso da UPP do Santa Marta." *Sociologias*, Porto Alegre, vol. 14, no. 30, pp. 194–221, May–August 2012.

Fraiha, Silvia, and Tiza Lobo. *Bairros do Rio (neighborhoods): Gávea, Rocinha e São Conrado*. Rio de Janeiro: Fraiha, n.d.

Freire-Medeiros, Bianca. "A favela que se vê e que se vende: Reflexões e polêmicas em torno de um destino turístico." *Revista Brasileira de Ciências Sociais*, vol. 22, pp. 61–72, 2007.

———. *Touring Poverty*. New York: Routledge, 2013.

Freire-Medeiros, Bianca, Marcio Grijo Vilarouca, and Palloma Menezes. "Gringos no Santa Marta: Quem são, o que pensam e como avaliam a experiência turística na favela." In Angela Moulin S. Penalva Santos, Glaucio José Marafon, and Maria Josefina Gabriel Sant'Anna, eds., *Rio de Janeiro: Um território em mutação*. Rio de Janeiro: Gramma / Fundação de Amparo à Pesquisa do Estado do Rio de Janeiro, 2012. pp. 183–206.

Fridman, Fania. *Donos do Rio em nome do Rei: Uma história fundiária da cidade do Rio de Janeiro*. Rio de Janeiro: Garamond, 1999.

Fried, Albert, and Richard Elman. *Charles Booth's London*. Harmondsworth, UK: Penguin, 1971.

Friedman, John. *Empowerment: The Politics of Alternative Development*. Cambridge, Mass.: Blackwell, 1992.

Fundação Oswaldo Cruz. "Brasil ser tão Canudos." Special issue of *História, Ciências, Saúde*, Manguinhos, vol. 5, July 1998.

———. *Oswaldo Cruz: Inventário analítico*. Rio de Janeiro: 2003.

Garcia, Maria Japor de Oliveira, and Vera Maria Fürtenau. *O acervo de Euclides da Cunha na Biblioteca Nacional*. Rio de Janeiro: Fundação Biblioteca Nacional; Campinas: Editora da UNICAMP, 1995.

Garreau, Lydie. *L. J. Lebret, un homme traqué (1897–1996)*. Villeurbanne, France: Golias, 1997.

Gilbert, Alan. "The Return of the Slum: Does Language Matter?" *International Journal of Urban and Regional Research*, vol. 31, no. 4, pp. 697–713, 2007.

Gilbert, Alan, and Peter Ward. *Housing, the State, and the Poor*. New York: Cambridge University Press, 1985.

Glass, Ruth. "Urban Sociology in Great Britain: A Trend Report." *Current Sociology* (UNESCO), vol. 4, no. 4, pp. 2–76, 1955.

Godoy, Armando Augusto de. *A Urbs e os seus problemas*. (Articles published between 1925 and 1936.) Rio de Janeiro: Jornal do Commercio, 1943.

Goffman, Erving. *Stigma*. Englewood Cliffs, N.J.: Prentice-Hall, 1963.

Goirand, Camille. *La politique des favelas*. Centre d'études et de recherches internationales (CERI). Paris: Karthala, 2001.

Goldstein, Donna. *Laughter Out of Place: Race, Class, Violence, and Sexuality in a Rio Shantytown*. Berkeley: University of California Press, 2003.

Goldwasser, Maria Julia. *O palácio do samba: Estudo antropológico da escola de samba Estação Primeira de Mangueira*. Rio de Janeiro: Zahar, 1975.

Gomes, Angela de Castro. "Ideologia e trabalho no Estado Novo." In Dulce Pandolfi, ed., *Repensando o Estado Novo*. Rio de Janeiro: Fundação Getúlio Vargas, 1999. pp. 53–72.

Gomes, Angela de Castro, and Marieta de Moraes Ferreira. "Industrialização e classe trabalhadora no Rio de Janeiro: Novas perspectivas de análise." *Boletim Informativo e Bibliográfico de Ciências Sociais*, Rio de Janeiro, 2nd semester, no. 24, pp. 11–40, 1987.

Gomes, Manoel. *As lutas do povo do Borel*. Preface by Luiz Carlos Prestes. Rio de Janeiro: Muro, 1980.

Gomes, Maria de Fátima C. M., Ana Izabel de Carvalho Pelegrino, C. E. Reginensi, and L. L. Fernandes. *Desigualdade e exclusão nas metrópoles brasileiras: Alternativas para seu enfrentamento nas favelas do Rio de Janeiro*. Rio de Janeiro: HPComunicações, Arco-Iris, 2006.

Gonçalves, Rafael Soares. *Favelas do Rio de Janeiro: História e direito*. Rio de Janeiro: Pallas, Pontifícia Universidade Católica do Rio de Janeiro, 2013.

———. *Les favelas de Rio de Janeiro: Histoire et droit, XIXe et XXe siècles*. Paris: L'Harmattan, 2010.

Gondim, Linda Maria. "A manipulação do estigma de favelado na política habitacional do Rio de Janeiro." *Revista de Ciências Sociais*, no. 1/2, pp. 27–44, 1982.

Goulart, José Alípio. *As favelas do Distrito Federal*. Rio de Janeiro: Ministério da Agricultura, Serviço de Informação Agrícola, 1957.

Grabois, Gisélia Potengy. "Em busca da integração: A política de remoção de favelas do Rio de Janeiro." M.A. thesis, Universidade Federal do Rio de Janeiro, 1973.

Grafmeyer, Yves. *Sociologie urbaine*. Paris: Nathan, 1994.

Grafmeyer, Yves, and Isaac Joseph. *L'École de Chicago: Naissance de l'écologie urbaine*. Paris: Éditions du Champ urbain, 1979. Reprint, Paris: Aubier Montaigne, 1984.

Grignon, Claude, and Jean-Claude Passeron. *Le savant et le populaire: Misérabilisme et populisme en sociologie et en littérature*. Paris: Hautes Études, Gallimard, Seuil, 1989.

Guerrand, R. H., and M. A. Rupp. *Brève histoire du service social en France, 1896–1976*. Toulouse: Privat, 1978.

Guia de ruas Maré 2012. Rio de Janeiro: Redes de Desenvolvimento da Maré, Observatório de Favelas, 2012.

Guimarães, Alberto Passos. "As favelas do Distrito Federal." *Revista Brasileira de Estatística*, Rio de Janeiro, vol. 14, no. 55, pp. 250–78, July–September 1953.

Guimarães, Eloísa. *Escola, galeras e narcotráfico*. Rio de Janeiro: Editora da Universidade Federal do Rio de Janeiro, 1998.

Guimarães, Dinah, and Lauro Cavalcanti. *Morar: A casa brasileira*. Rio de Janeiro: Avenir, 1984.

Gunn, Philip, and Telma de Barros Correia. "Urbanismo, a medicina e a biologia nas palavras e imagens da cidade." *Revista PÓS*, São Paulo, 2002. pp. 34–61.

Gutierrez, Adriana C., Elyne Engstrom, and G. W. de Sousa Campos. "Território integrado de atenção à saúde: A experiência do TEIAS Escola Manguinhos como um novo modelo de atenção e gestão na garantia do direito à saúde." *Saúde e Direitos Humanos*, vol. 7, no. 7, pp. 39–51, 2010.

Halbwachs, Maurice. "Chicago, expérience ethnique." In *Annales d'Histoire Économique et Sociale*, vol. 4. Paris: Armand Colin, 1932. Reprinted in Yves Grafmeyer and Isaac Joseph, eds., *L'École de Chicago: Naissance de l'écologie urbaine*. Paris: Aubier, 1984.

Hasenbalg, Carlos, and Nelson do Valle Silva. *Estrutura social, mobilidade e raça*. São Paulo: Vértice, 1998.

Herpin, Nicolas. *Les sociologues américains et le siècle*. Paris: Presses Universitaires de France, 1973.

Herschmann, Micael, Simone Kropf, and Clarisse Nunes. *Missionários do progresso: Médicos, engenheiros e educadores no Rio de Janeiro, 1870–1937*. Rio de Janeiro: Diadorim, 1996.

Herschmann, Micael, and Carlos Alberto Messeder Pereira. *A invenção do Brasil moderno: Medicina, educação e engenharia nos anos 20–30*. Rio de Janeiro: Rocco, 1994.

Heye, Ana Margareth. "Mata Machado: Um estudo sobre moradia urbana." M.A. thesis, Universidade Federal do Rio de Janeiro, 1979.

Himmelfarb, Gertrude. *The Idea of Poverty: England in the Early Industrial Age*. Boston: Faber and Faber, 1984.

Hochman, Gilberto. *A era do saneamento: As bases da política de saúde pública no Brasil*. São Paulo: HUCITEC / Associação Nacional de Pós-graduação e Pesquisa em Ciências Sociais, 1998a.

———. "Logo ali, no final da avenida: Os sertões redefinidos pelo movimento sanitarista da 1a República." *História, Ciências, Saúde: Manguinhos*, supplement, no. 5, pp. 217–35, July 1998b.

Hoenack, Judith. "Marketing, Supply and Their Social Ties in Rio Favelas." Paper presented at XXXVII Congreso Internacional de Americanistas, Mar del Plata, 1966.

Hoffman, Elizabeth Cobbs. *All You Need Is Love: The Peace Corps and the Spirit of the 1960s*. Cambridge, Mass.: Harvard University Press, 1998.

Hoffman, Helga. *Desemprego e subemprego o Brasil*. São Paulo: Ática, 1977.

Houée, Paul. *Un éveilleur d'humanité: Louis Joseph Lebret*. Paris: L'Atelier, Ouvrières, 1997.

Hughes, Everett C. *Le regard sociologique: Essais choisis*. Ed. Jean-Michel Chapoulie. Paris: Éditions de l'École des Hautes Études en Sciences Sociales, 1996.

IPLAN-RIO. *Cadastro de favelas*. 2nd ed. Vol. 1, January. Rio de Janeiro: Prefeitura da Cidade do Rio de Janeiro, Secretaria Municipal de Desenvolvimento Social, 1983a.

———. *Cadastro de favelas: Manual do usuário*. Vol. 2, January. Rio de Janeiro: Prefeitura da Cidade do Rio de Janeiro, Secretaria Municipal de Desenvolvimento Social, 1983b.

———. *Favelas cariocas: Alguns dados estatísticos*. Rio de Janeiro: Prefeitura da Cidade do Rio de Janeiro, IPLAN-RIO, 1993.

———. *Favelas cariocas: Índice de qualidade urbana*. Estudos da Cidade. Rio de Janeiro: Prefeitura da Cidade do Rio de Janeiro, 1997.

Jamur, Marilena. "Imaginaire du changement et idéologie de la permanence: La formation des assistants sociaux au Brésil (1936–1988)." PhD diss., École des Hautes Études en Sciences Sociales, 1990.

Jesus, Carolina Maria de. *Quarto de despejo*. Rio de Janeiro: Francisco Alves, 1960.

Jones, Gareth Stedman. *Outcast London: A Study in the Relationship between Classes in Victorian Society*. Harmondsworth, UK: Penguin, 1976.

Júnior, Otávio. *O livreiro do Alemão*. São Paulo: Panda, 2011.

Kalaora, Bernard, and Antoine Savoye. "Frédéric Le Play, un sociologue engagé." In *Frédéric Le Play, Ouvriers des deux mondes*. Paris: À l'Enseigne de l'Arbre Verdoyant, 1983. pp. 320–23.

Kant de Lima, Roberto. *A antropologia da academia: Quando os índios somos nós*. 2nd ed. Niterói: Editora da Universidade Federal Fluminense, 1997.

Kant de Lima, Roberto, Michel Misse, and Ana Paula Mendes Miranda. "Violência, criminalidade, segurança pública e justiça criminal no Brasil: Uma bibliografia." *Boletim Informativo e Bibliográfico das Ciências Sociais*, Rio de Janeiro, no. 50, pp. 45–124, 2000.

Kantor, Iris, Débora A. Maciel, and Júlio Assis Simões, eds. *A Escola Livre de Sociologia e Política: Anos de formação, 1993–1953*. São Paulo: Escuta, 2001.

Kaufmann, Jean-Claude. *L'entretien compréhensif*. Paris: Nathan, 1996.

Knauss, Paulo, and Mário Sérgio Brum. "Encontro marcado: A favela como objeto da pesquisa histórica." In Marco Antônio da Silva Mello, Luiz Antonio Machado da Silva, Letícia de Luna Freire, and Soraya Silveira Simões, eds., *Favelas cariocas: Ontem e hoje*. Rio de Janeiro: Garamond, 2012. pp. 121–40.

Kowarick, Lúcio. *Capitalismo e marginalidade na América Latina*. Rio de Janeiro: Paz e Terra, 1975.

———. *A espoliação urbana*. Rio de Janeiro: Paz e Terra, 1979.

———. *Trabalho e vadiagem: A origem do trabalho livre no Brasil*. São Paulo: Brasiliense, 1987.

Kropf, Simone Petraglia. "Sonho da razão, alegoria de ordem: O discurso dos engenheiros sobre a cidade do Rio de Janeiro no final do século XIX e início do século XX." In Micael Herschmann, Simone Kropf, and Clarisse Nunes, eds., *Missionários do progresso: Médicos, engenheiros e educadores no Rio de Janeiro, 1870–1937*. Rio de Janeiro: Diadorim, 1996.

Lago, Luciana Corrêa do. "A 'periferia' metropolitana como lugar do trabalho: Da cidade-dormitório à cidade plena." *Cadernos IPPUR*, vol. 21, no. 2, pp. 9–28, August–December 2007.

Lambert, Jacques. *Os dois Brasis*. Rio de Janeiro: Instituto Nacional de Estudos e Pesquisas Educacionais Anísio Teixeira, 1959.

Lamparelli, Celso Monteiro. "O ideário do urbanismo em São Paulo em meados do século XX: Louis-Joseph Lebret e a pesquisa urbano-regional no Brasil." *Cadernos de Pesquisa do LAP*, São Paulo. Universidade de São Paulo / Faculdade de Arquitetura e Urbanismo, no. 5, pp. 27–54, March–April 1995.

Landim, Leilah. *Para além do mercado e do Estado? Filantropia e cidadania no Brasil*. Rio de Janeiro: Instituto de Estudos da Religião, 1993.

———, ed. *Ações em sociedade: Militância, caridade, assistência, etc*. Rio de Janeiro: Núcleo de Ativação Urbana, 1998.

Laplantine, François. *La description ethnographique*. Paris: Nathan, 1996.

Lassave, Pierre. *Les sociologues et la recherche urbaine dans la France contemporaine*. Toulouse: Presses Universitaires du Mirail, 1997.

Lebret, Louis-Joseph. "Introduction générale à l'économie humaine." In *Curso ministrado na Escola Livre de Sociologia e Política de São Paulo, de 14 de abril a 5 de junho*, 4 vols., 1947.

———. "Sondagem preliminar a um estudo sobre a habitação em São Paulo." *Revista do Arquivo*, vol. 139, pp. 7–52, 1951.

———. *Manuel de l'enquêteur*. Paris: Presses Universitaires de France, 1952.

Bibliography

Lebret, Louis-Joseph, and R. Bride (in collaboration with H. Hollard et al.). *L'enquête urbaine: L'analyse du quartier et de la ville*. Paris: Presses Universitaires de France, 1955.

Leclerc, Gérard. *L'observation de l'homme: Une histoire des enquêtes sociales*. Paris: Seuil, 1979.

Leeds, Anthony. "Economic Cycles in Brazil: The Persistence of a Total Culture-Pattern: Cacao and Other Cases." PhD diss., Columbia University, 1957.

———. "Brazilian Careers and Social Structure: An Evolutionary Model and Case History." *American Anthropologist*, vol. 66, pp. 1321–47, 1964.

———. "The Anthropology of Cities: Some Methodological Issues." In Elizabeth Eddy, ed., *Urban Anthropology: Research Perspectives and Strategies*. Southern Anthropological Society Proceedings, no. 2. Athens: University of Georgia Press, 1968.

———. "The Significant Variables Determining the Character of Squatter Settlements." *América Latina*, Rio de Janeiro, vol. 12, no. 3, pp. 44–86, July–September 1969.

Leeds, Anthony, and Elizabeth Leeds. *A sociologia do Brasil urbano*. Rio de Janeiro: Zahar, 1978.

Leeds, Elizabeth. "Forms of 'Squatment' Political Organization: The Politics of Control in Brazil." PhD diss., University of Texas, Austin, 1972.

———. "Political Complementarity of Favelas with the Larger Society of Rio de Janeiro." Paper presented at XXXVII Congreso Internacional de Americanistas, Mar del Plata, 1966.

———. "Cocaine and Parallel Politics in the Brazilian Urban Periphery: Constraints on Local Level Democratization." *Latin American Research Review*, vol. 31, no. 33, pp. 47–83, 1996.

Leitão, Gerônimo. *Dos barracos de madeira aos prédios de quitinetes: Uma analise do processo de produção da moradia na favela da Rocinha, ao longo de cinquenta anos*. Niterói: Editora da Universidade Federal Fluminense, 2009.

Leite, Marcia Pereira. "Entre o individualismo e a solidariedade: Dilemas da política e da cidadania no Rio de Janeiro." *Revista Brasileira de Ciências Sociais* (Associação Nacional de Pós-graduação e Pesquisa em Ciências Sociais), vol. 15, no. 44, pp. 73–90, October 2000.

———. "Religião e politica no espaço publico: Moradores de favelas contra a violência e por justiça." In Claudia Mafra and Ronaldo de Almeida, eds., *Religiões e cidades: Rio de Janeiro e São Paulo*. São Paulo: Terceiro Nome / Fundação de Amparo à Pesquisa do Estado de São Paulo, 2009. pp. 207–28.

Leite, Marcia Pereira, and Luiz Antonio Machado da Silva. "Circulação de fronteiras no Rio de Janeiro: A experiência urbana de jovens moradores de favelas em contexto de 'pacificação.'" In Neiva Vieira da Cunha and Gabriel Feltran, *Sobre periferias*. Rio de Janeiro: Lamparina e Fundação de Amparo à Pesquisa do Estado do Rio de Janeiro, 2013.

Leme, Maria Cristina da Silva. "Apresentação: A pesquisa pioneira de Lebret sobre as condições de habitação em São Paulo." *Espaço e Debates*, vol. 24/25, pp. 110–13, January–July 2004.

Leme, Maria Cristina da Silva, and Celso Lamparelli. "A politização do urbanismo no Brasil: A vertente católica." In *IX Encontro Nacional da ANPUR*, vol. 2. Rio de Janeiro, 2001. pp. 675–87.

Le Play, Frédéric. *La méthode sociale*. Ed. Antoine Savoy. 1879. Paris: Méridiens Klincksieck, 1989.

Lepoutre, David. *Coeur de banlieue: Codes, rites et langages*. Paris: Odile Jacob, 1997.

Letalien, Bethany Lynn. "Vexations, Volumes, and Volunteers: Institutionalization and the Veneration of Information at a Small International NGO." PhD diss., University of Texas, Austin, 2009.

Lewis, Oscar. *Five Families: Mexican Case Studies in the Culture of Poverty*. New York: New American Library, Mentor, 1959.

———. *The Children of Sanchez: Autobiography of a Mexican Family*. Harmondsworth, UK: Penguin, 1961.

———. "The Culture of Poverty." *Scientific American*, vol. 215, no. 4, pp. 19–25, October 1966.

Lima, Arlete Alves. *Serviço social no Brasil: A ideologia de uma década*. 3rd ed. São Paulo: Cortez, 1987.

Lima, Nísia Verônica Trindade. "O movimento de favelas do Rio de Janeiro: Políticas do estado e lutas sociais (1954–1973)." M.A. thesis, Instituto Universitário de Pesquisas do Rio de Janeiro, 1989.

———. *Um sertão chamado Brasil: Intelectuais e representação geográfica da identidade nacional*. Rio de Janeiro: Revan / Instituto Universitário de Pesquisas do Rio de Janeiro / Universidade Cândido Mendes, 1999.

Limongi, Fernando. "A Escola Livre de Sociologia e Política em São Paulo." In Sérgio Miceli, ed., *História das ciências sociais no Brasil*, vol. 1. São Paulo: Vértice (Editora Revista dos Tribunais), IDESP, 1989. pp. 217–33.

Lins, Paulo. *Cidade de Deus*. São Paulo: Companhia das Letras, 1997.

Lira, José Tavares de. "Mots cachés: Les lieux du mocambo à Recife." *Genèses*, no. 33, pp. 77–106, December 1998.

———. "O urbanismo e o seu outro: Raça, cultura e cidade no Brasil (1920–1945)." *Revista Brasileira de Estudos Urbanos e Regionais*, no. 1, pp. 47–78, May 1999.

Loew, Jacques. *Enquête sur les dockers de Marseille (1941–1943)*. Paris: Économie et Humanisme, 1945.

Lopes, Paulo Victor Leite. "Sexualidade e construção de si em uma favela carioca: Pertencimentos, identidades, movimentos." M.A. thesis, Universidade Federal do Rio do Janeiro, 2011.

Lopes, Valdecir. "Duas favelas do Distrito Federal." *Revista Brasileira dos Municípios*, Rio de Janeiro, vol. 8, no. 32, pp. 283–98, October–December 1955.

Lynd, Roberto, and Helen Lynd. *Middletown: A Study in Modern American Culture*. New York: Harcourt Brace, 1929.

Machado, Carly. "'É muita mistura': Projetos políticos, sociais, midiáticos, de saúde e segurança pública nas periferias do Rio de Janeiro." *Religião e Sociedade*, Rio de Janeiro, vol. 33, no. 2, pp. 13–36, December 2013.

———. "Morte, perdão e esperança de vida eterna: 'Ex-bandidos,' policiais, pentecostalismo e criminalidade no Rio de Janeiro." In Patricia Birman et al., eds., *Dispositivos urbanos e tramas dos viventes*. Rio de Janeiro: Fundação Getúlio Vargas, 2015. pp. 451–72.

Machado da Silva, Luiz Antonio. "A política na favela." *Cadernos Brasileiros*, Rio de Janeiro, vol. 9, no. 3, pp. 35–47, May–June 1967.

———. "O significado do botequim." *América Latina*, Rio de Janeiro, vol. 12, no. 3, pp. 160–82, July–September 1969.

———. "Mercados metropolitanos de trabalho manual e marginalidade." M.A. thesis, Universidade Federal do Rio de Janeiro, 1971.

———. "Violência e sociabilidade: Tendências na atual conjuntura urbana no Brasil." In Luiz César de Queiroz Ribeiro and Orlando Alves Santos Júnior, eds., *Globalização, fragmentação e reforma urbana*. Rio de Janeiro: Civilização Brasileira, 1994. pp. 147–68.

———. *Vida sob cerco: Violência e rotina nas favelas do Rio de Janeiro*. Rio de Janeiro: Nova Fronteira, 2008.

———. "Afinal, qual é a das UPPs?" www.Observatoriodasmetropoles.ufrj.br, 2010, pp. 1–7.

———. "As UPPs, a linguagem da violência urbana e a sociabilidade no Rio de Janeiro." In Angela Moulin S. Penalva Santos, Glaucio José Marafon, and Maria Josefina Gabriel Sant'Anna, eds., *Rio de Janeiro: Um território em mutação*. Rio de Janeiro: Gramma / Fundação de Amparo à Pesquisa do Estado do Rio de Janeiro, 2012. pp. 115–31.

———. "A experiência das UPPs: Uma tomada de posição." *Dilemas*, vol. 8, pp. 7–24, 2015.

Machado da Silva, Luiz Antonio, and Carlos Nelson Santos. "Les politiques d'intervention." *Économie et Humanisme*, no. 186, pp. 53–60, March–April 1969.

Machado de Assis, Joaquim Maria. *Esaú e Jacó*. Rio de Janeiro: Garnier, 1904.

Magalhães, Alex Ferreira. *O direito das favelas*. Rio de Janeiro: Letra Capital, 2013.

Magalhães, Alexandre Almeida de. "Transformações no 'problema favela' e a reatualização da 'remoção' no Rio de Janeiro." PhD diss., Universidade do Estado do Rio de Janeiro, 2013.

Magri, Susanna. "Normalisation et différenciation sociale de l'usage du logement par les politiques de l'État." In *Vie quotidienne en milieu urbain*. Actes du Colloque de Montpellier, January 1978. Paris: CRU, 1980.

Maio, Marcos Chor. "A história do projeto UNESCO: Estudos raciais e ciências sociais no Brasil." PhD diss., Instituto Universitário de Pesquisas do Rio de Janeiro, 1997.

———. "Costa Pinto e a crítica ao negro como espetáculo." In L.A. da Costa Pinto, ed., *O negro no Rio de Janeiro: Relações de raças numa sociedade em mudança*. Rio de Janeiro: Editora da Universidade Federal do Rio de Janeiro, 1998. pp. 17–50.

Mangin, William. "Latin American Squatter Settlements: A Problem and a Solution." *Latin American Research Review*, no. 2, pp. 65–98, 1967.

Mariano Filho, José, Alberto Pires Amarante, and Américo Campelo. "As 'favelas' do Rio de Janeiro." Paper presented at I Congresso Brasileiro de Urbanismo, Rio de Janeiro, Departamento de Urbanismo do Centro Carioca, 1941.

Maricato, Ermínia. "Autoconstrução, a arquitetura possível." In Ermínia Maricato, ed., *A produção da casa (e da cidade) no Brasil industrial*. São Paulo: Alfa-Omega, 1979. pp. 17–93.

Marié, Michel. *Les terres et les mots: Une traversée des sciences sociales*. Paris: Méridiens Klincksieck, 1989.

Marin, Richard. *Dom Helder Camara, les puissants et les pauvres: Pour une histoire de l'Église des pauvres dans le Nordeste brésilien (1955–1985)*. Paris: L'Atelier, 1995.

Martinière, Guy. *Aspects de la coopération franco-brésilienne*. Paris: Maison des Sciences de l'Homme, 1982.

Martins, Carlos Benedito, et al. "Mestres e doutores em sociologia." In Jacques Velloso, ed., *A pós-graduação no Brasil: Formação e trabalho de mestres e doutores no país*. Brasília: CAPES/UNESCO, 2002. pp. 343–71.

Martins, Luís. *João do Rio: Uma antologia*. Rio de Janeiro: Sabia, 1971.

Massi, Fernanda. "Franceses e norte-americanos nas ciências sociais brasileiras, 1930–1960." In Sérgio Miceli, ed., *História das ciências sociais no Brasil*, vol. 1. São Paulo: Vértice (Editora Revista dos Tribunais), IDESP, 1989. pp. 410–59.

Mattos Mar, José. "Migration and Urbanization: The *Barriadas* of Lima, an Example of Integration into Urban Life." In Philip Hauser, ed., *Urbanization in Latin America*. New York: Columbia University Press, 1961.

Mattos, Carla. "No ritmo neurótico: Cultura funk e performances proibidas em contexto de violência no Rio de Janeiro." M.A. thesis, Universidade do Estado do Rio de Janeiro, 2006.

———. "Viver nas margens: Gênero, crime e regulação de conflitos." PhD diss., Universidade do Estado do Rio de Janeiro, 2014.

Mattos Pimenta, José Augusto de. *Para a remodelação do Rio de Janeiro: Discursos pronunciados no Rotary Club do Rio de Janeiro*. Rio de Janeiro, 1926.

Mauger, Gérard. "Enquêter en milieu populaire." *Genèses*, no. 6, pp. 125–43, 1991.

Medeiros, Lídia Alice. "Atendimento à pobreza no Rio de Janeiro durante a Era Vargas, do Albergue da Boa Vontade aos Parques Proletários: A atuação do Dr. Victor Tavares de Moura (1935–1945)." M.A. thesis, Universidade do Estado do Rio de Janeiro, 2002.

Medina, Carlos Alberto de. *A favela e o demagogo*. São Paulo: Martins, Coleçao Leituras do povo, 1964.

———. "A favela como uma estrutura atomística: Elementos descritivos e constitutivos." *América Latina*, Rio de Janeiro, vol. 12, no. 3, pp. 112–36, July–September 1969.

Medina, Carlos Alberto de, and Licia do Prado Valladares. *Favela e religião: Um estudo de caso*. Rio de Janeiro: Centro de Estatística Religiosa e Investigações Sociais, 1968.

Meihy, José Carlos S. Bom, and Robert M. Levine. *Cinderela negra: A saga de Carolina Maria de Jesus*. Rio de Janeiro: Editora da Universidade Federal do Rio de Janeiro, 1994.

———, eds. *Carolina Maria de Jesus: Meu estranho diário*. São Paulo: Xama, 1996.

Melatti, Júlio Cézar. "A antropologia no Brasil: Um roteiro." *Boletim Informativo e Bibliográfico das Ciências Sociais*, Rio de Janeiro, no. 17, pp. 3–52, 1984.

Mello, Marco Antônio da Silva, Luiz Antonio Machado da Silva, Letícia de Luna Freire, and Soraya Silveira Simões, eds., *Favelas cariocas: Ontem e hoje*. Rio de Janeiro: Garamond, 2012.

Melo, Marcus André B. C. de. "A cidade dos mocambos: Estado, habitação e luta de classes no Recife (1920–1960)." *Espaço e Debates*, São Paulo, vol. 14, pp. 45–66, 1985.

Memmi, Dominique. "L'enquêteur enquête: De la 'connaissance par corps' dans l'entretien sociologique." *Genèses*, no. 35, pp. 131–45, June 1999.

Mendonça, Tassia. "Batan: Tráfico, milícia e 'pacificação' na Zona Oeste do Rio de Janeiro." M.A. thesis, Universidade Federal do Rio de Janeiro, 2014.

Menezes, Palloma. "Interseções entre novos sentidos de patrimônio, turismo e politicas publicas: Um estudo de caso sobre o Museu a Céu Aberto do Morro da Providência." M.A. thesis, Instituto Universitário de Pesquisas do Rio de Janeiro, 2009.

———. "Os rumores da 'pacificação': A chegada da UPP e as mudanças nos problemas públicos no Santa Marta e na Cidade de Deus." *Dilemas*, vol. 7, pp. 665–83, 2014.

———. "Entre o 'fogo cruzado' e o 'campo minado': Uma etnografia do processo de 'pacificação' de favelas cariocas." PhD diss., Universidade do Estado do Rio de Janeiro, 2015.

Miceli, Sérgio, ed. *História das ciências sociais no Brasil*. Vol. 1. São Paulo: Vértice (Editora Revista dos Tribunais), IDESP, 1989.

————, ed. *História das ciências sociais no Brasil*. Vol. 2. São Paulo: Vértice (Editora Revista dos Tribunais), IDESP, 1995.

Mills, C. Wright. *A imaginação sociológica*. Rio de Janeiro: Zahar, 1965.

Mingione, Enzo, ed. *Urban Poverty and the Underclass: A Reader*. Oxford: Blackwell, 1996.

Misse, Michel, Carolina Christoph Grillo, César Pinheiro Teixeira, and Natasha Elbas Neri. *Quando a polícia mata: Homicídios por "autos de resistência" no Rio de Janeiro (2001–2011)*. Rio de Janeiro: NECVU, Booklink, 2013.

Moncorvo Filho, Carlos Arthur. *Histórico da proteção à infância no Brasil: 1500–1922*. Rio de Janeiro: Empreza Graphica, 1926.

Moraes, C. "Museu de favela: Pensando turismo patrimônio no Pavão, Pavãozinho e Cantagalo." M.A. thesis, Universidade do Estado do Rio de Janeiro, 2011.

Morocco, David. "Carnival Groups: Maintainers and Intensifiers of the Favela Phenomenon in Rio de Janeiro." Paper presented at XXXVII Congreso Internacional de Americanistas, Mar del Plata, 1966.

Morse, Richard. "Recent Research on Latin American Urbanization: A Selective Survey with Commentary." *Latin American Research Review*, vol. 1, no. 1, pp. 35–74, 1965.

————. "Trends and Issues in Latin American Urban Research, 1965–1970." *Latin American Research Review*, vol. 6, no. 1, pp. 3–52, 1971.

Moura, Victor Tavares de. "Esboço de um plano para estudo e solução do problema das favelas do Rio de Janeiro." Rio de Janeiro, Archive and Documentation Department of the Casa de Oswaldo Cruz, 1940.

————. "Favelas do Distrito Federal." In *Aspectos do Distrito Federal*. Rio de Janeiro: Academia Carioca de Letras, 1943. pp. 255–72.

Naro, Nancy. "Eviction! Land Tenure, Law, Power and the Favela." Paper presented at XXXVII Congreso Internacional de Americanistas, Mar del Plata, 1966.

Neves, Rogério Aroeira, and Carlos Nelson Ferreira dos Santos. "Um tema dos mais solicitados: Como e o que pesquisar em favelas." *Revista de Administração Municipal*, vol. 27, no. 161, pp. 8–19, October–December 1981.

Nun, José. "Sobre población relativa, ejército industrial de reserva y masa marginal." *Revista Latinoamericana de Sociología*, Buenos Aires, no. 2, pp. 174–236, 1969.

Oliveira, Jane Souto. "A reposição do suor." M.A. thesis, Universidade Federal do Rio de Janeiro, 1980.

————. "Repensando a questão das favelas." *Revista Brasileira de Estudos Populacionais*, Campinas, vol. 2, no. 1, pp. 9–29, January–June 1985.

————. "Os outros lados do funk carioca." In Hermano Vianna, ed., *Galeras cariocas*. Rio de Janeiro: Editora da Universidade Federal do Rio de Janeiro, 1997. pp. 59–93.

Oliveira, Jane Souto, et al. *Favelas do Rio de Janeiro*. Rio de Janeiro: Fundação Instituto Brasileiro de Geografia e Estatística, 1983.

Oliveira, Jane Souto, and Maria Hortense Marcier. "A palavra é: Favela." In Alba Zaluar and Marcos Alvito, eds., *Um século de favela*. Rio de Janeiro: Fundação Getúlio Vargas, 1998. pp. 61–114.

Oliveira, Lúcia Lippi. "As ciências sociais no Rio de Janeiro." In Sérgio Miceli, ed., *História das ciências sociais no Brasil*, vol. 21. São Paulo: Sumaré / Fundação de Amparo à Pesquisa do Estado de São Paulo, 1995. pp. 233–307.

———. "Interpretações sobre o Brasil." In Sérgio Miceli, ed., *Que ler na ciência social brasileira: Sociologia*, vol. 2. São Paulo: Sumaré / Associação Nacional de Pós-graduação e Pesquisa em Ciências Sociais / CAPES, 1999. pp. 147–81.

———. "Revolução de 1930: Uma bibliografia comentada," *Boletim Informativo e Bibliográfico de Ciências Sociais*, Rio de Janeiro, no. 4, pp. 8–18, 1978.

Oliveira, Ney dos Santos. "Parque proletário da Gávea: Uma experiência de habitação popular." Rio de Janeiro. M.A. thesis, Universidade Federal do Rio de Janeiro, 1981.

Oliven, Ruben George. "Favelados não são marginais?" *Coojornal*, Porto Alegre, vol. 3, no. 32, p. 35, September 1978.

Olivier de Sardin, Jean-Pierre. "La politique du terrain: Sur le production de donnés en anthropologie." *Enquête*, no. 1, pp. 71–109, 1995.

O'Neill, Charles. "Some Problems of Urbanization and Removal of Rio Favelas." Paper presented at XXXVII Congreso Internacional de Americanistas, Mar del Plata, 1966.

Paiva, Ângela Randolpho, and Marcelo Baumann Burgos, eds. *A escola e a favela*. Rio de Janeiro: Pontifícia Universidade Católica do Rio de Janeiro, Mallas, 2009.

Pandolfi, Dulce. *Camaradas e companheiros: História e memória do PCB*. Rio de Janeiro: Relume Dumará, 1995.

———. *Pernambuco de Agamenon Magalhães: Consolidação e crise de uma elite política*. Estudos e Pesquisas no. 32. Recife: Fundação Joaquim Nabuco / Massangana, 1984.

Pandolfi, Dulce, and Mário Grynspan. "ONGs, poder público e favelas: Algumas questões." Mimeograph. 2000.

Pandolfi, Dulce, and Mário Grynspan, eds. *A favela fala: Depoimentos ao CPDOC*. Rio de Janeiro: Fundação Getúlio Vargas, 2003.

Parisse, Lucien. "Favelas do Rio de Janeiro: Evolução, sentido." *Caderno do CENPHA*, no. 5, Rio de Janeiro: Centro Nacional de Pesquisas Habitacionais (CENPHA), 1969a.

———. "Bibliografia cronológica sobre a favela do Rio de Janeiro a partir de 1940." *América Latina*, Rio de Janeiro, vol. 12, no. 3, pp. 221–32, July–September 1969b.

———. "Las favelas en la expansión urbana de Rio de Janeiro: Estudo geográfico." *América Latina*, Rio de Janeiro, vol. 12, no. 3, pp. 7–43, July–September 1969c.

———. "Favelas de l'agglomération de Rio de Janeiro: Leur place dans le processus d'urbanisation." PhD diss., Université de Strasbourg, 1970.

Park, Robert E., and Ernest W. Burgess, eds. *The City*. Chicago: University of Chicago Press, 1925.

Pastuk, Marilia. "Favela como oportunidade." In Rubens Penha Cysne et al., *O Brasil de amanhã*. Rio de Janeiro: Forum Nacional, 2013. pp. 197–220.

Paugam, Serge. *L'exclusion: L'état des savoirs*. Paris: La Découverte, 1996.

Pearse, Andrew. "Integração social das famílias dos favelados." *Educação e Ciências Sociais*, Rio de Janeiro, vol. 2, no. 6, pp. 245–77, 1957.

———. "Some Characteristics of Urbanization in the City of Rio de Janeiro." In Philip Hauser, ed., *Urbanization in Latin America*. New York: Columbia University Press, 1961. pp. 191–205.

Pécaut, Daniel. *Os intelectuais e a política no Brasil: Entre o povo e a nação*. São Paulo: Ática, 1990.

Pechman, Robert Moses. "O urbano fora do lugar? Transferências e traduções de ideais urbanísticas nos anos 20." In Luiz César de Queiroz Ribeiro and Robert Pechman, eds., *Cidade, povo e nação*. Rio de Janeiro: Civilização Brasileira, 1996. pp. 331–62.

Peirano, Marisa. *A favor da etnografia*. Rio de Janeiro: Relume-Dumará, 1995.

Pelletier, Denis. *Économie et humanisme: De l'utopie communautaire au combat pour le Tiers Monde, 1941–1966*, Paris: CERF, 1996.

Pereira, Margareth da Silva. "A cidade planificada: O discurso dos médicos e a noção de interesse público entre o Império e a República, o caso do Rio de Janeiro." Paper presented at Seminário "Centenário da República," Rio de Janeiro, 1989.

———. "O pan-americanismo e seu impacto na institucionalização do urbanismo no Brasil (1920–1945)." In *IV Seminário de História da Cidade do Urbanismo: Herança, identidade e tendência da cidade latino-americana*, vol. 2, 2nd ed. Rio de Janeiro: Universidade Federal do Rio de Janeiro, 1996a.

———. "Pensando a metrópole moderna: Os planos de Agache e Le Corbusier para o Rio de Janeiro." In Luiz César de Queiroz Ribeiro and Robert Pechman, eds., *Cidade, povo e nação*. Rio de Janeiro: Civilização Brasileira, 1996b. pp. 363–76.

Perlman, Janice. *The Myth of Marginality: Urban Poverty and Politics*. Berkeley: University of California Press, 1976.

———. *O mito da marginalidade: Favelas e política no Rio de Janeiro*. Preface by Fernando Henrique Cardoso. Translated by Valdivia Portinho. Rio de Janeiro: Paz e Terra, 1977.

———. *Favela: Four Decades of Living on the Edge in Rio de Janeiro*. Preface by Fernando Henrique Cardoso. Oxford: Oxford University Press, 2010.

Piccolo, Fernanda Delvalhas. "A gramática nativa: Reflexões sobre as categorias morro, rua, comunidade e favela." In Heitor Frugoli Júnior, Luciana T. Andrade, and Fernanda A. Peixoto, eds., *As cidade e seus agentes: Práticas e representações*. Belo Horizonte: Pontifícia Universidade Católica de Minas Gerais / Editora da Universidade de São Paulo, 2006. pp. 330–52.

Pierson, Donald. *Negroes in Brazil: A Study of Race Contact at Bahia*. Chicago: University of Chicago Press, 1942.

———. *Teoria e pesquisa em sociologia*. 15th ed. São Paulo: Melhoramentos, 1973.

Pinçon, Michel, and Monique Pinçon-Charlot. *Voyage en grande bourgeoisie: Journal d'enquête*. Paris: Presses Universitaires de France, 1997.

Pino, Júlio César. "Dark Mirror of Modernization: The Favelas of Rio de Janeiro in the Boom Years, 1948–1960." *Journal of Urban History*, vol. 22, no. 4, pp. 419–53, May 1996.

———. *Family and Favela: The Reproduction of Poverty in Rio de Janeiro*. Westport, Conn.: Greenwood, 1997a.

———. "Sources on the History of Favelas in Rio de Janeiro." *Latin American Research Review*, vol. 32, no. 3, pp. 111–22, 1997b.

———. *An Annotated Historical Bibliography of the Rio de Janeiro Favelas*. Latin American Labor Studies Publications, vol. 8. Miami: Center for Labor Research and Studies, Florida International University, 2000.

Pires-Saboia, Anita. "Catalogue général de thèses soutenues en France sur le Brésil (1823–1999)." *Cahiers du Brésil Contemporain (CRBC)* (École des Hautes Études en Sciences Sociales), n.s., Paris, 2000.

Platt, Jennifer. *A History of Sociological Research Methods in America, 1920–1960*. Cambridge: Cambridge University Press, 1996.

Platt, Damian, and Patrick Neate. *Cultura é nossa arma: Afroreggae nas favelas do Rio*. Rio de Janeiro: Civilização Brasileira, 2008.

Poggiese, Héctor Atilio. "Urbanização e propriedade da terra nas favelas do Projeto Rio." *Revista Brasileira de Planejamento*, Porto Alegre, vol. 8, no. 15/16, pp. 53–76, 1985.

Polanyi, Karl. *A grande transformação: As origens da nossa época*. Rio de Janeiro: Campus, 1980.

Pontifícia Universidade Católica do Rio de Janeiro, Escola de Sociologia e Política. "Três favelas cariocas: Levantamento socio-econômico das favelas de Mata Machado, Morro União e Brás de Pina, dados preliminares." Mimeograph. 1967.

Pontual, Virginia. "A cidade e o bem comum: O engenheiro Antônio Bezerra Baltar no Recife dos anos 50." Paper presented at IX Encontro Nacional da ANPUR, Rio de Janeiro, 2001. *Anais ANPUR*, vol. 2. pp. 797–809.

Prefeitura da Cidade do Rio de Janeiro. *O Rio de Janeiro e seus prefeitos: Evolução urbanística da cidade*. Vol. 3. Rio de Janeiro: Lidador, 1977.

Prefeitura do Distrito Federal. *Código de obras de 1937*. Rio de Janeiro: Prefeitura do Distrito Federal, 1937.

———. *Censo das favelas: Aspectos gerais*. Rio de Janeiro: Prefeitura do Distrito Federal / Secretaria Geral do Interior e Segurança / Departamento de Geografia e Estatística, 1949.

Préteceille, Edmond. "Ségrégations urbaines: Introduction au dossier." *Sociétés Contemporaines*, no. 22/23, pp. 5–14, June–September 1995.

Préteceille, Edmond, and Licia do Prado Valladares. "Favelas no plural." Paper presented at XXIII Encontro Anual da ANPOCS, Caxambu, October 1999.

———. "Favela, favelas: Unidade ou diversidade da favela carioca." In Luiz César de Queiroz Ribeiro, ed., *O futuro das metrópoles: Desigualdades e governabilidade*. Rio de Janeiro: Revan / FASE, 2000. pp. 375–403.

Préteceille, Edmond, and Luiz César de Queiroz Ribeiro. "Tendências da segregação social em metrópoles globais e desiguais: Paris e Rio de Janeiro nos anos 80." *Revista Brasileira de Ciências Sociais*, vol. 14, n. 40, pp. 143–62, June 1999.

Queiroz, Maria Isaura Pereira de. "O Brasil dos cientistas sociais não-brasileiros." In *Ciências Sociais Hoje / Anuário ANPOCS*. São Paulo: Vértice (Editora Revista dos Tribunais), 1990. pp. 65–49.

Quijano, Aníbal. "La formación de un universo marginal en las ciudades de América Latina." In Manuel Castell and P. P. Velez, eds., *Imperialismo y urbanización en América Latina*. Barcelona: Gustavo Gili, 1971.

Quoist, Michel. *La ville et l'homme*. Paris: Ouvrières / Économie et Humanisme, 1952.

Rabinow, Paul. *Reflections on Fieldwork in Morocco*. Preface by Robert Bellah. Postface by Pierre Bourdieu. Berkeley: University of California Press, 1977.

Ramalho, Cristiane. *Noticias da favela*. Rio de Janeiro: Aeroplano, 2007.

Ramalho, José Ricardo. "Uma prática de assessoria à pastoral popular." In Vanilda Paiva, ed., *Perspectivas e dilemas da educação popular*. Rio de Janeiro: Graal, 1984. pp. 267–82.

Reis, Fernando, and Fernando Aragão. *Retratos históricos: Rotary Club do Rio de Janeiro, 70 anos*. Rio de Janeiro: Rotary Club do Rio de Janeiro, 1993.

Reis, Irene Monteiro. *Bibliografia de Euclides da Cunha*. Rio de Janeiro: Instituto Nacional do Livro, 1971.

Rezende, Vera Lúcia Ferreira Motta. *Planejamento urbano e ideologia: Quatro planos para a cidade do Rio de Janeiro*. Rio de Janeiro: Civilização Brasileira, 1982.

Ribeiro, Luiz César de Queiroz. *Dos cortiços aos condomínios fechados: As formas de produção da moradia na cidade do Rio de Janeiro*. Rio de Janeiro: Civilização Brasileira / Instituto de Pesquisa e Planejamento Urbano e Regional / Universidade Federal do Rio de Janeiro / FASE, 1997.

―――. "Cidade desigual ou cidade partida? Tendências da metrópole do Rio de Janeiro." In Luiz César de Queiroz Ribeiro, ed., *O futuro das metrópoles: Desigualdades e governabilidade*. Rio de Janeiro: Revan / FASE. 2000. pp. 63–98.

Ribeiro, Luiz César de Queiroz, and Luciana Lago. "A oposição favela-bairro no espaço social do Rio de Janeiro." *São Paulo em perspectiva*, vol. 15, no. 1, pp. 144–54, 2001.

Ridinger, Robert B. Marks. *The Peace Corps: An Annotated Bibliography*. Boston: G. K. Hall, 1989.

Rio, João do. "Os livres acampamentos da miséria." In *João do Rio: Uma antologia*. Rio de Janeiro: Instituto Nacional do Livro / Sabiá, 1911. pp. 51–59.

Rios, José Arthur. *Educação dos grupos*. Rio de Janeiro: Serviço Nacional de Educação Sanitária, 1957.

―――. "Favela." In *Dicionário das ciências sociais*. Rio de Janeiro: Fundação Getúlio Vargas, 1987. pp. 466–68.

―――. "Aspectos humanos das favelas cariocas, 50 anos: Uma avaliação." In Marco Antônio da Silva Mello, Luiz Antonio Machado da Silva, Letícia de Luna Freire, and Soraya Silveira Simões, eds., *Favelas cariocas: Ontem e hoje*. Rio de Janeiro: Garamond, 2012, pp. 35–50.

―――. "Lebret: Uma reflexão inatual." Mimeograph. n.d.

Rios, Rute Maria Monteiro Machado. "Amando de modo especial os menos favorecidos, 1945–1954." In Victor Vincent Valla, ed., *Educação e favela: Políticas para as favelas do Rio de Janeiro, 1940–1985*. Petrópolis: Vozes, 1986a. pp. 43–61.

―――. "O desenvolvimento e as favelas: Adaptar o favelado à vida urbana e nacional, 1955–1962." In Victor Vincent Valla, ed., *Educação e favela: Políticas para as favelas do Rio de Janeiro, 1940–1985*. Petrópolis: Vozes, 1986b. pp. 62–84.

Rizzini, Irma. *O século perdido: Raízes históricas das políticas públicas para a infância no Brasil*. Rio de Janeiro: Amais, 1997.

Rocha, Lia M. *Uma favela 'diferente das outras'? Rotina, silenciamento e ação coletiva na favela do Pereirão no Rio de Janeiro*. Rio de Janeiro: Quartet, 2013.

―――. "O 'repertório dos projetos sociais': Política, mercado e controle social nas favelas." In Patricia Birman, Marcia Leite, Carly Machado, and Sandra de Sá Carneiro, eds., *Dispositivos urbanos e trama dos viventes: Ordens e resistências*, vol. 1. 1st ed. Rio de Janeiro: Fundação Getúlio Vargas / Fundação de Amparo à Pesquisa do Estado do Rio de Janeiro, 2014. pp. 291–312.

Rocha, Lia M., and Doriam Borges. "UPPs e os múltiplos significados de 'paz' na perspectiva dos jovens moradores de favelas 'pacificadas.'" In Adalberto Cardoso, ed., *Juventudes na cidade: Violência, cultura, religião, escola*. Rio de Janeiro: Azougue, 2014. pp. 13–37.

Rocha, Oswaldo Porto. *A era das demolições: Cidade do Rio de Janeiro, 1870–1920*. Rio de Janeiro: Prefeitura da Cidade do Rio de Janeiro / Secretaria Municipal de Cultura, 1986.

Rocha, Sonia. "Renda e pobreza nas metrópoles brasileiras." In Luiz César de Queiroz Ribeiro and Orlando Alves dos Santos Júnior, eds., *Globalização, fragmentação e reforma urbana: O futuro das cidades brasileiras na crise*. Rio de Janeiro: Civilização Brasileira, 1994. pp. 121–45.

Rockfeller, Margaret Dulany. "Voluntary Associations and Social Evolution: A Case Study of Brazilian Favela Associations." Final course project, Radcliff College, 1969.

Rodrigues, André. *Trinta dias de UPP: Um relato e algumas questões pertinentes à implantação da Unidade de Polícia Pacificadora do Morro da Providência.* Comunicações do Instituto de Estudos da Religião, December 2012.

Rodrigues, André, and Raiza Siqueira. "As Unidades de Polícia Pacificadora e a segurança pública no Rio de Janeiro." *Comunicações do Instituto de Estudos da Religião*, pp. 9–52, December 2012.

Rodrigues, Robson. "The Dilemmas of Pacification: News of War and Peace in the 'Marvelous City.'" *Stability International Journal of Security & Development*, vol. 3, no. 1, pp. 1–16, 2014.

Rodríguez, Alfredo, et al. "De invasores a invadidos." *Revista EURE*, Santiago, vol. 2, no. 4, pp. 101–42, 1972.

Rodríguez, Alfredo, Vicente Espinoza, and Hilda Herzer. "Argentina, Bolivia, Chile, Ecuador, Peru, Uruguay: Urban Research in the 1990s, a Framework for an Agenda." In Richard Stren, ed., *Urban Research in the Developing World: Latin America*. Toronto: Center for Urban and Community Studies, 1995. pp. 223–80.

Rubim, Christina de Rezende. "Um pedaço de nossa história: Historiografia da antropologia brasileira." *Revista Brasileira de Informação Bibliográfica em Ciências Sociais*, Rio de Janeiro, no. 44, pp. 31–72, 1997.

Russell-Wood, A. J. R. *Fidalgos and Philanthropists: The Santa Casa da Misericórdia of Bahia, 1550–1755.* Ann Arbor: UMI Books on Demand, 1968.

Sachs, Céline. "Le 'mutirão' brésilien: La tradition de l'entraide rurale au secours de l'urbain." *Annales de la Recherche Urbaine*, Paris, no. 28, pp. 61–69, October 1985.

SAGMACS, Comissão Municipal da Pesquisa Urbana, São Paulo. "Estrutura urbana da aglomeração paulistana." Research report directed by F. Louis-Joseph Lebret for the Municipal Commission for Urban Research of São Paulo (unpublished manuscript). São Paulo, 1958.

———. *Aspectos humanos da favela carioca: O Estado de São Paulo.* Special supplements 13 and 15 April 1960.

Salmen, Lawrence. "A Perspective on the Resettlement of Squatters in Brazil." *América Latina*, vol. 12, no. 1, pp. 73–93, January–March 1969.

———. "Housing Alternatives for the Carioca Working Class: A Comparison between Favelas and *Casas de Comodos*." *América Latina*, vol. 13, no. 4, pp. 51–70, October–December 1970.

Sanjek, Roger. *Cities, Classes and the Social Order: Anthony Leeds.* Ithaca, N.Y.: Cornell University Press, 1990.

———, ed. *Cities, Classes and the Social Order.* Ithaca, N.Y.: Cornell University Press, 1994.

Sant'Anna, Maria Josefina Gabriel. "Família e moradia em espaços de favela e não favela na cidade do Rio de Janeiro." In Angela Moulin S. Penalva Santos, Gláucio José Marafon, and Maria Josefina Gabriel Sant'Anna, eds., *Rio de Janeiro: Um território em mutação*. Rio de Janeiro: Gramma / Fundação de Amparo à Pesquisa do Estado do Rio de Janeiro, 2012.

Sant'Anna, Maria Josefina Gabriel, and Carlos Augusto Ferreira Lima Júnior, eds. *Quem faz a pesquisa urbana no Brasil? Catálogo de pesquisadores.* Rio de Janeiro: URBANDATA-Brasil / Universidade Candido Mendes: GURI / Conselho Nacional de Pesquisa / Universidade do Estado do Rio de Janeiro, 2001.

Santos, Boaventura de Souza. "The Law of the Oppressed: The Construction and Reproduction of Legality in Pasargada." *Law and Society Review*, vol. 12, no. 1, pp. 5–126, October 1977.

———. "Sociologia na primeira pessoa: Fazendo pesquisa nas favelas do Rio de Janeiro." *Revista da Ordem dos Advogados do Brasil*, São Paulo, vol. 49, pp. 39–79, Spring 1988.

Santos, Carlos Nelson Ferreira dos. "Volviendo a pensar en 'favelas' a causa de las periferias." *Nueva Sociedad*, San José de Costa Rica, vol. 30, pp. 22–38, May–June 1977.

———. "Estarão as pranchetas mudando de rumo?" *Revista Chão*, no. 1, pp. 22–31, 1978.

———. "Como projetar de baixo para cima uma experiência em favela." *Revista de Administração Municipal*, no. 156, pp. 6–27, July–September 1980a.

———. "Como e quando pode um arquiteto virar antropólogo?" In Gilberto Velho, ed., *O desafio da cidade*. Rio de Janeiro: Campus, 1980b. pp. 37–57.

———. *Movimentos urbanos no Rio de Janeiro*. Rio de Janeiro: Zahar, 1981.

———. "Habitação: O que é mesmo que pode fazer quem sabe?" In Licia do Prado Valladares, ed., *Repensando a habitação no Brasil*. Rio de Janeiro: Zahar, 1983. pp. 79–107.

Santos, Carlos Nelson Ferreira dos, and Vogel Arno, eds. *Quando a rua vira casa: A apropriação de espaços de uso coletivo em um centro de bairro*. 2nd ed., revised and updated. Rio de Janeiro: Instituto Brasileiro de Administração Municipal / Financiadora de Inovação e Pesquisa, 1981.

Santos, Cecília, et al. *Le Corbusier e o Brasil*. São Paulo: Tessela/Projeto, 1987.

Santos, Milton. *A urbanização brasileira*. São Paulo: HUCITEC, 1993.

Santos, Nubia M., and José Antonio Nonato. *Era uma vez o Morro do Castelo*. Rio de Janeiro: IPHAN / Depron / Petrobras / Casa da Palavra, 2000.

Santos, Wanderley Guilherme dos. *Cidadania e justiça: A política social na ordem brasileira*. Rio de Janeiro: Campus, 1987.

Sarmento, Carlos Eduardo. *O Rio de Janeiro na era de Pedro Ernesto*. Rio de Janeiro: Editora da Fundação Getúlio Vargas, 2001.

Scalon, Celi. *Mobilidade social no Brasil: Padrões e tendências*. Rio de Janeiro: Evan / Instituto Universitário de Pesquisas do Rio de Janeiro, 1999.

Schwartz, Olivier. Preface to Nels Anderson, *Le hobo: Sociologie du sans-abri*. Paris: Nathan, 1993a. pp. 5–21.

———. "L'empirisme irréductible." In Nels Anderson, *Le hobo: Sociologie du sans-abri*. Paris: Nathan, 1993b. pp. 265–308.

Segala, Lygia. "O riscado do balão japonês: Trabalho comunitário na Rocinha (1977–1982)." M.A. thesis, Universidade Federal do Rio de Janeiro, 1991.

Shaw, Clifford R. *The Jack-Roller: A Delinquent Boy's Own Story*. Chicago: University of Chicago Press, 1930.

Shaw, Clifford R., and Henry D. McKay. *Juvenile Delinquency and Urban Areas*. Chicago: University of Chicago Press, 1942.

Sheriff, Robin E. *Dreaming Equality: Color, Race, and Racism in Urban Brazil*. New Brunswick, N.J.: Rutgers University Press, 2001.

Sieber, R. Timothy. "The Life of Anthony Leeds: Unity in Diversity." In Roger Sanjek, ed., *Cities, Classes and the Social Order*. Ithaca, N.Y.: Cornell University Press, 1994. pp. 3–26.

Silberstein, Paul. "Favela Living: Personal Solution to Larger Problems." *América Latina*, Rio de Janeiro, vol. 12, no. 3, pp. 183–200, July–September 1969.

Silva, Eduardo. *As queixas do povo*. Rio de Janeiro: Paz e Terra, 1988.

Silva, Eliana Sousa. *Testemunhos da Maré*. Rio de Janeiro: Aeroplano and Fundação de Amparo à Pesquisa do Estado do Rio de Janeiro, 2012.

Silva, Elionalva Sousa. "Ampliando futuros: O curso pré-vestibular comunitário da Maré."

Master's thesis, Centro de Pesquisa e Documentação de História Contemporânea do Brasil, Fundação Getúlio Vargas, 2006.

Silva, Lúcia. "A Trajetória de Alfred Donat Agache no Brasil." In Luiz César Queiroz Ribeiro and Robert Moses Pechman, eds., *Cidade, povo e nação*. Rio de Janeiro: Civilização Brasileira, 1996. pp. 397–410.

Silva, Marcella Carvalho de Araújo. "A transformação da política na favela: Um estudo de caso sobre os agentes comunitários." Master's thesis, Programa de Pos-graduação em Sociologia e Antropologia, Instituto de Filosofia e Ciências Sociais, Universidade Federal do Rio de Janeiro, 2013.

Silva, Maria Hortência do Nascimento e. *Impressões de uma assistente sobre o trabalho na favela*. Rio de Janeiro: Prefeitura do Distrito Federal / Secretaria Geral de Saúde e Assistência, Instituto Social, 1942.

Silva, Maria Laís Pereira da. "A 'Batalha do Rio de Janeiro': Combatentes e combatidos nas favelas cariocas, 1947–1948." Mimeograph. 2001.

———. "Percursos, significados e permanência das favelas cariocas (1930–1964)." PhD diss., Universidade Federal do Rio de Janeiro, 2003.

———. *Favelas cariocas, 1930–1964*. Rio de Janeiro: Contraponto, 2005.

Simmel, George. *Les pauvres*. Introduction by Serge Paugam and Franz Schultheis. Paris: Quadrige / Presses Universitaires de France, 1998.

Simões, Soraya. *Histoire et ethnographie d'une cité de Rio: La Cruzada São Sebastião*. Paris: Kartala, 2010.

Slob, Bart. "Do barraco para o apartamento: A 'humanização' e a 'urbanização' de uma favela situada em um bairro nobre do Rio de Janeiro." Final course project, Universiteit Leiden, 2002.

Soares, Luiz Eduardo, ed. *Violência e política no Rio de Janeiro*. Rio de Janeiro: Instituto de Estudos da Religião / Relume-Dumará, 1996.

Soares, Luiz Eduardo, and Leandro Piquet Carneiro. "Os quatro nomes da violência: Um estudo sobre éticas populares e cultura política." In Luiz Eduardo Soares, ed., *Violência e política no Rio de Janeiro*. Rio de Janeiro: Instituto de Estudos da Religião / Relume-Dumará, 1996.

Sorj, Bernardo. *Brasil@povo.com: A luta contra a desigualdade na sociedade da informação*. Rio de Janeiro: Zahar, 2003.

Souza e Silva, Jailson de. "Por que uns e não outros? Caminhada de estudantes da Maré para a universidade." PhD diss., Pontifícia Universidade Católica do Rio de Janeiro, 1999.

———. *Por que uns e não outros? Caminhada de estudantes da Maré para a universidade*. Rio de Janeiro: 7Letras, 2003.

Souza e Silva, Jailson de, and Jorge Luís Barbosa. *Favela: Alegria e dor na cidade*. Rio de Janeiro: Serviço Nacional de Aprendizagem Comercial, 2005.

Stuckenbruck, Denise Cabral. *Plano Agache e o ideário reformista dos anos 20*. Rio de Janeiro: Observatório de Políticas Urbanas / Instituto de Pesquisa e Planejamento Urbano e Regional / Universidade Federal do Rio de Janeiro / FASE, 1996.

Taschner, Suzana Pasternak. "Favelas do Município de São Paulo: Resultados de pesquisa." In Eva Blay, ed., *A luta pelo espaço*. Petrópolis: Vozes, 1978. pp. 125–48.

———. "Favelas e cortiços no Brasil: 20 anos de pesquisas e políticas." *Cadernos de Pesquisa do LAP*, no. 18, March–April 1997.

Taschner, Suzana Pasternak, and Lucia Bogus. "A cidade dos anéis." In Luiz César de

Queiroz Ribeiro, ed., *O Futuro das metrópoles: Desigualdades e governabilidade*. Rio de Janeiro: Revan / FASE (São Paulo), 2000. pp. 247–84.

Telles, Sarah da Silva. "Pobreza e desigualdade na escola da favela." In Ângela Randolpho Paiva and Marcelo Baumann Burgos, eds., *A escola e a favela*. Rio de Janeiro: Pontifícia Universidade Católica do Rio de Janeiro, Pallas, 2009. pp. 133–71.

Thery, Hervé, and Martine Droulers, eds. *Pierre Monbeig: Un géographe pionnier*. Paris: Centre de Recherche et de Documentation sur l'Amérique Latine (CREDAL) / Institut des Hautes-Études de l'Amérique Latine (IHEAL), 1991.

Thomas, Hélène. *La production des exclus: Politiques sociales et processus de désocialisation socio-politique*. Paris: Presses Universitaires de France, 1997.

Thomas, William Isaac, and Florian Znaniecki. *The Polish Peasant in Europe and America*. New York: Dover, 1927.

Tolosa, Hamilton. "Dualismo no mercado de trabalho urbano." *Pesquisa e Planejamento Econômico*, vol. 5, no. 1, pp. 1–35, 1975.

Tolosa, Hamilton. "Rio de Janeiro as a World City." In L. O. Fu-Chen and Yue-man Yeung, eds., *Globalization and the World of Large Cities*. New York: United Nations University Press, 1999. pp. 203–27.

Tommasi, Livia de. "'Naturellement créatifs': Pacification, entrepreneuriat et créativité dans les favelas cariocas." *Brésil(s): Sciences humaines et sociales*, vol. 6, pp. 55–74, November 2014.

Topalov, Christian. *Naissance du chômeur, 1880–1910*. Paris: Albin Michel, 1994.

———, ed. *Laboratoires du Nouveau Siècle: La nébuleuse réformatrice et ses réseaux en France, 1880–1914*. Paris: École des Hautes Études en Sciences Sociales, 1999.

Topalov, Christian, Laurent Coudroy de Lille, Jean-Charles Depaule, and Brigitte Marin, eds. *L'aventure des mots de la ville à travers le temps, les langues, les sociétés*. Paris: Robert Laffont, 2010.

Torquato da Silva, Rodrigo. *Escola-favela e favela-escola: "Esse menino não tem jeito!"* Petrópolis: De Petrus; Rio de Janeiro: Fundação de Amparo à Pesquisa do Estado do Rio de Janeiro, 2012.

Trindade, Helgio. *Integralismo: O fascismo brasileiro na década de 30*. São Paulo: Difel, 1979.

Turner, John. "Uncontrolled Urban Settlement: Problems and Policies." In Gerald Breese, ed., *The City in Newly Developing Countries: Readings on Urbanism and Urbanization*. Englewood Cliffs, N.J.: Prentice-Hall, 1969.

———. *Housing by People*. London: Marion Boyars, 1976.

Valla, Victor Vincent, ed. *Educação e favela: Políticas para as favelas do Rio de Janeiro, 1940–1980*. Petrópolis: Vozes, 1986.

Valladares, Licia do Prado. "Opération de relogement et réponse sociale: Les cas des résidents des favelas à Rio de Janeiro." PhD diss., Université de Toulouse–Le Mirail, 1974.

———. "Favela, política e conjunto residencial." *Dados*, vol. 12, pp. 74–85, 1976.

———. "Associações voluntárias na favela." *Ciência e Cultura*, vol. 29, no. 12, pp. 1390–1403, December 1977.

———. *Passa-se uma casa: Análise do programa de remoções de favelas do Rio de Janeiro*. Rio de Janeiro: Zahar, 1978a.

———. "Working the System: Squatter Response to Resettlement in Rio de Janeiro." *International Journal of Urban and Regional Research*, vol. 2, no. 1, pp. 12–25, March 1978b.

———. "A proposito da urbanização de favelas." *Espaço e Debates*, São Paulo, vol. 1, no. 2, pp. 5–18, May 1981.

———. "Políticas alternativas de habitação popular: Um vôo sobre a literatura internacional." *Espaço e Debates*, São Paulo, vol. 5, no. 16, pp. 33–51, 1985.

———. "Family and Child Work in the Favela." In Datta Satya, ed., *Third World Urbanization: Reappraisals and New Perspectives*. Stockholm: HSFR, 1990a, pp. 149–67.

———. "La investigación urbana en Brasil, una breve revisión." In Fernando Carrión, ed., *La investigación urbana en América Latina: Caminos recorridos y por recorrer, una aproximación desde los países*. Quito: CIUDAD, 1990b.

———. "Cem anos pensando a pobreza (urbana) no Brasil." In Renato Boschi, ed., *Corporativismo e desigualdade: A construção do espaço público no Brasil*. Rio de Janeiro: Instituto Universitário de Pesquisas do Rio de Janeiro / Editora Rio Fundo, 1991. pp. 81–112.

———. "La recherche urbaine au Brésil: Parcours et tendances." In Anita Joussement, ed., *La recherche sur la ville au Brésil: Actes des Journées Franco-Brésiliennes du PIR Villes, 28–29 novembre 1994*. Paris: CNRS, 1997. pp. 37–64.

———. "Qu'est-ce qu'une favela?" *Cahiers des Amériques Latines*, no. 34, pp. 61–72, 2000a.

———. "A gênese da favela carioca: A produção anterior às ciências sociais." *Revista Brasileira de Ciências Sociais / ANPOCS*, Rio de Janeiro, vol. 15, no. 44, pp. 5–34, October 2000b.

———. "Favela.com." Paper presented at Forum América Latina Habitar 2000, Salvador, May 2001.

———. "Favelas, mondialisation et fragmentation." In Françoise Navez-Bouchanine, ed., *La fragmentation en question: Des villes entre fragmentation spatiale et fragmentation sociale?* Paris: L'Harmattan, 2002a. pp. 209–21.

———. "Le langage de la coopération internationale: Peace Corps et ONG dans les favelas à Rio de Janeiro." In Daniel Cefai and Isaac Joseph, eds., *L'héritage du pragmatisme: Conflits d'urbanité et épreuves de civisme*. Paris: L'Aube, 2002b. pp. 175–91.

———. *La favela d'un siècle à l'autre: Mythe d'origine, discours scientifiques et représentations virtuelles*. Paris: Éditions de la Maison de Sciences de l'Homme, 2006.

———. "Educação e mobilidade social nas favelas do Rio de Janeiro: O caso dos universitários (graduandos e graduados) das favelas." *Dilemas*, no. 5–6, pp. 153–72, July–August–September–October–November–December 2008.

Valladares, Licia do Prado, and Magda Prates Coelho. "Urban Research in Brazil and Venezuela: Towards an Agenda for the 1990's." In Richard Stren, ed., *Urban Research in the Developing World: Latin America*. Toronto: Centre for Urban and Community Studies, 1995. pp. 43–142.

Valladares, Licia do Prado, and Ademir Figueiredo. "Habitação no Brasil: Uma introdução à literatura recente." *Boletim Informativo e Bibliográfico de Ciências Sociais*, Rio de Janeiro, no. 11, pp. 25–49, 1981.

Valladares, Licia do Prado, and Regina Kayat. *Invasões de terras no Rio de Janeiro de 1983: Uma cronologia*. Estudos. Rio de Janeiro: Instituto Universitário de Pesquisas do Rio de Janeiro, 1983.

Valladares, Licia do Prado, and Roberto Kant de Lima. "A Escola de Chicago: Entevista com Isaac Joseph." *Revista Brasileira de Informação Bibliográfica em Ciências Sociais*, Rio de Janeiro, no. 49, pp. 3–13, 2000.

Valladares, Licia do Prado, and Lídia Medeiros. *Pensando as favelas do Rio de Janeiro: Uma bibliografia analítica, 1906–2000*. Rio de Janeiro: Relume-Dumará / URBANDATA / Universidade Candido Mendes / Fundação de Amparo à Pesquisa do Estado do Rio de Janeiro, 2003.

Valladares, Licia do Prado, and Rosa Maria Ribeiro. "The Return of the Favela: Recent Changes in Intra-metropolitan Rio." *Urbana*, Caracas, no. 14/15, pp. 59–73, 1994.

Valladares, Licia do Prado, and Maria Josefina Gabriel Sant'Anna, eds. *Rio de Janeiro em teses catálogo bibliográfico (1960–1990)*. Rio de Janeiro: URBANDATA / Instituto Universitário de Pesquisas do Rio de Janeiro / CEP-RIO / Universidade do Estado do Rio de Janeiro, 1992.

Valladares, Licia do Prado, Maria Josefina Gabriel Sant'Anna, and Ana Maria Caillaux, eds. *1001 teses sobre o Brasil urbano: Catálogo bibliográfico (1940–1989)*. Rio de Janeiro: Instituto Universitário de Pesquisas do Rio de Janeiro / URBANDATA / ANPUR, 1991.

Valladares, Licia do Prado, et al. *Alternative Housing Policies in Brazil: Self-Help Experiments in Rio de Janeiro*. Rio de Janeiro: IDRC / Instituto Universitário de Pesquisas, 1986.

Vaz, Lillian Fessler. "Notas sobre o Cabeça de Porco." *Revista Rio de Janeiro*, vol. 1, no. 2, pp. 29–35, January–April 1986.

———. "Dos cortiços às favelas e aos edifícios de apartamentos: A modernização da moradia no Rio de Janeiro." *Análise Social* (Instituto de Ciências Sociais da Universidade de Lisboa), vol. 24, no. 127, pp. 581–97, 1994.

Vekemans, Roger, and Ramón Venegas. *Marginalidad, incorporación e integración*. Santiago de Chile: DESAL, 1966.

Velho, Gilberto. *A utopia urbana: Um estudo de antropologia social*. Rio de Janeiro: Zahar, 1972.

———. "Favelas cariocas: O problema da marginalidade." *Anuário Antropológico*, Rio de Janeiro, no. 76, pp. 321–24, 1977.

———. "Observando o familiar." In Edson de Oliveira Nunes, ed., *A aventura sociológica*. Rio de Janeiro: Zahar, 1978. pp. 36–46.

———, ed. *O desafio da cidade: Novas perspectivas da antropologia brasileira*, Rio de Janeiro: Campus, 1980.

Velho, Gilberto, and Marcos Alvito, eds. *Cidadania e violência*. Rio de Janeiro: Editora da Universidade Federal do Rio de Janeiro / Fundação Getúlio Vargas, 1996.

Velho, Gilberto, and Luiz Antonio Machado da Silva. "Organização social no meio urbano." *Anuário Antropológico*, Rio de Janeiro, vol. 76, pp. 71–82, 1977.

Velho, Otávio Guilherme. "Processos sociais no Brasil pós-64: As ciências sociais." In Bernardo Sorj and Maria Hermínia Tavares de Almeida, eds., *Sociedade e política no Brasil pós-64*. São Paulo: Brasiliense, 1983. pp. 240–61.

Velloso, João Paulo dos Reis, Marilia Pastuk, and Vicente Pereira Jr. *Favela como oportunidade: Plano de desenvolvimento de favelas para sua inclusão social e econômica*. Rio de Janeiro: Instituto Nacional de Altos Estudos, 2012.

Velloso, João Paulo dos Reis, and Marilia Pastuk, eds. *Favela como oportunidade: Plano de desenvolvimento de favelas para sua inclusão social e econômica*. Forum Nacional. Cantagalo, Pavão-Pavãozinho, Rocinha, Borel, Complexo de Manguinhos, Complexo do Jacarezinho, Complexo do Alemão. Rio de Janeiro: Instituto Nacional de Altos Estudos, 3 vols., 2012–13.

Ventura, Zuenir. *Cidade partida*. São Paulo: Companhia das Letras, 1994.

Véras, Maura Pardini Bicudo, and Suzana Pasternak Taschner. "Evolução e mudanças das favelas paulistanas." *Espaço e Debates*, vol. 10, no. 31, pp. 52–71, 1990.

Vianna, Hermano, ed. *Galeras cariocas: Territórios de conflitos e encontros culturais*. Rio de Janeiro: Editora da Universidade Federal do Rio de Janeiro, 1997.

Vianna, Luiz Werneck. *Liberalismo e sindicato no Brasil*. 4th ed. Belo Horizonte: Editora da Universidade Federal de Minas Gerais, 1976.

Vianna, Luiz Werneck, Maria Alice Rezende de Carvalho, and Manuel Palácios Cunha Melo. "As ciências sociais no Brasil: A formação de um sistema nacional de ensino e pesquisa." *Boletim Informativo e Bibliográfico de Ciências Sociais*, Rio de Janeiro, no. 40, pp. 27–64, 1995.

Vidal, Dominique. "Concevoir la communauté: L'efficacité d'une catégorie socio-spatiale au Brésil." In Jérôme Monnet, ed., *Espace, temps et pouvoir dans le Nouveau Monde*. Paris: Anthropos, 1996. pp. 213–33.

———. *La politique au quartier: Rapports sociaux et citoyenneté à Recife*. Paris: Éditions de la Maison des Sciences de l'Homme, 1998.

Vila Nova, Sebastião. *Donald Pierson e a Escola de Chicago na sociologia brasileira: Entre humanistas e messiânicos*. Lisbon: Vega, 1998.

Vital, C. "Ocupação evangélica: Efeitos sociais do crescimento pentecostal na favela de Acari." Master's thesis, Department of Social Sciences, Universidade do Estado do Rio de Janeiro, 2002.

Vogt, Carlos. "Trabalho, pobreza e trabalho intelectual: O *Quarto de despejo* de Carolina Maria de Jesus." In Robert Schwartz, ed., *Os pobres na literatura brasileira*. São Paulo: Brasiliense, 1983. pp. 204–13.

Wacquant, Loïc. "Banlieues françaises et ghetto noir américain: De l'amalgame à la comparaison." *French Politics & Society*, Paris, vol. 10, no. 4, pp. 81–103, Fall 1992.

Wagley, Charles, Thales Azevedo, and Luiz Costa Pinto. "Uma pesquisa sobre a vida social no estado da Bahia." *Publicações do Museu do Estado*, Salvador, no. 11, 1950.

Warner, William Lloyd, and Paul Sanborn Lunt. 1946. *The Social Life of a Modern Community*. New Haven: Yale University Press, 1946.

Whitaker Ferreira, Francisco. "Dans le sillage de Lebret au Brésil." In Paul Houée, *Louis Joseph Lebret: Un éveilleur d'humanité*. Paris: L'Atelier/Ouvrières, 1997. pp. 134–48.

Whyte, William Foote. *Street Corner Society: The Social Structure of an Italian Slum*. Chicago: University of Chicago Press, 1943.

Wilson, William Julius. *Les oubliés de l'Amérique*. Translation by Ivan Ermakoff. Paris: Desclée de Brouwer, 1994.

Wirth, Louis. *The Ghetto*. Introduction by Hasia Diner. New Brunswick, N.J.: Transaction, 1998.

World Bank. allginis_2013.xls, 2013. http://siteresources.worldbank.org/INTRES /Resources/469232-1107449512766/allginis_2013.xls. Accessed 16 December 2017.

Zaluar, Alba. *A máquina e a revolta: As organizações populares e o significado da pobreza*. São Paulo: Brasiliense, 1985.

———. *O Rio contra o crime: Imagens da justiça e do crime*. Rio de Janeiro: Instituto Universitário de Pesquisas do Rio de Janeiro, 1989.

———. "Violência e crime." In Sérgio Miceli, ed., *O que ler na ciência social brasileira (1970–1995)*, vol. 1, *Antropologia*. São Paulo: Sumaré / Associação Nacional de Pós-graduação e Pesquisa em Ciências Sociais / CAPES, 1999. pp. 13–107.

———. *Integração perversa: Pobreza e tráfico de drogas*. Rio de Janeiro: Fundação Getúlio Vargas, 2004.

Zaluar, Alba, and Marcos Alvito. *Um século de favela*. Rio de Janeiro: Fundação Getúlio Vargas, 1998.

Zilly, Berthold. "A guerra como painel e espetáculo: A história encenada em *Os Sertões*." *História, Ciências Saúde Manguinhos*, vol. 5, pp. 13–37, July 1998.

Zylberberg, Sonia, ed. *Morro da Providência: Memórias da "favela."* Vol. 1 of *Memória das favelas*. Rio de Janeiro: Prefeitura da Cidade do Rio de Janeiro / Secretaria Municipal de Cultura Turismo e Esportes, 1992.

Index

Page numbers in italics refer to illustrations.

et Humanisme and, 85–91; Pierson and, 72–73; sociology and, 66, 85, 86. *See also* anthropologists; anthropology; fieldwork

childcare centers, 67, 68

Child of the Dark (1961), 97

children and youth, 26, 33, 45, 56, 61, 166, 167; abandoned, 23, 33; problems of, 133, 166; violence and, 8, 133, 159

Chile, 71, 78, 103

Chombart de Lauwe, Paul-Henri, 85–86, 90

Cidade de Deus: favela, 158, 166; housing complex, 138, 139

Cidade Maravilhosa (Marvelous City). *See* Marvelous City, Rio as

cinema, cinemas, 33, 135, 165, 189n32, 203n63

citizenship, 8, 134, 151, 154

city, 31, 86, 148; favela vs., 27, 119; formal/legal and informal/illegal, 131, 142, 166

City, The (Park and Burgess, 1925), 86, 92

City Center of Rio, 16, 143, 157

class, social, 5, 90

clientelism, political, 40, 47, 49, 93, 117, 141; favelas and, 76–77, 85, 93, 106, 151

Clube de Engenharia (Engineering Club), 30

clusters, 9, 58–59, 75, 130; subnormal, 137, 141, 149

Código de Posturas Municipais (Code of Municipal Orders), 30

Cold War, 65, 95

Colégio Sion, 48

collective action, 100, 126, 127

Columbia University, 102, 103, 199n4

Comissão de Estudo do Problema das Favelas (Commission for the Study of the Problem of Favelas), 46–47

Comissão de Recenseamento dos Mucambos (Commission for a Census of Mocambos), 46

Comissão de Saneamento do Rio de Janeiro (Rio de Janeiro Sanitation Commission), 30

Comissão do Bem Estar Social (Social Welfare Commission), 71

common land ownership, 24

communism, communists, 58, 67, 70, 94, 101, 192n4, 192n6. *See also* Partido Comunista Brasileiro

community, 25, 78, 107; favela and, 7, 27, 65, 69, 76, 89, 106, 168, 195n58; residents' associations and, 150, 151

community development, 77, 125; Peace Corps and, 94–96, 99, 103, 196n76; as principle, 68–69

Companhia de Desenvolvimento de Comunidades (Community Development Company, CODESCO), 111, 123–27, 138, 185n5, 198n97

Companhia de Habitação Popular do Estado da Guanabara (State of Guanabara Affordable Housing Authority, COHAB-GB), 97, 200n25

Companhia Estadual de Águas e Esgotos (State Water and Sewer Company, CEDAE), 163

comparative studies, 137, 158

complexity of favelas, 47, 52, 63, 100, 167

Complexo da Maré, 137–39, 148, 157–58

Complexo da Penha, 166

Complexo do Alemão, 148, 158–60, 163, 166, 167

Complexo do Jacarezinho, 167

conference annals and presentations, 127, 131, 200n23

Conferência Nacional dos Bispos do Brasil (National Conference of Brazilian Bishops, CNBB), 5, 68, 185n9

Conjunto Habitacional Cidade de Deus (City of God Housing Complex), 137

Conjunto São Sebastião, 68

Conniff, Michael, 39, 41

Conselheiro, Antônio (the Counselor), 24–25, 187n14

Conselho Nacional de Pesquisa (National Council for Research, CNPq), 114

Conselho Nacional do Desenvolvimento Urbano (National Council for Urban Development, CNDU), 115

Constitutionalist Revolt of 1932, 31

Constitution of 1988, 110

contagion and contagious illness, 26, 28, 31, 32, 37

195n64; convents of, 75, 198n99; Lebret as, 66, 72

Dowdney, Luke, 159

Doxiadis Plan, 185n2

drug trafficking, traffickers, 10, 139, 141, 147, 159, 166, 168, 203n62; favelas and, 161, 162

dualization, 144, 154

Durkheim, Émile, 2, 72, 193n20

dwellings, 54, 59, 84. *See also* shacks and shanties

ecology and ecological analysis, 87, 103, 111; human, 86, 91

Economic Commission for Latin America (ECLA), 71, 192n16

economics, 51, 80, 90, 115, 119, 135; humane: 71, 73

Économie et Humanisme movement, 70, 72, 73, 76–78, 81, 84, 105; Chicago School and, 85–91; Lebret and, 66, 69, 80

Edmundo, Luiz, 25, 26; *O Rio de Janeiro do meu tempo* (The Rio de Janeiro of my time, 1938), 22–23

education, 85, 165; cuts to, 162; in favelas, 51–52, 68, 84

elderly, 23, 33

electricity and electrification, 59, 76, 99, 106, 124, 162–63

elites, 39, 65, 70, 73, 79

empirical research, 73, 74, 82, 86

engineering, engineers, 18, 28, 30, 31, 45, 71, 73, 96, 135, 188n24, 190n53; Agache and, 34, 36; discourse of, 135, 188n24; favela and, 12, 27, 47; Lebret and, 72, 88, 90; municipal, 30, 41

England, 8, 43, 88, 116, 186n5

entrepreneurship, 148, 167, 168

environment, 18, 30–31, 50, 203n63

epidemics, 14, 28, 30, 37, 164. *See also* contagion and contagious illnesses; diseases

Erlanger, Luís, *José Júnior no fio da navalha* (José Júnior on the razor's edge, 2015), 165

Escola Livre de Sociologia e Política (Free School of Sociology and Politics, ELSP),

71, 73, 80–82, 113, 194n49, 198n101; Lebret and, 70, 72

Escondidinho favela, 195n54

espaço provisório (transitory space), 53

Espírito Santo state, 60

Esqueleto favela, 195n54

Estado Novo (New State) regime, 39, 45, 192n11

Estatística Predial do Distrito Federal (Federal District Building Statistics), 1933, 53

Estatuto da Cidade (City Statute), 110, 140, 163

Estrutura urbana da aglomeração paulistana (Urban structure of the São Paulo Agglomeration), 74

ethnology, ethnologists, 81, 99

eugenics, 49, 56, 191n66

Europe, 7, 8, 16, 32, 43, 96, 186n5, 188n30, 189n42, 199n14; Brazil and, 39, 116; culture of, 34, 187n14; reform in, 30, 38, 190n46; social sciences in, 14, 47

evangelicalism, 141, 166

Evaristo da Veiga Street (Rio), 16

Evenson, Norma, 101

extinction of favelas, 62

family, families, 39, 56, 76, 84, 85, 89

Fátima district, Rio, 2

favela, favelas: administration and control of, 38–52; archetype of, 18, 139, 145; Catholic Church and, 66–69; city vs., 27, 119; culture and, 141, 166; definition of, 9–10, 43, 54, 57–59, 149; eradication of, 13, 56; evolution of scholarly production on, 127–34; expansion of, 118, 129–30, 157; foreigners and, 36, 189n43; government and, 28, 188n27, 190n54; images of, 20–21, 189n43, 203n63; informal networks in, 99–100; invention of, 1, 2, 11; Lebret and, 74–78; as locus of poverty, 93, 134, 141–42, 155, 167; maps of, 186n8, 191n71; Mattos Pimenta and, 31–34; myths of, 4, 13, 18–27; number of, 54, 59, 152, 185n1; Peace Corps and, 96–102, 104, 196n76, 196n77; as phenomenon, 16, 62, 63, 104; photographs of, 33, 45, 188n22; politics

and, 69, 76, 85; population numbers
of, 54, 190n55; as problem, 26, 27–38,
29, 62, 85, 119–27; publications on, 127,
128, 128–34, 134–39, *135*, *136*, 136–37, *138*,
139–44, 157; removals and, 2, 42, 111,
163, 200n25; representations of, 11, 12,
54–55, 63, 106, 111, 112; research on, 92,
130, 161–62; of social sciences, 109–44; as
solution, 119–27; studies of, 8–9, 45, 142,
195n54, 198n97, 198n99, 203n56; as term,
16, 20, 62; understanding of, 43–52; unity
of, 143, 167; urbanization and, 12, 111, 123,
124, 162; Web and, 145–55
favelados, 1, 7, 27, 41, 43, 60, 120, 140,
142, 155, 158, 160, 165, 166, 168, 190n53;
population numbers of, 59, 75; removal
and relocation of, 51–52, 121, 138
Favela Pastoral, 139
favela plant, 19, 187n15
favelas, As (film), 33, 189n32
favelization, 1, 9, 16, 29–30, 43, 129
Federação das Associações de Favelas
do Estado da Guanabara (Federation
of Favela Associations of the State of
Guanabara, FAFEG), 2, 98, 101, 104, 123,
125
Federação das Indústrias do Estado de São
Paulo (Federation of Industries of the
State of São Paulo, FIESP), 73
Federal District, 30, 31, 54, 60, 61, 67, 75, 81,
83, 186n2, 189n38, 191n71; former, 2, 93;
population of favelas in, 50, 52
federal government, 57, 67, 68, 121, 132, 160,
163, 165, 187n14
Ferreira dos Santos, Carlos Nelson, 6, 111, 112,
123, 125, 198n97, 201n31, 201n35, 202n45
fieldwork, 3, 4, 7, 65, 66, 73, 82, 87, 110, 120,
140; of author, 4, 11, 98; in favelas, 6, 66;
Lebret and, 78, 195n60; U.S. researchers
and, 104, 128
Filho, Albuquerque, 35
Filinha, Dona, 98
Financiadora de Estudos e Projetos
(Financing Agency for Studies and
Projects, FINEP), 9, 131
First Brazilian Urbanism Conference
(1941), 43, 45

First Republic, 19
Fischer, Fritz, 101
Fleury, Sonia, 166
Fontes Ferreira, Maria Luiza de, 47
Food and Agriculture Organization (FAO)
of UN, 71
Ford Foundation, 94, 103, 115, 131
Fraga, Clementino, 33
France, 7, 43, 52, 66, 70, 78, 108, 189n37,
194–95n52; Agache and, 34, 35, 189n42;
Catholics and Dominicans in, 66, 70,
195n64; Lebret and, 69, 90–91; social
science of, 47, 113; urban studies in, 85,
89. *See also* Paris
functionalism, 118
Fundação Leão XIII (Leo XIII
Foundation), 53, 68, 77, 82, 100, 191n62,
195n54, 197n88; creation of, 63, 67
Fundo Nacional para o Desenvolvimento
Científico e Tecnológico (National
Fund for Scholarly and Technological
Development), 114
funk, 141, 166
Fürtenau, Vera Maria, 19

gangs, 159, 162
Gans, Herbert, 121
Garcia Japor de Oliveira, Maria, 19
Gávea district, Rio, 2, 59
Gávea Proletarian Park (Parque Proletário
da Gávea), 3, 50, *51*, 52; as a favela, 60,
195n54
Gazeta de Notícias (newspaper), 20
General Census of 1950, 13, 52, 57–64, 83, 93,
104, 117, 121, 128, 137
gentrification, 164
geographers, 66, 72, 80, 115, 140, 158, 194–
95n52, 199n10; SAGMACS study and,
82, 83
geography, 9, 21, 82, 110, 159, 195n52, 198n99;
human, 78, 91
George, Pierre, 91
Germany, 52, 185n9
Glass, Ruth, 8
globalism, 11, 65, 87, 134, 146, 147, 151, 154
Globo, O (newspaper), 31, 161, 162
Godard, Francis, 7

Godoy, Armando Augusto de, 36
Goldwasser, Maria Julia, 112
Gomes, Angela de Castro, 39, 190n48
Gomes, Manoel, 67, 192n5, 192n6
Goulart, José Alípio, *Favelas do Distrito Federal* (Favelas of the Federal District, 1957), 63
Grabois, Gisélia, 111, 112
graduate programs and students, 115, 116, 127, 131
Gravier, Jean-François, 91
Grynspan, Mário, 158
Guanabara state, 2, 3, 93, 94, 106, 123, 194n51, 197n79
Guaratiba district, Rio, 158
Guimarães, Alberto Passos, 53, 57–58, 61, 62, 84
Guimarães, Francisco, 34, 189n32
guns, 160, 162

Halbwachs, Maurice, 85, 195n57
Haussmann, Georges-Eugène ("Baron"), 32
head of household, 148
health, 68, 165
heterogeneity of favelas, 148
Heye, Ana Margareth, 112
higher education, 113, 115. *See also* universities
hills and hillsides, 21; Canudos and, 23–24; favelas and, 16, 29, 36, 58, 67, 75
history, historians, 8, 9, 11, 158, 159, 166
Hoffman, Elizabeth Cobbs, 101; *All You Need is Love* (1998), 95
home ownership, 33, 39, 51
hospitals and clinics, 41, 67, 68, 146
housing, 8, 20, 29, 32, 58, 67–69, 83, 121, 141, 164, 197n79; construction of, 28, 38, 42; market for, 10–11, 92, 106; policies for, 7, 121–23; for poor, 28, 37, 38; for workers, 10, 33, 39, 51, 65, 75, 78
Hoyt, Homer, 86
Hughes, Everett, 86, 185n4
humanitarian ideal, 95
human rights, 133, 165
hustlers, 26
hybridism, 91

hygiene and hygienism, 16–18, 30–32, 37, 39, 41, 51, 56, 68, 141, 190n48; concerns of, 12, 51; demolitions and, 36, 38; favelas and, 18, 36; hygienist discourse and, 14, 28, 31

identity of *favelados*, 141
ideology, ideologies, 56, 114, 121, 125–26, 151, 154
Ilha do Fundão, 138
illiteracy, 55, 74, 116
immigrants, 16, 190n56
inclusion, 161, 167
indigenous groups, 111, 187n18
individualism, 97
indolence, 26, 32, 50
inequality, 8, 74, 134
informality, 166
infrastructure, 68, 96, 148, 149, 163; lack of, 97, 118
insecurity in Brazilian cities, 132–33
Institut International de Recherche et de Formation en vue du Développement Harmonisé (International Institute for Research and Training for Harmonized Development, IRFED), 70
Institute for Juvenile Research of Chicago, 88
Institut National de la Statistique et des Études Économiques (National Institute of Statistics and Economic Studies, INSEE), 90
Instituto Brasileiro de Análises Sociais e Econômicas (Brazilian Institute for Social and Economic Analyses, IBASE), 53, 57, 57–64, 59, 202n47
Instituto Brasileiro de Geografia e Estatística (Brazilian Institute of Geography and Statistics, IBGE), 2, 52–53, 57, 57–59, 80, 93, 137, 141, 148, 149, 185n1, 191n68, 203n60; on subnormal clusters, 137, 149
Instituto Brasileiro de Opinião Pública e Estatística (Brazilian Institute of Public Opinion and Statistics, IBOPE), 132
Instituto de Arquitetos do Brasil (Institute of Brazilian Architects, IAB), 131
Instituto de Educação Social e Familiar

neoliberalism, 109

Neves, Rogério Aroeira, 6, 201n32

Neves, Tancredo, 114

newspapers, 16, 17, 20, 31, 47, 66, 79, 91, 145, 186n12; favelas in, 2, 4, 10

NGOs (nongovernment organizations), 11, 132, 133, 137, 151–52, 159, 165, 168, 201n30, 202n47, 203n58 (chap. 3), 203n59 (chap. 3), 203n1 (chap. 4), 204n8; favelas and, 109, 132, 139, 164–65; research by, 110, 131, 134

Niemeyer, Oscar, 163

Nogueira Garcez, Lucas, 71, 72, 80

Northeast Brazil, 45, 57, 58, 68, 74, 97, 113, 187n14; *favelados* from, 54–55, 60

North Zone of Rio, 16; favelas in, 59, 60, 143, 158, 163

Nós do Morro (NGO), 165

Notícia, A (newspaper), 31

Nova Holanda favela, 138, 139

Nova Iguaçu, 168

Nun, José, 120, 200n16

Oberg, Kalervo, 81, 194n49

observation, 82, 86, 92. *See also* participant observation

Observatório de Favelas (Favela Observatory, NGO), 165, 202n48, 203n59

O Estado de São Paulo (newspaper), 66; favela study in, 4, 66, 78–80

Offices of Inspection, 42

official publications, 134

Ogburn, William, 90

Oliveira, Jane Souto, 112

Oliven, Ruben George, 120

Olympic Games (2016), 158–59, 162, 163

Operação Lava Jato (Operation Car Wash), 162

Organization of American States, 69

origin myth of favela, 12–13, 18–27

Oswaldo Cruz Foundation School of Public Health, 138

otherness, 4

overpopulation, 199n14, 200n16

overurbanization, 118

Palmer, Vivien, 90

Pan-American Union, 103

Pandolfi, Dulce, 158

pardos, 55

Paris, 32, 190n45

Parisse, Lucien, 6, 66, 92, 94, 105, 198n99

Park, Robert, 73, 90; Chicago School and, 85, 88; *The City* (1925), 86, 92

Parque Acari favela, 139, 158

Parque Royal favela, 158

Parque União favela, 148

Parsons, Talcott, 2

participant observation, 4, 5, 86, 99, 102–5, 110, 125, 131

Partido Comunista Brasileiro (Brazilian Communist Party, PCB), 58, 67, 71, 114, 123

Partido Trabalhista Brasileiro (Brazilian Labor Party, PTB), 67

Pasmado favela, 2, 101

Passa-se uma casa (Passing by a house, 1978), 7, 126

Passeron, Jean-Claude, *The Craft of Sociology*, 5

Pastuk, Marila, 167

Paul VI (pope), 69

Pavão-Pavãozinho favela, 138–39, 158

Peace Corps, 95, 196n71, 196n73, 196n74; community development and, 94–96; in Rio favelas, 96–102. *See also* Peace Corps volunteers

Peace Corps volunteers, 105, 112, 197n80; Anthony Leeds and, 6, 66, 102–5, 112; in Brazil, 196n77, 198n95; in favelas, 94, 196n76, 198n97; numbers of, 96–97; in Rocinha, 197n84, 197n91; training of, 95–98, 103, 197n85, 197n87

Pearse, Andrew, "Some Characteristics of Urbanization in the City of Rio de Janeiro" (1961), 4

Pécaut, Daniel, 132, 152

Pechman, Robert, 32

Peixoto, Afrânio, 23

Pelletier, Denis, 69, 192n14

Pensando as favelas do Rio de Janeiro, 1906–2000, 139

People's Pastorals, 124

Pereira, Margareth da Silva, 36

Pereirão favela, 158

Rotary Club of Rio de Janeiro, 45, 188n26, 188n29; Agache and, 34–35; favela campaign and, 32–33; Mattos Pimenta and, 31, 188n28; speeches at, 188n29, 188n30
Ruth Ferreira favela, 98

Saint Sebastian Crusade. *See* Cruzada São Sebastião
Salgueiro favela, 97
Salmen, Lawrence, 6
Salvador, 2, 60
samba, 24, 139, 141, 166, 187n17
samba schools (*escolas de samba*), 4, 41, 99–100, 139, 185n6
Sampaio, Carlos, 36, 188n2
sampling, 110, 131, 137
sanitation, 17, *17*, 31, 32, 33, 45, 84, 186n11
Sanjek, Charles, 103
Santa Cruz district, Rio, 158
Santa Marta favela, 137, 139, 158, 163, 164, 165–66
Santo Antônio Hill, 16
São Gonçalo district, Rio, 168
São Paulo, 66, 70, 71, 74, 78–79, 112, 187n14, 188n25, 192n12, 192n14, 193n26, 193n28, 194n34, 195n52, 198n101; favelas of, 4, 97
São Paulo state, 71, 115
São Sebastião district, Rio, 77
Sauvy, Alfred, 71, 90
schools, 41, 67, 84, 92, 166
Seabra, J. J., 28
Sebastian, Saint, 191n73
Secondi, Father, 75
Second Vatican Council, 124
Secretariat of Culture of Rio de Janeiro, 165, 166
security, 160
segregation, 32, 134, 144; sociospatial, 10, 119, 142, 154
serenaders, 26
Serra Morena favela, 16
Serrinha favela, 139
sertanejo (backlander), *21*, 25, 187n14, 187n18
sertão (backlands of Northeast Brazil), 25, 187n14
Sertões, Os: Campanha de Canudos (Cunha,

1902), 13, 19, 20, 27; as canonical work, 186–87n14; influence of, 23–24
service facilities, 84
service sector, 61
Serviço Brasileiro de Apoio às Micro e Pequenas Empresas (Brazilian Micro- and Small Business Support Service, SEBRAE), 146
Serviço de Estatística da Rede Ferroviária Federal (Statistical Service of the Federal Railway), 58
Serviço Especial de Reabilitação das Favelas e Habitações Anti-higiênicas (Special Service for Recovery of Favelas and Antihygienic Housing, SERFHA), 93, 106
Serviço Especial de Saúde Pública (Public Health Special Service), 81
Serviço Federal de Habitação e Urbanismo (Federal Housing and Urban Planning Service, SERFHAU), 115
Serviço Social da Indústria (Social Service for Industry, SESI), 73, 193n25
Serviço Social Rural (Rural Social Service), 81
shacks and shanties, 33, 75; building material of, 20, 23, 29, 37; in definition of favela, 43; demolition of, 34, 42; *mocambo* as, 45–46; of Morro da Favela, 28, 29
Shaw, Clifford, 87; *The Jack-Roller* (1930), 86
Sieber, Timothy, 104
Silberstein, Paul, 6, 199n2
Silva, Maria Hortência do Nascimento e, 55; *Impressões de uma assistente . . .* (Impressions of a social worker . . . , 1942), 45, 47–49
Simonsen, Roberto, 73
Sindicato dos Corretores de Imóveis (Realtors Association), 31
Sistema de Assentamentos de Baixa Renda (System on Low-Income: Settlements, SABREN), 137, 185n1, 186n10, 202n45
Sistema de Avaliação do Programa Favela-Bairro (Programa Favela-Bairro Evaluation System), 131
slavery, 117; legacies of, 49–50

urban ecology, 119, 195n61
urban geography, 134
urban growth and expansion, 23–24, 34, 41, 65, 83, 85, 105, 117–18
urbanism, 31, 32, 35, 36, 140, 188n24
urbanization, 30, 118, 122, 138, 155, 198n97, 200n18; favelas and, 13, 59, 83, 123, 149, 162, 198n99; process of, 8, 92, 163, 201n35
urban law, 116
urban planners, 70, 74, 140, 158; favelas and, 12, 47
urban planning, 6, 10, 13, 32, 37, 45, 101, 134, 188n27, 193n26; U.S., 82, 193n27
urban policy, 7; favelas and, 1, 8
urban poor and poverty, 111, 116, 118, 142, 152
urban reform, 14, 28
urban renewal, 187n16, 189n32
urban research, 115–16
urban segregation, 155
urban social movements, 8
urban social order, 18
urban sociology, 134, 154
urban studies, 9, 115, 195n58
USAID (U.S. Agency for International Development), 2, 97, 197n79, 200n25

vagabundos (bums), 14
Valla, Victor Vincent, 77
Valladares, Licia do Prado, biography, 2–8
Valverde, Orlando, 82
Vargas, Getúlio, 39, 41, 47, 71, 117, 188n25, 190n58, 191n61, 192n11, 192n15; fall of, 56, 67, 70; Proletarian Parks and, 3, 12–13, 50–52; Revolution of 1930 and, 31, 38–39
Vatican, 5
Vaz, Abreu, 16
Vaz, Lillian Fessler, 14, 16
vecindades (large tenements in Mexico City), 119
Veja (magazine), 155
Velho, Gilberto, 4, 111, 120
Ventura, Zuenir, *Cidade partida* (Divided city, 1994), 133, 142
verticalization, urban growth and, 41
Vianna, Hermano, 133
Vidal de la Blache, Paul, 91

video, 166
Vidigal favela, 139, 148, 164
Vigário Geral favela, 98, 133, 139
Vila Aliança, 2, 5
Vila Autódromo favela, 158–59
Vila do Vintém favela, 195n54
Vila Kennedy, 2, 5
Vila Proletária da Penha favela, 195n54
violence, 10, 160, 168; children and youth and, 8, 159; drug trafficking and, 139, 147; favela and, 141, 161; urban, 132, 159
virtual reality, 145
Viva Favela (Long Live Favela, NGO), 165
Viva Rio (Long Live Rio, NGO), 139, 164–65, 202n47, 203n58 (chap. 3), 203n1 (chap. 4)

Wagley, Charles, 103
War Ministry, 19
Warner, William Lloyd, 86
water and sewage systems, 29, 68, 151, 163
Weber, Max, 2, 195n55
websites, World Wide Web, 131–32, 145–55, 165, 202n48, 203n58, 204nn1–4
welfare state, 39, 117
West Zone of Rio, 143
Whitaker Ferreira, Francisco, 69, 74
Whyte, William Foote, 86; *Street Corner Society* (1943), 4, 89, 197n87
women, 48, 61, 75
work ethic, 8, 117
working class and workers, 14, 26, 39, 98, 117, 133, 190n48, 190n50; housing for, 6, 10, 20, 29, 33, 38, 51, 65, 75, 78; neighborhoods of, 109, 143
working groups, 125
World Bank, 131
World Cup (2014), 162, 163
World War II, 56, 65

Zaluar, Alba, 132, 133; *Um século de favela* (A century of the favela; with Alvito, 1998), 91–92, 141
Zilly, Berthold, 19
Znaniecki, Florian, 86, 87
Zuzu Angel Tunnel, 7

www.ingramcontent.com/pod-product-compliance
Lightning Source LLC
Chambersburg PA
CBHW031414270326
41929CB00010BA/1449